ZAMBIA
AT FIFTY YEARS

ZAMBIA
AT FIFTY YEARS

What went right, what went wrong and
wither to? A treatise of the country's
socio-economic and political developments
since independence

ROYSON MUKWENA & FANUEL SUMAILI (EDITORS)

PARTRIDGE
A Penguin Random House Company

To order additional copies of this book, contact
Toll Free 0800 990 914 (South Africa)
+44 20 3014 3997 (outside South Africa)
orders.africa@partridgepublishing.com

www.partridgepublishing.com/africa

Contents

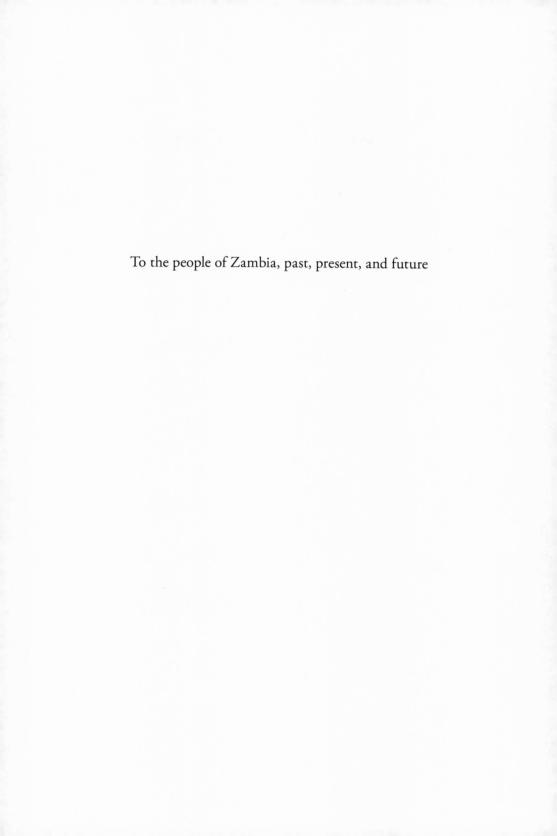

To the people of Zambia, past, present, and future

Preface

This book looks at what went wrong and right during Zambia's first fifty (50) years of nationhood and based on this makes some recommendations, where necessary, on the way forward for the country in the areas covered in the book. The cut-off point for the book is 24 October 2014.

The book is a systematic discourse on a range of socio-economic and political developments in the country since independence. The discourse covers political history, constitutional history, political culture and citizen participation in public affairs, sovereignty and democracy, foreign policy, civilian control of armed forces, dependency syndrome, employment creation through micro, small, and medium enterprises, tourism, marketing systems, library and information services, labour matters, the civil service, and social welfare.

With the exception of Dr Njunga-Michael Mulikita who lectures at the Copperbelt University's Dag Hammarskjöld Institute for Peace and Conflict Studies and Ms Petra Chinyere who is a former lecturer of Mulungushi University, all the contributors to this book are members of staff at Mulungushi University. The editors would, in the first place, like to thank most sincerely all the contributors to this book for working so hard to ensure that the book materialises.

Secondly, our great appreciation goes to Dr John Simwinga for his fine professional assistance with language editing.

Thirdly, we wish to also acknowledge and thank our families for the support they rendered while we worked on the book. In this regard Royson Mukwena wishes to express his gratitude to wife Ruth Kanjanga Phiri Mukwena, daughter Masho, and sons Kanjanga and Mandandi; and Fanuel Sumaili wishes to express his gratitude to wife Godfrida, daughters Mwewa, Marylyn, and Wanga, and sons Mibenge and Mumba.

Finally, we wish to acknowledge that this book project was made possible by a special loan from Mulungushi University and a financial contribution from Ambassador Professor Royson Mukwena. We are grateful to Mulungushi University for the special loan.

Royson Mukwena
Mulungushi University
Kabwe, Zambia

Fanuel Sumaili
Mulungushi University
Kabwe, Zambia

Chapter 1

Zambia's Political History: From Colonialism to the Third Republic

R. Samuel Sakala

Introduction

Before independence, present-day Zambia was known as Northern Rhodesia. It was a protectorate in South Central Africa, formed in 1911 by the amalgamation of the two earlier protectorates of North-Western Rhodesia and North-Eastern Rhodesia. It was initially administered by the British South African Company (BSAC), a chartered company on behalf of the British government.

Zambia is a landlocked country which lies approximately between latitudes 8 and 16 degrees south and longitudes 22 and 36 degrees east, covering a total surface area of 752,614 square kilometres (of which 740,724 sq. km is land and 11,890 sq. km water). It occupies the northern part of the southern African plateau and is surrounded by eight countries: the Democratic Republic of Congo in the north, Tanzania and Malawi in the north-east and east, Mozambique in the south-east, Zimbabwe, Botswana, and Namibia in the south and south-west, respectively, and Angola in the West (Phiri 2006).

Zambia's political history can be divided into two broad categories: the pre-independence and the post-independence periods. The pre-independence era is further divided into two periods, the precolonial era, which ran from around 1890 to about 1924 when the country was placed under the administration

1

of the BSAC, and the colonial period, which ran from 1924 to 1964 under Britain. During this period, the country was placed under direct control of the Colonial Office in Britain. The post-independence dispensation is from independence in 1964 to the current period. This era is divided into three periods, viz. the First Republic from 1964 to 1972, the Second Republic from 1972 to 1991, and the Third Republic from 1991 forward (Phiri 2006).

This chapter will endeavour to highlight the major successes, challenges, and/ or failures encountered from the precolonial through the colonial periods into independence. It will attempt to bring to the fore the prominent features of Zambia's political history from 1890 and then relate them to events since independence (Tordoff 1974). It is true that every nation is a product of its past. Zambia is by no means an exception to this fact. Thus, in order to understand the problems, policies, and political developments in present-day Zambia, it is imperative to address the past and assess how the historical political developments have impacted the political and social developments in Zambia since independence in 1964.

THE PRECOLONIAL AND COLONIAL ERA
The BSAC Administration

Colonial rule came to Zambia at the extreme end of the nineteenth century. The area of what became Northern Rhodesia, including Barotseland and lands as far as Nyasaland to the east and Katanga and Lake Tanganyika to the north, was placed under BSAC administration by an Order-in-Council of 9 May 1891 (Galbraith 1974). Before 1911, Northern Rhodesia was administered as two separate territories named North-Western Rhodesia and North-Eastern Rhodesia. The former was recognized as British territory by the Barotseland and North-Western Rhodesia Order-in-Council of 1899 and the latter by the North-Eastern Rhodesia Order-in-Council of 1900. Tordoff (1974) states that while the causes were those underlying the general 'scramble for Africa', the most immediate factor was the large gold discoveries of 1886 in South Africa. However, these new mines were located in Transvaal, the Boer-controlled territory. Cecil Rhodes, who was the prime minister of the Cape Colony, decided to bypass the Boer-occupied territories and establish British colonies to the north. By so doing, he hoped to find new minerals there. As a result, he founded the British South Africa Company (BSAC), which established itself in present-day Zimbabwe. He then sent agents to sign treaties with various chiefs to the north of the Zambezi. The most significant of the treaties was that signed with Lewanika, the king of Barotseland, in 1890. This became the basis of the company's claims to mineral rights over the country far beyond Lozi control in later years (Tordoff 1974).

Tordoff (1974) further states that there were a number of features that obtained in Northern Rhodesia which have had continuing relevance in the independent state. One of these was that the new colony was made up of not one traditional state but a large number of fragmented polities of varying sizes, state systems, languages, and cultures. To this effect he reckons that the colonial period was too short for the members of these fragmented precolonial societies to be completely integrated into a single united nation.

Secondly, the absence of prolonged and destructive wars that was characteristic of the imposition of colonial rule in other parts of Southern Africa helped the traditional authority systems in Zambia to survive though in an increasingly modified and weakened way. This is evident even to this day, fifty years after independence, where these traditional authority systems such as the Litunga of Barotseland and Chitimukulu of the northern region have continued to be the major focus for subnational group loyalty which repeatedly threatens national integration and unity.

Further, British common law became the basis of the administration of Southern and Northern Rhodesia while Roman Dutch law applied in South Africa. In 1889, the British South African Company assumed the power to establish a police force and to administer justice within Northern Rhodesia. In the case of African natives appearing before courts, the company was instructed to have regard to the customs and laws of their tribe or nation. An Order-in-Council of 1900 created the High Court of North-Eastern Rhodesia which took control of civil and criminal justice. It was not until 1906 that this British legal system provision was extended to North-Western Rhodesia. In 1911 the two were amalgamated into the High Court of Northern Rhodesia (Gann 1958). He also argues that the BSAC considered that its territory north of the Zambezi was more suitable for a largely African police force than a European one. However, at first the British South Africa Police patrolled the north of the Zambezi in North-Western Rhodesia, although its European troops were too expensive to maintain and prone to diseases. This force was replaced by the Barotse Native Police force, which was formed between 1899 and 1902.

THE END OF BRITISH SOUTH AFRICAN COMPANY RULE

According to Slinn (1971), the settlers in Northern Rhodesia were hostile to the BSAC administration and its commercial position from the very beginning of the company. This was mostly because the company opposed the settlers' political aspirations, and refused to allow them to elect representatives to the advisory council but only limited them to a few nominated members.

However, following a judgment by the Privy Council that the land in Southern Rhodesia belonged to the British Crown, not BSAC, opinion among settlers in Southern Rhodesia turned to favour responsible government and in 1923 this was granted. This development left Northern Rhodesia in a difficult position since the BSAC had believed it owned the land in both territories and some settlers suggested that land ownership in Northern Rhodesia should also be referred to the Privy Council. However, the BSAC insisted that its claims were unchallengeable and persuaded the United Kingdom government to enter into direct negotiations over the future administration of Northern Rhodesia. As a result, a settlement was achieved by which Northern Rhodesia remained a protectorate but came under the British government, with its administrative machinery taken over by the Colonial Office, while the BSAC retained extensive areas of freehold property and the protectorate's mineral rights. It was also agreed that half of the proceeds of land sales in the former North-Western Rhodesia would go to the company. On 1 April 1924, Herbert Stanley was appointed governor and Northern Rhodesia became an official protectorate of the United Kingdom, with Livingstone as capital. The capital was later moved to Lusaka in 1935 for administrative convenience (Slinn 1971).

Under the administration of the BSAC, the administrator had similar powers to those of a colonial governor, except that certain powers were reserved for the high commissioner for South Africa. There was neither an executive council nor a legislative council, but only an advisory council, consisting entirely of nominees. The Northern Rhodesia Order in Council of 1924 transferred to the governor all power or jurisdiction previously held by the administrator or vested in the high commissioner for South Africa. The order also provided for an executive council consisting of six ex-officio senior officials and any other official or unofficial members the governor wished to appoint. At the same time, a legislative council was established, consisting of the governor and up to nine official members, and five unofficial members who were to be elected by the small European minority consisting of 4,000 people only, as none of the African population had the right to vote (Gann 1958).

The political development of Northern Rhodesia was shaped by Cecil Rhodes' belief that the territory was to be ruled by whites, developed by Indians, and worked by Africans. This became essentially the philosophy of British colonialism in Central and Southern Africa. However, BSAC rule did not survive for very long because the company was not really designed to govern.

Phiri (2006) argues that as a commercial company, BSAC's primary objective was to make profit and not to spend on administration. As such since Europeans had to be encouraged to come to Northern Rhodesia, they were given heavy tax exemption incentives. The fear was that heavily taxing the Europeans would have discouraged many from coming to the territory.

THE COLONIAL PERIOD AND ITS IMPACT

The BSAC ruled Zambia from the 1890s until 1924 when it handed over its administrative role to the British Colonial Office. Britain retained ultimate control over the territory until independence in 1964 (Tordoff 1974). Present-day Zambia was officially created as a British colony in 1911 when the separate administrations of North-Western Rhodesia and North-Eastern Rhodesia, first divided by the Kafue River and then by the railroad line, were amalgamated by the BSAC to cut down cost (Phiri 2006). The resident commissioner, who was answerable to the high commissioner, was appointed to preside over the affairs of the newly created territory. The BSAC ruled the vast region with the financial support from Cecil Rhodes. However, its powers in Northern Rhodesia were limited and the Colonial Office felt that it was not advisable to strengthen the company's hand in Northern Rhodesia.

In the early stages of European occupation, the BSAC had little interest in Northern Rhodesia. This is because it was never envisioned that the territory would develop into a white colony in the same way as in Kenya, where European settlement was adopted as official policy as early as 1902. The original reason for occupying the territory was, according to Ian Henderson, that it would be a labour reserve for the development of white areas of Southern Rhodesia and South Africa (Phiri 2006). However, the outlook changed gradually as it is evidenced by the growing number of white settlers in the region. For example, between 1904 and 1911 a total of 159 farms were established between Kalomo in the south and Kabwe in the north.

Phiri (2006) further stresses that with this increased European population came an increased European participation in local politics. The white population of Northern Rhodesia attained membership on various quasi-political bodies from which they sought and secured great influence on the colonial officials towards the colony. It must be understood that European participation in local politics developed over a long period and that the process itself was influenced by both fear of the indigenous population and the desire to be free from BSAC administration.

The discovery of large quantities of copper sulfide ores in Ndola attracted large mining companies to the area which developed into Northern Rhodesia's Copperbelt. The emergence of the Copperbelt had three major consequences. Firstly, it attracted increased white migration, including large numbers of skilled and semi-skilled mineworkers, mostly from South Africa. They all shared the determination to protect their privileged financial and social position by preserving a white monopoly of the more highly paid jobs (Phiri 2006). In the second instance, it is argued that copper mining also stimulated trade, leading to considerable development not only on the Copperbelt but also on the whole stretch along the railroad line. This area became an area of increased economic development and white domination. However, uneven development grew as the railroad area flourished while most of the country remained poverty-stricken. Thirdly, the development of the Copperbelt attracted a large African labour force. At first the labour force stayed for shorter periods, but later many began to settle almost permanently in unplanned settlements or compounds that sprouted in the mining towns and later along the Line of Rail.

However, because of cultural differences and the superiority complex of the white labour force, Africans were treated with a lot of disrespect. As a result of this perception by the whites, regardless of their origin, mining was made unpopular among Africans in the early years of the development of the mining industry. Thus, colonial Zambia's political history is essentially a story of race relations characterized more by the doctrines of paramountcy than that of partnership. That is, European demands on one hand, first for the amalgamation with Southern Rhodesia and later for a federation of the two Rhodesias and Nyasaland, and African responses to these initiatives, on the other. The stage for these political events was largely the Copperbelt and the railroad line that formed the economic base of the territory (Phiri 2006).

The BSAC first introduced hut tax in North-Eastern Rhodesia in 1901 which was slowly extended through North-Western Rhodesia between 1904 and 1913. It was charged at different rates in different districts, but was supposed to be equivalent to two months' wages. The aim of the hut tax was to persuade or force the Africans into the system of wage labour in order to raise funds for administering the territory and provide labour for the mines. Its introduction generally caused little unrest, and any protests were quickly suppressed by the British South African Police force. Before 1920, it was commonly charged at five shillings a year, but in 1920 the rate of hut tax was sharply increased, and often doubled, to provide more workers for the Southern Rhodesian mines, particularly the coal mines of Wankie. At this time the company considered the principal economic benefit of Northern Rhodesia as that of serving as reservoir for migrant labour which could be called upon for the development of Southern Rhodesia where the white settlers had established themselves. However, a sharp increase in the rate of hut tax in 1920 caused unrest in the territory. Unrest also occurred on the Copperbelt in 1935 following tax rate increase. In 1935, the Northern Rhodesian government proposed to increase the rates of tax paid by African miners working on the Copperbelt, while reducing it in rural areas. Although the provincial commissioners had been told about the change in early 1935, it was not until later in May that year that the Native Tax Amendment Ordinance was signed, with rates implemented retrospectively to 1 January 1935. This retrospective implementation outraged the miners, who already had grievances regarding low pay and poor conditions. They also had issues with the Pass Laws (Chitupa) which had been introduced in 1927 requiring Africans to have permits to live and work on the Copperbelt. The tax rate increase provoked an all-out Copperbelt strike in three of the four mines in the area, namely Mufulira, Nkana (Kitwe), and Roan Antelope.

The British South Africa Police were sent from Southern Rhodesia to Nkana to suppress it. When police in Luanshya attempted to disperse a group of Africans, violence erupted and six Africans were shot dead. The loss of life shocked both sides and the strike was suspended while a Commission of Inquiry was set up. In its report, the commission concluded that the strike action had been caused by the abrupt manner in which the increases were announced, adding that if they had been introduced calmly, they would have been accepted. One of the major outcomes of the strike was the establishment of tribal elders' advisory councils for Africans across the Copperbelt, following the system which had been introduced at the Roan Antelope mine earlier. These councils acted as minor courts referring major issues to the mine compound manager or district organizer. Initially the native courts operated outside the urban areas but eventually were introduced to the towns as well, starting with Mufulira in 1938. By the end of 1940 they had been extended to Kitwe, Luanshya, Ndola and Chingola on the Copperbelt, Lusaka and Kabwe (Broken Hill) in the centre of the country, and Livingstone on the border with Southern Rhodesia. Simultaneously, African Urban Advisory Councils were established in the main Copperbelt towns because of strained relations between Africans and Europeans.

A second round of labour hostilities broke out in March 1940. This was prompted by successful wildcat strike action by European miners at two Copperbelt mines, who demanded increased basic pay, a war bonus, and a closed shop to prevent the advancement of African miners. The European strikers' demands were largely conceded, including an agreement on preventing the permanent 'dilution of labour'. This was followed by a refusal to grant a proportionate increase of pay to African miners, who then went on strike despite the offer of slightly increased bonus payments. In the violence that followed, the troops fired on the strikers, causing thirteen deaths immediately and four later.

The colonial secretary forced the governor to hold a Commission of Inquiry, which found that conditions at Nkana and Mufulira had not changed much since 1935, but no strike had happened as compared to the situation at Nchanga and Roan Antelope. It recommended increases in pay and improvements in conditions to which the mine owners agreed. The commission also recommended that African miners should be eligible for jobs previously reserved for European miners. This recommendation was not implemented immediately but was gradually introduced after 1943.

It must be noted that the Northern Rhodesian colonial system not only shaped the nationalist movement which emerged to oppose and eventually overthrow it but also had far-reaching consequences for independent Zambia. Northern Rhodesia's dependence on the south had considerable effects for Zambia. For example, it was from South Africa and Southern Rhodesia that most of Northern Rhodesia's whites hailed. It was also through Southern Rhodesia that Northern Rhodesia accessed its first outlet to the sea for both exports and imports through major trading partners including the giant Anglo-American Corporation.

Tordoff (1974) argues that this orientation to the south has created numerous problems for Zambia since independence, particularly following Southern Rhodesia's Unilateral Declaration of Independence (UDI) in 1965 and closure of its railway line in 1966. The onset of UDI resulted in severe fuel and other shortages which to a larger extent impacted negatively on the implementation of Zambia's first National Development Plan. Southern Rhodesia's closure of its railway line and border in 1966 caused more serious economic disruptions to Zambia. There were also threats of border closure in 1973. In order to address these challenges, Zambia had to take the immensely costly construction of alternative routes through Tanzania to the sea after 1965, such as the Tanzania Zambia Railway (TAZARA) in 1970 and Tanzania Zambia Mafuta (TAZAMA) pipeline in 1968 as well as the Great North Road up to Nakonde Border and the Benguela Railway through Angola. However, the Benguela railway could not be used because of the civil war that broke out in the late 1970s in Angola as the Portuguese were withdrawing from that country.

According to Tordoff (1974), colonial rule also introduced into Northern Rhodesia European and Asian minorities. The former monopolized managerial, professional, and skilled artisan occupations and the latter controlled the country's middle-range retail commerce. Both of these groups were highly committed to a private enterprise economy. However, not many of them were ready to take on Zambian citizenship in 1964 or to invest in long-term projects necessary for the development of the economy. As a result of their dominant position in the economic structure, UNIP was forced to adopt a non-racialist policy at a time when many of its African supporters deeply resented the wealth, exploitation, social exclusiveness, and arrogance of these minority groups. The citizenship policy and fears of 'paper Zambians' have been recurrent issues throughout the First, Second, and Third Republics.

The European minority also successfully institutionalized racialist practices against the African majority which included the establishment of a virtual political monopoly for Europeans until 1959 (Davidson 1948, cited in Tordoff 1974: 7). In as much as racialism created a convenient target for the nationalist movement, for example, the boycott of butchers' shops in the 1950s, it also created a number of post-independence problems. For example, many Europeans hastily left after 1963, before citizens could be trained to replace them. On the other hand, the economic divide between Africans and other racial groups diverted popular attention from the evolving intra-African class formation which took place at independence and paved the way to African entry into the private sector and domination of the public bureaucracy.

Another consequence of colonial rule was that the colonial system was an authoritarian one. The colonial government had wide-ranging and arbitrary powers which contravened all the important civil liberties. To this effect, force was used to suppress divergent views while movement and association were extensively curtailed among the Africans. The Zambian government inherited these powers from the governor of Northern Rhodesia and has continued to invoke them whenever need arises.

Hence, it can be deduced that the colonial era did little to develop a political culture in Zambia which placed a high value on limited government powers and respect for individual rights. To this effect, any divergent political views or opinions have been taken to mean direct attack on the political elites throughout all the three political dispensations since independence in 1964. After fifty years of independence, it is still common place for the ruling elements to suppress individual political rights and freedoms and to consider any such divergent views as acts of disloyalty to the regime.

Lastly, colonialism had impact on national integration. To a large extent, it is true that Zambia would not have existed in its current form without colonial rule, and that colonialism, particularly the imposition of federation in 1953, evoked a nationalist response and was therefore itself functionally integrative. However, colonialism also took certain measures that were aimed at retarding the growth of national consciousness (Tordoff 1974). Such measures included the introduction of indirect rule after 1929 and the prolonged degree of loyalty to the precolonial governmental structures such as the chiefs. Furthermore, there was deliberate withholding of secondary education until the 1940s and locally based higher education throughout the colonial period, which retarded the emergence of a nationalist leadership. Consequently, Zambia entered independence in 1964 with a relatively smaller pool of educated human resources than any other former British colony.

OPPOSITION TO MINORITY RULE

On the economic front, both the BSAC and later the Colonial Office alienated considerable quantities of the best land to European settlers. Following large-scale copper exploitation in the 1930s, there was a rapid and large increase in the number of Europeans in the territory, on one hand and the formation of the African Mineworkers' Union in 1949. Tordoff (1974) asserts that the vehicle for African protest against colonial rule was initially in form of religious sects and in particular the African Watch Tower Movement. The Watch Tower and other related movements rejected all governmental authority, and since they retained large numbers of followers even into the post-independence period, they came into sometimes violent conflict with the United National Independence Party (UNIP) government after 1963.

However, more explicit resistance to colonial rule began with the voluntary welfare societies organized by the tiny minority of Africans with primary-level school education. These were Africans educated by missions or abroad who sought social, economic, and political advancement through voluntary associations. Their protests were muted until the early 1930s and concentrated mainly on improving African education and agriculture, with political representation a distant aspiration.

Phiri (2006) asserts that these societies became amalgamated into the Federation of African Societies (FAS) in 1946. He goes on to argue that the fundamental aim of FAS was to secure improved positions for its members within the colonial system. FAS served only as the base on which the first African nationalist party was to be built. Hence, the federation came to be known as the Northern Rhodesia African National Congress (NRANC) in 1948 and in 1951 it changed its name to the African National Congress (ANC). The NRAC was the first political party to be formed by Africans prior to independent Zambia. Its successor, the African National Congress (ANC), led the unsuccessful anti-federation struggle of the early 1950s. In 1959, a more militant offshoot, the Zambia African National Congress (ZANC) was formed after the ANC was banned. ZANC (UNIP, as it later came to be known) spearheaded the final stage of the independence struggle which was victorious in 1964.

During this period, the nationalist activities were generally aimed at securing the rights of the emerging African elite who were essentially interested in some limited access to both political and economic power. Evidence suggests that settler demands for self-governance after the Southern Rhodesia model radicalized African nationalism in colonial Zambia (Phiri 2006). It must be noted, therefore, that the nature of the nationalist struggle had very important effects on the political culture, political conflict structure, and party and state institutions of independent Zambia. To begin with, though the struggle was more intense than in several other British-ruled African territories, it was not prolonged. For instance, the ANC was formed only after the Second World War and its failure to stop the federation had a demoralizing effect and the organization was almost inert in the middle and late 1950s (Hall 1965). When certain ANC leaders, led by Kenneth Kaunda, broke away from ANC in 1958 to form their own party so as to wage a more militant struggle and to break the Central African Federation, a new phase of nationalist-colonialist conflict began. The struggle was won by early 1962 when the near chaos, in three rural provinces, caused by the 'Cha Cha Cha' campaign had forced the British colonial administration to revise the new constitution so as to clear the way for majority rule.

Further, the nationalist movement's impact was uneven. Its roots go back furthest in the urban areas, in the southern and eastern provinces, which were largely affected by land alienation, and in Northern and Luapula provinces, which developed close ties with the Copperbelt through returning migrants. At the other extreme, parts of Western and North-Western provinces only heard of the nationalist message to any significant extent at the very end of the 1950s. Further still, a small number of Africans remained faithful and loyal to the colonialists throughout, while certain religious groups such as Watch Tower and Alice Lenshina's Lumpa Church in Northern and some parts of Eastern provinces never responded to the nationalist call (Kaunda 1962; Hall 1965). Therefore, the unevenness of the nationalist impact, as well as the short duration of the anti-colonial struggle within a culturally and linguistically fragmented society, meant that the unity which UNIP established was fragile (Kaunda 1962). As a result Kaunda coined and developed the slogan of 'One Zambia, one nation', to try and inculcate in the people a sense of unity and oneness. It became his deliberate policy to have the slogan heard on every public meeting and event as well as on national radio and television.

FEDERATION OF RHODESIA AND NYASALAND

The Bledisloe Commission reported in March 1939, and suggested that Africans could benefit socially and economically from European enterprise. However, it thought that two major changes would be necessary: firstly, to moderate Southern Rhodesian racial policies, and secondly, to give some form of representation of African interests in the legislatures of each territory. The commission considered the complete amalgamation of the three territories, and thought that it would be more difficult to plan future development in a looser federal union. It did not favour an alternative under which Southern Rhodesia would absorb the Copperbelt. Despite the almost unanimous African opposition to amalgamation with Southern Rhodesia, the commission advocated for it. However, a majority of commission members ruled amalgamation out as an immediate possibility, because of African concerns and objections. This majority favoured a union of Northern Rhodesia and Nyasaland into one unit which would co-operate economically with Southern Rhodesia as a possible first step to uniting all three territories later. Northern Rhodesia's white population were severely disappointed, but the outbreak of World War

II fundamentally changed the economic and political situation, as Northern Rhodesian copper became a vital resource in winning the war.

During the Second World War, co-operation between the three territories increased with a joint secretariat in 1941 and an advisory Central African Council in 1945, made up of the three governors and one leading European politician from each territory. Post-war British governments were persuaded that closer association in Central Africa would cut costs, and they agreed to a federal solution, not the full amalgamation that the Southern Rhodesian government preferred. After further revisions of the proposals for federation, agreement was reached. Following a positive referendum result in Southern Rhodesia, Northern Rhodesia joined the Federation of Rhodesia and Nyasaland when it was created in 1953.

OPPOSITION TO FEDERATION

As earlier stated, the Federation of African Welfare Societies which was formed in 1946 united all the welfare societies set up by educated Africans in towns in the 1930s to discuss local affairs. In 1948 the federation became the Northern Rhodesia National Congress (NRNC) under Godwin Mbikusita Lewanika as president. In the same period several local trade unions representing African miners merged to form the Northern Rhodesian African Mineworkers' Union. Under Lewanika, the NRNC gradually developed as a political force. It had some radical policies, but Lewanika favoured gradualism and dialogue with the settler minority.

In 1951 Lewanika was voted out of office and replaced by the more radical Harry Mwaanga Nkumbula, a schoolteacher from Kitwe. At this time, the congress advanced two major objections to the federation. The first was that political domination by the white minority of Southern Rhodesia would prevent greater African political participation. The second was that control by Southern Rhodesian politicians would lead to an extension of racial discrimination and segregation. Mr Nkumbula's radicalism caused some chiefs and conservatives to withdraw their support from the congress. However, the African National Congress, as the party was renamed in 1951, was able to persuade the African Representative Council to recommend two of its members to be African-nominated members of the Legislative Council in 1951.

The Northern Rhodesian African National Congress had been a rather small, largely urban party under Mbikusita Lewanika, but Nkumbula used opposition to federation to increase its membership. In 1951, Kenneth Kaunda, formerly a teacher, became organizing secretary for the congress in the Northern Province, and in 1953 he moved to Lusaka as secretary general of the congress, under Nkumbula's presidency. The efforts of the congress, including a failed general strike in March 1953, could not prevent the imposition of the federation which, apart from some urban protests, was resentfully accepted by the African majority.

Both Kaunda and Nkumbula began to advocate for self-government under African majority rule, rather than just increased African representation in the existing colonial institutions. In addition to demanding the break-up of the federation, the congress targeted local grievances, such as the colour bar, the denial of certain jobs or services to Africans and low pay and poor conditions of service for African workers. Kaunda was prominent in organizing boycotts and sit-ins, but in 1955 both he and Nkumbula were imprisoned for two months. As a result, the imprisonment radicalized Kaunda, who intensified the campaign of economic boycotts and disobedience upon his release, but it had the opposite effect on Nkumbula, who had already acted indecisively over the 1953 general strike. Nkumbula's leadership became increasingly autocratic and it was alleged he was using party funds for his own benefit.

However, Kaunda continued to support Nkumbula even though in 1956 Nkumbula attempted to end the campaign against the colour bar. Kaunda's estrangement from Nkumbula grew when he spent six months in Britain working with the Labour party on decolonization, but the final rupture came only in October 1958 when Nkumbula tried to purge the congress of his opponents and assume sweeping powers over the party. In that month, Kaunda and most of the younger, more radical members left to form the Zambia African National Congress, with Kaunda as president (Phiri 2006).

END OF FEDERATION AND INDEPENDENCE

After the defection of Kaunda and the radicals, Nkumbula decided that the African National Congress would contest the Legislative Council elections to be held under the 1959 Order-in-Council in October 1959. In order to increase the chances of the congress, he entered into electoral pacts with white liberals. Kaunda and the Zambia African National Congress planned to boycott these elections, regarding the 1959 franchise as racially biased.

However, before the elections a state of emergency had been declared in Nyasaland, and Banda and many of his followers had been detained without trial, following claims that they had planned the indiscriminate killing of Europeans and Asians, and of African opponents, in the so-called murder plot. Shortly afterwards, the governor of Northern Rhodesia also declared a state of emergency there, and arrested forty-five Zambia African National Congress including Kaunda and banned the party (Kaunda 1962). Kaunda later received a nineteen-month prison sentence for conspiracy, although no credible evidence of conspiracy was produced.

The declaration of states of emergency in both Northern Rhodesia and Nyasaland marked the end of attempts by their nationalist parties to work within the colonial system, and the start of a push for immediate and full independence. Although Nkumbula and his party won several seats in the October 1959 elections, he made little use of Kaunda's enforced absence and managed to alienate another section of the African National Congress who, with former Zambia African National Congress members, formed the United National Independence Party (UNIP) in October 1959.

When Kaunda was released from prison in January 1960, he assumed its leadership. Nkumbula and what was left of the congress retained support in the south of the country, where he had always maintained a strong following among the Ila and plateau Tonga peoples, but the United National Independence Party was dominant elsewhere. This was the beginning of regional and sectional politics that would become characteristic of the independent Zambian State after 1963 and beyond, into the Second and Third republics.

Roy Welensky, a Northern Rhodesian settler who was the federal prime minister from 1956 convinced the colonial secretary, Alan Lennox-Boyd, from 1954 to 1959, to support federation and to agree that the pace of African advancement would be gradual. This remained the view of the British cabinet until after the declaration of the state of emergency in 1959, when it decided to set up a Royal Commission, the Monckton Commission, on the future of the Federation of Rhodesia and Nyasaland held in 1960. The commission concluded that the federation could not be maintained except by force or through massive changes in racial legislation. It advocated a majority of African members in the Nyasaland and Northern Rhodesian legislatures and giving these territories the option to leave the federation after five years.

Epstein (1958, cited in Tordoff 1974: 9) asserts that UNIP and ANC together won a majority of Legislative Council seats against the settler United Federal Party (UFP) in the election held at the end of 1962. In December of that year, they participated in the government of Northern Rhodesia in an uneasy coalition. Nkumbula agreed to work in a coalition which had Kaunda as prime minister, and the two and their parties worked in reasonable harmony until a pre-independence election in 1964 where, with a much wider franchise, the United National Independence Party gained the majority seats. In that election, UNIP won fifty-five (55) of the seventy-five (75) main roll seats and 69.6 per cent of the votes cast (Epstein 1958, cited in Tordoff 1974: 9).

This led to immediate negotiations with the British administration over the timing of independence and the constitution of the new state. The Federation of Rhodesia and Nyasaland was formally dissolved on 31 December 1963, and the country became the independent Republic of Zambia on 24 October 1964, with Kaunda as the first president.

Therefore, it can be asserted that the nationalist struggle in colonial Zambia was closely connected with the politics of the Federation of Rhodesia and Nyasaland: firstly, to prevent its creation and then to secure its dissolution. Hence the decolonization process in colonial Zambia had a federal dimension. Further, because of the racially polarized circumstances of colonial Zambia at the time, the ANC-UFP alliance played into the hands of UNIP when it became public. Nkumbula was accused of selling out to Europeans and UNIP exploited this alliance to the maximum, increasingly appearing populist and truly concerned with the interests and aspirations of the masses (Phiri 2006).

THE POST-INDEPENDENCE ERA:
THE FIRST AND SECOND REPUBLICS

The major figure in Zambian politics from 1964 to 1991 was Kenneth Kaunda, who led the fight for independence and successfully bridged the rivalries among the country's various regions and ethnic groups. Kaunda tried to base government on his philosophy of humanism, which condemned human exploitation and stressed cooperation among people, but not at the expense of the individual.

Kaunda's political party, the United National Independence Party (UNIP), was founded in 1959 and was in power under Kaunda's leadership from 1964 to 1991. Before 1972, Zambia was under a multiparty political dispensation with three significant political parties. These were the United National Independence Party (UNIP), the African National Congress (ANC) and the United Progressive Party (UPP). The ANC drew its strength from Western and Southern provinces, while the UPP found some support among Bemba speakers in the Copperbelt and Northern provinces. Of the three political parties, only UNIP had a nationwide following.

Phiri (2006) argues that following the country's independence in 1964, two issues dominated the actions of the UNIP government. He states that firstly, UNIP was preoccupied with maintaining its political dominance under a constitution designed to guarantee liberal democracy and secondly, the drive for political supremacy was entangled with its search for national unity, which was seen as a prerequisite for nation-building.

In the 1968 multiparty elections, Kaunda was re-elected as president, running unopposed. But the political situation in the country was tense. The 1968 elections were characterized by regional violence. The country was ravened by deep divisions with the ANC under Harry Mwaanga Nkumbula winning Southern and Western provinces. In 1971, Simon Kapwepwe, a former Republican vice president, broke away from UNIP and formed the United Progressive Party (UPP) and went on to win a parliamentary by-election (Tordoff 1980). This development threatened the support UNIP enjoyed in the Northern and Copperbelt regions.

As a result of these elections, Zambia was declared a one-party state in 1972. This marked the beginning of the second republic in Zambia's political history. Following this adoption of the one-party state system, all political parties except UNIP were banned. This was formalized in a new constitution that was adopted in 1973. That constitution framed a system called One-Party Participatory Democracy, which in practice meant that UNIP became the sole political factor in the country. It provided for a strong <u>president</u> and a <u>unicameral</u> <u>National Assembly</u>.

It must be noted here that UNIP's search for political dominance predated independence. Phiri (2006) argues that as Zambia African National Congress (ZANC) was formed in 1958, the decision to name the new party Zambia African National Congress was made deliberately, to replace the ANC. ZANC's primary objective was to become the only nationalist party by completely destroying the ANC. Up until the legislation of the one-party participatory democracy in 1972, UNIP enjoyed political dominance but this dominance had been on the decline. It was this decline that greatly influenced the UNIP government's decision to move away from plural political system to a one-party system with political power being concentrated in the hands of the executive and the president (Phiri 2006).

Following the adoption of the one-party participatory democracy political system, the party (UNIP) and government activities become intertwined. For example, the national policy was formulated by the central committee of UNIP, and the cabinet executed the central committee's policy. In legislative elections, only candidates running on UNIP's platform were allowed to participate. However, though inter-party competition was out of question, the contest for seats within UNIP was energetic. In the presidential elections, the only candidate that was allowed to run was the one elected as president of UNIP at the party's general conference. Under this bill, no person was allowed to attempt to form a political party or any organization other than UNIP. Further, no one was allowed to 'belong to or assemble associate, express opinion, or do anything in sympathy with any such political party or organization' (Phiri 2006).

As a result of this policy, Kaunda was re-elected unopposed with a yes or no vote in the <u>1973</u> election. President Kaunda's mandate was renewed in

December 1978, October 1983, and October 1988. In the 1983 election, more than 60 per cent of those registered participated and gave President Kaunda a 93 per cent yes vote.

However, this did not mean that there was no dissension to the imposition of the one-party rule in the country or within UNIP. For example, <u>Sylvester Mwamba Chisembele</u>, who was cabinet minister for Western province, together with UNIP leaders from seven out of the eight provinces established a committee of fourteen. The objective of the committee of fourteen was to establish a democratically elected council of two leaders from each province to rule the country by consensus with the president as head of state. If this had been achieved, it would have meant the curtailing of the absolute power residing in the president. However, later the president banned the committee of fourteen and Sylvester Chisembele and several leaders were suspended or sacked (*Zambia Daily Mail*, 21 April 1971).

Phiri (2006) points out that under the one-party participatory democracy, the party president became the only presidential candidate. He would become the country's president if elected by at least 51 per cent of the total vote cast in a presidential election. However, this was a political myth or fallacy in that it had people believe that they were participating in electing the country's president in an election when in effect Kaunda was a de facto life president for Zambia and UNIP was the supreme political institution in the country.

The myth of one-party participatory democracy was itself a subsequent outcome of earlier myths about political opposition. It is safe to deduce that it had its origin in the colonial era. This is so in that throughout the independence negotiations and struggle, African nationalists portrayed the picture that they were united and stood for the oneness of the will of the people. Phiri (2006) points out that the Colonial Office insisted on some form of unity among the Africans for it to relinquish power. Kenneth Kaunda once alluded to this myth when he said, while addressing the National Assembly, 'In accordance with our African way of life we intend that the president should be no mere figurehead but that he will have strong executive powers'. By appealing to African traditions, Kaunda was trying to invoke the masses' fanatical faith in the leader and therefore sought to neutralize every form of political opposition to his rule.

In 1978, Simon M. Kapwepwe and Harry M. Nkumbula, who, before the declaration of a one-party state, had been leaders of the UPP and ANC political parties respectively as well as Robert Chiluwe, a Lusaka businessman, decided to take a shot at the country's presidency. However, the UNIP general conference held at Kabwe Mulungushi Rock of Authority, approved amendments to the constitution in which the candidates for the presidency must have held continuous party membership for five years and without any criminal record. This provision effectively disqualified the contenders and declared Kaunda the sole UNIP candidate for the presidency of Zambia.

However, Simon Kapwepwe and Harry Nkumbula challenged the resultant 1978 election of President Kaunda in the High Court, but it was not surprising that their action was not successful. This act by UNIP demonstrated its failure to allow a free and fair election for the presidency within the party, and it was evident that there was lack of democracy within the party machinery and Zambia's political system as a whole.

In the meantime, UNIP tightened its grip on political power in Zambia by systematically filling positions by those who would flatter the party leadership with unrealistic praises. Those who could challenge the system or posed threat to the system from within were either fired, resigned, or were sent abroad into diplomatic missions so as to keep them out of the way. Sending any potential challenges abroad was the most effective method used in dealing with leadership conflict within the party and the government as a whole (Phiri 2006).

MULTIPARTY DEMOCRACY: THE THIRD REPUBLIC

The one-party rule and the declining economy created disappointment among the people, especially among the urban elite. Several strikes hit the country in the 1980s. The government responded by arresting several union leaders, among them Frederick Chiluba, leader of the Zambia Congress of Trade Unions (ZCTU). When 70 per cent of the population was in rural areas and the economy was in good shape, it was economically feasible to implement very costly politically motivated policies such as subsidizing food and other societal requisites. However, the urban population rise to 78 per cent had profound effect on social, political, and economic situation in the country. The government found it extremely hard to continue subsidizing the urban population. Food riots became a prominent feature in the urban areas.

In 1986 and 1987 protests arose again in <u>Lusaka</u> and the <u>Copperbelt</u>. The food riots that took place in June 1990 culminated into the June 30 coup attempt. It was this coup attempt that effectively broke President Kaunda's grip on power and led to the formation of a pressure group called the Movement for Multiparty Democracy (MMD), which was later transformed into a political party.

However, because of growing opposition to UNIP's monopoly on power from the civil society, the church, and the public at large, Kaunda realized the need for political <u>reforms</u>. He promised a <u>referendum</u> on <u>multiparty democracy</u> and lifted the ban on formation of political parties. It can be argued therefore that UNIP and the Kaunda regime were toppled by popular struggle and that the MMD was just the avenue representing the aspirations of various social forces and political disillusionment caused by almost three decades of one-party state rule.

President Kaunda agreed to a referendum on the one-party state, but in the face of continued opposition, he dropped the referendum and signed a constitutional amendment bill making Zambia a multiparty state. The amendment to the constitution that lifted the ban on political parties and restriction of association resulted in the quick formation of seven new parties. Among these were the <u>Movement for Multiparty Democracy</u> (MMD), the National Democratic Alliance (NADA), the Multiracial Party (MP), the People's Liberation Party (PLP), the Democratic Party (DP), the Movement for Democratic Process (MDP), and the Theoretical Spiritual Political Party (TSPP).

The MMD assembled an increasingly impressive group of important Zambians, including prominent UNIP defectors and labour leaders. Zambia's first multiparty elections for parliament and presidency since the 1960s were held on 31 October 1991. The MMD candidate Frederick Chiluba resoundingly carried the presidential election over Kenneth Kaunda with 81 per cent of the vote. Further, in the parliamentary elections, the MMD won 125 of the 150 elected seats and UNIP the remaining 25. However, UNIP swept the Eastern Province, gathering 19 of its seats there.

The 1991 multiparty elections did not only result in the toppling of UNIP and the Kaunda regime by the MMD, but also demonstrated the success of the popular will of the people (Phiri 2006). Besides the business interests, the intelligentsia, labour leaders and politicians, the informal sector producers, peasants, and the lumpenproletariat contributed massively to the all-powerful social movements with the objective of bringing about a multiparty political system. These were the most affected by the political and economic decline in the Second Republic. They also constituted the vast majority of the voters in Zambia.

When one-party rule was abolished in 1991, many expected a more democratic future for Zambia. These expectations were, however, clouded by the MMD's vengeful treatment of the opposition through questionable amendments of the constitution and detentions of political opponents, which caused major criticism. The MMD began to experience similar problems that UNIP had faced as the dominant political party in the First Republic. The MMD was a coalition of many interest groups that were generally agreed that there was a need to remove the Kaunda regime from power, and once that objective was achieved, the various interests began to look more towards their own interests as opposed to those of the collective whole. Nonetheless, the Third Republic was relatively open to and accommodative of divergent views and interests. As a result, the MMD and the political leadership were openly attacked and criticized in the crudest ways at times.

Phiri (2006) observes that soon after the MMD came into power, several other political parties were born. Among these were the National Party (NP) in 1993, the Liberal Progressive Front (LFP) in 1994, the Zambia Democratic Congress (ZDC) in 1995, the Lima Party (LP) in 1996, the Agenda for Zambia (AZ) in 1996, the United Party for National Development (UPND) in 1998, the Forum for Democracy and Development (FDD) in 2001, and the Patriotic Front (PF) in 2001. The other political parties formed include the National Citizens Coalition (NCC) in 1998, the Zambia Republican Party (ZRP) in 1998, the Social Democratic Party (SDP), the Zambia Alliance for Progress

(ZAP) in 1999, and the Heritage Party (HP) in 2001. The formation of these political parties had the greatest impact on the politics of Zambia. Furthermore, by the end of 2001, there were approximately thirty-seven registered political parties in Zambia.

By the end of Chiluba's first term as president in 1996, the MMD's commitment to political reform had faded in the face of re-election demands. Relying on the MMD's overwhelming majority in parliament, in May 1996 President Chiluba pushed through constitutional amendments that eliminated former President Kaunda and other prominent opposition leaders from the 1996 presidential elections. In November 1996, Chiluba was re-elected as president of Zambia, and the MMD won 131 of the 150 seats in the National Assembly. Kaunda's UNIP party boycotted the parliamentary polls to protest the exclusion of its leader from the presidential race as well as alleging that the outcome of the election had been predetermined by a faulty voter registration exercise.

Despite the UNIP boycott, the elections took place peacefully, and five presidential and more than 600 parliamentary candidates from eleven parties participated. Afterwards, however, several opposition parties and non-governmental organizations declared the elections neither free nor fair. As President Chiluba began his second term in 1997, the opposition continued to reject the results of the election amid international efforts to encourage the MMD and the opposition to resolve their differences through dialogue. Early in 2001, supporters of President Chiluba mounted a campaign to amend the constitution to enable Chiluba to seek a third term of office. Civil society, opposition parties, and many members of the ruling party complemented widespread popular opposition to exert sufficient pressure on Chiluba to force him to back away from any attempt at a third term.

The presidential, parliamentary, and local government elections were held on 27 December 2001 in which eleven parties contested the elections. The MMD's presidential candidate Levy Mwanawasa was declared the victor by a narrow margin, and was sworn into office on 2 January 2002. However, opposition parties alleged that serious irregularities had occurred and petitioned the election results in court. The courts acknowledged that there had been some irregularities in the election process but stated that they were not serious enough to have affected the overall result, thus the election result was upheld. The opposition parties won a majority of parliamentary seats in the December 2001 election, but subsequent by-elections gave the ruling MMD a slim majority in parliament.

In the 2006 elections, the Patriotic Front (PF) and Michael Sata participated and lost for the second time to MMD's candidate Levy Mwanawasa, who was elected for his second term as president of Zambia. Following the death of Mwanawasa two years into his second term in 2008, Rupiah Banda, who had delivered the UNIP, dominated Eastern Province to Mwanawasa, and his MMD party in the 2006 election became the acting president and subsequently the president after defeating Michael Sata of the PF with a narrow margin of victory in the by-elections. Sardanis (2014) asserts that Banda's elevation to the highest position in the nation was pure luck. He further contends that like Mwanawasa, Banda just happened to have been at the right place at the right time.

The Banda administration lasted for three years only. In 2011, a new election was held in which he only managed to secure 35.63 per cent or 987,866 of the vote. The Patriotic Front (PF), under the leadership of Michael Sata won with 42.24 per cent or 1,170,966 votes. In the third position was Hakainde Hichilema of the United Party for National Development (UPND), who got 18.28 per cent or 506,763 votes. In parliament, Sata's PF got 60 seats, the MMD got 55, and the UPND got 28 seats. There were three independent seats; one went to FDD and another to ADD (Electoral Commission of Zambia 2011).

Unlike many other presidents across the African continent who lost an election and refused to go, Banda gracefully stepped aside, following the tradition established by Kenneth Kaunda in 1991 when UNIP lost power to Frederick Chiluba and the MMD (Sardanis 2014). He goes on to argue that Sata's support in 2011 election victory stemmed mainly from towns and cities along the Line of Rail. He had, in his unique populist fashion, promised jobs within ninety days for all the unemployed and to double the salaries for all those in low-level employment.

Sata's reign was both spectacular and controversial, more than any other president's. Sardanis argues that upon assuming office in 2011, Sata petitioned the results of all parliamentary seats won by the opposition political parties with total disregard to the astronomical costs in legal fees and court time. These petitions resulted in by-elections throughout the first three years of Sata's reign. However, very few gains ensued for his party from these by-elections.

This is further affirmed by the Episcopal Conference which states, 'much as we acknowledge that there are by-elections occasioned by deaths of office holders, we are also seeing more and more by-elections motivated by greed, individual interests, and a selfish propensity for political dominance. This is being done without care, serious prior consideration of the views and feelings of the electorate, and sensitivity to the colossal amount of money these by-elections are imposing on the economy' (cited in Sardanis 2014: 251).

However, the PF did not need all the opposition MPs to cross the floor in order to for the party to govern, especially if such a process meant that Sata had to pack half of the parliament on the government front bench at tremendous cost to the nation. At the beginning of 2013, there were about seventy-one ministers and deputy ministers in government. This number rose to eighty-one by the end of that year. This suggests that about 51 per cent of parliament was sitting on the front bench (Sardanis 2014).

These tendencies speak against the ability of political players in Zambia to be amenable to divergent views in a maturing democracy fifty years after independence. President Sata could have still governed without requiring opposition MPs to cross the floor through by-elections and appointments of opposition MPs to government positions, if only the opposition was made not to feel targeted or persecuted and their views and opinions considered.

CONCLUSION

The political developments in Zambia from the colonial period through the First, Second, and Third republics gave rise to and then demise of liberal democracy in independent Zambia. The vices of the one-party participatory democracy state were influenced by the fact that the one-party system turned out to be a one-party dictatorship which did not allow any other political party to exist or individual citizen to express a divergent political view or opinion from that of the political elite. There was no democracy within the party itself and it was a fallacy to expect a nondemocratic party to produce political machinery at national level that was democratic and accommodative to divergent ideas and opinions. The supremacy of the party, besides the de facto life presidency of the sitting president, who was surrounded by people who were inclined to flattery in the Central Committee, worked against the development of democracy.

Phiri (2006) has rightly argued that the rise and demise of liberal democracy in Zambia reflected the nature of politics in a country where for a long time opposition politics, were condemned by those in power—both before and after independence. By the 1980s, there were widespread demonstrations pulling large crowds similar to those that had rallied for the removal of one-party states in Eastern Europe in the early 1990s. The government was forced to amend the constitution so as to restore the multiparty political system in 1990 and had scheduled a referendum on multiparty system for 1991. However, because of mounting pressure from across social, political, and economic boundaries, the referendum was cancelled and instead the constitution was amended to pave the way for multiparty politics and a presidential and parliamentary election was scheduled for October 1991. Two major political parties participated in the ensuing elections: UNIP and the MMD, which had been transformed from a pressure group into a political party. This newly found freedom of expression and association resulted in several other political parties being formed from 1992 through to 2001. The Zambian society managed to create an autocrat out of a seeming democrat in the first Republican president, because of praise-singing and flattery. It is hoped that as a nation, Zambia shall guard against repeating such an error by avoiding flattering the president as was the case with Kaunda in the First and Second republics and Chiluba in the Third Republic.

Furthermore, it is hoped that in order to foster democratic institutions at national level, political parties would avoid vesting so much power in the single individual or the president of their respective parties so as to encourage intra-party democracy as well as inter-party tolerance. It must be borne in our minds that holding divergent political views is healthy and should be encouraged in order to enhance the flourishing of the political, social, and economic aspects of the Zambian society.

REFERENCES

Electoral Commission of Zambia (2011), available www.elections.org.zm/media/28092011 publicnotice 2011 presidential election results.pdf, accessed 15 February 2015 at 13:11.

Gann, L. H. (1958), *The Birth of a Plural Society: The Development of Northern Rhodesia under BSAC, 1894–1914* (Manchester: Manchester University Press).

Galbraith, J. S. (1974), *Crown and Chanter: The Early Years of the BASC* (Los Angeles: University of California Press).

Hall, R. (1965), *Zambia* (London: Pall Mall Press).

Kaunda, K. D. (1962), *Zambia Shall Be Free: An Autobiography* (London: Heinemann).

Lunn, J. (1992), 'The Political Economy of Primary Railway Construction in the Rhodesias, 1890–1911', *Journal of African History*, 33/2: 239–244.

Mutesa, Fred (2007), *The State, Privatization and the Public Sector in Zambia* (Harare: SAPSN).

Phiri, Bizeck J. (2006), *A Political History of Zambia: From Colonial Period to the 3rd Republic* (Trenton, NJ: African World Press).

Sardanis, Andrew (2014), *Zambia: The First 50 Years, Reflections of an Eyewitness* (London: I. B. Tauris & Co. Ltd.).

Slinn, P. (1971), *Commercial Concessions and Politics During the Colonia Period: Role of the BSAC in Northern Rhodesia—1890–1964* (London: Cambridge University Press).

Tordoff, William (1974), *Politics in Zambia* (Manchester: Manchester University Press).

Tordoff, William (1980), *Administration in Zambia* (Manchester: Manchester University Press).

Zambia Daily Mail (1971), 21 April.

Chapter 2

A Critique of the Constitutional History of Zambia

Petra Rumbidzai Chinyere and Shakespear Hamauswa

Introduction

Zambia attained independence in 1964 and since then successive governments have tried to come up with a home-grown constitution that fulfils the aspirations of the Zambian people. There have been several draft constitutions initiated by the different governments. Since independence, the constitution has been successfully amended three times: in 1973, 1991, and 1996. As Zambia celebrates its golden jubilee, it is worth noting that as one of the oldest independent African states, it is sad that it still grapples with constitutional issues as the nation and the government are failing to agree on certain issues. The complications are mainly a result of the changing world dynamics such that the process of catching up with world speed is taking its toll on most national constitutions, Zambia inclusive. This far it has been a growing democracy where power swiftly and peacefully changes hands.

Any country embarking on constitution making should ensure that the process is all-inclusive to guarantee legitimacy among all the stakeholders. During the Northern Rhodesia Constitutional Conference at Lancaster House on 19 December 1960, the Secretary of State for the colonies noted:

> As with any major step in the political evolution of a country, the solution which we seek must on the one hand meet the natural aspirations of the peoples of the territory and on the other provide for the maintenance of stable government and an efficient and developing administration. It must surely be founded upon the present conditions and capabilities of the territory, whilst looking forward to its future needs.

In a democratic state, all stakeholders have the right to participate in the governance of their country and such participation takes the form of being involved in national processes such as constitution making. Popular participation in constitution making is particularly important because, as Chanda (2001: 1) observes, 'A constitution is the supreme law, the embodiment of the values—political, social, and economic, of the people'. As such it binds all citizens equally and defines the arrangement of governmental offices. In the case of Zambia, there have been allegations of non-involvement of the public in constitution making. This is because over the years, government has not adopted most of the public submissions on critical issues whenever such have been recommended by Constitution Review Commissions. The irony is that all the Constitutional Review Commissions whose recommendations have been rejected have been set up by government. The Zambian case is typical of governments in Africa which have been labelled non-democratic in that they ignore the aspirations and will of the population while pursuing their own interests and those of the governing elite. This scenario is what has been witnessed in the constitution-making processes that Zambia has undergone so far. The government and the civil society have continuously accused each other of not being committed to the process. This chapter discusses the constitutional developments that Zambia has witnessed for the past fifty years of its independence and analyses why there have been failed attempts at coming up with a new constitution that will stand the test of time, if the aspirations of the public remain the same.

Constitutional Changes Since Independence

To date, Zambia has witnessed five major constitutional developments comprising three constitutions and two constitutional amendments. The three constitutions are the 1964 Constitution, the 1973 Constitution, and the 1991 Constitution while the two constitutional amendments are the 1969 Constitutional (Amendment) Act and the 1996 Constitutional (Amendment) Act. Apart from these, there have been other attempts to change the constitution where commissions were appointed but the process was not seen through to the end. These include the 2003 Mung'omba Constitutional Review Commission and the 2011 Technical Team on Drafting the Constitution. As the changes are related, questions on the purpose of a constitution in a nation will be attempted as well.

The Pre-Independence Era

The Federation of Northern Rhodesia (now Zambia), Southern Rhodesia (now Zimbabwe), and Nyasaland (now Malawi) through the Order in Council of 1953 brought the three territories under one administration. In 1962 there was a constitution written by the colonial administration to cater for the inclusion of the native Africans in the legislative body of Northern Rhodesia as it prepared for its independence from the federation. The negotiations leading to independence mainly centred on ensuring peaceful coexistence of different races to allow both sides to pursue their aspirations in relative peace. The Northern Rhodesia territory did not have a protracted armed struggle for independence; it was more of a negotiated settlement. Probably it was because the territory was considered more of a resource base where the British extracted copper while they were settled in the Southern Rhodesian territory where they developed modern social, economic, and infrastructural services using the extracted resources. The lack of development in Northern Rhodesia made it lag behind, thereby posing no threat to the welfare of the white settler community. As such, they granted Zambia independence without much resistance. At the Lancaster House negotiations, all the major stakeholders were represented. These included members of the African National Congress, chiefs, Dominion Party, Liberal Party, independent members of Legislative Council, United Federal Party, United National Independence Party, government of Northern Rhodesia, and legal advisors. Having representatives from all these sectors made the process all-inclusive and participatory as they tried to cater for the aspirations of all sectors of the mixed-race community.

The main issues arising out of the negotiations focused on increasing the number of Africans in the legislature which, until then, had been dominated by the white minority, having political advancement being related to social responsibility which would gradually translate into universal suffrage, protection of minority groups, and granting chiefs a special place in the central councils of government. These negotiations mainly considered making everyone feel part of the new creation and that is what any constitutional process should be, all participative and inclusive of all relevant stakeholders. Brandt (2011: 15) holds 'the constitution has come to be regarded as a contract among the people on how they would like to be governed.'

The Constitution that came out of the process included a bill of rights that was designed to safeguard the rights of individuals and the interests of minorities, noting that Northern Rhodesia was a diverse community. The chiefs were also considered important as they are the people's representatives, for they reflect the opinion of the people by custom. They were given an important role in the administration of the new independent nation. According to the proposals at the February 1961 Meeting for Constitutional Change, they were to be consulted on all matters of public importance so that they could offer their views on behalf of their people since they knew the people's needs and aspirations better. This was mainly done because the administration appreciated the importance of the public voice in national issues. As shall be noticed later, as the republics changed, there was a considerable shift on the role of the chiefs, in some cases being rendered irrelevant while in others being overtaken by events.

The Postcolonial Era

Zambia attained independence on 24 October 1964 under the leadership of Kenneth Kaunda and the United National Independence Party (UNIP), which was the main party during the struggle for independence. Following the dissolution of the federation in 1963, a new constitution based on the Westminster model and designed to resolve the conflicting interests of the indigenous Africans, the settler white community, and the colonial government was negotiated by the major stakeholders (International IDEA 2010: 1). The Independence Constitution provided for a multiparty democracy with an executive president (Mbao 2010: 1). The multiparty scenario, dominated by

Kaunda's UNIP, was meant to cater for all parties that were there at the negotiating table for the independence settlement, as mentioned earlier. The first constitution was therefore all-inclusive and tried to uphold the rights of all and safeguard the aspirations of all citizens despite their different inclinations. Surprisingly, the seemingly fair and democratic constitution has been subjected to reviews and amendments.

Mainza Chona Constitutional Review Commission

Multi-partyism lasted for a few years as opposition parties presented a challenge to the Kaunda regime more than the regime could take. Consequently, Kaunda's regime decided to nip it in the bud by creating a one-party state to foster national unity and cohesion. This was done by amending the Constitution in 1969 and consolidated later by the appointment and engagement of the Mainza Chona Constitutional Review Commission in 1972. This exercise ultimately resulted in the 1973 Constitution that declared UNIP the only legally recognized political party. The Kaunda regime popularised the 'One Zambia, one nation' slogan to foster national unity and patriotism.

The 1973 Constitution mainly managed to bring in a new restriction on the freedom of association, choice, and free participation in the politics of the nation, in the name of uniting the nation. It brought in the one-partyism which meant curtailment of the freedom of expression where people are free to choose the party to align with or to support. This resulted in the creation of the one-party participatory democracy where all belonged to one party although they had the right to choose among different candidates of the same party. Kaunda believed in African humanism, which he explained in his *A Humanist in Africa: Letters to Colin Morris from Kenneth Kaunda, President of Zambia* as human-centred compared to the power-centred European society; as such, he believed in unity in diversity. Further, Kaunda saw his humanism as related to Christian humanism and sought to see the whole of Africa free. The one-party state meant that different aspirations and views of the people were expressed within one party to avoid ethnic rivalries in a highly ethnic diverse community. Such practices implied the existence of authoritarian tendencies in the ruling government. This perspective is supported by Sithole (1998: 26) who states, 'total elimination of all opposition requires extremely effective mobilisation and the full integration of all institutions and social groups into the structures of the regime'. There was need to suppress all opposition in order to effectively maintain the one-party regime.

Since then Zambia continued under the one-party system but as more and more African countries gained independence, the democratic wave intensified and was exacerbated by the collapse of the Soviet Union in 1991. According to Cummings (2012) the fall of the then Soviet Union is partly attributed to wide ranging sweeping economic and political changes championed by Mikhail Gorbachev who became the general secretary in 1985. The changes were guided by the philosophy of perestroika, which meant restructuring. On the economic front, the reforms allowed for more freedoms in the economy, including some market economy mechanisms, while on the political front, competition was introduced as well as allowing the opposition groups to criticise communism. Consequently, in leading to the collapse of the Soviet Union the changes had ripple effects on socialist-inspired nations across the world that had nothing to do but embrace democratic values and capitalism. Within this context, the Zambian people, because of frustrations from the autocratic tendencies of the Kaunda regime, began getting agitated against the one-party rule. What happened in Zambia during this period fits well into Sithole's analysis: 'authoritarianism is a pathology against which humankind has a tendency to always rebel' (1998: 26). The gaps in the 'authoritarian' regime led to the continued opposition among the population, continually calling for democratic practices. This wind of change swept across Africa, resulting in increased demand for democracy by citizens. Further, the economic problems experienced after the fall of copper prices on the world market resulted in Zambia experiencing balance-of-payment problems and requiring financial assistance from the democracy-driven Western countries. This development meant democratic inclination was inevitable for the country. The intensified pressure for multiparty democracy resulted in the appointment of the Patrick Mvunga–led Constitutional Review Commission in 1990, meant to restore multi-partyism.

The Mvunga Constitutional Review Commission

The efforts of the Mvunga Commission resulted in the Constitutional (Amendment) Act of 1991 as a transitional document meant to meet the desires of the population for multi-partyism, following the demise of the Soviet Union in 1989. In Zambia, multi-partyism was associated with the democratic wave that had triumphed over the Soviet ideals, resulting in the strengthening of the labour movement in Zambian politics under the leadership of Frederick Chiluba. The labour movement became a formidable force which was joined by different interest groups to form the opposition Movement for Multiparty Democracy (MMD), which wrestled power from UNIP in the 1991 elections. This development heralded a new political dispensation for Zambia where everyone expected the various freedoms, rights, and liberties to be upheld to the letter since the MMD had been very critical of the UNIP governance style and had promised the nation a better and more democratic regime during its campaign.

The Mwanakatwe Constitutional Review Commission

Following ascendancy to political power, the Chiluba government initiated its own constitutional review under the chairmanship of John Mwanakatwe. The Mwanakatwe Commission was appointed in December 1993 with a wider mandate to enable democratic consolidation and to draft a constitution that would stand the test of time, according to the Government Paper number 1 of 1995. Among other things, the Mwanakatwe Commission recommended the restoration of the House of Chiefs, which had become redundant. However, in the Government White Paper Number 1 of 1995, the Chiluba government rejected most of the recommendations made by the Mwanakatwe Commission. This rejection pointed to the perpetuation of the trend by most governments in Africa of wanting to safeguard their stay in power for as long as they could possibly do under the prevailing circumstances. The tendency of African governments to pursue long incumbency was slowly creeping into this newly formed government that claimed to be highly democratic. This trend reflected Gandhi's observation that possession of power makes men blind and deaf (Blaug 2010: 1) and affirms Lord Acton's contention, in a letter to Bishop Mandel in 1887: 'power tends to corrupt and absolute power corrupts absolutely. Great men are almost always bad men' (*Phrases Finder*). Accordingly it can be observed that opposition parties see the wrongs done by the ruling party when outside, but the moment they get into power, they continue with the same ills which they had previously criticised. The Chiluba government continued in the same tracks that the Kaunda regime was being criticised of; the only difference was that the Chiluba government had popular support initially for proclaiming the gospel of democracy. During the initial stages, the government had a lot of money flowing in and managed to sustain the population by providing social adequate services which gave satisfaction to the people, who in turn were blinded to the inadequacies of the government. Other evils, particularly corruption, began to creep in, leading to the loss of popularity of the Chiluba regime by 2001.

The Mwanakatwe Constitutional Review Commission's recommendations had however been rejected by the Chiluba government inasmuch as they had been comprehensive and representative of the views and opinions of the people. The 1996 Amendment Act was basically to block Kaunda from contesting in any election since it is alleged that his parents were not of Zambian origin and the amendment was mainly on parentage of presidential aspirants. Thus far the Zambian constitutional review processes were considered a government prerogative where the government can easily reject public opinion, thereby raising questions as to who the government is meant to serve: the people's interests or those of government officials? Dewey's observation that all special privileges limit the outlook of those who possess it (Blaug 2010: 1) is particularly fitting.

The Mung'omba Constitutional Review Commission

In the 2001 elections, Levy Mwanawasa became the president of Zambia and initiated his own constitutional review in 2003 under the chairmanship of Willa Mung'omba. The trend since independence has been that of government-initiated constitutional review to cater for the ruling elite or ruling party's ideals. The Mung'omba Commission is reported to have produced a comprehensive and progressive report.

> The main thrust of the Commission's recommendation was that the people should define the constitution-making process and that the constitution should be a product of the sovereign will of the people. It should be made and amended through popular mandate and not through the *Inquiries Act* and that

in order for the constitution to stand the test of time it ought
to be a product of the will of the people expressed directly by
the people. (Mbao 2007: 21)

The Mung'omba recommendations focused on making a people-driven
constitution, which is the main issue in any constitution-making process.
Unfortunately, the process was dragged for too long as the government and
civil society failed to agree on the proposed time frame. The government
announced a 285-week-long time frame while civil society had a 71-week
schedule. The Zambian Centre for Interparty Dialogue (ZCID) intervened
and only managed to bridge the gap between government and civil society by
coming up with a plan that emphasized on the need for a body to adopt a new
constitution, dubbed the National Constitutional Conference (NCC).

The National Constitutional Conference

However, this NCC did not have legislative powers; it only went as far
as drafting a new constitution by reviewing the Mung'omba draft and
recommendations (part II clause 3 of the NCC Act of 2007). This meant that
the initial Mung'omba process was a waste of time and financial resources.
Following the demise of President Mwanawasa and subsequent takeover by
Rupiah Banda, NCC continued working amid pressure from civil society
and opposition parties for completion of the process prior to holding the 2011
elections. The process of adopting the constitution remained one of the major
bones of contention in the NCC review process. This was because legislative
power remained solely the role of parliament, which had the ruling party in the
majority, thereby rendering the role of the NCC futile. It is noted that under
the NCC as an extension of the Mung'omba era, Zambia had set itself on a
good path in terms of constitution making. As observed by Mbao (2007: 29),
'it is therefore important to recognise that for the first time in the history of
constitution making in Zambia, a genuine attempt has been made to involve a
very broad spectrum of Zambian society in the constitution-making process'.
The requirement for the presidential candidate to attain 50 per cent plus one
of the valid votes was another rejected recommendation since it was viewed as
an expensive exercise apart from the effectiveness it impliedly imparts.

The Technical Committee of the Constitution

The 2011 elections saw the coming into power of the Patriotic Front (PF) under the leadership of Michael Sata. During his campaign President Sata had promised the people a new constitution within a year of his ascendency to power. That promise was never met as the Sata government went beyond a year to institute a review process to change the constitution and the same process is still dragging to this day. The technical committee constituted by the Sata government managed to come up with a draft but it is yet to release the draft to the people, resulting in political tension within the country as civil society and opposition political parties accused government of bad faith and subverting the people's will by refusing to make the draft available to the public. The PF government has continued to refuse to avail to the public the draft constitution that was handed to the president by the Technical Committee on Drafting the Constitution, allegedly in 2012, according to the Zambian Voice. However, on 23 October 2014, the government bowed down to pressure from the civil society organizations by releasing the Draft Constitution. At the time of writing this chapter, the civil society organizations have continued lobbying government to uphold the will of the people arguing that the only way to deliver a people-driven constitution is to subject it to a national referendum. On the other hand, government is insisting that they do not have the required financial resources to see the process through. Sports Minister Kambwili challenged NGOs and civil society organizations to fund the constitution-making process as government-prioritised development (The Zambian Voice 2014). However, when the *Draft Constitution* was released in October 2014, the then acting Minister of Justice Simbyakula reiterated government's commitment to producing a people-driven constitution (Kuyela 2014). The government's option was to give the draft to the people for them to make further recommendations on how they would want the process to proceed. Opposition political parties and the civil society could not trust the government and continued to demand for a road map to the release of the final constitution as well as specific timelines.

Based on inconsistent utterances by senior government officials, allegations of acting in bad faith and lack of political will have been levelled on government. This development has resulted in suspicion that there is a deliberate act of sabotage by government to stall the people-driven process with the intention of manipulating the document. This is more so following utterances by the president himself, who was quoted to have said there is no need for so much noise about the constitution-making process when the country has a functioning constitution (*Lusaka Times* 9 April 2014). This culture of government officials pursuing their will at the expense of general will has been a trend in Zambia since independence, in relation to constitution making as alluded to earlier. All governments have managed to manoeuvre their way through the will of the people and attain their selfish goals without due consideration of public will (Simutanyi 2013).

Salient Issues in Zambia's Constitutional History

After the observations from the several constitutional review processes that the nation has embarked on since independence, one would question the objectivity of embarking on such a costly process, taking a heavy toll on the budget, and disrupting the implementation of development programmes only to abort it in the end. The Zambian Voice noted that the ruling Patriotic Front (PF) condemned the MMD for failing to give Zambians a constitution despite spending K120 billion on the process. The technical committee appointed by the PF government has used close to K150 billion (K150 million rebased) since it was set up (The Zambian Voice 2014).

It is also worth observing that all the governments have deliberately used the Inquiries Act to institute constitutional review commissions, thereby giving themselves excessive power to manipulate the process. Mbao as quoted by Motsamai (2014: 3) notes, 'in the case of constitutional review commissions, the Act empowers the president to determine the terms of reference of the review commissions and have exclusive right of access to and control of commission reports.' In short the government has power to reject or accept the recommendations, thereby overriding the wishes of the people.

However, the principles of democracy allow for public participation as one of the key pillars. In a country that claims to be democratic, popular participation in national issues is a must. This position is aptly summed up by Brandt et al (2011: 15), who note, 'Due to the notion of people's sovereignty and the fundamental right of the people to participate in public affairs, there is a tendency . . . to promote people's participation in constitution making.' In this regard, popular participation in the constitution-making process is a legitimate expectation because the role of any constitution is to unite and bind all people in a nation. It is the case that in Zambia the constitution making has been characterised by the perpetuation of the culture of popular exclusion, where the public have been allowed to make contributions during commission outreach meetings yet feedback has been withheld and the government in most cases, if not all, has rejected the recommendations made by their mandated commissions.

Further, the current Constitution (the one being reviewed) stipulates that the adoption of any new constitution remains the prerogative of parliament, where only members of parliament have the power to consider the drafts. However, natural justice demands that the adoption of a national project of such magnitude, which directly affects the lives of individuals, should involve all the stakeholders by being subjected to a national referendum as recommended by the Mung'omba Constitution Review Commission. Notwithstanding the uncontested truth that parliament is vested with legislative powers, the procedure ought and must be different with regard to constitution making, which is purported to be people-driven. Again the parliamentarians could not be allowed to exclude the public at the final and crucial stages on account of the flawed constitution which the people of Zambia are seeking to repeal. In this regard, the voice of the people through a national referendum should remain sovereign and sacrosanct.

It has also been observed that all constitutional reviews have been initiated by government. The expectation is that the rest of the process would follow David Easton's political cycle whereby citizens make demands and give support as input into the political system, which is the government, where debate and deliberations take place with the output of decisions and policies (Easton 1965). These decisions and policies are given out to the public in response to the demands already made. After receiving the decisions and policies, the people give feedback to the political system again on their view of the policies and decisions. That cycle goes on and on in a normally functioning political system. In the case of Zambia, the demand for the new constitution has been emanating from the political system itself. While the initiative itself is welcome, what is unacceptable is government's disrespect for their people's views, especially after consulting them.

In Zambia, the trend has been that as soon as a government comes into power, it initiates a constitutional review process to suit their intentions. The wide consultation takes place well after the need to review has been identified by the government of the day. The major drawback has been lack of transparency and accountability on the part of the governments to revert to the people, whose views they had solicited to enable the public to identify more with the constitutional provisions which they had crafted for themselves.

Conclusion

From the discussion, it can be concluded that fifty years on constitution making in Zambia have been characterised by manipulation and mutilation of the people's will. The intention has always been to safeguard one's rule and hold on power, as illustrated by the imposition of single-partyism during the Kaunda era and the insertion of the parentage clause by the Chiluba regime as well as attempts by Chiluba to change the Constitution to enable him to run for the third term as president. As stated by Mbao (2007: 18), 'Prior to 2001 presidential and parliamentary elections, Chiluba tried to amend the constitution so as to allow him to run for a third term.' It is the case, therefore, that leaders have used their different machinations to perpetuate their hold on state power. In such circumstances, it can safely be assumed that such leaders stand to gain more by amending or changing the constitution than the nation stands to gain.

As a way forward, it is important for the civil society and government to work together to push the country forward, especially looking at how far Zambia has gone in terms of development for the past five decades. There are serious considerations that the nation as a whole has to make in a bid to move the nation forward. Most notable of these are

(i) a complete overhaul of the system of governance to ensure that leaders are held accountable to the people of Zambia and nurture political will to see national projects through to their conclusive ends

(ii) cultivation of a culture of being participative because a passive political
culture is fertile breeding ground for political ill rule by the leaders
since nobody is inclined to oppose the status quo; instead, they
passively obey

(iii) forging of unity of purpose by civil society to have a greater impact.
In this regard, civil society should be autonomous, self-generating,
and self-sustaining to avoid being compromised by government. A
divided civil society cannot withstand pressure from government,
especially considering that civil society in Africa has been regarded
by governments as enemies of the state mainly because of their
confrontational approach. Mbao (2007: 18) noted, 'the opposition
parties and others opposing government policies were not seen as
people holding different opinions but as enemies of the state'

(iv) ensuring closer complementary working relations between civil society
and government for the benefits of the citizenry. Civil society should
complement government work and not be confrontational all the
time. The two should work as partners in development if indeed their
mission is to better the lives of Zambians

5.   ensuring respect for the will of the people on the part of government
with regard to constitution making. A constitution is the supreme law
of any land therefore it has to be drafted with the full participation
of all the stakeholders in good faith. These include government,
civil society, academics, constitutional law experts, and the public at
large. Those who do not know should be educated to appreciate the
importance of participating in constitution-making processes.

References

Books

Blaug, R. (2010), *How Power Corrupts: Cognition and Democracy in Organisations*
(London: Palgrave Macmillan).

Brandt, M. et al. (2011), *Constitution Making and Reform: Options for the Process*
(Geneva, Switzerland: Interpeace).

Chanda, A. W. (ed.) 2001, 'Constitutionalism in Southern Africa: Old Wine
in New Bottles', *The Human Rights Observer* vol. 5, July, Southern

Africa Human Rights NGO Network (SAHRINON) and Inter-African Network for Human Rights and Development (Afronet).

Easton, D. (1965), *A Systems Analysis of Political Life*. (New York: John Wiley and Sons).

Makumba, M. M. (2007), *Introduction to African Philosophy* (Nairobi: Paulines Publications Africa).

Simutanyi, N. (2013), *Zambia: Democracy and Political and Political Participation* (discussion paper) A Review by AfriMAP and the Open Society Foundations, Johannesburg.

Sithole, M. (1998), *Zimbabwe's Public Eye: Political Essays (October 1997– October 1998)* (Harare: Rujeko Publishers).

Articles and Papers

Banda, T. I. (2008), *An Evaluation of the Constitution Making Process in Zambia and the Legitimate Sources of a Constitution*, LLB dissertation submitted to the University of Zambia.

Blaug, R. (2010), *How Does Power Corrupt?* Roundhouse Journal pamphlet.

Colonial Office Northern Rhodesia Proposals for Constitutional Change Presented to Parliament by the Secretary for State of the Colonies by Command of Her Majesty, February 1961, (London, Her Majesty's Stationery Office).

Cummings, L. (2012), *Gorbachev's Perestroika and the Collapse of the Soviet Union*. http://www.lagrange.edu/resources/pdf/citations/2012/08_Cummings_History.pdf Accessed 03 February 2015.

International IDEA (2010), Constitutional History of Zambia, 2010, http://www.constitutionnet.org.

Kuyela, T. (2014), 'Draft Constitution Released', *Zambia Daily Mail*, 24 October, accessed online, available at https://www.daily-mail.co.zm/?p=8886.

Lusaka (2014), 'Zambia Has a Functional Constitution—President Sata', 9 April.

Lusaka Times (2014), 21 May.

Lusaka Times (2014), 8 June.

Lusaka Times (2014), 'Interview with Non-Governmental Organisations Coordinating Council (NGOCC) Executive Director Engwase Mwale', 10 June.

Lusaka Voice (2014), 'Lewanika and Others v Chiluba (1998)—The Most Significant Court Ruling in Zambia's 50 Year Jurisprudence', 25 August.

Mbao, M. (2007), *The Politics of Constitution Making in Zambia: Where Does the Constituent Power Lie?* Paper presented at African Network of Constitutional Law Conference on Fostering Constitutionalism in Africa, Nairobi, April 2007.

Motsamai, D. (2014), *Zambia's Constitutional Making Process: Addressing the Impasse and Future Challenges*, Institute for Security Studies, Situation Report, Pretoria.

ncczambia.org December 2014.

Republic of Zambia Government Paper Number 1 of 1995, Summary of the Recommendations of the Mwanakatwe Constitutional Review Commission and Government Reaction to the Report, Government Printers, Lusaka.

Republic of Zambia, Draft Constitution of Zambia, 30 April 2012.

Phrases Finder. http://www.phrases.org.uk/meanings/absolute-power-corrupts-absolutely.html.

The Southern Times (The Newspaper for Southern Africa), 20 December.

Wired Project 316 16 November 2011.

The Zambian Voice (2014), 'Michael C. Sata and His PF in a Battle Front', 3 February.

Zambiaconstitutionnet.org November 2011.

Chapter 3

The Nexus of Political Culture and Citizen Participation in Public Affairs: Critical Reflections on Zambia's Fifty Years of Independence

Shakespear Hamauswa and Petra Rumbidzai Chinyere

1.1 Introduction

As the people of Zambia celebrate fifty years of independence in 2014 the pertinent question which remains mind boggling to many is how political culture has been influencing political participation since 1964. Academic enquiries to this fundamental question have inordinately bypassed the cultural factors in their quest to provide explanations to Zambia's political development. This dearth in information set the stage for this piece of work which fundamentally focuses on political culture currently prevailing in the country, relating it to the participation of citizens in public affairs. This chapter advances the position that although cultural imperatives are often ignored, they have a considerable bearing on the involvement of the public in national affairs, yet the subject remains insufficiently explored. In achieving this goal, this chapter examines factors that have influenced Zambian political culture from the precolonial period to the present. As illustrated in this chapter, the precolonial traditional system of governance and values continue to shape and guide the political culture of leaders, political parties, and individuals in Zambia. The same is true to the vagaries of colonialism and other historical developments such as the establishment of indirect rule, cultural imperialism, establishment of one-party system, and technological revolution. It is also important to note that the postcolonial political developments have been products of various political cultures as well as influencing political culture in different ways. These events and historical developments have resulted in the development of various modes of political culture which in turn have a bearing on the general participation of the citizens in public affairs.

2. Conceptual Framework

2.1 *Political culture*

Political culture has been variably defined by different scholars. Ball and Peters (2005: 56) define political culture as 'the set of attitudes, beliefs, and values of society that relate to the political system and to the political issues'. Roskin et al. (2006: 115) define political culture as 'beliefs, symbols, and values about the political system'. From the above definitions it can be noted that political culture relates to beliefs, attitudes, orientations, and values that a particular society has towards its political system and society in general. These values are not static but are developed and change over an extended period and are transferred from one generation to another in various forms and processes including political socialisation and education. According to Chilton (1998: 419), 'culture must refer specifically to something shared among the people'. This means that within a particular community, society or state, the generalised culture has to manifest itself in the attitudes and beliefs of the people concerned. Political culture can take different forms. As a result, various scholars such as Almond and Verba (1963), Elazar (1970), and Lowery and Sigelman (1982) have suggested different types of political culture. In examining the nexus of political culture and participation in Zambia, Almond and Verba's classifications were found befitting. However, it is worth noting that no state or nation will exhibit uniform political culture at any given time.

According to Roskin et al. (2006), Gabriel Almond and Sidney Verba identify three different types of political culture, which are participant, subject, and parochial. In a participant political culture, the citizens of the country concerned are well versed with the political system in their country and are proud of taking part in national politics. In most cases participant citizens are ever willing to discuss national politics as they have the belief that they can influence their national politics through protest, group formation, and voting (Roskin et al. 2006: 118). Participant political culture sees the citizens being actively involved in the input side of the governing system (Almond and Verba 1963: 19). In this case the input comes in form of support and demands. Accordingly, Klesner (2007: 1) submits that citizens with participant political culture are expected to form the basis of active civil society and hence form the foundations of democracy.

Subject political culture relates to a situation whereby the citizens are looking forward to receiving outputs from the government. Citizens under this type are aware of political and government systems but just choose not to participate. According to Roskin et al. (2006), citizens with subject political culture follow national developments probably through watching political news but do not take pride in their country's political system. As a result, such people do not show emotional attachment to their political system. They feel they can influence politics only to the extent of speaking with a local official (ibid.: 118).

Parochial culture is where citizens generally expect nothing from the political system and are oblivious of the political arrangement. For Roskin et al. (2006), citizens under parochial political culture have a narrow or limited appreciation of national politics and display little or no interest in politics. More often than not, these citizens identify themselves with their immediate locality since they are not proud of their national political system. Parochial culture can be related to an individual political system. According to Lowery and Sigelman (1982: 376), although individualistic culture regards the participation of the public in national affairs as integral in maintaining political order, the public are kept outside the policymaking processes. In this regard, professionals are preferred to the ideas of the public. As illustrated in this chapter, Zambian people have exhibited a hybrid type of political culture with the characteristics of all the three types identified by Almond and Verba. It is even becoming difficult to identify a single dominant political culture prevailing in the country.

2.2. Political participation

According to Smith (2003), participation of citizens in public affairs relates to a 'process in which individuals, groups, and organisations have the opportunity to participate in making decisions that affect them, in which they have an interest'. With the increasing dominance of democratic system of governance, governments are being called upon and put under pressure to consider the participation of the citizens and other stakeholders in public affairs. Simutanyi (2013) observes that citizens can take part in public affairs through 'civil society organisations, or by directly making submissions, writing letters to the newspapers or through public discussion on radio and television'. Political participation of the citizens also manifests itself during elections and referendums as well as through public opinion polls. With regard to civil society organizations, the citizens can be represented by non-governmental organizations or directly forming their own interest and pressure groups. Political participation can be influenced by various factors, such as institutional capacity of the state, the nature of a political system as well as the level of development, among others. This study examines the role political culture plays in shaping or influencing political participation.

2.3. *The link between culture and political participation*

The democratic debate in Southern Africa has inordinately downplayed the interface between political culture and public participation, with scholars and analysts alike directing their attention on elections and electoral systems (Matlosa 2003). Political culture may have either negative or positive implications on public participation of citizens. According to Wiarda (1989: 193) cultural factors are as important in shaping national development as other factors such as technological advancement and education. For Wiarda this is true because traditional political culture and institutions have proved to be remarkably long-lived and persistent. This view is applicable to Zambia, where the present cultural traits and beliefs have their roots in the precolonial systems and institutions of governance. These cultural traits and beliefs continue to guide not only the general populace but also the political elite as they participate in public affairs. Boelkelman (1991) conducted a study on how political culture shapes the developmental policies in different states and came to the conclusion that it will be a mistake to assume that economic factors alone explain state policies. In explaining the importance of political culture, Boelkelman argues that political culture is pertinent because it may be rooted in orientations towards political economy. Therefore, the orientations, beliefs, and attitudes developed by a people or their ruling elite affect how the general people will participate in national politics. Heywood (1997) notes that political culture shapes people's perceptions and expectations regarding the running of national affairs by governments. This means that an analysis of the governance system of a particular society cannot be complete without an examination of its political culture.

The second reason why political culture is important is that it appears to manifest itself more readily in the behaviour of the political leaders than in the general 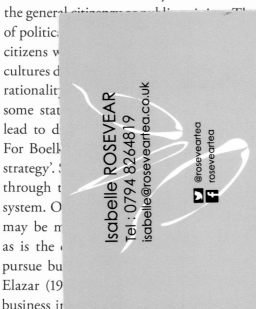 efore, the dominant manifestation of politic: litical elite has a bearing on how citizens v th noting that different political cultures d ept the marketplace and economic rationality (Boelkelman 1991). As a result, some stat individualistic. These attitudes lead to d omic and development policies. For Boelk ted to incline toward a creation strategy'. with the creation of public goods through t en participation in the political system. O t individualistic political culture may be n riented policies. Unfortunately, as is the eveloping countries, politicians pursue bu sonal self-interest. According to Elazar (19 ented politicians and organised business ii perform favours for each other in a "marketplace that emphasises commercial considerations and economic development'. The ultimate results of economic policies that are developed in these circumstances do not benefit the general public but the business people and the politicians. Boelkelman succinctly captures this scenario arguing that

> These policies, then, may be less an attempt to improve a state's overall economy than a favour that the political side of the alliance grants to the business side in the hope that the favour will be returned in political support. (1991)

Consequently, the reaction of the citizens to the above scenario may result in resentment towards the entire political system. In the case of Zambia, complex types of political culture have been in the making, not only among the citizens but among the ruling elite as well. It is important to understand the fundamental factors that shape the political culture in Zambia before we identify features of that culture and how they impact or relate to political participation.

3. Determinants of Zambia's Political Culture

There are many factors that shape the political culture of a given people at a particular time in history. According to Johari (2009: 226), 'political culture is a product of several interrelated factors that include historical, geographical as well as socio-economic conditions'. Johari also remarks that political culture is dynamic in that it responds to the needs generated from inside the concerned political system and to those that could be imposed from the outside. Ensuing is an analysis of how Zambia's political history, geographical conditions as well as socio-economic conditions have shaped the country's political culture.

3.1 *Historical factors*

According to Johari (2009: 226) traditions of a country have a bearing on the making of political culture. Thus, Zambia's political culture in the twenty-first century reflects the building up of attitudes, beliefs, orientations, and assumptions of many centuries that have been transmitted from one generation to another. In supporting the importance of history in shaping a country's political culture, Johari notes that the British people have a history of conservatism which influences them to favour slow and gradual change. Historically, Zambia has passed through a number of phases that have shaped and in some instances transformed the country's political culture. Firstly, the country had been governed by small and disparate kingdoms before the coming of colonial powers. Just like in any other precolonial society in Africa, decision-making was centrally organised in Zambia before the coming in of the colonial powers (Chiluba 1995: 21). The influence of the precolonial political practices to such an attitude was aptly captured by Lungu as cited by Chiluba (1995: 21) arguing, 'An individual's right to speak out his mind or advise the village headman or king on matters of public concern was taken for granted in almost all ethnic groups in Zambia.' It can also be noted that in almost all traditional systems in Africa, the chief had an elevated position over the subjects with the right to command them. This right, it is argued, was believed to have a divine basis leading to hereditary kind of succession. This view is glaringly clear in Kaunda's writings and pronouncements. For instance he claimed that

> the enduring importance of chiefly authority was representative of an authentically African model of consensual and communitarian decision-making that made competing political parties not only inappropriate but also politically destabilising basis for tribally based conflict. (Kaunda 1966)

The colonial period is part of the historical developments that have influenced Zambia's political culture. The coming of the British colonial power to Zambia had altered the governance system leading to the current set-up with a central government. The colonial government employed a system of separate development marked by racial and political segregation. The blacks were not given the right to vote and participate in politics. According to Wim (1995), colonialism had brought in cultural imperialism whereby the African culture and political systems were derided. This created an inferiority complex among the black majority, resulting in the development and internalisation of parochial political attitudes and beliefs by the subjects. However, as Wim (1995) observes, colonialism did not only humiliate the African people but also presented opportunities for political participation though to a limited extent. As such, the people in Zambia during the colonial period were socialised to participate in public affairs through involvement in missionary organizations as evangelists, local government administrators, junior teachers in schools, and drillers in mining companies (Wim 1995). As a result, the participating citizens, though few, were exposed to the exercise and manipulation of power in a formal organization. This exposure had an influence on the people of Zambia's attitudes and beliefs towards the political system and participation. Simutanyi (2013) concurs with this view, arguing that during the colonial period, traditional leaders were recognized by colonial masters to administer rural communities through what came to be known as traditional rule. Although these traditional rulers were not recognized to advance the wishes of their respective communities, they provided some opportunities for political participation.

3.2 *The postcolonial period*

The attainment of independence in 1964 inevitably brought into being new sets of beliefs, orientations, and attitudes towards politics and other related issues in Zambia. The introduction of the one-party state is regarded in this chapter as both the result of traditional governance systems and cause for the parochial culture among the citizens in the twenty-first century. In advancing the idea of the one-party state, Kaunda cited reasons that were being pushed forward by other authoritarian leaders in Africa. One of the arguments was to introduce a participatory democracy. However, history shows that the political system under Kaunda was never participatory but pushed the majority will to the periphery of political life. Even the much vaunted intra-party democracy was nowhere to be practiced. According to Chiluba (1995: 26), members of parliament were actually vetted by the party's central committee, and even before the introduction of the one-party system, the majority of the central committee came to be determined by the party leader, whose own candidacy for the presidency of the country was not allowed to be challenged.

One of the major implications of such a system to the development of political culture in Zambia is that the general populace came to accept the individual leaders and their respective political parties as all-knowing and that contestation for political, economic, and national policies was antagonistic. Thus while Zambia, from one angle, can be described as a thriving democracy, it can be noted that it is just democracy in form. This is mainly because as centralisation and concentration of power increased, so did the fear to criticise the government and to challenge the leadership.

While the political system was turning more and more towards statist and traditionalistic culture, the citizens at large became increasingly individualistic as a result of suppression of freedom of expression. Therefore, with the statist approach that was advanced from President Kaunda's time, decision-making excluded the participation of the majority in politics. In support of this, Simutanyi (2013) observes that in 1969 the government removed the constitutional provisions that limited its ability to make decisions without consulting the people. This development in Zambia supports Uchendu's view of the postcolonial state in Africa: 'consensus, an important ingredient of traditional African polity, has been replaced by coercion in modern African states' (1977: 99). Although Uchendu accepts the inevitability of coercion in any state, the fundamental difference between the use of coercion in the modern and traditional times is that during the precolonial period, force was used as an option of last resort. Therefore, when the incumbent political leaders easily resort to force or use it as their primary way of compelling compliance, citizens will end up developing resentment towards public affairs.

3.3 *Geographical location and conditions*

Zambia's political culture has also been influenced by its geographical location and conditions. According to Johari (2009: 227), 'the geographical make-up of a country also plays a part in the determination of the political culture of a people.' It is therefore important to examine how the geographical position of Zambia has shaped its political culture. Zambia is a landlocked country. According to Joffe (2013: 25), 'landlocked states do not have the type of unlimited and unconstrained access to freedom of movement on the high seas.' As a consequence, landlocked states negotiate to secure and maintain transit routes with their neighbours more often from a position of normative diplomatic weakness. Besides being landlocked, it can be noted that Zambia is also centrally located in the southern part of Africa, sharing its borders with eight countries. To the north of Zambia there is Tanzania, to the north-east there is Malawi, while to the east there is Mozambique, and to the southern part there is Zimbabwe, Botswana, and Namibia, and Angola to the west, and to the north-west the Democratic Republic of Congo (DRC). Following Joffe's point of view (2013) it can be argued that Zambian politics and political culture are affected by what happens in its neighbouring countries. As far as political culture is concerned, Zambia assisted most of its neighbouring countries such as Namibia, Zimbabwe, DRC, Mozambique, and Angola either during their struggles for independence or in dealing with civil war as was the case with DRC in 1998.

Surprisingly, Zambia's heroic history in building peace has not been well publicised, yet its position and such historical influences could have given its leaders and people an assertive attitude towards foreign policy.

Because of its central geographical location, Zambia has always been home to thousands of refugees from its neighbouring countries especially during times of crises, political and economic turmoil. According to the World Refugee Survey of 2009 published by the US Committee for Refugees and Immigrants, there were almost 88,900 refugees and asylum seekers in Zambia. About 47,300 of these refugees and asylum seekers came from the DRC, 27,100 from Angola, 5,400 from Zimbabwe and 4,900 from Rwanda (ibid.). This situation was correctly observed by Gewald, Hinfelaar, and Macola (2008: 18) arguing that one of Zambia's geopolitical weaknesses was its permeability to external efforts at destabilisation. As far as political culture is concerned, it seems plausible to suggest that the above-mentioned foreign people that are now residing in Zambia have capacities of varying degrees to bring in their political beliefs, attitudes and values. As a result, the political culture in Zambia becomes complex and multifaceted such that it is difficult to draw clear-cut lines distinguishing various forms of political culture.

3.4 *Socio-economic development*

The socio-economic conditions of a particular society may also influence the development of attitudes, beliefs, and orientations among the citizens towards their political system. According to Johari (2009: 227) a predominantly urban industrialised society is a more complex society, putting a premium on rapid communications. He adds that when educational standards are higher, groups proliferate and participation in the decision-making process of the state in question is also broadened. However, in a predominantly rural population with the peasants constituting the majority of the population, the situation and political culture thereof is different. Since Zambia is largely rural, it is not surprising that most of the people in rural areas are more of the traditionalistic category of political culture. While this form of political culture can be regarded as strength especially in maintaining institutions and their values, it also acts as a barrier to political progress. This is because in most cases rural people are more likely to have subject and parochial political culture. When the economy of the country is performing well, the citizens are likely to partake in public affairs. However, when the performance of the economy is poor and its weaknesses attributed to politics and corruption, citizens will have negative attitudes towards politics. Simutanyi (2013) supports this view, arguing that the rise of popular movements against Kaunda's one-party state in 1990 was based on the perception that Zambia's poor economic performance was a result of UNIP's misrule. This perception disregarded the contributions of the other factors such as the mono economy which had been heavily dependent on copper and the political instabilities in the region. As a result, civil society groups especially the trade unions, students, farmers, the poor, and the business community had to combine their forces, demanding the return to the multiparty political system of governance.

The effects of modernization and information communication technology cannot be ignored as far as political participation in the twenty-first-century Zambia is concerned. Because of technological revolution, information is now readily available to the general populace. Citizens can now post their comments on issues of public concern through social media. For instance daily newspapers have created platforms on social media where pertinent issues such as the health of the president, the economic performance and politics of succession, among others, can be debated. The only challenge is that participants use pseudo names or identities leading to the use of abusive language which sometimes is not racially, politically, or tribally neutral. As such, some are dissuaded from effective participation.

3.5 *Political violence*

Political violence has also played a pivotal role in shaping and reshaping Zambia's political culture. According to Rahman (1990: 3), 'one important feature of contemporary political culture is the instrumental use of violence as a method of political competition.' In Zambia the issue of violence has not been confined or peculiar to a singular historical period in the development of the country's political history but permeates almost all historical periods, though with varying degrees. In this chapter, the authors randomly picked a few violent historical events not because they were the most violent and/or the only ones but just to illustrate the continued effects of violence on building and shaping a country's political culture. The Lumpa uprising is one classic example that can be used to show how violence has shaped Zambia's political culture. As Gordon (2008) argues, 'the Lumpa uprising occurred when the United National Independence Party (UNIP) was in control of government while the colonial administration was still in charge of security.' As a result there are multiple explanations to what really transpired leading to the death of an estimated 1,000 Lumpa church followers. For Gordon (2008), the established and conventional history of the Lumpa-UNIP conflict is a culmination of the church's rebellion against authority which started during the colonial period. It is argued that the Lumpa church had a history of rebellious behaviour as they rebelled against the colonial regime and the chiefs (especially the latter's insistence on revering the ancestral spirits) and at the time of the crisis they rebelled against the UNIP-led government.

While the results of the Lumpa uprising are regarded in this chapter as a cause of what would be Zambia's political culture, the incident itself brings to the fore the fact that Zambian people have always shown some aspects of resistance. What could have overturned such traits is the reaction of the authorities at whom the resistance was directed. Uchendu (1977) notes that politics can fundamentally be regarded as a form of warfare, meaning that violence can be justified.

Despite some scattered incidents of political violence, Zambian people have been conducting their political activities without engaging in violence. However, Ndlovu (2014: 1) argues that violence slowly entered Zambian politics towards the end of Chiluba's rule and the coming into power of the Patriotic Front (PF). While there are different versions to the causes of violence and even to the major culprits of violence, it is clear that political violence has come to be used as a tool for enforcing compliance by politicians. Ndlovu (2014) cites some specific cases of violence that could have left some scars among the Zambian people with the capacity of altering the attitudes, beliefs, and views of the general populace about politics. These incidents include but are not limited to the by-elections that were conducted shortly after PF assumed power. For instance, the case of Mufumbwe in North-Western province, the arrest of opposition party leaders and barring them from exercising their freedom of association are cases in point. Other striking cases cited by Ndlovu (ibid.) include the arrest of the Movement for Multiparty Democracy leader Nevers Mumba for merely visiting a traditional leader in the Copperbelt province and the case in which United Party for National Development president Hakainde Hichilema had to escape suspected PF party cadres after giving live address at a private radio station in Ndola on 10 April 2014. In all these cases the accused always give reasons to refute the claims of violence but the argument is that political violence is slowly moving in to affect the way people think and feel about politics.

The observation that violence is taking root in Zambia was echoed by the United States of America embassy chargé d'affairs David Young, who in 2014 expressed concern over the culture of violence in Zambia. Young remarked that in a democracy, disagreements are settled with words and not with machetes as witnessed in Zambian politics (*Lusaka Times* 6 June 2014). However, it is important to note that isolated cases where machetes were used cannot be a basis for making sweeping generalisations about the conduct of politics in Zambia. What is clear is that violence engenders violence as such isolated cases will lead to more complicated incidence of political violence.

4. Implications of political culture on political participation in Zambia

From the determinants of political culture in Zambia presented above, it can be argued that the implications to the general involvement of people in public affairs have been both positive and negative. On the positive side, Zambia's long record of peace and mutual coexistence has influenced Zambians to treat each other with dignity as well as to exhibit the spirit of patriotism. This is evident when there are national events such as independence celebrations. For instance towards, during, and after the fiftieth independence celebrations, most of the people including children could be seen in Zambian flag colours. While Zambians have always been peaceful, more often than not, they have shown capacity of measurable magnitude to resist authoritarianism and dictatorial tendencies. Before and during the federation which brought together Nyasaland now Malawi, Northern and Southern Rhodesia, now Zambia and Zimbabwe respectively, under a single administration in 1953, Zambians expressed their resistance and through protests influenced its dissolution (Sardanis 2014).

In addition it was due to widespread protest and popular pressure by the citizens that the first president of Zambia, Kaunda, agreed to revert to the multiparty political system in 1991. The people of Zambia also exhibited their resolve to defend their will when they rejected the Second Republican president Chiluba's attempt to manipulate the constitution in order to secure a third presidential term (Simutanyi 2013). This also partly explains why and how the people of Zambia have managed to peacefully change their presidents four times. This capacity to communicate through the ballot has seen successive governments being put under pressure to deliver on their promises to the people. However, there is a notable trend in Zambia whereby the politicians are not prepared to provide citizens with the opportunity to meaningfully participate in their national affairs beyond voting. Simutanyi (2013) notes that the present situation is highly centralised thereby limiting additional grounds for political participation.

Lack of participant political culture in Zambia has led to an increasingly lower voter turnout in national elections. Probably, this could be attributed partly to the poor performance of the economy during Kaunda's time and to the continued constrained space for public participation. Simutanyi (2013) notes, 'since 1991, voter turnout in general elections as a percentage of eligible voters has only averaged 32.5 per cent.' Simutanyi suggests that the probable reason for limited interest in national politics among Zambians from 1991 to the present was that the MMD was guided by transient goals. In this regard, the MMD found its legitimacy and source of public support in advancing the reintroduction of the multiparty system of government.

Subject and parochial political cultures in Zambia have also led to the systematic exclusion of the people in the formulation and implementation of developmental and national policies. These negative developments resulted from convoluted experiences with authoritarian leadership that was guided by traditionalistic and individualistic political beliefs and orientations. As a result, the majority continue to play peripheral roles in matters of public concern such as policymaking and constitution making. The introduction of the one-party state during the Second Republic did much in dissuading the citizens from active politics as well as leading to the glorification of political leaders as the only fountains of wisdom (Simutanyi 2013). Zambia's constitutional reform process is one classic example of how the citizens have been systematically excluded from active participation even by the regimes that seemed to be championing political liberalism. Simutanyi (2013) correctly observes that constitutional changes sought by successive regimes in Zambia were done to suit and serve the interests of the succeeding regimes without seeking the views of the people. For instance when the one-party state was introduced, citizens were not consulted on its efficacy to Zambian society but on how it would be applied. Such an approach to issues of national concern continues to lower citizens' level of interest in political participation.

Another observation is that because of the political culture prevailing in Zambia, the voice of the general populace in policy formulation and holding politicians to account has not been as strong as it should be in a democratically governed state. Therefore, the grass-roots population cannot be fully represented if those in power are not opening up the space for effective citizenry participation. It is, however, worth noting that at the time of writing this chapter, the government of Zambia is coming up with a policy document to ensure that future policies will represent the aspirations of the people. It can also be observed that because of technological revolution and the increase in literacy rate, citizens are resorting to new forms of participation as they can now use social media and social networks to air their views on pertinent issues. In this regard, online media such as the *Watch Dog*, the *Economist*, the *Lusaka Voice*, and other daily newspapers are providing citizens with platforms to participate and contribute to national debates through the Internet. Some politicians as well as political parties have Facebook accounts where citizens can share information and raise issues of concern. Therefore, the contributions of the people through such platforms will definitely alert the responsible officials about the people's preferences to particular policy options and other developments in the country.

Subject and parochial political cultures have also affected the attitudes of people on issues of national development. The Zambian deputy minister of commerce, trade, and industry, Miles Sampa, argued that citizens need to change their mindset and be more industrious to effectively contribute to poverty reduction. In support of his argument, the deputy minister remarked, 'since independence, our people have always aspired and worked hard to improve living conditions to be a prosperous and successful nation' (*Daily Mail* 7 August 2014). Unfortunately, the deputy minister's view seems to suggest that people just chose to be lazy without even being influenced by their political system. It is important for government officials to understand that their approach to politics and how they view their citizens greatly influences the people's political culture. As such, a government that treasures the contributions of its people will likely prioritise opening opportunities for the citizens especially in the mainstream economy and political participation.

5. Conclusion

As this chapter tried to show, there is a close relationship between political culture and the participation of citizens in public affairs. Sadly, political scientists and other social scientists have always shown the tendency of excluding cultural factors in the political participation matrix. Therefore, as the people of Zambia are celebrating their jubilee independence from the former British colonial masters, it was important to examine how political culture developed and evolved in Zambia. The ultimate aim was to identify those positive and negative cultural traits in Zambia and to show their linkages to the patterns of political participation. It has been argued in this chapter that Zambia's political culture is shaped by various factors such as traditional and historical experiences, the experience with colonialism, its central position in southern Africa, socio-economic conditions, technological revolution, and the conduct of politics by successive governments. As a result the political culture has been complex.

Therefore, it can be noted that Zambia has developed a hybrid political culture with multiple traits of different types or forms of political culture manifesting themselves in various circumstances. Succeeding regimes and political leaders have adhered to different political systems, thereby promoting certain types of political culture. In brief, one can identify individualistic, traditionalistic, moralistic, and statist political attitudes and beliefs towards the political system. These have been evident among the political leaders who in turn affected the direction of national institutions as well. Policies have also been crafted guided by the forms of political culture of the ruling elite. As a negative development, citizens have shown more of parochial and subject political cultures only to be active during elections. Nevertheless, because of the advent of information communication technology, citizens are increasing their participation through social media and other social networks.

Political violence and intolerance of different opinions appear to be on the increase in Zambia. As indicated in this chapter, Zambians have been known to be peace-loving people but the coming in of multiparty politics in 1991 has been paralleled by an increase in political violence. Therefore, statist type of political culture and political violence greatly pushes people out of political participation. What is important to note is that politicians and other factors such as political violence, corruption, and dependence on foreign capital unconsciously affect the political culture of a given people. It is therefore important for the government to identify the factors that bring in positive political culture that will contribute to the growth of democracy in the country.

Since the attitudes of politicians towards political systems can be both products of and factors that shape a country's political culture, it is important for politicians to take stock of how their actions have shaped Zambia's political culture throughout the past five decades. In this regard, political leaders in Zambia can adopt and put in place various strategies that help to build positive political attitudes among the citizens. Adoption of and putting into practice the concept of deliberative democracy will help in nurturing a political system where the citizens positively contribute to the development of their nation. Deliberative democracy is defined by Carcasson and Sprain (2010) as 'an approach to politics in which citizens, not just experts or politicians, are deeply involved in public decision-making and problem-solving'. Therefore the general populace, through the adoption of deliberative democracy, can find ways in which they can contribute to national policy and decision-making process. When the people effectively participate in the affairs of their nations, their attitudes toward their governments and representatives as well as their perception of their nation as a whole will change positively. The citizens become proud of their nations as they feel respected by their leaders.

References

Almond, G. A. and Verba, S. (1963), *The Civic Culture: Democracy in Five Nations* (Princeton: Princeton UP).

Ball, A. R. and Peters, B. G. (2005), *Modern Politics and Government* 7th edition (New York: Palgrave Macmillan).

Boelkelman, K. (1991), 'Political Culture and State Development Policy', *Publicus* 21/2.

Carcasson, M. and Sprain, L. (2010), 'Key Aspects of the Deliberative Democracy Movement', *Public Sector Digest*, 2010, available online at https://www.publicsectordigest.com/articles/view/722 accessed on 13 August 2014.

Chilton, S. (1988), 'Defining Political Culture', *Western Political Quarterly*, 41/3: 419–445, available online at http://www.jstor.org/stable/448596 accessed on 15 August 2014.

Chiluba, F. J. T. (1995), *Democracy, the Challenge of Change* (Lusaka: Multimedia Publications).

Elazar, D. J. (1970), *Cities of the Prairie: The Metropolitan Frontier and American Politics* (New York: Basic Books).

Gewald, J. B., Hinfelaar, M., and Macola, G. (2008) (eds.), *One Zambia, Many Histories: Towards a History of Post-Colonial Zambia*, Afrika-Studiecentrum Series, Volume II. Available online at http://saipar.org/wp-content/uploads/2013/09/One-Zambia.pdf accessed 10 August 2014.

Gordon, D. M. (2008), 'Rebellion or Massacre, The UNIP-Lumpa Conflict Revisited', in *One Zambia, Many Histories: Towards a History of Post-Colonial Zambia*, edited by Gewald, J. B., Hinfelaar, M., and Macola, G., Afrika-Studiecentrum Series, Volume II. Available online at http://saipar.org/wp-content/uploads/2013/09/One-Zambia.pdf accessed 10 August 2014.

Heywood, A. (1997), *Politics* (London: Macmillan).

The International Encyclopaedia of the Social Sciences (1968), (New York: Macmillan).

Joffe, G. (2013) 'Chad: Power Vacuum or Geopolitical Focus', in *Land-Locked Sates of Africa and Asia*, edited by William, R. H., Lloyd, S., and McLachlan, K. (London: Routledge).

Johari, J. C. (2009), *Principles of Modern Political Science* (New York: Sterling Publishers).

Kaunda, K. D. (1966), *A Humanist in Africa: Letters to Colin Morris from Kenneth Kaunda, President of Zambia* (Tennessee: Abingdon Press).

Klesner, J. (2007), *Political Attitudes, Social Capital and Political Participation: The United States and Mexico Compared* (Ohio: Kenya College). Available online at http://lasa.international.pitt.edu/Lasa2001/KlesnerJoseph.pdf accessed on 2 August 2014.

Lowery, D. and Sigelman, L. (1982), 'Political Culture and State Public Policy: The Missing Link', *The Western Political Quarterly*, 35/3. Available at http://www.jstor.org/stable/447552 accessed on 25 July 2014.

Lusaka Times, 'US government bemoans levels of political violence in Zambia', available online at https://www.lusakatimes.com/2014/06/06/us-government-bemoans-levels-political-violence-zambia/ accessed on 26 July 2014.

Matlosa, K. (2003), 'Political Culture and Democratic Governance in Southern Africa', *African Journal of Political Science*, 8/1: 85–112.

Mazrui, A. A. A. (1977), 'The Warrior Tradition in Modern Africa', *International Studies in Sociology and Social Anthropology Studies in Medieval and Reformation Thought*.

Ndlovu, G. (2014), 'Violence Taking Root in Zambia', *The Independent Observer*, available at http://www.tiozambia.com/headlines/political-violence-taking-root-in-zambia accessed on 16 August 2014.

Rahman, H. Z. (1990), 'Landscape of Violence and Political Culture in Bangladesh', *Economic and Political Weekly*, 24 November.

Roskin, M. G., Cord, R. L., Medeiros, J. A., and Jones, S. W. (2006), *Political Science: An Introduction* 9th edition (New Jersey: Pearson Education, Inc.).

Sardanis, A (2014), Zambia: The First 50 years, London: IB Taurus

Smith, B. L. 'Public Policy and Public Participation: Engaging Citizens and Community in the Development of Public Policy', B. L. Smith Groupwork Inc. A paper prepared for the Population and Public Health Branch Atlantic Regional Office, Health Canada. Available online at http://www.sasanet.org/documents/Curriculum/ConceptualFramework/pub_policy_partic_e.pdf accessed 20 October 2014.

Uchendu, V. (1977), 'The Cultural Roots of Aggressive Behaviour in Modern Africa Politics', in *The Warrior Tradition in Modern Africa*, edited by Mazrui, A. (Brill: Leiden).

US Committee on Refugees and Immigrants (2009), The World Refugee Survey, available online at http://www.refugees.org/resources/refugee-warehousing/archived-world-refugee-surveys/2009-world-refugee-survey.html accessed on 13 August 2014.

Wiarda, H. J. (1989), 'Political Culture and National Development', *Fletcher Forums* 13: 193–204.

Wim, V. B. (1995), 'Aspects of Democracy and Democratisation in Zambia and Botswana: Exploring African Political Culture at the Grassroots', *Journal of Contemporary African Studies*, 13/I: 3–33. Available online at http://www.quest-journal.net/publications/ASC-1239806-061.pdf accessed 19 November 2014.

The Zambia Daily Mail (2014), 'Sampa Calls for Industrious Attitudes', Thursday, 7 August.

Chapter 4

Sovereignty and Democracy: Zambia's Challenges

Torben Reinke

Introduction

One of Zambia's enduring challenges has been how to build a strong nation, which protects the sovereignty gained at independence along with developing a strong democracy representing the people. The post-independence state sought to achieve this by using rents from copper exports. Zambia's development has been very dependent on its connections to the global economy through copper exports and the relationship with foreign donors. From being among Africa's most prosperous countries, which benefitted from high copper exports in the 1960s, Zambia descended into severe economic crisis as the copper price collapsed in the mid-1970s. This was the starting point of heavy dependence on foreign aid as the World Bank and IMF assisted the government economically, requiring economic and political reform in return. The country's bad economic situation both facilitated the change towards multiparty democracy in 1991 and also made Zambia stuck in transition towards democracy as its sovereignty remained constrained due to aid dependency. This chapter will analyse the relationship between sovereignty and democracy using a political economy approach. The following section will explain why a dependency on either natural resources or aid is problematic in facilitating democracy. Subsequently three different periods will be analysed to provide a comparative study over time of Zambia's sovereignty and democracy.

The curse of natural resources and aid

In a country where the economy is entirely reliant on just one commodity rather than on broad taxation of companies and citizens, the prime challenge is how to secure long-term benefits from such a commodity, particularly if it is characterised by price fluctuation. There is strong evidence from the resource-curse literature that countries having large deposits of natural resources, such as minerals or oil, are not performing well economically (Collier and Hoeffler 2007; Sachs and Warner 1995; Hallum 2011). These countries furthermore tend to face higher risks of developing internal conflicts and becoming authoritarian. In Africa, countries with large natural resources have, in most cases, had an intensified struggle for the control of this wealth (Collier 2008). Most of the newly independent African countries have had to contend with the challenge of how to achieve nation-building in territories demarcated by the former colonial powers rather than precolonial structures. It has been particularly difficult to attain nation-building, which requires creating a shared identity of the state within ethnically diverse territories. In many cases, little was done to create the political and institutional conditions conducive to transference of power (Clapham 1996). When this is combined with the availability of large deposits of natural resources, there is a rise in the stakes for territorial control by a new independent government. In the case of resource-rich Belgian Congo, it was thus not surprising that independence in 1960 quickly turned into civil war, as the newly elected government of Patrice Lumumba quickly faced secessionist movements in the absence of proper institutional structures left behind by the Belgians (ibid.: 38–39). Since then DR Congo has remained unstable and poor despite the vast amounts of natural resources available.

In the oil-rich Middle East, the presence of wealth has not led to failed states as in Africa, but to stable authoritarian regimes, where the ruling elite has used authoritarianism to protect their grip on both power and resources. However, the wealth has not trickled down to the majority of the people. The recent Arab Spring uprisings in the Middle East and North Africa showed public dissatisfaction with authoritarian leaders in these countries (Danahar 2013). The initial optimism from the uprisings has however turned out to be an illusion due to the fight for control over resources. Religious differences become part of a larger struggle for the resources. In Iraq and Syria, an Islamic state benefits from capturing oilfields to fund the struggle for control in the region.

In the developed world, Norway is one of the few exceptions to the negative pattern of resource-rich states. The country first discovered its oil in 1969. The Government Pension Fund was created by the government to invest oil revenue for future generations, rather than spending the revenue. The government is accountable with a high degree of transparency for all revenue and investments. The secret in the Norwegian case is particularly the late discovery of oil: Norway was a consolidated democracy reliant on taxes before the oil was discovered. This development ensured proper long-term strategy to the benefit of the country, where Norway diversified and relies on exports of other goods, such as fish and timber, in addition to investment in science and a highly educated population. Furthermore, Norway has one of the highest tax levels in the world, which has contributed to making them the highest-ranked country on the Human Development Index (World Bank 2014).

A relevant theoretical starting point to explain why Norway is an exceptional case, compared to other resource-rich countries, is to account for the typical resource curse happening in many resource-rich countries. Mick Moore's research (1998) on the importance of the tax state as essential for countries to become developed can explain why natural resources as well as aid dependency are problematic in fostering development. Moore argues that a government's dependency on broadly levied taxes is important for a country's development as it will constrain government borrowing while at the same time enhancing accountability to the citizens. The history of modernization in Western countries shows that becoming successful tax states was essential for development and democratization. A country with natural resources differs from the tax state as it does not rely on taxing its citizens. Instead it relies on rents. Moore distinguishes between two types of rents, which are natural resource rents and strategic rents. Natural resource rents include products like oil and minerals such as copper and diamonds and others. This type of rent has become particularly valuable to developing countries because of increased demand and hence higher world market prices. Strategic rents represent rents for countries, which are considered strategic for other countries. In Africa this rent has mainly consisted of foreign aid, offered with conditionalities of economic reforms and good governance. Both resource rents and strategic rents affect state-society relations because the rents are unearned income. *'Earnedness depends on the bureaucratic and organizational effort put into raising revenue by the government and also the degree of effective reciprocity between citizens and state, i.e. services in return for tax contributions'* (ibid.: 85). The type of income that fulfils these requirements of earnedness the most are direct taxes, which consist of personal and corporate income taxation and corporate income taxation. It requires the highest organizational effort to both collect and meet the service provision demands of the people in return. When citizens contribute to the state by paying taxes, they expect services in return. In this regard, the state is more accountable to the taxpayers on how it spends the taxpayers' money. It does not have to display the same accountability on how it spends unearned income such as royalties from mine extraction. Timmons (2005) has found strong support for this causality that citizens and state have an implicit fiscal contract, where states actually deliver welfare and other services according to how much tax is contributed. States do so because taxpayers demand to be heard in policymaking and particularly democratically elected governments need to care as we assume they want to be re-elected. To analyse this in the case of Zambia, an important indicator is if the people are able to hold the government accountable at elections. Is there a meaningful debate over distribution of benefits at elections and is the government actually being held accountable, as should be the purpose of elections? Opposition parties play an important role in expressing public dissatisfaction. Following the return to multiparty democracy in Zambia, presidential elections will be analysed in this chapter to establish changes in democratic accountability. Moore's theory leads us to the expectation that at times when Zambia has been too reliant on either copper or aid, there has been lack of democratic accountability in the country. On the other hand as the government relies increasingly on earned income, it is expected that there will be enhancement democratic accountability.

Earned income is also important for building state institutions and state capacity (Moore 1998; Bräutigam 2000). Studies on aid effectiveness point towards the problems of states lacking the incentives to strengthen capacity in revenue collection (Bräutigam 2000; van de Walle 2001). Van de Walle (2001) furthermore argues that African governments has been able to remain in power due to the aid received, which often have sustained the use of clientelism and patronage. Without aid they would not have been able to postpone unpopular economic reforms. Aid recipients have applied the strategy of partial reform implementation that could utilise the World Bank and IMF's inclination to keep on lending despite conditionalities that were not completely met (van de Walle 2001: 223–224). The choice of African governments to only partially reform their economies has been an efficient coping-strategy of balancing the reform pressure with the need to satisfy domestic stakeholders necessary for re-election. In the early 1990s, most of the African countries adopted multiparty democracy but only in 12 per cent of all presidential elections from 1990 to 2009 did the incumbent lose (Cheeseman 2010: 142). The benefits of incumbency explain a lot of the dominance of incumbent parties. The incumbent party typically has access to state resources, controls the media, and is faced with weak non-institutionalised opposition parties.

Scholars disagree about the responsibility for the failure of aid in facilitating development. Van de Walle's (2001) criticism of aid-recipient governments has been met with criticism targeted at aid as an efficient way of assisting countries to develop, particularly because donors and recipients do not have the same interests. Whitfield (2009) argues that donors want to be too much in control over the policies in aid-receiving countries instead of allowing the recipient government genuine ownership. Ownership is defined as *the degree of control recipient governments are able to secure over implemented policy outcome* (ibid.: 4). The government must take leadership and donors should align their assistance with these priorities. Aid has the main purpose of creating long-term sustainable development and mobilising state capacity. The donor community and aid recipients have identified these important concerns of ownership and have targeted it as one of the important elements in improving aid effectiveness. This dimension was most significantly established with OECD DAC's agreement on the Paris Declaration (OECD 2008) setting the terms of relationship between donors and recipient governments. Donors have remained committed to the recommendations of the Paris Declaration in general and to creating ownership in particular. The problem however remains that the Paris

Declaration assumes a partnership perspective with shared interests between donors and recipient countries. However, this assumption does not reflect reality. Instead the relationship is rather influenced by power struggles and conflicts (Andersen and Therkildsen 2007). Donors are not just altruistic as they have own geopolitical and economic interests to serve through the aid they are providing.

A bureaucracy, such as a country's aid agency is, also has a life of its own. It has a basic interest to expand its budget and be in control (Barnett and Finnemore 2004). Multilateral organizations, such as the World Bank and IMF, have managed to become so powerful that they are deeply involved in the domestic politics of recipient countries (ibid.). Barnett and Finnemore describe the IMF to have become an authority acknowledged by their expert knowledge with some of the best economists. However, the economists of IMF have macroeconomic stability as their concern, which is only one of the many concerns an elected government has to consider. This incongruity of interest has often led to conflicts between recipient governments and the IMF. For example, structural adjustment programmes prioritized the shock treatment of liberalizing the economy, which was politically difficult for recipient governments to implement. This conflict of interest and the tendency of donors to try to micromanage aid is still very much present despite donors' focus on aid effectiveness and new aid modalities (Whitfield 2009). The conflict poses a risk to aid recipients' sovereignty as donors have the interest to interfere in domestic politics of the recipient country to maintain control. Contrary to van de Walle's (2001) position of placing blame for aid failure on attention to the problems on the aid recipient government's side, donors can be said to constrain democracy and even compromise a country's sovereignty by choosing how aid is targeted (Whitfield 2009).

Having accounted for the problems of unearned income, such as natural resources and aid, sovereignty, and democracy in general, the chapter will now focus on the Zambia case. The theoretical expectation in the case of Zambia is that high dependence on copper earnings or high aid dependency will constrain Zambia's democracy. The impact on sovereignty is mostly expected to be caused by aid dependency due to donors' interest in influencing domestic politics through conditionalities. Although sovereignty is often threatened in resource-rich African countries, its potential to lead to instability depends on other factors, particularly how challenging nation-building was at the time of independence.

Nation-building in Zambia (1964–1991)

At independence in 1964, Zambia had a very viable economic foundation, being among the richest countries in Africa as measured by GDP per capita (Rakner 2003: 44). Foreign investment in copper mining from the 1930s and onwards in Northern Rhodesia created one of Africa's most industrialized territories. However, from the beginning the pattern of development was lopsided and did not spread sufficiently from mining to other sectors. Zambia's main challenge after independence was nation-building. Being a newly created state with high ethnic diversity and large copper deposits, the contest for power intensified in the newly independent country. Zambian humanism was an attractive strategy for nation-building and for the government to control both mineral resources and opposition. Starting in 1968 with the Mulungushi reforms, many companies were nationalised, including acquisition of 51 per cent of shares in foreign-owned mining companies. By the mid-1970s around 80 per cent of the Zambian economy was state controlled (ibid.). Nationalising the economy was important for the government to assert its sovereignty. Specifically it enabled the government to use tribal balancing to maintain support through patronage.

Tribal balancing was an essential nation-building strategy applied by President Kaunda. Zambia's diversity with at least thirty-nine ethnic groups (see Posner 2005: 52–55 for discussion of the number of ethnic groups) posed a challenge for nation-building. However, it has the benefit over ethnically polarised countries, that ethnicity cannot mobilise voters on its own as no ethnic group or language group in Zambia can claim to constitute the majority (Posner 2005; Lindemann 2010). As identified by Posner (2005), political parties in Zambia have mobilised support based on the four main language groups (Bemba, Nyanja, Tonga, and Lozi) at times of multiparty democracy. Kaunda deliberately created an over-representation of Tonga- and Lozi-speaking groups in government to cope with the opposition strength of ANC in Southern Province as well as to please Barotseland (the Lozis) who had drawn concessions from the government to maintain special status in return for accepting to be part of Zambia (Lindemann 2005: 13). A careful consideration of economic power sharing, according to language groups, was also ensured to maintain national support through the distribution of patronage. The nationalised economy enhanced the opportunity to use patronage through appointments and Lindemann's tabulation of appointments to board of directors and management of parastatals shows that the distribution was fair according to language groups (ibid.: 23). Appointments to parastatals were valuable and constituted an efficient strategy for co-opting important opposition candidates as well as leaders of strong societal groups such as the labour movement ZCTU (ibid.). As the government was the biggest employer in the country, such appointments enabled the office-bearers to run the offices effectively, thereby enhancing the target of nation-building without tribal tensions. By deliberately appointing people to serve in different provinces from where they were born, there was promotion of ethnic diversity. This was strengthened by the increased urbanisation making cities ethnic melting pots, which has made intertribal marriages particularly common in Zambia (Posner 2005: 92).

Copper constituted as much as 68 per cent of state revenue in 1965 (Chisala 2006: 109). While this was obviously a favourable situation for the government at the time, it was a dangerous source of dependency on unearned income. As argued by Moore (1998: 85) this leads to lack of organizational effort in raising alternative revenue for the government as well as lack of democratic accountability from the government to the people. The timing of the nationalisation of the copper mines turned out to be inappropriate as the price of copper fell substantially in the mid-1970s. The government considered the economic crisis temporary and obtained loans to maintain government spending (Rakner 2003: 54). Zambia had not diversified its economy during the boom period, which was also difficult as a 'Dutch disease' occurred, where high copper earnings made the kwacha appreciate, thereby making other sectors lose the competitiveness for export. A Dutch disease is, however, not inevitable and should rather be considered a political phenomenon of mismanagement rather than a pure economic phenomenon (Hallum 2011: 9). If the government had taken the responsibility of investing the large rents from copper into diversification and development of other sectors, the Dutch disease could have been avoided. In reality the government did not manage the rents from the copper boom well. The money was spent on sustaining the patronage networks and satisfying ordinary people with food subsidies, with little attention to diversification. When the price of copper declined, the state had a large budget deficit and little earned income to minimise the consequences of the drop in revenue. Therefore, Zambia fell into the trap of relying on unearned income (ibid.). Unearned income became a problem as predicted by Moore because when copper earnings were high, the revenue was not invested in building state capacity and diversifying the economy. State-society relations were not improved either. The revenue came from the mines and not from the people, and it was more beneficial to satisfy the groups in society that posed immediate challenge to the government's power.

The election of Margaret Thatcher as prime minister of the UK and Ronald Reagan as American president initiated a shift in the economic policies promoted by donors as well as the international financial institutions from the early 1980s. Comprehensive market reforms were required to solve the balance of payment crisis which was being experienced by the indebted countries (Rakner 2003: 27). President Kaunda prioritised the compliance with the donor strategy of solving Zambia's economic problems. However, this strategy had to be adopted at the political cost of having to reject the demands of the powerful domestic groups such as the bureaucracy, labour unions, and parastatal enterprises. The economic reforms also severely affected ordinary Zambians. The removal of government subsidies on maize in 1986, as required by donors, led to unrest in Lusaka and the Copperbelt, pressuring Kaunda to restore the subsidies (ibid.: 58). The programmes with the IMF and the World Bank were abandoned and the government introduced their own New Economic Recovery Programme (ibid.: 59–61). In an attempt to meet the domestic demands, the liberalisation process was halted and debt servicing minimised. The programme was not sustainable, and as bilateral donors decided to cut aid, the government had to return to the IMF and the World Bank to negotiate again in 1989.

As the government doubled the price of maize meal, three days of riots broke out in 1990 causing the death of twenty-seven people. Unlike the 1986 uprising, the blame was on the political system itself and UNIP, not on the IMF (ibid.: 63). At this time, the Zambia Congress of Trade Unions (ZCTU) had an important role in mobilising a movement pressuring for the return of multiparty democracy as well as in providing the organizational structure for such a movement. ZCTU's demands were supported by students, academics, the business community as well as backbenchers from UNIP who had politically began mobilising from July 1990 (Lewanika and Chitala 1990). These interest groups formed the Movement for Multiparty Democracy (MMD) and held its first convention in February 1991. As the pressure built up, President Kaunda eventually accepted the widespread demands for multiparty elections, which were held on 25 October 1991. MMD enjoyed widespread public support and won a landslide victory taking 75 per cent of the votes. MMD won the election by campaigning on the donor-encouraged neo-liberal agenda, despite the fact that it was the same structural adjustment that had caused dissatisfaction with the UNIP government (Rakner 2003: 65).

While UNIP failed in the end economically, their effort in creating nationhood must be recognized. Where many other newly independent African countries descended into violent conflict and civil war, President Kaunda managed to maintain Zambia peaceful by the sacrifices of developing an expensive parastatal sector used for patronage. It was preferred to please powerful interest groups, to co-opt challengers to the regime, and to use authoritarian means to maintain stability. As evident from this period, economics and politics are very interlinked. UNIP could probably have avoided the collapse of the economy by not letting the state control the majority of the economy, but it is doubtful if the party could have maintained its grip on power, which could have led to instability seen in many of Zambia's neighbouring countries. The Kaunda era also showed how dependency on one type of unearned income (copper) led to an unsustainable situation due to lack of diversification and effort into taxing other sectors. This made Zambia dependent on another type of unearned income—aid. Zambia's sovereignty was fairly strong after independence until there was an urgent need for foreign assistance. The autonomy of the government was constrained because of structural adjustment programmes initiated by the World Bank and IMF and eventually the hardship felt by Zambians led to pressure for democracy and the fall of the one-party state. The next section will further analyse the constraints on Zambia's sovereignty caused by continued aid dependency.

Aid dependency and the pressure on Zambia's sovereignty (1991–2004)

As MMD was elected into office, Zambia's reform challenges were comprehensive. The new government inherited a very large debt of 7 billion US$ (World Bank 2014), which made the government very dependent on bilateral donors as well as the international financial institutions: the World Bank and the IMF. The aim was further economic liberalisation to make the Zambian economy viable and to stimulate long-term growth for Zambia to pay off her debt. Most comprehensive and politically challenging was the process of privatising the many parastatal companies. MMD also committed to remove subsidies, abolish import and export licenses, and abandon price control. More than 250 companies were listed for privatisation, which was equal to around 85 per cent of the Zambian economy (Larmer 2005: 5).

The initial commitment to liberalisation by the MMD government and donors being attracted by a possible democratic success story made aid to Zambia reach its highest point in the early and mid-1990s. As evident from figure 1, the Chiluba government attracted large amounts of aid as it assumed power, with aid constituting 36 per cent of GDP during MMD's first full year in power (1992).

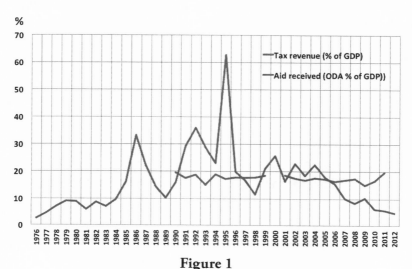

Figure 1
World Bank 2014
(Tax revenue data not available before 1990 and for 2000)

In comparison to aid figures, total tax revenue has generally been lower than aid, a trend which is however broken from 2005, where taxes finally become a more important source of income than aid. The political implication of the revenue distribution before 2005 was that it became more rational for the Zambian government to be more accountable to donors than to the Zambian people when the interests of the two differed.

Tax revenue consists of direct taxes (which include both personal income and corporate taxation), taxes on goods and services (mainly VAT), and taxes on international trade. According to Moore's classification, the direct taxes are the most important ones (high earnedness), followed by taxes on goods and services (medium earnedness). Figure 2 shows the development in the taxes of most interest: direct taxes, as they are expected to lead to increased democratic accountability. This is particularly the case with personal income taxation, as it is ultimately the people holding the government accountable at the elections.

Figure 2

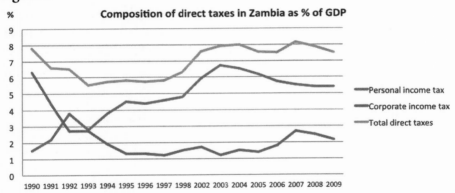

Fjeldstad and Heggstad 2011: 123 (1999–2001 are omitted from figure 2 because of biased figures caused by the sale of the copper mines during these years.)

In the early 1990s, personal income taxation was very low. The creation of semi-autonomous revenue authorities in much of Africa in the early 1990s boosted the personal income taxation. In Zambia, ZRA was created in 1994 and it did improve tax collection. From as low for this period as 1.5 per cent of GDP in 1990, it increased to 6.8 per cent at the highest in 2003. While this is evidence of people paying more taxes and Zambia collecting more earned income, the problem of too few formal jobs being created in Zambia remains. Measuring the share of direct taxes out of total tax revenue Zambia is performing well. With 45 per cent direct tax share, Zambia is ranked third after South Africa and Egypt (OECD 2010: 87).

Having clarified the importance of aid in the early 1990s, we now look at the political implications of aid dependency with regard to the government's accountability to donors and the electorate. Despite MMD coming to power with a strong mandate, it did not mean there was unity on the right development strategy. What brought together the diverse interests in forming MMD was the ambition to end one-party rule more than a full commitment to structural adjustment programmes and liberalisation. According to Fraser (2009: 310) the neo-liberal commitment was '*an anti-ideological pragmatism that considers Zambia's international reputation its greatest asset. The MMD's eagerness to please donors and investors was encouraged by massive aid increases in the early 1990s*'. During the first years, the government was able to act quite independently from the interest groups that Kaunda had difficulties handling in the 1980s and the government adopted an '*almost uncritical acceptance of the donor policy agenda*' (Rakner 2003: 155). The relationship to donors was a well-functioning partnership during these first years.

The World Bank and the IMF focused on the long-term macroeconomic stability without much attention to what was likely to be politically feasible for a government being accountable to its electorate and the economic interest groups that brought the MMD to power. Implementing comprehensive economic reforms would, at least in the short run, hurt most Zambians and the economic interest groups that mobilized the MMD coalition. MMD chose to abandon the inclusion of the relevant interest groups (ibid.: 67). ZCTU was willing to agree to some sacrifices and had understanding as Chiluba told them '*to convince the workers to die a little*', for the economy to recover (Larmer 2005: 38). The labour movement was also weakened as labour legislation was amended in 1993 and 1997 to remove ZCTU's monopoly representation of the unions. This appeared as a deliberate move to weaken the labour movement that was so united and politically powerful during the Kaunda era. The labour movement fragmented and four unions broke away from ZCTU. As a result of job losses from the combined effects of public sector reforms and privatisation, the membership base of ZCTU declined from 359,000 in 1990 to 230,000 in 1996 (Rakner 2003: 98).

President Chiluba's strategy did serve the interest of avoiding Kaunda's destiny by keeping the aid and loans flowing while at the same time weakening interest groups, MMD was able to cope economically (Larmer and Fraser 2007: 616). The government was however still increasingly challenged as there was lack of results from the reforms and MMD had to use authoritarian measures to protect its power. The 1996 elections were not considered free and fair, particularly as MMD changed the electoral law with the sole purpose of banning former President Kaunda from running for president. This led to a boycott of the elections by large parts of the opposition (Rakner 2003: 109). MMD did however challenge the donor conditionalities that were hardest to accomplish politically. One of them was privatising the national mining company: Zambia Consolidated Copper Mines Ltd (ZCCM). Considering Zambia's history of creating large revenue from the copper mines, it was difficult politically to sell the company that had the potential to generate much state revenue if the copper price recovered. The mines were, however, a large economic burden on the state as the copper price continued to decline throughout the 1990s. MMD's strategy was to delay the sales process as a way to show commitment without actually proceeding with the sale (Fraser and Lungu 2007: 10).

The 2001 elections became a big challenge for the ruling MMD as the government still struggled economically after ten years in power. GDP had only grown by a total of 24 per cent from 1991 to 2001 (a negative growth rate if measured as a constant of GDP per capita) while Zambia's external debt only decreased from 7 billion in 1991 to 6.2 billion US$ in 2001 (World Bank 2014). President Chiluba wanted to run for a third term, which required an amendment of the constitution. There was pressure from civil society to block this amendment and in the end Chiluba did not manage to acquire the two-thirds majority in Parliament for changing the constitution (Venter 2003: 12). Instead, Levy Mwanawasa contested the presidential elections for MMD. Despite the internal conflicts in MMD over succession, Mwanawasa won the election with only 28.7 per cent of the votes, followed by Mazoka from UPND gaining 26.8 per cent of the votes (Electoral Commission of Zambia 2001). The rest was shared among many smaller parties. Rakner (2003: 124) describes the competition to the elections as follows:

> It was virtually impossible to separate the parties along ideological or programmatic lines. According to the party manifestos all parties vowed to continue the current economic policies, albeit manage them better than MMD had done for the past 10 years

An analysis of Zambia's three largest national newspapers (*The Post, Times of Zambia, Daily Mail*) also shows lack of debate of different positions among the parties running for presidency in 2001 (Reinke 2012). The newspapers' coverage mainly focused on personalities and negative campaigning targeting opponents' inabilities to govern. Much of the explanation of why we did not see any parties seriously challenge MMD despite its poor performance and voter apathy should be related to the influence donors had through granting Zambia a possible debt relief. The joint World Bank and IMF Heavily Indebted Poor Countries (HIPC) initiative was created in 1996 to relieve poor countries of the increasingly unmanageable debt that had been accumulated. It had at this point increasingly been acknowledged by the donor community that a high debt combined with large donor influence severely constrains the aid recipient countries and limits the benefit of aid (Whitfield 2009). The HIPC initiative is a two-step process, with a decision point determining if the country qualifies for debt relief, and a completion point where it is decided if the conditionalities on the recipient country have been sufficiently met to grant the debt relief. All parties at the 2001 elections thus had to consider the aim of debt relief and that MMD had reached HIPC decision point in 2000, which constrained democratic competition at the elections. Opposition parties could not credibly challenge the development agenda of MMD, as it would mean Zambia would not qualify for completion point.

In Zambia, the government qualified for the decision point in 2000. It was when donors were able to use the HIPC debt relief to strengthen their bargaining position, that the sales process of ZCCM speeded up, and made

GRZ sell at the time they least wanted it and the copper price was at the lowest (Fraser and Lungu 2007: 10). As foreign investors were aware that the mines had to be sold no matter what, it gave the investors the upper hand and it made the government sell on conditions much more beneficial to the investors than to Zambia. At the time the process was not transparent to the public, as the agreements with the mining companies (development agreements) were not published. A Christian Aid report (Fraser and Lungu 2007) published the leaked development agreements, which finally created public debate over mining taxation, particularly as it became part of the Patriotic Front's election campaign in 2006, which will be covered later.

Zambia was at this point a clear example of an unfortunate aid dependency where a country becomes too reliant on donors and actually ends up destroying the democracy that the donors at the same time wanted to consolidate. Considering the lack of economic results MMD could present after ten years of rule in 2001, the elections should be considered a 'most likely' case of an electoral defeat for MMD. The outcome of the 2001 elections does support van de Walle's argument of African governments being protected by aid and structural adjustment programs to remain in power (van de Walle 2001). The choice of MMD to be more accountable to donors than the electorate was understandable considering the much higher dependency on aid (ODA) compared to tax revenue (figure 1). Paradoxically, the return of multiparty democracy did not enhance democratic accountability, as donors were deeply involved in the country's domestic policymaking.

Improved Zambian economy and contested elections (2005–2014)

Zambia did reach the HIPC completion point in 2005 and was granted debt relief worth more than $3.8 billion from both multilateral and bilateral donors (Chisala 2006: 246). In 2006 the World Bank and IMF granted an additional multilateral debt relief to countries having achieved the HIPC completion point. This reduced the Zambian debt stock further from around $4.5 million after HIPC to only $500 million with the Multilateral Debt Relief Initiative (Fraser and Lungu 2007: 60). Debt relief lowered Zambia's aid dependency (see figure 1), as much aid was used to serve debt. Key economic indicators have improved for this period. Most importantly GDP growth has stabilised at above 6 per cent a year (see figure 3 below) compared to the very unstable 1990s figures. Inflation from 1991 to 2004 averaged 48.9 per cent a year, while from 2005 to 2012 it has averaged only 9.3 per cent (World Bank 2014).

Figure 3

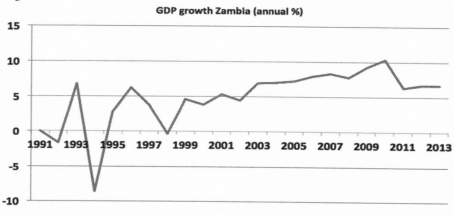

(World Bank 2014)

SAPs had put pressure on Zambia's sovereignty and democracy since they were initiated in 1977 as argued in the analysis of the previous periods. The long-term benefits of SAPs have however finally become evident in the 2000s, where the investor-friendly environment had created much inflow of FDI (see figure 4 below). Much of the increased investment comes from the emerging economies, where particularly China has become a large investor in Zambia (Kragelund 2014). Exact figures of the Chinese investments are not available, and agreements between GRZ and China are generally confidential. It is however apparent that Chinese investments in Zambia are not of a small scale anymore and China's ability to combine trade with aid makes China an attractive alternative to Western donors (ibid.).

Figure 4

(Zambia Development Agency 2014)

While the increase in FDI is important for Zambia, and has brought stable GDP growth figures of not below 6 per cent annually since 2005, it should be noted that a large increase in FDI does not automatically lead to high tax revenue. This is especially the case for mining taxation, where Zambia has not collected much tax. From an average world market copper price of only 1,880 USD/ton in 2003, the price gradually increased to its highest level of 9,880 USD/ton on average in February 2010 (Index Mundi 2014). However between 2002 and 2007, taxes originating from the copper mines constituted less than 1 per cent of state revenue (Fraser and Larmer 2010: 125), yielding almost no benefit to the Zambian government from the higher copper price. IMF has offered technical assistance to the Zambian government to assist in tax collection. According to IMF resident representative, Perry Perone, *'It's not so much the tax rate that is the problem, it's the collection that is the main problem'* (Reinke 2012: 55). Among the problems Zambia is faced with is abusive transfer pricing, where a multinational company trades internally between its subsidiary companies with the purpose of making the profit in the country with the lowest taxation (Fraser and Larmer 2010).

Zambia is also still faced with the problem of too little job creation despite economic growth. According to the 2008 Labour Force Survey Zambia

(Central Statistical Office 2008: 53) 5.2 million people are in employment, but only 10 per cent are employed in the formal sector. Of the 90 per cent working in the informal sector, 79 per cent worked in agriculture/forestry/fishing. For the majority it should be considered subsistence agriculture. Zambia needs to improve the formal employment percentage. The informal sector is difficult to tax, which is also evident from Moore's categorisation of countries according to income levels: in 1988, 69 per cent of state revenue for low-income countries had low earnedness while only 12 per cent for high-income countries (Moore 1998: 101). High-income countries are able to collect more direct taxes with high earnedness, as the formal sector is prevailing.

The improved economy in Zambia has resulted in a decline in foreign aid since 2005 following the granting of debt relief. At the same time tax revenue became more important than aid and has with tax revenue being equal to 20 per cent of GDP in 2011, which is more than three times as much as aid for the same year (figure 1). The theoretical expectations are that this has led to improved state-society relations in Zambia as unearned income has declined. Neither copper earnings nor aid constitutes a large share of state revenue for an improved Zambian economy and we should expect a more contested democracy compared to the earlier periods where Zambia depended heavily on either copper earnings or aid.

In measuring if the government has been held accountable at elections, this period shows a new pattern during election campaigns. While MMD could present progress and economic growth ahead of the 2006 elections, opposition parties were able to target the injustice and the lack of benefit to ordinary Zambians that had been the outcome of the comprehensive liberalisations taking place during the past decades. The Patriotic Front (PF) party had in the years up to the 2006 elections mobilised the party as critics of the impact of SAPs. PF led protests against the privatisation of Zambia National Commercial Bank, and in 2005 when mineworkers went on strike and rioted, the PF president Michael Sata stated he had supported the protests (Larmer and Fraser 2007: 625). At the 2006 elections, the PF continued to focus on injustice to ordinary people compared to foreign investors (Larmer and Fraser 2007). They managed to articulate particularly Chinese investors and traders as doing nothing good to Zambia and instead taking away jobs from Zambians. PF also raised the issue of taxation and the injustice in the mines paying almost no taxes. According to PF president Michael Sata:

> Zambians are paying high taxes, while the mines pay little tax. This will change when we come into power. (Michael Sata, quoted in *The Post* 19/11/2006)

The 2006 elections became the first elections where a party was successful in articulating popular resentment to the liberalisation donors had pushed hard to make the government implement. This worked particularly well in urban areas where PF was the most popular party (Reinke 2012: 63). While the PF did not win despite an effective campaign, the elections were significant as the government came under pressure and was held accountable through the polls. The pressure continued after the elections, where the MMD government was under increased popular pressure to protect Zambian priorities. President Mwanawasa rejected IMF's tax recommendation of reintroducing VAT on food and agricultural products, and the government even lowered income taxation in the 2007 budget (Larmer and Fraser 2007: 635). The government also surprised donors as well as investors by introducing a windfall tax on the mining companies in 2007—an initiative that the government however reversed as the global economic crisis set in (Fraser and Larmer 2010). The 2006 elections should be considered a positive development in improving democratic accountability. First of all by holding the government accountable at the elections but also subsequently as MMD adapted to opposition priorities and prioritised popular pressure above donor recommendations.

In 2011, PF managed to win the elections after twenty years of MMD rule. Particularly urban voters were attracted by promises of lower taxes and the 'more money in your pockets' slogan. The PF advocated for more taxation of multinational corporations and promised to crack down on all corruption (Reinke 2012). The corruption issue became very important in mobilising the public voice to hold the government accountable. Zambia's most read newspaper, *The Post*, effectively became the mouthpiece of the Patriotic Front with allegation of corruption by the ruling party. This was media coverage previously unseen at Zambian elections. The elections in Zambia in 1996 and 2001 were without any real differences among the parties, and there was no critical media coverage as well (Rakner 2003; Reinke 2012). The shift in media coverage by *The Post* began in 2006 when the paper gave a lot of coverage to issues raised by the PF during the election campaigns, earning the paper popularity among a large section of Zambian voters (Larmer and Fraser 2007; Reinke 2012).

The Patriotic Front's campaigns in both 2006 and 2011 should not be considered as actually bringing in ideology to Zambian politics. It is rather evidence of successful populist campaigns. Populism is recognized as a particular mode of articulation appealing to the sentiments of most people. This is particularly successful when there are a variety of frustrations not being addressed by the ruling party. These frustrations share a negative dimension, which can lead to a successful campaign when the unmet demands are combined (Panizza 2005: 6). Parties will absorb these demands in institutionalized party systems with political differences along a traditional left- to right-wing scale. This is the case for the many successful social democratic parties found in Europe, where left-wing social democratic parties typically have close ties to the labour movement. In Zambia where a minority is formally employed, the labour movement has lost its power as a consequence of SAPs and MMD's gradual effort to weaken the economic interest groups in the 1990s (Rakner 2003). This means demands are unmet which PF successfully could combine in campaigns promising more money in your pockets, creating more jobs and fighting corruption. Populism reveals some institutional deficiencies such as a non-institutionalized party system. This does, however, not mean it is not a step in the right direction towards democracy. Populism has opened a channel to hold the government increasingly accountable in Zambia. Populist pressure holding the government accountable can give the government incentives to be more attentive to Zambian priorities rather than just committing to donor priorities. This happened after the 2006 and 2011 elections as the government prioritised popular policies.

A comparison of the voting patterns at the Zambian presidential elections in 1996, 2001, 2006, 2008, and 2011 shows a change occurring from 2006 and onwards which supports the finding of more contested elections based on issues. The Patriotic Front won thirteen out of fourteen of the high-density urban constituencies in 2006 and 2008, and won all fourteen in 2011. This voting pattern is much in line with the campaigns targeting urban frustrations. Combined with the rural Bemba strongholds of Northern and Luapula province, the PF combined issue-based campaigns with the more traditional tribal/regional-based voting (Reinke 2012: 76).

While democracy does not consolidate overnight even after a positive development such as an electoral turnover of government in 2011, it is of importance that election campaigns have included real political debates with more public attention to the distribution of the country's wealth in recent general elections. With the increased policy space coming from less reliance on donors, Zambians and the political parties representing them are able to discuss the development path of the future.

Kragelund (2014) argues that Zambia has increasingly become assertive in negotiations with donors. Rhetorically we have seen stronger incentives to dismiss donor requirement and criticize them publicly. This is a consequence of increasingly contested elections since 2006 and less dependency on the donor funds. There is also evidence of a government actually demanding to be more in control and assert ownership of the development agenda. The Sixth National Development Plan (2011-2015) was drafted without direct donor involvement and is more founded on Zambian priorities (ibid. p. 10). Donors have together with the Zambian government agreed on a new partnership strategy, the Joint Assistance Strategy for Zambia II (JASZ II), to target aid around Zambia's sixth National Development Plan and ensure aid effectiveness. According to a civil servant from Ministry of Finance there is reason for optimism with the new strategy:

> In the JASZ the donors called the shots. In the JASZ II it is going to be different. Now, the government will drive the process and decide the division of labour among the donors . . . The donors resisted this idea very much in the beginning. We were far apart in the discussions, but now we agree much more. (Quoted in Kragelund 2014: 10)

The Zambian government's improved ability to negotiate from a stronger position with donors is not only a reaction to less aid dependency; it is also evidence of more financing options available as China increasingly offers aid to Zambia without the conditionalities typically attached to Western aid (Kragelund 2014). The traditional donors need to adjust to this new reality, which brings a healthy competition the Zambian government can benefit from. One of the choices made by the PF government is to finance development through obtaining loans. This has been made possible from improved international credit rankings of Zambia and bilateral loans being offered from non-traditional donors such as China. The improved credit ranking has enabled Zambia to raise money by launching two Eurobonds, the first one of 750 million USD in 2012 and the second one of 1 billion USD in 2014. This has created concern whether the debt created is viable for the country and targeting long-term development (Mukanga 2014). There is a lack of transparency with regard to how the money is actually spent and the concern that it is mainly used to finance budget deficits. The risk of a government having more autonomy to make its own decisions is the attention to short-term gains for democratically elected governments. The temptation to finance campaign promises such as higher salaries and lower taxes through loans is a concern that requires the people to hold the government accountable of how loans are spent for development. Collier (2014) identifies the main challenge for the PF government to make tough decisions in managing Zambia's copper wealth properly. There is a need to allocate an increasing percentage of the copper revenue towards savings as the resources are gradually being depleted. The savings must be wisely used for domestic investments. This has however not been the case in Zambia, where budget deficits have prevented savings (ibid.: 23)

The last period analysed (2005–2014) shows how politics is fundamentally interlinked with the economy. As the economy has improved, it has made elections increasingly competitive, where it has been easier to hold the government accountable. This has made governments more attentive to public priorities and to gain more ownership over the development agenda. As aid dependency has decreased, it has also been easier for governments to assert their sovereignty and reject donor priorities when they do not serve the interest of the government. The downside of increased democratic accountability has however been more attention to fulfilling generous campaign promises rather than investing in Zambia's development.

Conclusion

In this chapter it has been argued that it is essential for Zambia to become a tax state, which is increasingly reliant on earned income, as unearned income has been a problem for the country's sovereignty and democracy. Moore's theoretical expectations of unearned income not being likely to create development and democratic accountability have been true in the case of Zambia. Through analysing elections it has been possible to identify the shifts in democratic accountability in Zambia.

During the Kaunda era from 1964 to 1991, Zambia's main achievement was nation-building and maintaining the peaceful nation Zambians still enjoy today. As the copper price was high, President Kaunda had the state revenue needed to spend on patronage and maintenance of support for UNIP. There was no democratic accountability except for the elite being kept loyal because of patronage. State revenue was not invested in diversification and creation of other sources of state income, which was needed because of the price shocks likely to occur for commodities. As the copper price tumbled, a severe economic crisis was inevitable. The collapse of the Zambian economy created a new dependency, the aid dependency, which it has taken long for Zambia to recover from. Kaunda's attempt to abandon structural adjustments did not succeed because of the severe economic situation the country was in. MMD followed a strategy of compliance with donor requirements while largely rejecting popular societal demands. This made democracy in Zambia very constrained as no political party could credibly suggest an alternative to the government's development agenda which was deeply linked to structural adjustments at the 1996 and 2001 elections. The government was accountable to donors rather than to the electorate and aid dependency resulted in lack of responsibility by the government to develop Zambia. The country's sovereignty thus suffered along with democracy. The government prioritised compliance with donor requirements of continued structural adjustments to maintain the aid flow, thereby preventing democratic accountability at elections.

The elections of 2006 and 2011 have shown improved democratic accountability. Zambia is no longer dependent on unearned income resulting in improved state–society relations. Successful populist campaigns backed by media attention to the issues of a more fair distribution of Zambia's wealth have held the government accountable. Opposition parties have been able to suggest a credible alternative to the ruling party as the economy has improved and Zambia has more options to finance development, which includes access to loans. The aftermath of the 2006 elections showed the connection between the government being held accountable at elections and the ruling party's interest in increasingly asserting Zambia's sovereignty to defend itself against increased opposition strength.

Despite there being enough reasons for optimism, based on the last period since 2005, it should be emphasized that Zambia still has a long way towards becoming a tax state, which Moore argues is essential for development and consolidation of democracy. The majority of Zambians are not formally employed, are not paying tax, and are quite distanced from politics. This puts a lot of responsibility on politicians to work on long-term benefits for most Zambians. Politicians can no longer excuse themselves by being constrained by structural adjustment programmes. Economic progress has led to increased sovereignty, which needs to be used wisely to create diversification, jobs creation, and, consequently, sustainable national social and economic development.

References

Andersen, O. W. and Therkildsen, O. (2007), *Harmonisation and alignment: The double-edged swords of budget support and decentralised aid administration*, Copenhagen, DIIS working paper no. 2007/4.

Barnett, M. and Finnemore, M. (2004), *Rules for the World* (New York: Cornell University Press).

Bräutigam, D. (2000), *Aid Dependence and Governance* (Washington DC: Expert Group on Development Issues).

Central Statistical Office (2008), *Labour Force Survey Zambia* (Lusaka).

Cheeseman, N. (2010), 'African Elections as Vehicles for Change', *Journal of Democracy*, 21/4: 139–153

—— and Hinfelaar, M. (2010), 'Parties, platforms, and political mobilisation: The Zambian presidential election of 2008', *African Affairs*, 109/434: 51–76.

Chisala, V. (2006), *Foreign Aid Dependency: The Case of Zambia*, PhD dissertation at School of Oriental and Africa Studies (London: University of London).

Clapham, C. (1996), *Africa and the international system—The politics of state survival* (Cambridge: Cambridge University Press).

Collier, P. (2008). *The Bottom Billion—Why the Poorest Countries Are Failing and What Can Be Done About It* (Oxford: Oxford University Press).

—— (2014), 'Zambia: A Time of Big Opportunities and Tough Decisions' in Adam, C. A., Collier, P., and Gondwe, M. (eds.) *Zambia—Building Prosperity from Resource Wealth* (Oxford: Oxford University Press).

—— and Hoeffler, A. (2009), 'Testing the neocon agenda: Democracy in resource-rich societies', *European Economic Review*, 53/3: 293–308.

Danahar, P. (2013), *The New Middle East—The World After the Arab Spring* (London: Bloomsbury Publishing).

Fjeldstad, O. and Heggstad, K. (2011), *The tax systems in Mozambique, Tanzania and Zambia—Capacity and constraints* (Bergen: Chr. Michelsen Institute).

Fraser, A. (2009), 'Zambia: Back to the future', in Whitfield, Lindsay (ed.), *The politics of aid: African strategies for dealing with donors* (Oxford: Oxford University Press).

—— (2010), 'Introduction: Boom and Bust on the Zambian Copperbelt' in Fraser and Larmer, *Zambia, Mining, and Neoliberalism* (New York: Palgrave Macmillan).

—— and Larmer, M. (2010), *Zambia, Mining, and Neoliberalism* (New York: Palgrave Macmillan).

—— and Lungu, J. (2007), *For Whom the Windfalls? Winners & losers in the privatisation of Zambia's copper mines* (Lusaka: Christian Aid).

Hallum, C. (2011), *Privatization and liberalisation of the extractive sector in Zambia—Implications for the resource curse* (Aarhus: Aarhus University).

Index Mundi (2014), 'Copper, grade A cathode monthly price', accessible online at http://www.indexmundi.com/commodities/?commodity=copper&months=180.

Kragelund, P. (2014), '"Donors go home": Non-traditional state actors and the creation of development space in Zambia', *Third World Quarterly*, 35/1: 145–162.

Larmer, M. (2005), *Reaction and Resistance to Neo-liberalism in Zambia*, Pretoria: working paper for presentation at the Centre for Civil Society.

—— and Fraser, A. (2007), 'Of cabbages and King Cobra: Populist politics and Zambia's 2006 election', *African Affairs*, 106/425: 611–637

Lewanika, A. and Chitala, D. (1990), *The Hour Has Come! Proceedings from the National Conference on the Multi-Party Option* (Lusaka: Zambia Research Foundation).

Ministry of Finance, Norway (2014), *The Government Pension Fund* http://www.regjeringen.no/en/dep/fin/selected-topics/the-government-pension-fund.html?id=1441

Moore, M. (1998), 'Death Without Taxes', in Mark Robinson and Gordon White (eds.), *The democratic developmental state: Politics and institutional design* (Oxford: Oxford University Press).

Mukanga, C. (2014), 'Zambia's New Eurobond', *Zambian Economist* http://www.zambian-economist.com/2014/04/zambias-new-eurobond.html.

OECD (2008), *The Paris Declaration on Aid Effectiveness and the Accra Agenda for Action* (Paris: OECD Publishing).

OECD (2010), *African Economic Outlook 2010* (Paris: OECD Publishing).

Panizza, F. (2005), *Populism and the Mirror of Democracy* (New York: Verso Books).

Posner, D. (2005), *Institutions and Ethnic Politics in Africa* (New York: Cambridge University Press).

Rakner, L. (2003), *Political and Economic Liberalisation in Zambia 1991–2001* (Stockholm: Nordic Africa Institute).

Reinke, T. R. (2012), *Zambian ownership in aid relations—Decreased aid dependency and expanded policy space* (Aarhus: Aarhus University), MA thesis.

Sachs, Jeffrey and Warner, Andrew (1995), *Natural Resource Abundance and Economic Growth*, NBER Working Paper Series, No. 5398.

Timmons, J. F. (2005), 'The Fiscal Contract: States, Taxes, and Public Services', *World Politics*, 57/4: 530–567.

van de Walle, N. (2001), *African Economies and the Politics of Permanent Crisis, 1979–1999* (New York: Cambridge University Press).

Venter, D. (2003), 'Democracy and Multiparty Politics in Africa—Recent Elections in Zambia, Zimbabwe, and Lesotho', *Eastern Africa Social Science Research Review*, 19/1: 1–39.

World Bank (2014), *World Development Indicators*, World Bank Databank, http://databank.worldbank.org

Chapter 5

A Critical Analysis of Zambia's Foreign Policy During the First Fifty Years

Royson M. Mukwena

Introduction

This chapter analyses Zambia's foreign policy during the first fifty years of nationhood. The material used in this chapter is drawn from secondary sources and the author's own observations based on his experience as an ambassador for a period of slightly above six years. The major limitation of the chapter is that due to the closed and secretive nature of Foreign Service, it is not easy to access information and statistics. Further, in order not to compromise on national interest and national security, access to information on foreign policy may be denied or where one has such information, by virtue of having served in the Foreign Service, the information thus obtained may not be discussed or used in public. Thus, in some cases the real reasons behind certain foreign policy actions may not be revealed to the general public or indeed to researchers. Furthermore, many reports relating to a country's relations with other countries are classified and cannot be brought in the public domain. Thus, although the conduct of foreign policy has become more open in recent times mainly because of rapid globalisation, massive advances in information communication technology (ICT) and growing public demand for governments to adhere to the tenets of good governance (such as transparency and accountability), a lot of aspects of a country's foreign policy remain closed and secretive.

In analysing Zambia's foreign policy performance, the author will use various theories highlighted in the section that follows. In other words, the author will scrutinize Zambia's foreign policy during her first fifty years by placing the various foreign policy actions in a broad context of academic knowledge which is defined by various theories and approaches. The list of the theories and approaches used in this chapter is not exhaustive. Based on the conclusions drawn from the discussion in the chapter, the author ends the chapter by generating some suggestions that can be used to improve on foreign policy implementation and maximize benefits derived from the country's engagements with other countries and international organizations.

The coverage period for the discussion is from 24 October 1964 (when Zambia gained independence from British colonial rule) to 24 October 2014 when she turned fifty years. For ease of analysis, the discussion will be categorised in terms of the various foreign policy actions pursued under the five presidents that have ruled Zambia in her first fifty years of nationhood, namely presidents Kenneth Kaunda, Frederick Chiluba, Levy Mwanawasa, Rupiah Banda, and Michael Sata.

DEFINITIONAL CLARIFICATIONS AND THEORETICAL CONSIDERATIONS

A foreign policy refers to a set of political goals whose object is to outline how a particular country will interact with other countries of the world (Wikibook 2014). Similar to Wikibook, Jackson and Sorenson (2013: 252) conceptualise foreign policy as involving 'goals, strategies, measures, methods, guidelines, directives, understandings, agreements, and so on, by which national governments conduct international relations with each other and with international organisations and non-governmental actors'. Clark (1999) defines foreign policy as a range of actions taken by varying sections of government of a state in its relations with other bodies similarly acting in the international system, in order to advance the national interest. Clark's definition and those of other several scholars highlight the central position of national interest in the pursuance of foreign policy. There are several facets to the concept of national interest. They include providing for the physical safety of a country; attainment of economic prosperity given a country's available resources, investments, and other enabling conditions; and provision of an enabling political environment for the good governance of a country, which includes creation and maintenance of a system that enables a country's citizens to freely choose their form of government and its leadership. Thus, in a country's interactions with other countries, any policy actions that are directed at promoting the above-mentioned interests are seen to be in the national interest. For instance, in the case of promoting economic prosperity, policy actions that constitute national interest will include improving the balance of trade, encouraging free trade, gaining access to the markets of the world, attracting foreign investments, enhancing industrialisation, securing and maintaining access to oil, natural gas, and other forms of energy (Papp 2002; Akapelwa 2010).

Ideally, foreign policies are designed to help protect a country's national interests. The main objective of pursuing a foreign policy for any country is to secure and protect its several vital interests such as achieving economic prosperity, safeguarding national security and peace, maintaining ideological goals, and promoting international peace and security. The foregoing can be achieved through peaceful cooperation with other countries, or through aggression, war, and exploitation (Wikibook 2014).

There is an abundance of theories, theoretical frameworks, concepts, and approaches that are used in foreign policy analysis and some of these will be used in this paper to analyse Zambia's foreign policy. The list of these include, inter alia, geopolitics, globalisation, constructivism, realism, liberalism, international society approach, international political economy, traditional approach, comparative approach, bureaucratic structures and processes approach, cognitive processes and psychology approach, multilevel analysis and multidimensional approach. Most of the theories used in foreign policy analysis belong to the general international relations theories (Jackson and Sorenson 2013). In turn, various approaches are derived from international relations theories. There are however some approaches that are specific to foreign policy analysis (Jackson and Sorenson 2013: 253). In addition, some approaches are derived from other disciplines such as economics and social psychology (Jackson and Sorenson 2013: 253). In the sections that follow, the author gives brief explanations of the theories, theoretical frameworks, concepts, and approaches mentioned above.

Geopolitics: It is the study of the effects of geography (both human and physical) on international politics and international relations. Geopolitics is a method of foreign policy analysis which seeks to understand, explain, and predict international political behaviour primarily in terms of geographical variables. The geographical variables used in this method include the physical location, size, climate, topography, demography, natural resources, and technological advances of the state being evaluated (Wikibook 2014).

Globalisation: It is the process of international integration arising from the interchange of world views, products, ideas, and other aspects of culture. Advances in transportation and telecommunications infrastructure, including the rise of the telegraph and its posterity the Internet, are major factors in globalisation, generating further interdependence of economic and cultural activities (Wikipedia 2014*d*). Globalisation is perceived as a process of interaction and integration among the people, companies, and governments of different nations and a process that is driven by international trade and investment and aided by information technology. It has several effects on relations between and among nations and certainly affects any country's foreign policy. Globalisation does not only relate to economic matters. It is a multidimensional phenomenon that affects all aspects of life: economic, cultural, environmental, social, and political. It is one of the major factors that shape foreign policies.

Constructivism: This approach focuses on 'human awareness or consciousness and its place in world affairs' (Jackson and Sorensen 2013: 209). In defence of constructivism, its proponents argue that much of international relations theory, and especially neorealism, is materialistic, focusing on how the distribution of material power, such as military forces and economic capabilities, defines the balances of power between states and explains the behaviour of states (Jackson and Sorensen 2013: 209). Constructivists reject this materialistic focus, arguing that the most important aspect of international relations is social, not material (Jackson and Sorensen 2013: 209). They further argue that the social reality is not objective, or external to the observer of international relations. Recognizing that the social and political world, including international relations (and foreign policy) is not a physical or material entity outside human consciousness, constructivists argue that the study of international relations (which includes foreign policy) must focus on the ideas and beliefs that inform the actors on the international scene (Jackson and Sorensen 2013: 209). The proponents of constructivism see foreign policymaking as an intersubjective world, whose ideas and discourse can be scrutinised in order to arrive at a better theoretical understanding of a process. In the study of foreign policy, the constructivists trace the influence of ideas, as one factor among others on the processes and outcomes in foreign policy. It should be noted here that there are various shades of constructivism. Some shades emphasize ideas while others emphasize identity. Ideas refer to mental constructs held by individuals, sets of distinctive beliefs, principles, and attitudes that provide broad orientations for behaviour and policy. Ideas include ideologies (shared belief systems), normative beliefs or principles (beliefs about what is wrong and right), cause effective beliefs, and policy prescriptions. Identity on the other hand refers to individual characteristics by which a person is recognized. According to constructivists, ideas and identity are the basis for a definition of interests and thus lie behind any foreign policy (Jackson and Sorensen 2013).

Realism: This theory underlines the value of national security. According to realists, national military and power balancing is the major way of achieving national security. The proponents of realism see the outcomes of a country's relations with other countries as being determined by its relative state power. The theorists that are concerned with defence and security matters are likely to adopt a realist approach to the analysis or study of foreign policy (Jackson and Sorensen 2013: 253).

Liberalism: This approach focuses on freedom and democracy, arguing that the two values are the core values in international relations. Liberals are convinced that liberal democracies will support peaceful international cooperation based on international institutions (Jackson and Sorensen 2013: 253). It should be noted here that foreign policy theorists 'concerned with multilateral questions are likely to take a liberal approach, emphasizing international institutions— such as the United Nations (UN) or the World Trade Organization—as a means of reducing international conflict and promoting mutual understanding and common interests' (Jackson and Sorensen 2013: 253).

International society approach: International society scholars emphasize the values of order and justice. To these scholars, a rule-based and well-ordered international society is the major goal (Jackson and Sorensen 2013: 253).

International political economy (IPE): This approach focuses on the importance of socio-economic wealth and welfare (Jackson and Sorensen 2013: 253). Foreign policy theorists who emphasize the importance of socio-economic wealth and welfare as the central goal of foreign policy are likely to take an IPE approach. For these theorists, the promotion of a stable international economic system that can support economic growth and welfare progress is the chief objective (Jackson and Sorensen 2013: 253). The IPE is a more appropriate approach for explaining the vulnerable position of weak states in international relations and best explains their limitations and constraints in terms of manoeuvre in foreign policy (Jackson and Sorensen 2013).

Traditional approach: The focus of this approach is on the decision maker (Jackson and Sorensen 2013: 253). The approach involves 'being informed about a government's external policies, knowing their history or at least their background, comprehending the interests and concerns that drive the policies, and thinking through the various ways of addressing and defending those interests and concerns' (Jackson and Sorensen 2013: 253). Further, the approach also includes knowing the consequences of past foreign-policy decisions and actions. Furthermore, it also involves 'an ability to recognize the circumstances under which a government must operate in carrying out its foreign policy' (Jackson and Sorensen 2007: 223). The traditional foreign policy study can be summed up as 'a matter of gaining insight into the activity of foreign policymakers either from experience or by careful scrutiny of past and present foreign policies' (Jackson and Sorensen 2007: 223).

Comparative approach was inspired by the behaviouralist turn in political science, beginning in the 1950s and 1960s when many political scientists became persuaded by the methodology of behaviouralism (Jackson and Sorensen 2007: 223). As observed by Jackson and Sorensen (2007: 223), the behaviouralist approach believes in the unity of science, meaning that social science is not fundamentally different from natural science, and that the same analytical methods, including quantitative methods, can be applied in both areas. The approach also believes in interdisciplinary studies among the social sciences. Thus, as noted by Jackson and Sorensen (2007: 223), political behaviouralists 'seek to apply scientific attitudes and methods to the interdisciplinary study of politics'. The advocates of behaviouralism argue that, in order to study politics scientifically, one should focus on human behaviour as it involves politics and government (Jackson and Sorensen 2007: 223). According to Eulau (1963: 21), behaviouralism investigates 'acts, attitudes, preferences, and expectations of people in political contexts.' Eulau, who is one of the leading advocates of behaviouralism, gives the key elements of the approach as follows: '(i) the individual person is the basic unit of analysis, (ii) politics is seen as only one aspect of the behaviour of people, and (iii) political behaviour is to be examined at different levels of analysis, including the social level and the personal level' (Eulau 1963: 21). The roles of people in social systems constitute the core focus of the study of political behaviour, with the political system being regarded as the central social structure (Eulau 1963: 21). The aim of the comparative approach to foreign policy was to build systematic theories and explanations of the foreign-policy process in general (Jackson and Sorensen 2013: 254). This was done through the amalgamation of large bodies of data, describing the content and context of the foreign policy of a large number of countries (Jackson and Sorensen 2013: 254).

Bureaucratic structures and processes approach focuses on the organizational context of decision-making, which is perceived to be conditioned by the dictates and demands of the bureaucratic settings in which decisions are made (Jackson and Sorensen 2013: 255). According to the advocates of this approach, analysing processes and channels through which organizations arrive at their policies is a superior way of acquiring empirical knowledge of foreign policy (Jackson and Sorensen 2013: 255). The objective of this approach is not only to find out what happened but also why it happened the way it did (Jackson and Sorensen 2013: 255).

Cognitive processes psychology approach focuses on the individual decision maker, but with particular attention to the psychological aspects of decision-making, such as perceptions of actors (Jackson and Sorensen 2007: 223; 2013: 255). Among the prominent proponents of this approach are Robert Jervis and Margaret Herman. Jervis (1968 and 1976) focused on misperceptions. His interest was to find out why actors see what they want to see instead of what is really going on. He argued that such actors were guided by ingrained, pre-existing beliefs (for example the tendency to perceive other states as more hostile than they really are). He observed that such actors tended to engage in 'perceptual satisficing' and 'wishful thinking' (Jackson and Sorensen 2007: 223; 2013: 255). Herman (1984) focused on the personality characteristics of leaders. She studied the personality characteristics of 54 Heads of Government, the result of which she made claim that "such factors as the leaders' experience in foreign affairs, their political styles, their political socialisation and their broader views of the world all should be drawn into the analysis in order to understand the ways in which leaders conduct foreign policy" (Jackson and Sorensen 2013: 255).

Multilevel, multidimensional approach: This approach was developed following the realisation that there will never be one, big, all-encompassing theory of foreign policy (Jackson and Sorensen 2013: 255). The proponents of this approach argue, 'many scholars now use the various major theories as approaches to study particular aspects of foreign policy making' (Jackson and Sorensen 2013: 255). For example, realism best explains the value of national security in foreign policy decision-making while IPE best explains the vulnerable position of weak states in foreign policy and their limitations and constraints in terms of manoeuvre in foreign policy (Jackson and Sorensen 2007: 223; 2013: 255).

FACTORS INFLUENCING FOREIGN POLICY

A country's foreign policy is influenced by several factors. The range of these factors include, inter alia, historical background, geopolitical location, ideology, national values, religious beliefs, demographic features, membership to regional and international organizations, and national security (already explained earlier in the chapter). As earlier pointed out in this chapter, the question of national interest is one major factor that influences a country's foreign policy.

With regard to the influence of historical background on a country's foreign policy, one can point out here that, for instance, generally countries that were colonised have close relations with their former masters. For example, former French colonies are generally closer to France than to other Western countries and similarly former British colonies are generally closer to Britain than to other Western countries. On the same issue of history, one can also point out here that countries that share a history, for instance the history of the struggle to free Africa, tend to have close relations.

As earlier pointed out in this chapter, geopolitical location (physical location) of a country is one of the variables of geopolitics. This variable is fixed and cannot be changed and should be factored when relating to other countries, especially neighbouring countries. For example, a landlocked country has to maintain cordial relations with neighbouring and coastal countries for easy access to the sea.

Ideologies, national values, and religious beliefs also play a major role in influencing foreign policies. Ideologies, or put simply, shared belief systems, play important roles in determining countries' foreign policies. For example, during the Cold War, the United States of America's foreign policy was dominated by its anti-communist ideology (Sylvan and Majeski 2008). Another good example of the influence of ideology on foreign policy is that of China. The ideologies of both Marxism-Leninism and Maoism have had an important influence on China's interpretations of world events. The ideological components of China's foreign policy, whose influence has varied over time, have included a belief that conflict and struggle are inevitable; a focus on opposing imperialism; the determination to advance communism throughout the world, especially through the Chinese model; and the Maoist concept of responding with flexibility while adhering to fundamental principles (Country Studies 2014). This author now wishes to elaborate on one major component of Chinese foreign policy arising from ideology—opposition to imperialism. As result of China's opposition to imperialism, China's foreign policy has been characterised by focusing on opposing United States imperialism in the 1950s, on opposing collusion between United States imperialism and Soviet revisionism in the 1960s, on combating Soviet social imperialism or hegemony in the 1970s, and on opposing hegemony by either superpower in the 1980s (Country Studies 2014). China's opposition to imperialism coupled with her determination to advance communism throughout the world led to her support for worldwide armed struggle against colonialism and 'reactionary' governments (Country Studies 2014).

Like ideology, religious beliefs play a role in influencing the foreign policies of some countries. For instance, Islamic states are more inclined to have closer bilateral and multilateral relations with fellow Islamic states. Further, such states will also be influenced by Islamic teachings in the way they view world events.

National values are also a factor that influences foreign policies of countries. National values include tolerance for religious beliefs, respect for human freedoms and rights including the right to self-determination and independence of other people in the entire world, and generally adherence to the ideals of democracy. National values may also be commonly shared by member countries of a regional or international organization such as the European Union (EU) and Southern African Development Community (SADC). These values have an impact on how a country views international events and relates with other countries. Where such values are violated, some countries have been known to impose sanctions on the violating country or withdraw from certain relations and engagements with such a country. The imposition of sanctions on Zimbabwe by the EU in 2002 and the USA in 2003 as a result of human rights abuses in that country (European Sanctions 2014) is a case in point in this regard.

Demographic features in the context of racial and ethnic composition and whether some ethnic and racial groups have same origins as those in neighbouring countries have an influence on foreign policies of some countries. In the case of people along borders, especially in Africa, many boundaries are artificial in that they have divided members of the same ethnic groups and families into separate countries. Such countries have to be mindful of certain foreign policy actions to avoid antagonising their own citizens in situations where some foreign policy actions might be perceived as victimising or injurious to members of their own families or ethnic group in neighbouring countries.

Membership to regional and international organizations such as Southern Development Community (SADC), the Common Market for Eastern and Southern Africa (COMESA), the African Union (AU), the United Nations (UN), and the Commonwealth of Nations influence a country's foreign policy (Akapelwa 2010: 36). Membership to such organizations may, for instance, require member countries to abide by certain principles on good governance and human rights and follow agreed upon practices in international trade and foreign investments.

RESPONSIBILITY FOR FOREIGN POLICY FORMULATION

In most countries the formulation of foreign policy is undertaken by the ministry of foreign affairs in consultation with the collective leadership, academics, civil society, non-governmental organizations (NGOs), and missions abroad (Akapelwa 2010: 35). After formulation of a foreign policy, the consideration and approval of the formulated policy is the responsibility of the Cabinet and head of state. The key players in foreign policy formulation include presidents, prime ministers, foreign ministers, defence ministers, and their respective advisors (Jackson and Sorensen 2013: 252).

FOREIGN POLICY DURING ZAMBIA'S FIRST FIFTY YEARS

1964–1991

In pursuit of her national interests, upon attainment of political independence in 1964, Zambia's foreign policy went through several phases of transformation that were determined by a number of regional and international dynamics. President Kenneth Kaunda, who served as republican president from 1964 to 1991, made several pronouncements on how to pursue the newly independent country's national interests. These pronouncements focused on, among other factors, colonialism, racism, apartheid, and neocolonialism. During the Kaunda presidency, Zambia operated without an approved foreign policy document. Various pronouncements and statements, written and unwritten, by the head of state, Cabinet, and Ministry of Foreign Affairs constituted the country's foreign policy.

Immediately after attainment of independence, Zambia had to establish cordial relationships with the rest of the world, especially neighbouring countries, given the country's geopolitical situation. Landlocked and surrounded by several countries, Zambia needed to peacefully coexist with her neighbours in order to secure easy access to the sea for her exports and imports. Thus, since independence Zambia's foreign policy has been that of peaceful coexistence with her neighbours as well as with the international community.

One major factor at independence that shaped Zambia's foreign policy was the liberation of the rest of the continent of Africa. As Kaunda stated,

Zambia's independence was meaningless if other African countries were still in bondage. Kaunda rightly felt that among colonised neighbours, Zambia's independence would not bring any economic benefits. Thus, in addition to the liberation of neighbouring countries that were still in bondage, Kaunda made disengagement from Rhodesia his immediate foreign policy goal and looked for alternative routes to the sea.

When the white settlers in Rhodesia announced the Unilateral Declaration of Independence on 11 November 1965 (Sklar 1974), it became very clear to the government of newly independent Zambia that the country needed to quickly disengage from Rhodesia and explore alternative routes to the sea. Before UDI was declared, Kaunda had requested the British government to use military force to stop the rebellion by the white settlers in Rhodesia and implored Britain that it was her responsibility to establish majority rule in Rhodesia (Sklar 1974: 322). Kaunda even offered Britain a military base in Zambia from which an attack could be launched on Rhodesia in the event of a unilateral declaration of independence (Sklar 1974: 322). Britain refused to use military force and also made it clear that she would not require the immediate introduction of majority rule in Rhodesia, arguing that time was needed to alleviate racial fears and suspicions (Sklar 1974: 323). Britain instead opted for economic and financial sanctions in the event of white settlers declaring UDI (Sklar 1974: 323). Indeed, when UDI was declared, 'Britain immediately imposed a number of economic and financial sanctions' on Rhodesia (Sklar 1974: 323). When requesting Britain to use military force on Rhodesia, Kaunda seemed to have not appreciated the important role ethnicity plays in foreign policy. There was no way the British could have agreed to rain bombs on their own kith and kin in Rhodesia. Such an action could have resulted in political consequences for the British government back at home.

Sanctions on Rhodesia became extensive on 17 November of the same year when the United Nations Security Council adopted a resolution which called upon all states to break all economic relations with Southern Rhodesia, including an embargo on oil and petroleum products (Sklar 1974: 323). UDI and the resulting sanctions on Rhodesia had negative economic consequences on Zambia. It disrupted the smooth transportation of Zambian exports and imports and increased the cost of transportation (Sklar 1974). For instance, in the case of oil imports, when Britain, following the UN Security Council resolution in December 1965, banned the delivery of petroleum products by British nationals to Rhodesia, the Rhodesian regime retaliated by prohibiting the conveyance of petroleum products through her territory to Zambia (Sklar 1974: 335). Following this retaliation by the Rhodesia regime, Zambia was forced to import petroleum products via precarious land routes and by air (Sklar 1974: 335–336).

In response to the dislocation of the transportation system for Zambian imports and exports in the aftermath of UDI, in '1966 the Zambian and Tanzanian governments joined with the Italian Fiat organization to form Zambia-Tanzania Road Services Ltd' (Sklar 1974: 340). The Zambia-Tanzania Road Services Ltd activated a fleet of lorries, including dual-purpose tankers, which carried both petroleum imports and copper exports on the Great North Road. The Great North Road route went up to the Port of Dar es Salaam (Sklar 1974: 340). In 1966–67 the United States Agency for International Development and the World Bank commissioned studies for improvements in road transport between Tanzania and Zambia (Sklar 1974: 345). With the financial assistance from Britain, Sweden, the United States of America, and the World Bank, a vastly improved Tanzam Highway was constructed (Sklar 1974: 345). Zambia also made use of the southern Tanzanian port of Mtwara. Zambia even went to the extent of financing the improvements of the harbour facilities and airport at Mtwara (Sklar 1974: 340).

The most significant response to the UDI was the construction of the Tanzania Zambia Railway (TAZARA) stretching 1,860 km from Dar es Salaam to Kapiri Mposhi in central Zambia. In 1967 a firm commitment to build the Tanzania Zambia Railway was made by the People's Republic of China, which made available to Zambia and Tanzania an interest-free loan amounting to K286.6 million to be repaid over a thirty-year period (Sklar 1974: 345). Construction of the railway commenced in 1970 and was completed in 1975. The governments of Zambia, Tanzania, and China built the railway in order to eliminate landlocked Zambia's dependence on minority white-ruled Rhodesia and apartheid South Africa (Wikipedia 2014p).

Another major response to UDI was the decision by the Zambian government to construct, jointly with Tanzania, the Tanzania Zambia Mafuta (TAZAMA) pipeline. In June 1966 the Zambian government announced that it was awarding the contract for building the oil pipeline to Snamprogetti, a subsidiary of the Italian state oil company ENI at the total cost of £16 million. The construction of the pipeline commenced in March 1967 and was commissioned in September 1968 (Sardanis 2003: 204). The pipeline stretches 1,710 km from Dar es Salaam to Ndola (Wikipedia 2014*o*). At the time of commissioning, the management of the pipeline was given to the Italian State oil company ENI (Sardanis 2003: 205). The pipeline is currently managed by TAZAMA Pipelines Limited, a company jointly owned by Zambia (66.7 per cent) and Tanzania (33.3 per cent) (Wikipedia 2014*o*).The Zambian government followed up construction of the pipeline with the setting up of the INDENI Refinery in 1973 and the Ndola Fuel Terminal, which is adjacent to the refinery (Oil Gas Africa 2014). The management of the Indeni Refinery was placed under the Indeni Petroleum Refinery Company Limited with a shareholding of 50 per cent for the Zambian government and 50 per cent for the Italian company Total (Oil Gas Africa 2014). The management of the Ndola Fuel Terminal was placed under TAZAMA Pipelines Limited (Oil Gas Africa 2014). The purpose of constructing the TAZAMA pipeline, INDENI refinery, and Ndola terminal was to keep costs of transportation, processing, supply, and distribution of oil products low and predictable arising from the consequences of UDI (Economics Association of Zambia 2008: 6; Zambia Reports 2014; Nuttahmumbi 2014). Following the declaration of UDI, Zambia had been left with no choice but to reduce her dependence on an oil supply chain which ran through apartheid South Africa and white-minority-ruled Rhodesia.

The sudden closure of Zambia's southern border at Livingstone by the Rhodesian regime in January 1973 'in reprisal for the actions of nationalist guerrillas who were alleged to operate from Zambia' (Sklar 1974: 345) sent a clear message to Zambia that the Rhodesian rail route was no longer a viable route for Zambian imports and exports.

Kaunda's government pursued its foreign policy mainly through the framework of the Organization of African Unity (OAU), with the object of safeguarding the country's sovereignty, territorial integrity, and political independence (Zambia 1996). In addition to the OAU, during the era of the UNIP government, Zambia joined several other international and regional organizations in order to effectively pursue her foreign policy and safeguard her national interests. These organizations included the Commonwealth, Non-Aligned Movement (NAM), Preferential Trade Area for Eastern and Southern Africa (PTA), and Southern African Development Coordination Conference (SADCC). Zambia joined the OAU on 16 December 1964 (Wikipedia 2014*k*), the Commonwealth in 1964 (royal.gov.uk 2014), NAM in 1964 (NTI 2014). From 1970 to 1974 Zambia was a member of the Mulungushi Club, which was comprised of leaders of Tanzania (Nyerere), Uganda (Obote, up to 1971), and Zambia (Kaunda). Oliver Tambo, the leader of the African National Congress (ANC) of South Africa who was in exile in Zambia used to attend all Mulungushi Club meetings (Mwakikagale 2010). The leaders of the other active liberation movements in the region were frequently invited to the summits of the club. Uganda's membership to the Mulungushi Club ended in 1971 when Idi Amin replaced Obote as president of Uganda in a military coup (ISS 1999). From 1973, Mobutu of Zaire attended club meetings (ISS 1999). The club was an informal group of respected heads of state rather than an interstate institution. The Mulungushi Club had its focus on the liberation of Southern Africa. It provided a platform for the coordination of efforts towards the liberation of countries that were still under colonial rule and white domination in the region. Because of its relatively small size, the club was able to meet frequently and at short notice. The Mulungushi Club was the predecessor to the Frontline States (FLS). Most of the features of the club were carried over to the FLS. In 1975, Zambia together with other countries in the region established the Frontline States. The FLS was established as an informal forum for the discussion of mainly political and, to a lesser extent, military problems that were common to the liberation movements. Security issues were discussed in the Inter-State Defence and Security Committee (ISDSC), which was a substructure of the FLS (ISS 2014). The FLS also discussed problems faced by the newly independent countries of Mozambique and Angola. At summit level, the FLS in addition to national governments included representatives of the various liberation movements in the region. At times the head of state of Nigeria attended FLS summits as an informal associate. The leaders of Botswana (Sir Seretse Khama), Tanzania (Julius Nyerere), and Zambia (Kenneth Kaunda), together with Samora Machel of Mozambique were considered as the founder members of the FLS. Angola joined the FLS in 1976, Zimbabwe in 1980, and Namibia in 1990. South Africa joined in 1994, the same year that the existence of the FLS came to an end (ISS 1999). Lesotho was never a member of the FLS, although Chief Leabua Jonathan sent representatives to attend a number of ISDSC meetings (ISS 1999). The FLS played a key role in the liberation of Rhodesia (Zimbabwe) and South West Africa (Namibia) and dismantling of apartheid in South Africa by providing material, logistical, diplomatic, and political support to the liberation movements of Zimbabwe, Namibia, and South Africa. The freedom fighters from Zimbabwe infiltrated their country from the front-line states of Mozambique, Tanzania, and Zambia; the ANC infiltrated South Africa from Angola, Mozambique, and Zambia; and SWAPO infiltrated Namibia from Angola and Zambia. Further, it should be mentioned here that these liberation movements were hosted in the various front-line states (SA History 2014). Zambia was also a founder member of SADCC in 1980 (Wikipedia 2014*n*) and the PTA in 1981 (FAO 2014). The national interests pursued through these organizations cover broad areas which include political, economic, and security matters. Membership to these regional and international organizations has had an influence in the way Zambia has conducted her international relations in that as a member she was expected to abide by the principles on which these organizations were founded and observe the various agreements and protocols to which she was a signatory. It should also be noted here that membership to the United Nations (UN), which Zambia joined in 1964, has had a major influence on Zambia's foreign policy in that as a UN member the country is expected to abide by certain principles of the UN and implement various UN resolutions. Zambia is also expected to participate in various UN programmes and activities, such as UN peacekeeping missions.

Surrounded by hostile colonial regimes to the west, east, and south and realising that such a situation was not in the newly independent country's national interests, the Kaunda government had no choice but to take a leading role in the liberation struggle. Thus, internationally, Zambia's sympathies lay with forces opposing colonial or white-dominated rule. Therefore, from the 1970s to the 1990s, she actively supported liberation movements in the region, namely the National Union for the Total Independence of Angola (UNITA), the Front for the Liberation of Mozambique (FRELIMO), the Zimbabwe African People's Union (ZAPU) and Zimbabwe African National Union (ZANU) in Southern Rhodesia, the African National Congress (ANC) in their struggle against apartheid in South Africa, and the South West Africa People's Organization (SWAPO) in their struggle for independence of Namibia. In this vein, Zambia also had to host some of the liberation movements like the ANC exile headquarters which was located in Lusaka, and ZAPU, which was based in Zambia throughout the liberation struggle. This resulted in security problems, as the South Africa and South Rhodesia military forces raided targets inside Zambia on several occasions (ChaCha 2014; Henderson 1978; Wikipedia 2014*c*).

In fact, from as early as the mid 1960s, Zambia was rendering some support to the liberation movements in the region. Soon after joining the OAU, Kaunda allowed a liberation centre to be set up in Lusaka which provided offices to those liberation movements that had received official recognition from the OAU. This centre allowed them to conduct the business of processing refugees, organising transit through Zambia, and providing access to propaganda and other benefits (Matsheumhlope 2010). With regard to military bases, it should be noted that during the mid-1960s and early 1970s, the People's Army for the Liberation of Angola (Exercito Pupular de Libertacao de Angola, or EPLA), the military wing of the Popular Movement for the Liberation of Angola (MPLA), operated very successfully from bases in Zambia against the Portuguese in Eastern Angola (Wikipedia 2014*a*). And by 1966, the South West Africa People's Organization (SWAPO) had also established military bases in Zambia (Wikipedia 2014*m*). In the case of Rhodesia, until the early 1970s the Zimbabwe African National Liberation Army (ZANLA), the military wing of the Zimbabwe African National Union (ZANU), was based in camps around Lusaka; and the Zimbabwe People's Revolutionary Army (ZIPRA), the military wing of the Zimbabwe African People's Union (ZAPU) operated from bases in Zambia throughout the liberation struggle (Wikipedia 2014*v*). At the time of Zimbabwean independence in 1980, ZIPRA had a modern military stationed in Zambia (Wikipedia 2014*e*).

Over and above supporting liberation movements, Kaunda's government attempted to serve the role of mediator between the entrenched colonial governments and the various guerrilla movements that were fighting to overthrow the respective colonial governments (Anderson and O'Dowd 1999). On 26 August 1975, President Kaunda and prime minister of South Africa B.

J. Vorster acted as mediators in the Victoria Falls Conference which took place at Victoria Falls to discuss possibilities for an internal settlement in Southern Rhodesia. The conference was held aboard a South African Railways train halfway across the Victoria Falls Bridge. The participants in the conference were a delegation led by the Rhodesian prime minister Ian Smith on behalf of his government and a nationalist delegation attending under the banner of Abel Muzorewa's African National Council (UANC), which for this conference also incorporated delegates from ZANU, ZAPU, and the Front for the Liberation of Zimbabwe (FROLIZI). The Victoria Falls Conference failed to produce a settlement (Wikipedia 2014*u*). On 30 April 1982, President Kaunda met with the South African prime minister Pieter Willem Botha in Botswana across South Africa's border with Botswana to discuss the political situation in South West Africa (Namibia) and South Africa (About.com 2014). Kaunda's meeting with P. W. Botha did not achieve anything.

Kaunda also on one occasion played the role of negotiator for the release of hostages. In August 1989, Farzad Bazoft, an Iranian-born freelance journalist was detained in Iraq for alleged espionage. He was accompanied by a British nurse, Daphne Parish, who was arrested as well. Bazoft was attempting to expose Saddam Hussein's mass murder of Iraq Kurds. Bazoft was later tried and condemned to death, but Kaunda managed to negotiate for the release of Daphne Parish (bufvc.ac.uk 2014).

Zambia under President Kaunda also established close military relations with other countries with the object of not only pursuing the liberation of the rest of Africa but also securing her territorial boundaries and ensuring national security. In this vein, Zambia entered into agreements to procure military equipment from several countries such as Germany, Russia, and China (*Buffalo News* 1998). It has also been conducting exchange programmes whereby military personnel from other countries train in Zambia and vice versa. For example, in 1987 the Zambia Army trained an intake of Mozambican recruits at Army Battle Training Area (ABTA) Recruit Training Centre under the Military Training Establishment of Zambia, or MILTEZ (*Buffalo News* 1998). Furthermore, Zambia has been conducting joint military exercises with other countries. The Kaunda government also adopted a deliberate policy to strengthen bilateral relations with each neighbouring country by creating Joint

Permanent Commissions (JPCs) to foster peace and security in the border areas.

Owing to her geopolitical position, Zambia has also been engaged in rendering services to refugees who left their countries during the liberation wars and those that later ran away from civil strife in their countries. According to Martin (1998), by hosting refugees, Zambia has been making efforts, in collaboration with United Nations High Commission for Refugees (UNHCR), to provide basic education for children. Women are trained in income-generating activities, thus making them a part of the development processes in Zambia, and not just recipients of aid. Zambia has been conducting voluntary repatriation of refugees who intend to leave for their countries. On the other hand, some refugees have opted to remain in Zambia because of their engagements in business, education, gainful employment, etc. Some refugees have married Zambians, and this has solidified the bond between Zambians and these nationals of other countries who have decided to make Zambia their home and be integrated into Zambian society.

Most of the progressive countries have prioritised attraction of foreign direct investments (FDIs) as one of their important foreign policy objectives. In the case of Zambia, it should be noted that the country has an advantage over many countries as a destination for foreign investments. Firstly, Zambia is endowed with abundant natural resources. It has very rich mineral resources, whose quality is 'equivalent, if not better, than those found in many successful mining economies' (UNCTAD 2006: 1). Further, Zambia is endowed with the most abundant surface and groundwater resources among the Southern African countries with about 45 per cent of the water supplies of the total water resources of Southern Africa (WWF 2014). The country also has unspoiled wilderness areas for tourism (UNCTAD 2006: 1). Zambia has also been peaceful and politically stable since independence, and the country's security situation has been the envy of many countries in the region. Despite these advantages, Zambia did not do well with regard to attracting foreign direct investments during Kaunda's presidency. The major reason for this was Kaunda's economic policies which worked to discourage foreign investments and created an atmosphere that was not conducive to promoting economic diplomacy. On 19 April 1968, Kaunda announced his Mulungushi Economic

Reforms wherein certain foreign companies were directed to sell 51 per cent of their enterprises to the government (Gupta 1974: 305; Sardanis 2003: 212). Following this directive, the government acquired majority shareholding in twenty-six principal companies (Gupta 1974: 305). The twenty-six affected companies were in the 'construction sector, commerce, road transport, and one or two other fields' (Gupta 1974: 365). On 11 August 1969, President Kaunda in his Matero Reforms announced the nationalisation of the copper industry, resulting in the government acquiring 51 per cent majority shareholding in the mining companies (Gupta 1974: 365). In 1970 the financial sector (insurance companies and building societies) were nationalised; the banks were excluded from the 1970 measures after successfully resisting the takeover (Gupta 1974: 365). Kaunda's nationalisation programme together with the new manufacturing ventures of the Industrial Development Corporation (INDECO) gave the government ultimate control over all major sectors of the economy, with the exception of large-scale commercial agriculture and the banks (Gupta 1974: 365). The nationalisation programme entailed an extensive expropriation of foreign investment, with an initial divestment of around US$300 million (UNCTAD 2006: 4 and 17).

In addition to the nationalisation policy, President Kaunda came up with another series of economic reforms which, although well intended, worked to discourage any new foreign investments and created an environment not conducive for promotion of economic diplomacy. The purpose of Kaunda's second set of economic measures was to increase participation of Zambians in the remaining private sector (Gupta 1974: 366). The same year (1968) that Kaunda announced his Mulungushi Economic Reforms, he put curbs on 'the right of resident expatriate enterprises to borrow money locally, in the hope that more credit would be made available to citizens' (Gupta 1974: 366). He also excluded foreigners from 'the retail trade outside the centres of ten major urban centres, and they were not to be granted any additional trading licences even in those areas' (Gupta 1974: 366). Foreigners were also excluded from the transportation sector and all building material permits and Public Works Department contracts worth K100,000 or less were reserved for citizens (Gupta 1974: 366). A year later (1969), Kaunda announced further measures wherein 'foreigners' participation in the wholesale trade was restricted to the ten major urban centres and the eight provincial headquarters' (Gupta 1974: 366). Finally

in 1970, Kaunda announced that from 1 January 1972, no foreigner would
be allowed to get a retail or wholesale licence anywhere in the country and
existing licences to retail prescribed goods as well as existing transport licences
and building material permits would become null and void from that date
(Gupta 1974: 366). Kaunda's economic reforms should be seen in the context
of his conviction that after overcoming colonialism the country needed to wage
war against neo-colonialism and achieve economic independence. Hence he
came up with various economic measures whose thrust was to economically
empower Zambians and wrestle the economy from foreign domination.

To fully comprehend the foreign policy of the newly independent Zambia, it
is also useful to look at other factors such as the personality and beliefs of the
leader of the country President Kaunda, national values and principles, culture,
ethnicity, and demography. Kaunda was a pan-Africanist who put the African
continent first, hence Zambia's activity participation in the OAU programmes.
Kaunda has Christian values of loving thy neighbour as you love yourself.
Kaunda propounded the ideology of humanism, which placed man at the centre
of all political, economical, social, cultural, as well as religious activities. These
ideals and values influenced his foreign policy of good neighbourliness and
liberating the rest of Africa. Kaunda was also a strong advocate of non-alignment
with regard to the two superpowers (USA and Soviet Union), hence Zambia's
active participation at NAM meetings. Zambia hosted the third NAM Summit
in 1970 and Kaunda served as NAM secretary general from 1970 to 1973
(Wikipedia 2014*j*). Kaunda even became a very close friend of the Yugoslavian
leader Josip Broz Tito, one of the founders of NAM (Henderson 1978).

Further, Kaunda was a strong voice of the oppressed people on the African
continent and elsewhere in the world. He frequently differed with President
Ronald Reagan of the USA and British Prime Minister Margaret Thatcher
over what he saw as a blind eye being turned towards South African apartheid.
However, it should be noted here that when it was convenient to Kaunda,
despite his strong beliefs in freedom and democracy, he forged very close ties
with some leaders that were oppressing their own people and certainly did
not share with him the values of freedom, democracy, and respect for human
rights. The case in point here is that of the Iraq strongman Saddam Hussein.
Prior to the first Gulf War, Kaunda cultivated a close friendship with Saddam

Hussein, with whom he secured oil resources for his nation. He even went to name a street in Lusaka in honour of Saddam Hussein (Wikipedia 2014*f*). This goes to show that at times for the sake of national interests, for example economic interests, national leaders and countries have to ignore their own principles and national values. In the case of Kaunda's close ties with Hussein, access to Iraq's oil resources seems to have overridden his personal principles and national values.

With regard to the relevance of ethnicity and demography to foreign policy, it should be noted here that Zambia is surrounded by countries whose people share the same origins, history, culture, and language and, in some cases, the same ethnic groups as Zambians. Good examples here are the Chewas of Malawi and Mozambique who pay allegiance to Paramount Chief Gawa Undi of Eastern Zambia and the Ngonis of Malawi and Mozambique who also pay allegiance to Paramount Chief Mpezeni of Eastern Zambia. These people are one and the same, having been divided by artificial boundaries created by the colonialists. Thus, given these close ties between the people of Zambia and those of neighbouring countries, it was imperative that Zambia maintained good neighbourliness with her neighbours.

The discussion on Zambia's foreign policy under the Kaunda presidency has clearly shown that several factors shaped the country's foreign policy. These factors have included, among others, colonialism and neocolonialism, geopolitics, demography, natural resource endowment, economy of the country, national interests, membership to regional and international organizations, history, national values and principles, and ideology.

Furthermore, the discussion has also shown that several theories and approaches can be used to explain Zambia's foreign policy under President Kaunda. These theories and approaches include, among others, multilevel, multidimensional approach; realism; constructivism; liberalism; international political economy (IPE); traditional approach; comparative approach; and cognitive processes psychology approach.

Realism, which is a theory that underlines the value of national security in foreign policy, can be used to explain the Zambian government's military cooperation with other countries, aimed at safeguarding national security. The comparative approach (which was inspired by behaviourism and focuses on, among other issues, attitudes, preferences, and expectations of people in political contexts and the roles of people in social systems) can also be used to explain the influence of Kaunda's preferences and expectations on Zambian foreign policy. For instance, Kaunda preferred non-alignment, hence Zambia's active participation in the affairs of the Non-Aligned Movement. Cognitive Processes Psychology Approach can also be used to understand Zambia's foreign policy. As earlier explained, this is an approach that focuses on the psychological aspects of the individual decision-maker. These aspects include, among others, political socialisation of a leader. In the case of Zambia, Kaunda and his fellow leaders' personal experiences with colonialism explains the unwavering support Zambia rendered to the liberation of the other countries in the region and beyond. The traditional approach is also relevant in explaining Zambia's foreign policy. As earlier explained, the traditional approach involves, among others, understanding a country's history and an ability to recognize the circumstances under which a government must operate in carrying out its foreign policy. In the case of Zambia, it can be noted that the country went through a similar colonial history with other countries like Tanzania and Nigeria. Thus, it was not surprising that Zambia forged a close alliance with Tanzania and Nigeria in the liberation of the other countries that were still under colonial and foreign domination on the continent. On the same issue of the traditional approach, one can refer back to the declaration of UDI, which created very difficult economic circumstances for Zambia, resulting in the Kaunda government turning to China for assistance to construct the Tanzania Zambia Railway in order to secure a viable route to the sea for the country's exports and imports. Another theory that can be used to understand some aspects of Zambia's foreign policy is the international political economy (IPE) approach—an approach that best explains the vulnerable position of weak states in international relations as well as their limitations and constraints. In the context of Zambia, this approach can be used to explain the vulnerable position Zambia found herself following the declaration of UDI. The theory of liberalism which is anchored on freedom and democracy can also be employed to enhance one's understanding of Zambia's foreign policy during Kaunda's presidency. In this regard, it can be noted that Kaunda's beliefs in freedom and democracy influenced his foreign policy with regard to the liberation struggle. Another theory dealing with ideas and beliefs and has relevance to the understanding of aspects of Zambia's foreign policy is constructivism. As earlier mentioned, this theory focuses on the ideas and beliefs that inform the actors on the international scene. Thus again, Kaunda's ideas and beliefs, for instance on humanism, non-alignment and pan-Africanism, explain Zambia's active participation in the programmes of the OAU and Non-Aligned Movement, deep involvement in the liberation struggle of other countries as well as the policy of good neighbourliness. Finally, as can be deduced from the discussion above, various theories and approaches explain different aspects of Zambia's foreign policy and thus a multilevel, multidimensional approach is particularly relevant to explaining Zambia's foreign policy.

Despite the political and economic challenges the country faced during the period 1964 to 1991, it should be noted here that Kaunda's government scored some notable foreign policy successes. The most prominent of these relate to the important role Zambia played in the liberation struggle, the hosting of refugees, the forging of regional and continental unity through SADCC, PTA, and the OAU. Kaunda's government should also be commended for the manner it responded to UDI through creation of alternative transportation routes for her imports and exports.

However, the foreign policy successes Kaunda's government scored came with negative consequences on the domestic front. Zambia's support and involvement in the liberation struggle impacted negatively on the country's economy, resulting in some sections of the Zambian society openly questioning, towards the end of the 1980s, the benefits of the liberation struggle to the nation (Akapelwa 2010: 38). They perceived the country's foreign policy as 'lending more weight and priority to pan-African interests at the expense of domestic economic and social interests of Zambia' (Akapelwa 2010: 38). The foregoing combined with other factors resulted in Kaunda's UNIP government becoming unpopular at home, resulting in electoral defeat to Frederick's Chiluba's Movement for Multiparty Democracy (MMD) at the 1991 general elections. Among other promises, Chiluba pledged that unlike Kaunda and UNIP, his MMD government would focus more on revitalising the national economy. The lesson that can be drawn here is that when pursuing a foreign policy, one has to tread carefully and weigh domestic expectations against regional and international interests (Akapelwa 2010: 37–38). If nationals of a country perceive a foreign policy to be more in favour of regional and international interests at the expense of national interests, such a foreign policy would become unpopular and cost a government politically and in some cases result in a government being voted out of power. Thus it is important that a government maintains a balance between national and regional/international interests by correctly reading the public mood and opinion and adjusting the foreign policy accordingly.

1991–2002

President Frederick Chiluba succeeded Kaunda on 2 November 1991 and left office on 2 January 2002. During the first four years of Chiluba's presidency (1991–1995), Zambia continued to operate without an approved foreign policy document. During this period, the MMD government worked on a foreign policy document in consultation with various stakeholders. In January 1996, Zambia's first foreign policy document was adopted. Thus, during President Chiluba's last six years in office (1996–2002) Zambia operated with a formal foreign policy, for the first time in the country's history. The policy focused on liberalisation of the economy and was also anchored on, among other values, respect for human rights, freedom and democracy, transparency and good governance. It also focused on safeguarding the sovereignty and national interests of the country and promotion of international peace and security (Zambia 1996).

Chiluba played an important role in African politics. His government played a constructive regional role sponsoring Angola peace talks that led to the 1994 Lusaka Protocols (Wikipedia 2014c). Zambia was also the first African country to cooperate with the International Tribunal investigation of the 1994 Rwanda genocide (Wikipedia 2014c). Further, in 1998 Zambia led the efforts to establish a ceasefire in the Democratic Republic of Congo and following the signing of the ceasefire agreement in July and August 1999 she actively participated in the Congolese peace effort (Wikipedia 2014c). However, activity pertaining to the Congolese peace process diminished considerably after the Joint Military Commission tasked with the implementation of the ceasefire relocated to Kinshasa in September 2001 (Wikipedia 2014c).

On the continental and global stages, the new MMD government also championed human rights, democracy, transparency, and good governance. Chiluba's government also championed the interests and aspirations of developing countries at the United Nations General Conference and other international conferences. As observed by Akapelwa, the Chiluba administration was 'credited for setting the pace for multiparty democracy in Africa and became the role model in the Organization of African Unity' (2010: 38). As Akapelwa (2010: 38) further observed, the Chiluba administration 'set the pace against unconstitutional governments through coup d'état in Africa'. It should also be noted here that the Organization of African Unity was transformed into the African Union (AU) in July 2001 at the Lusaka Summit under the chairmanship of Zambia.

To fulfil his campaign promise of solving the country's prevailing economic problems, Chiluba's government liberalised the economy and opened it up to foreign investors and privatised it. The new MMD government adopted a much greater economic orientation in the country's external relations. Thus in regard to matters related to the economy, liberalism best explains Chiluba's foreign policy. The opening up of the Zambian economy resulted in an increase in foreign direct investment (FDI). The increase in FDI inflows during Chiluba's presidency was largely attributed to 'an ambitious privatisation programme (1994–2001), investments in copper and cobalt extraction and greenfield investments in the agricultural sector, in particular horticulture and floriculture production, and in tourism' (UNCTAD 2006: 1). However, according to UNCTAD (2006: 37), 'Zambia has underperformed in using FDI in support of development and poverty reduction. Even though it has in many respects greater potential to attract FDI than other LDCs in the region, it is, relative to population and size of economy, being outpaced by its neighbours.' As UNCTAD (2006: 37) further observes, spillovers from FDI to local enterprises, including technology transfer, have been rather limited, and have not contributed to strengthening competitive production and diversifying Zambia's production and export base. A number of reasons account for Zambia's failure to attract more FDIs relative to the potential the country possesses. Firstly, being landlocked makes Zambia a high-cost area in comparison to neighbours that have outperformed her in attracting FDIs, such as Mozambique and Tanzania, who have direct access to the sea (Muweme

2004). Secondly, the high poverty levels in Zambia are a discouragement to FDIs. High poverty levels mean that people's ability to buy goods and services is very limited (Muweme 2004). Some investors certainly get discouraged by this factor. Third is the HIV/AIDS pandemic which continues to claim lives whose productive contribution is essential to any foreign firms investing in Zambia (Muweme 2004). Finally, the issue of corruption during Chiluba's presidency was a discouraging factor to foreign investments. In 2001, Transparency International placed Zambia at 76 out of 91 countries on its scale of Corruption Perception Index. This was 15 places from the bottom (Transparency International 2001).

With regard to military cooperation with other countries, the Chiluba government continued with this aspect of foreign policy. For instance, in 1994, Zambia trained African National Congress (ANC) officers at the Zambia Military Academy (ZMA) (*Buffalo News* 1998).

As earlier mentioned, Zambia is expected as a UN member to participate in programmes of the UN such as peacekeeping missions. During the Chiluba presidency, Zambia participated in UN missions as follows:

(a) Sent troops to the United Nations Assistance Mission for Rwanda (UNAMIR), which commenced in October 1993 and ended in March 1996 (Wikipedia 2014*q*);
(b) Sent experts and soldiers to the United Nations Organization Stabilisation Mission in the Democratic Republic of the Congo (MONUSCO), which commenced on 30 November 1999 and is to date ongoing (Wikipedia 2014*i*);
(c) Sent soldiers to the United Nations Mission in Ethiopia and Eritrea, which commenced in July 2000 and came to an end in July 2008 (Wikipedia 2014*r*);
(d) Sent military and police personnel to the United Nations Assistance Mission to Sierra Leone (UNAMSIL), which commenced on 22 October 1999 and came to an end on 31 December 2005 (UN 2005);

On a negative note, soon after Chiluba assumed power, Zambia experienced some isolation in the region because of the ill treatment Kaunda received from the new MMD government. Soon after losing power, Kaunda 'suffered political harassment, vilification, prosecution, and even imprisonment at the hands of his successor. He was denied his terminal benefits for two years, suffered the humiliation of being searched for suspected stolen books from State House, and only received recognition and full benefits when he retired completely from active politics in early 2000' (Simutanyi 2006: 74). Kaunda was also declared stateless (Maravi blog 2007).

It should be noted here that Kaunda is revered in the region and beyond for the role he played in the liberation struggle on the African continent and any perceived ill treatment of Kaunda is bound to invoke some reaction in sympathy to Kaunda from many countries on the continent, especially within the region. Thus in the case of Zambia, the Kaunda factor cannot be ignored as it has implications on the country's foreign relations. It should be further noted that since the liberation struggle days, the region has been politically interlinked with all the main liberation-struggle political parties still maintaining close links to date—UNIP in Zambia, MPLA in Angola, Chama Cha Mapinduzi (CCM) in Tanzania, FRELIMO in Mozambique, ZANU PF in Zimbabwe, ANC in South Africa, and SWAPO in Namibia. If you touch one of these organizations, you have touched all, and they are bound to unite in solidarity and support one of their own.

2002–2008

President Levy Mwanawasa succeeded President Chiluba on 2 January 2002 and occupied the office until 19 August 2008 when he passed on. Soon after assuming office, the Mwanawasa administration decided to revise the foreign policy document because circumstances on the domestic, regional, and international scenes had changed. Issues of climate change, international terrorism, human and drug trafficking, money laundering, and HIV/AIDS had brought a number of challenges to sub-Saharan Africa, including Zambia. With regard to HIV/AIDS and other health issues, it should be noted here that HIV/AIDS, TB, and malaria have had devastating impact on Zambia's developmental efforts. Thus, the revised policy was expected to emphasize closer cooperation with the rest of the world and various international bodies, including those under the UN, to address the health challenges in the country.

On the economic front, it was felt that there was need to realign the country's foreign policy towards more economic diplomacy.

During Mwanawasa's first term in office, from 2 January 2002 to 2 October 2006, Zambia attracted donor and investor confidence due to the new president's tough stance on corruption, disciplined fiscal management, and improvement in economic performance especially in the agriculture sector (Akapelwa 2010: 39; Wikipedia 2014*g*). The increase in donor confidence led to the country attracting more investors in mining, construction, and trade (Akapelwa 2010: 39). Foreign direct investment in 2004 increased by 11.7 per cent in 2004 to $334 million (UNCTAD 2006: 3). The pick-up in FDI from 2003 was mainly attributed to the 'commodity price boom, which saw copper prices increase by 80 per cent from $1,560 per metric ton in 2002 to $2,816 in 2004' (UNCTAD 2006: 5). During this period, two new large mines (the Kansanshi mine by First Quantum Minerals from Canada and the Lumwana mine by Equinox Minerals from Australia) started operations (UNCTAD 2006: 5). Other mines were rehabilitated and expanded by the new foreign owners after a period of decline, notably the RAMCOZ mine and Konkola Copper Mines (KCM), the largest producer in Zambia (UNCTAD 2006: 5). Zambia also received a relatively large amount of aid and debt relief because of liberalisation and Mwanawasa's 'solid efforts'. Overall, economic growth increased to about 6 per cent per year (Wikipedia 2014*g*).

Despite an increase in foreign investments during Mwanawasa's first term in office, 'poverty levels, unemployment, crime, low wages, and poor conditions of service for general workers continued unabated' (Akapelwa 2010: 39). With regard to the situation where the living conditions for Zambians were not improving despite the increase in foreign investments, the general view in the urban areas was that the investors who the government gave tax holidays were expropriating most of the money outside Zambia in form of profits (Akapelwa 2010: 39). The urbanites in Zambia were of the general view that the foreign investors were not creating more jobs and were paying low wages (Akapelwa 2010: 39). It was therefore not surprising that in the 2006 general elections, 'the majority of the electorate in urban and peri-urban areas voted for the opposition parties who promised them more jobs creation, improved wages, review of contracts signed with investors and improved working conditions'

(Akapelwa 2010: 39). The lesson to be drawn here is that a foreign investment policy should by all means strive to satisfy domestic interests, failure to which there will be political cost, such as loss of votes from certain sections of the electorate.

The donors, and the Western world in general, were also impressed with Mwanawasa's tough stance on the issue of Zimbabwe. Mwanawasa was one of the first African leaders to publicly criticise President Robert Mugabe of Zimbabwe on issues of bad governance in that country (Wikipedia 2014*g*). Mwanawasa held the rotating chair of SADC for one year from August 2007 to August 2008. It was at this time that the issue of Zimbabwe was one of the hot topics in world politics especially among the Western world who were united in opposition to Mugabe's governance style. During his tenure as SADC chair, President Mwanawasa brought the issue of Zimbabwe to the fore in the SADC, taking the lead role in pressuring President Mugabe for reforms in his country (Magagula 2009). During Mwanawasa's tenure as SADC chair, the economic and political situation in Zimbabwe had reached crisis point. The crisis was further worsened by the controversial outcome of the 29 March 2008 presidential and parliamentary elections, in which it was widely believed that Morgan Tsvangirai of the opposition Movement for Democratic Change (MDC) had been robbed of victory (Malupenga 2009: 215). Mwanawasa's handling of the Zimbabwe crisis resulted in the souring of relations between Zimbabwe and Zambia. His summoning of an urgent SADC in April 2008 to discuss the Zimbabwe crisis did not sit well with President Robert Mugabe (Malupenga 2009: 216). Mugabe boycotted the emergency SADC summit, opting to instead send a ministerial delegation (Malupenga 2009: 216). Mwanawasa had also invited to the summit Morgan Tsvangirai and Dr Simba Makoni, who had stood as presidential candidates in the March 2008 elections (Malupenga 2009: 216). Tsvangirai and Makoni were invited so that they could give their side of the story. Zimbabwe was not amused by the invitation of Tsvangirai and Makoni to the summit, arguing that only representatives of member states should have been in attendance (Malupenga 2009: 216). Mugabe's representatives at the summit went on to accuse Mwanawasa of being used by the United Kingdom and United States of America to effect regime change in Zimbabwe. Following Zimbabwe's protestations Tsvangirai and Makoni only managed to hold some informal consultations with some SADC leaders outside of the official programme of the summit (Malupenga 2009: 216). At this emergency summit, only President Khama of Botswana backed Mwanawasa (Malupenga 2009: 217). In the view of this author, the lack of support for Mwanawasa's stance on Zimbabwe at the summit is not surprising because of the tendency by countries led by liberation political parties to support one of their own, even when their own is in the wrong. From the observations of this author, Mwanawasa experienced isolation at SADC meetings because of his tough stance on the Zimbabwe issue.

Given President Mwanawasa's personality characteristics of being frank, honest, and courageous in expressing his views and his strong belief in the rule of law, it was not surprising that he tackled the Zimbabwe issue without any fear. Mwanawasa being a democrat and principled person would not accept a situation where a member state of SADC, in this case Zimbabwe, could with impunity disregard the SADC protocol on guidelines on elections, to which she was a signatory. Equally, Mwanawasa could not understand why the other SADC member states, with the exception of Botswana, could not support him on the stance he had taken with regard to the Zimbabwe crisis.

It should also be pointed out here that, to a certain extent, Mwanawasa's lack of diplomatic skills did not help matters with regard to the Zimbabwe crisis. In a speech at a state banquet in Windhoek, Namibia on the evening of Tuesday, 20 March 2007, Mwanawasa likened Zimbabwe to a sinking *Titanic* and said SADC had failed to achieve much in negotiations with Mugabe. He implored SADC to take a new approach to resolving the Zimbabwe crisis (Reuters 2007). Mwanawasa's likening of Zimbabwe to a sinking *Titanic* irked the leadership and people of Zimbabwe and contributed to the further worsening of relations between the two countries. It should be pointed out here that it is against diplomatic etiquette to use a state banquet to criticise other countries. A state banquet is not an occasion for criticising or attacking other countries. It is an occasion for welcoming a visiting head of state and reaffirming the good relations that exist between the host and visiting country, and expressing a desire to further strengthen those relations. It is not only unacceptable to the country being criticised but it is also embarrassing to the host country because it is being wrongly used as a platform by a visiting head of state to criticise a third country. Relations between Zimbabwe and Zambia became strained to the extent that President Mwanawasa had to send his vice president Rupiah Banda in August 2007 to help improve relations between the two countries prior to a planned SADC summit (Wikipedia 2014*l*). Banda is a former freedom fighter, former ambassador, and former foreign minister who is highly regarded in the region.

The Kaunda factor continued to haunt the MMD government during Mwanawasa's presidency, although on a scale less than was the case during the Chiluba presidency. There were allegations that Mwanawasa had referred to Kaunda as a chap who was decampaigning the MMD in foreign countries. Even Mwanawasa's predecessor Chiluba, who himself treated Kaunda very badly, is on record to have advised Mwanawasa to tone down on Kaunda (Maravi blog 2007). Mwanawasa denied calling Kaunda a chap (Lusaka Times 2007). Despite Mwanawasa denying the allegations, the story created some discomfort within certain sections of Zambian society and the SADC region. Even prior to these allegations, some SADC member countries continued being unhappy with what was perceived as ill treatment of Kaunda by the MMD government. Some members of the Zambian diplomatic corps serving in the SADC region had to engage in quiet diplomacy to defuse the negative impact the Kaunda factor was having on Zambia's relations with neighbouring countries. For instance, this author had to assure some key leaders in Tanzania that Kaunda was now being well treated by the MMD government. In a bid to ease the tension arising from the Kaunda factor, this author had to visit the secretary general of the ruling Chama Cha Mapinduzi (CCM) to persuade him to invite MMD to the Seventh Ordinary Meeting of the CCM National Congress slated for 24–25 June 2006. The CCM secretary general agreed to invite MMD but made it clear that UNIP, as a sister party of CCM, would as has always been the case be invited to the same congress. MMD was together with UNIP invited to the congress. To the disappointment of CCM and this author, MMD failed to honour the invitation and without even sending an apology. UNIP attended the Congress. By failing to attend the CCM Congress, the ruling MMD missed a golden opportunity to forge relations with CCM.

In the area of military cooperation the Mwanawasa administration, like previous governments, continued to cooperate with other countries in the region in order to secure national and regional security. For instance in 2007, Zambia hosted the inauguration of the SADC Standby Brigade, which was established to provide a collective self-defence system for the Southern Africa region. The standby brigade is comprised of military, police, and civilian personnel who provide peace and security assistance to the region (Meleka 2008). Under the Mwanawasa presidency, Zambia also continued participating in UN Peace Keeping missions. In 2003, Zambia sent police and military personnel to the United Nations Mission in Liberia (UNMIL), which commenced on 19 September 2003 and is ongoing (UN 2003). Zambia also participated in the United Nations Operation in Burundi (ONUB), which commenced on 21 May 2004 and ended on 31 December 2006 (Wikipedia 2014*t*).

2008–2011

President Rupiah Banda was Zambia's fourth president. He was in office from 29 June 2008 to 23 September 2011. It should be noted here that from 29 June 2008 to 2 November 2008 he was acting president. When President Mwanawasa suffered a stroke on 29 June 2008, while attending an AU summit in Egypt, Rupiah Banda, who was vice president, became acting president. And when President Mwanawasa died on 19 August 2008, Banda officially took over as acting president prior to a new presidential election. Banda won the presidential election that was held on 30 October 2008 and was sworn in as president on 2 November 2008 (Wikipedia 2014*l*). Rupiah Banda's administration continued with the revision of the 1996 foreign policy document.

Of all the presidents that have ruled Zambia during the fifty years of the country's existence, Banda was by far the most experienced in the area of foreign policy, prior to occupying the high office of president. During the independence struggle, he served as UNIP's representative in northern Europe during the early 1960s. Following Zambia's independence, he was appointed ambassador to Egypt in 1965. And on 7 April 1967 he was appointed ambassador to the USA and served there for about two years. Banda later served as permanent representative to the UN. While at the UN, Banda also headed the UN Council for Namibia. After serving about a year at the UN, Banda served as minister of foreign affairs from 1975 to 1976. During his brief stint as foreign minister, Banda was occupied by the task of attempting to broker a ceasefire in Angola (Wikipedia 2014*l*).

As observed by Akapelwa (2010: 40), under Banda's presidency, Zambia realigned itself away from what was perceived to be a 'confrontational stance in foreign policy to focus more on building bonds of friendship, good neighbourliness, diplomatic approaches, and networking particularly in the SADC region'. This move towards a more diplomatic approach to foreign policy was not surprising given Banda's solid foreign policy credentials and experience. During Banda's presidency, new bonds of friendship were created and relations with other countries remarkably improved. Notably, relations between Zambia and Zimbabwe significantly improved during Banda's presidency. The creation of new bonds of friendship and improvements in relations with other countries were made easy by the fact that Banda was an accomplished former diplomat who had a lot of old friends in Africa and overseas.

With regard to economic diplomacy, it should be noted here that the investment push in mining, tourism, and agriculture was reasonably successful. The foreign marketing policy and the branding of the country as an ideal investment destination contributed, among other factors, to this success. Further, it should also be noted here that in July 2011, the World Bank reclassified Zambia from a Least Developed Country to a Middle-Income Developing Country (*Zambia Daily Mail* 2011).

Just like other governments would act, when the Banda administration found itself in a situation where it had to choose between abiding by national values and securing economic interests, the Banda administration chose the latter. A case in point here is that of the issue of the recognition of the independence of Kosovo. Despite one of Zambia's national values being respect of other people's right to self-determination and independence, the Banda administration conveniently chose to turn a blind eye towards the issue of Kosovo's independence. In the view of this author, this was not surprising because there was more to gain economically by keeping quiet on the issue of Kosovo's independence, given that among the countries opposed to Kosovo's independence were China and Russia. It should be noted here that China and Russia are all-weather friends of Zambia and the country gains a lot economically from these two countries.

In February 2008 the Assembly of Kosovo unanimously declared independence from Serbia and established the Republic of Kosovo. This declaration was

formally legalised by the International Court of Justice on 22 July 2010. And
as at July 2010, out of 193 UN member countries, 110 had recognized the
Republic of Kosovo. Russia, China, and Zambia are among the countries
that had not yet recognized Kosovo. Russia and China are strongly opposed
to the sovereignty of Kosovo and have pronounced themselves to that effect
(Better World Campaign 2014; Kosovo Thanks You 2014). Zambia on the
other hand just chose to be quiet. This is not surprising as Zambia has very
strong economic ties with China and Russia. Zambia's ties to China have
already been explained earlier in this chapter. Russia is also a country that has
been politically close to Zambia for a long time. In addition, economically
Zambia benefits a lot from her relations with Russia. It is therefore unlikely
that Zambia would risk such benefits for the sake of abiding by national values
and principles. With regard to Russia, it should be pointed out here that the
Soviet Union (USSR) predecessor to Russian Federation was one of the first
states to recognize Zambia as an independent and sovereign state in 1964. Even
prior to that, Russia was one of the countries that rendered assistance during
the struggle for Zambian independence and the liberation of other countries
in the region (zambia.mid.ru 2014; Wikipedia 2014*b*). In the area of education
which is Russia's main investment in Zambia, out of 748 scholarships granted
to Africa annually, 85 are allocated to Zambia. More than 2,000 Zambians
have graduated from Russian universities. In addition, Russia provides training
for Zambian military and law enforcement officers in different fields, such as
peacekeeping, fight against terrorism, drug trafficking, illegal migration, and
transport security. Of the 350 officers from Africa that go to Russia for training
annually, 40 of them are Zambians (zambia.mid.ru 2014). With regard to
economic assistance, in 2001 Russia granted Zambia US$ 560 million of
debt relief and rescheduled US$ 138.3 million over the next 33 years (people.
com.cn 2001). In 2005, upon Zambia reaching the Highly Indebted Poor
Countries' Initiative Completion Point (HIPC), Russia granted Zambia $US
50 million debt relief. In June 2006, Russia cancelled more than US$ 100
million of Official Development Assistance (ODA) debt with Zambia under
a G8 Initiative (zambia.mid.ru 2014; people.com.cn 2006). In the view of this
author, the Zambian government at the time could not risk losing all these
benefits from Russia and indeed China by making a foreign policy decision
that might not sit well with these two big countries. The international political
economy (IPE) theory here best explains the vulnerability of weak countries

like Zambia in the area of international relations where their economic ties to big countries might constrain them from making independent foreign policy decisions.

Another factor that might also explain Zambia's decision to turn a blind eye to the issue of Kosovo's independence is the strong historical ties Zambia has with Serbia (former Yugoslavia). Zambia's strong ties with Yugoslavia date back to the early days of NAM when Kenneth Kaunda forged a very close relationship with the Yugoslavian leader Josip Broz Tito. This close relationship between the two leaders brought the two countries closer together. It was therefore unlikely that Zambia would support the independence of a territory (Kosovo) that broke off from a country that has been close to her for a long time. Thus, history here is also relevant in explaining Zambia's foreign policy position on Kosovo's independence.

During the Banda administration, Zambia continued participating in UN peacekeeping missions. For instance, the country sent both police and military personnel to the United Nations Mission in South Sudan (UNMISS), which commenced in July 2011 and is to date ongoing (Wikipedia 2014s).

Under the Banda administration, diplomatic training, which provides essential skills to diplomats on new posting to the Foreign Service, became mandatory (Akapelwa 2010: 40–41). Further, this training, which is undertaken at the Zambia Institute of Diplomacy and International Studies (ZIDIS), was opened up to private individuals (Akapelwa 2010: 41). Through this opportunity, many Zambians have been acquiring diplomatic skills, which is a good development because a lot of nationals interact with foreign nationals both within and outside the country (Akapelwa 2010: 41). Thus, the acquisition of diplomatic skills by private individuals through diplomatic training has the potential of contributing to the improvement of relations between Zambia and other countries.

23 September 2011 to 24 October 2014

In the general elections held on 20 September 2011, Michael Sata's Patriotic Front (PF) defeated the Movement for Multiparty Democracy, and on 23

September 2011, President Sata was sworn in as Zambia's fifth president (Wikipedia 2014*h*). Sata's administration continued with the revision of the 1996 foreign policy document.

Like previous Zambian governments, the PF government continued to maintain close and warm relations with China and reaffirmed the importance of Chinese investments to Zambia. To underscore the importance attached to the relations with China, President Sata's first official appointment at State House was with Chinese ambassador Zhou Yuxiao (China Africa Research Initiative 2011). And on 29 October 2011, Sata hosted a luncheon for the Chinese community at State House (*The Post* 2011). On 21 November 2011, President Sata sent President Kenneth Kaunda to China, as his special envoy, to go and renew Zambia's acquaintances with China and thank the Chinese people for the assistance they have been rendering to the Zambian people (AllAfrica 2011). From 5 to 12 April 2013, Sata visited China on a one-week state visit (*Zambia Daily Mail* 2013), during which he signed six bilateral agreements with the Chinese president on investments in various sectors of the economy (AidData 2013). The manner in which the PF government intensified efforts towards further strengthening relations with China goes to show that the anti-China rhetoric during the PF's years in opposition and during election campaigns was only for the purpose of getting more electoral votes.

The coming to power by the Patriotic Front (PF) saw further improvements in relations between Zambia and Zimbabwe. It should be noted in this regard that from the time the PF came to power up to the close of Zambia's fifty years of nationhood, Zimbabwean president Robert Mugabe is the only president to have visited Zambia.

Soon after coming to power, the PF government indicated that it was going to open more embassies in order to attract more foreign investments into the country and reposition the country in the global community. Thus, in February 2013 a new embassy was opened in Saudi Arabia and in May 2014 and September 2014 new embassies were opened in Turkey and South Korea respectively.

A SUMMARY OF FOREIGN POLICY IMPLEMENTATION CONSTRAINTS

During the first fifty years of nationhood, all Zambian governments faced various constraints with regard to implementation of foreign policy. These constraints have had impacts on the effectiveness of the country's foreign policy. From this author's experience and observations, these constraints have included, inter alia:

(a) poor quality of some of the staff posted to Zambian missions and in certain sections at Foreign Ministry headquarters;
(b) high levels of indiscipline in some Zambian missions among diplomats appointed from the ranks of party cadres and other diplomats with strong political connections back home;
(c) inadequate and delayed funding to Zambian missions;
(d) poor information and communications technology (ICT) infrastructure and poorly maintained websites;
(e) lack of staff with interest in ICT and maintenance of websites in Zambian missions;
(f) poor feedback from Foreign Ministry headquarters to Zambian missions;
(g) delays at Ministry of Foreign Affairs headquarters in processing correspondence from Zambian missions;
(h) poor state of government houses and equipment at Zambian missions;
(i) inadequate transport in some Zambian missions; and
(j) poor composition of Zambian delegations to various international conferences and negotiations; the quality of some of the individuals included on Zambian delegations leaves much to be desired.

CONCLUSIONS AND RECOMMENDATIONS

The discussion on Zambia's foreign policy under all the five presidents that ruled Zambia during the first fifty years of nationhood has shown that the country's foreign policy has been shaped by a broad range of factors. These factors have included, among others, colonialism and neocolonialism, geopolitics, demography, natural resource endowment, economy of the country, national interests, membership to regional and international organizations, history, national values and principles, ideology, personal characteristics of the leaders, and diplomatic skills and experience of the leaders. These factors individually or in various combinations shaped the foreign policy actions of the governments of presidents Kaunda, Chiluba, Mwanawasa, Banda, and Sata.

Further, the discussion has also shown that several theories and approaches can be used to explain the foreign policy actions of the governments of presidents Kaunda, Chiluba, Mwanawasa, Banda, and Sata. As earlier articulated in the sections on theoretical considerations and foreign policy during the Kaunda presidency, these theories and approaches include, among others, multilevel, multidimensional approach; realism; constructivism; liberalism; international political economy (IPE); traditional approach; comparative approach; and cognitive processes psychology approach.

In order to enhance efficiency and effectiveness in the implementation of the country's foreign policy, the Zambian government should take the following measures, among other measures:

(a) ensure that only persons that meet the prescribed qualifications and experience for positions in Zambian missions are appointed to those positions;

(b) continuously improve on the quality of ministry headquarters staff through training interventions and exposure;

(c) give heads of Zambian missions more power to discipline officers under their charge;

(d) improve on the levels and flow of funding to Zambian missions;

(e) improve on ICT infrastructure and website maintenance at Zambian missions;

(f) raise the levels of computer literacy among all diplomatic staff at Zambian missions through training;

(g) improve the communication channels between Ministry of Foreign Affairs headquarters and Zambian missions;

(h) improve on the capacity of ministry headquarters to timely provide feedback to Zambian missions;

(i)   regularly undertake maintenance of government houses at Zambian missions;

(j)   ensure that there is adequate equipment and transport at Zambian missions; and

(k) where necessary, include on Zambian delegations experts from universities, research institutes, and think tank organizations.

If the above and other measures are undertaken, efficiency and effectiveness will be enhanced in implementation of the foreign policy.

References

About.com (2014), 'This Day in African History: 30 April' http://africanhistory.about.com/od/april/a/td0430.html accessed on 30 August 2014.

AidData (2013), 'China and Zambia sign 100 million RMB funding for Confucius Institute', http://china.aiddata.org/projects/30680 accessed on 15 October 2014.

Akapelwa, S. (2010), *Diplomacy: Key to International Relations* (Lusaka: Zambia Educational Publishing House).

AllAfrica (2011), 'Zambia: Kenneth Kaunda Off to China', http://www.allafrica.com/stories/201111220685.html accessed on 15 October 2014.

Anderson, J. and O'Dowd, L. (1999), 'Borders, Border Regions and Territoriality: Contradictory Meanings, Changing Significance', *Regional Studies*, 33/7: 593–604.

Better World Campaign (2014), 'Kosovo (UNMIK)' http://www.betterworld campaign.org/un_peacekeeping/missions/Kosovo.html accessed on 15 October 2014.

Buffalo News (1998), issue number 10, January/April (Lusaka: Zambia Army Public Relations Department).

bufvc.ac.uk (2014), 'Nurse Daphne Parish released from Iraqi prison', http://bufvc.ac.uk/tvandradio/lbc/index.php/segment/0006600423003 accessed on 30 August 2014.

ChaCha (2014), http://www.chacha.com/question/what-is-an-example… accessed on 30 August 2014

China Africa Research Initiative (2011), 'Michael Sata and China in Zambia' http://www.chinaafricarealstory.com/2011/10/michael-sata-and-china-in-zambia.html accessed on 15 October 2014.

Clark, I. (1999), *Globalization and International Relations Theory* (Oxford: Oxford University Press).

Country Studies (2014), http://www.countrystudies.us/china/125.htm US Library of Congress, accessed 20 June 2014.

Economics Association of Zambia (2008), Position Paper on the Petroleum Sector in Zambia, (Lusaka) December.

Eulau, H. (1963), *The Behavioural Persuasion in Politics* (New York: Random House).

European Sanctions (2014), http://www.europeansanctions.com/zimbabwe/ accessed 20 September 2014.

FAO (2014), 'The Preferential Trade Area of Eastern and Southern Africa', http://www.fao.org/docrep/w5973e/w5973e06.htm accessed 20 September 2014.

Gupta, A. (1974), 'Trade Unionism and politics on the Copperbelt', in *Politics in Zambia*, edited by William Tordoff (Manchester: Manchester University Press) 288–319.

Henderson, L. W. (1978), *Angola: Five Centuries of Conflict* (Ithaca and London: Cornell University Press).

Herman, M. (1984), 'Personality and Foreign Policy Decision Making: A Study of 54 Heads of Government', in Foreign Policy Decision Making, edited by S. Chan and D. Sylvan (New York: Praegar) 53–80.

Institute for Security Studies (ISS) (1999), 'The Legacy of the Front-line States', Monograph No. 43: Building Security in Southern Africa, November, https://www.issafrica.org/pubs/Monographs/No43/TheLegacy.html

—— (2014), 'SADC Profile', https://www.issafrica.org/AF/RegOrg/unity to union/sadcprof.htm accessed on 30 September 2014.

Jackson, R. and Sorenson, G. (2007), *Introduction to International Relations: Theories and approaches* third edition (Oxford: Oxford University Press).

Jackson, R. and Sorenson, G. (2013), *Introduction to International Relations: Theories and approaches* fifth edition (Oxford: Oxford University Press).

Jervis, R. (1968), 'Hypotheses on Misperception', *World Politics*, 20: 454–479.

Jervis, R. (1976), *Perception and Misperception in International Politics* (Princeton, NJ: Princeton University Press).

Kosovo Thanks You (2014), http://www.kosovothanksyou.com accessed on 30 July 2014.

Lusaka Times (2007), http://www.lusakatimes.com 27 July, accessed on 30 August 2014.

Magagula, A. S. (2009), 'The Law and Legal Research in Zambia', http://www.nyulawglobal.org/globalex/Zambia.html accessed on 30 July 2014.

Malupenga, A. (2009), *Levy Patrick Mwanawasa: An incentive for posterity* (Grahamstown: NISC Pty Ltd).

Maravi blog (2007), 'My advice to Levy on KK was timely—Chiluba', http://maravi.blogspot.com/2007/08/my-advice-to-levy-on-kk-was-timely.html

Martin, G. A. (1998), *History of the Twentieth Century* (New York: William Morrow and Company, Inc.).

Matsheumhlope (2010), 'Zambia's Support for Liberation Movements, 1964–1979', http://matsheumhlope.wordpress.com/2010/05/14/zambias-support-for-liberation-movements-1964-1979/ accessed 30 July 2014.

Meleka, K. (2008), *The Role of Zambia–Zaire Joint Permanent Commission in Co-operation and Foreign Policy* (Lusaka: Zambia Publishing House).

Muweme, M. (2004), 'Foreign Direct Investment in Zambia', http://thezambian.com/2004/03/10/foreign-direct-investment-in-zambia/.

Mwakikagile, G. (2010), *Zambia: Life in an African Country* (Engelska: New Africa Press).

NTI (2014), 'Non-Aligned Movement (NAM)', http://www.nti.org/treaties-and-regimes/non-aligned-movement-nam/ accessed 20 September 2014.

Nuttahmumbi (2014), https://nuttahmumbi.wordpress.com/ accessed on 30 August 2014.

Oil Gas Africa (2014), www.oilgasafrica.com/downloads/ins... May 2014. Government of the Republic of Zambia (Draft), Institutional Framework and Storage and Transportation Infrastructure of the Zambian Petroleum Supply Chain.

Papp, D. S. (2002), *Contemporary International Relations* sixth edition (New York: Longman).

people.com.cn (2001), 'Russia Grants Zambia 560 Million Dollars of Debt Relief', http://english.people.com.cn/english/200108/26/eng20010826_78365.html accessed on 20 September 2014.

The Post (2011), 30 October.

Reuters (2007), 'Zambian president calls Zimbabwe sinking Titanic', http://www.reuters.com/article/us-zimbabwe-sadc-idUSL2140021620070321 accessed on 20 September 2014.

royal.gov.uk (2014), 'Commonwealth members', http://www.royal.gov.uk/monarchandcommonwealth/commonwealthmembers/membersofthe commonwealth.aspx accessed 20 September 2014.

SA History (2014), www.sahistory.org.za/organisations/frontline-States accessed on 30 August 2014.

Sardanis, A. (2003), *Africa, Another Side of the Coin: Northern Rhodesia's Final Years and Zambia's Nationhood* (New York: I. B. Tauris).

Simutanyi, N. (2006), 'The contested role of former presidents in Zambia', in *Legacies of Power: Leadership Change and Former Presidents in African Politics*, edited by Roger Southall and Henning Melber (Cape Town: Human Sciences Research Council) 73–97.

Sklar, R. L. (1974), 'Zambia's response to the Rhodesian unilateral declaration of independence', in *Politics in Zambia*, edited by William Tordoff (Manchester: Manchester University Press) 320–362.

Sylvan, D. and Majeski, S. (2008), 'Ideology and Intervention', paper prepared for presentation at the 49th Annual Convention of the International Studies Association, San Francisco, 26–29 March.

Transparency International (2001), Corruption Perception Index 2001.

UN (2005), 'UNAMSIL Facts and Figures', http://www.un.org/en/peacekeeping/missions/past/unamsil/facts.html accessed on 30 August 2014.

—— (2014), 'UNMIL Facts and Figures', http://www.un.org/en/peacekeeping/missions/unmil/facts.shtml accessed on 30 August 2014.

United Nations Conference on Trade and Development (UNCTAD) (2006), Investment Policy Review of Zambia (New York: United Nations).

Wikibook (2014), 'International', http://en.wikibook.org/wiki/international accessed 20 June 2014.

Wikipedia (2014*a*), 'Armed Forces', http://en.wikipedia.org/wiki/Armed_Forces... accessed 30 June 2014.

—— (2014*b*), 'Dates of esta', http://en.wikipedia.org/wiki/Dates_of_esta... accessed on 20 September 2014.

—— (2014*c*), 'Foreign relations', http://en.wikipedia.org/wiki/Foreign_relat... accessed 20 June 2014.

—— (2014*d*), 'Globalisation', http://en.wikipedia.org/wiki/Globalisation accessed 20 June 2014.

—— (2014*e*), 'Joshua Nkomo', http://en.wikipedia.org/wiki/Joshua_Nkomo accessed on 30 August 2014.

—— (2014*f*), 'Kenneth Kaunda', http://en.wikipedia.org/wiki/Kenneth_Kaunda accessed on 30 August 2014.

—— (2014*g*), 'Levy Mwanawasa', http://en.wikipedia.org/wiki/Levy_Mwanawasa accessed on 30 August 2014.

—— (2014*h*), 'Michael Sata', http://en.wikipedia.org/wiki/Michael_Sata accessed on 15 October 2014.

—— (2014*i*), 'MONUSCO', http://en.wikipedia.org/wiki/MONUSCO accessed on 30 September 2014.

—— (2014*j*), 'Non-Aligned Movement', http://en.wikipedia.org/wiki/Non-Aligned_M... accessed 20 June 2014.

—— (2014*k*), 'Organisation of African Unity', http://en.wikipedia.org/wiki/Organisation_... accessed 20 June 2014.

—— (2014*l*), 'Rupiah Banda', http://en.wikipedia.org/wiki/Rupiah_Banda accessed on 20 June 2014

—— (2014*m*), 'South African', http://en.wikipedia.org/wiki/South_African... accessed 30 July 2014.

—— (2014*n*), 'Southern African Development Coordination Conference', http://en.wikipedia.org/wiki/Southern_Afri... accessed 20 June 2014.

—— (2014*o*), 'TAZAMA pipeline', http://en.wikipedia.org/wiki/TAZAMA_pipeline accessed on 30 June 2014.

—— (2014*p*), 'TAZARA Railway' http://en.wikipedia.org/wiki/TAZARA_Railway accessed on 30 June 2014.

—— (2014*q*), 'United Nations Assistance Mission for Rwanda', http://en.wikipedia.org/wiki/United_Nations_Assistance_Mission_for_Rwanda

—— (2014*r*), 'United Nations Mission in Ethiopia and Eritrea', http://en.wikipedia.org/wiki/United_Nation... accessed on 30 June 2014.

—— (2014*s*), 'United Nations Mission in South Sudan', http://en.wikipedia.org/wiki/United_Nations_Mission_in_South_Sudan accessed on 30 September 2014.

—— (2014*t*), 'United Nations Operation in Burundi', http://en.wikipedia.org/
wiki/United_Nations_Operation_in_Burundi accessed on 30 August
2014.

—— (2014*u*), 'Victoria Falls', http://en.wikipedia.org/wiki/Victoria_Falls
accessed on 30 June 2014.

—— (2014*v*), 'Zimbabwe Africa', http://en.wikipedia.org/wiki/Zimbabwe_
Afri…

WWF (2014), 'Zambia: Freshwater (Rivers, Lakes, Fisheries, and Wetlands)',
http://wwf.panda.org/who_we_are/wwf_offices/wwf_zambia_
nature_conservation/focal_thematic_areas/freshwater/ accessed on 30
August 2014.

Zambia Daily Mail (2011), 14 July.

zambia.mid.ru (2014), 'Zambia and Russia Enjoying Good Relations', http://www.
zambia.mid.ru/doc/Zambia_and_Russia_Enjoying_Good_Relations.
htm accessed on 30 August 2014.

Zambia Reports (2014), 'Oil Politics in Zambia, Part 1', http://zambiareports.
com/2014/06/17/oil-politics-zambia-part-1/ accessed on 17 June 2014.

Zambia, Republic of (1996), Zambia's Foreign Policy (Lusaka: Government
Printer).

Chapter 6

Fifty Years of Civilian Control of Zambia's Armed Forces
Njunga M. Mulikita

1. BACKGROUND AND CONTEXT

This chapter seeks to provide an overview of civil–military relations since Zambia attained political independence in 1964. Zambia is one of the relatively few countries in postcolonial Africa never to have experienced military rule. The question that arises from this empirical fact is: why have Zambia's armed forces refrained from intervening in the country's political life, whilst soldiers in other parts of Africa, have ousted constitutionally elected civilian governments? It is therefore appropriate that this paper interrogates the modalities and strategies that successive Zambian governments have deployed to ensure civilian control over the armed forces. The paper is divided into six parts. After this introductory section, the next phase offers a cursory look at the pre-independence phase. Thereafter an overview of civil–military relations in the first republic (1964–1972) is provided followed by an examination of civil–military relations during the Second Republic of the one-party state while the fifth section assess civil-military relations during the third republic of pluralistic multi-party politics. The sixth and final section presents useful lessons and pathways for the next fifty years.

1.1. Civil–military relations: operational definition

Civil–military relations lay the groundwork for the smooth running of the government and the defence forces structured to defend and support the government (Lopa 2014: 1). Indeed civil–military relations describes the relationship between the civilian authority of a given society and its military forces (Ngoma 2004: 4). Civil–military relations is premised on the normative assumption that civilian control of the state and military is preferable to military control of the state, as stated by Samuel Huntington (1957).

Unstable civil–military relations in sub-Saharan Africa have caused death on a massive scale, destruction, and bad governance. Unstable civil–military relations have placed good governance, political stability, and peace in grave jeopardy. Unstable civil–military relations in Africa have established dictatorships, subverted democratic governance, precluded the exercise of people to constitute or change their governments, and led to gross violations of human rights and triggered horrendous civil wars (Mulikita 2010). Between the Egyptian revolution in 1952 and 1998, there were eighty-five violent or unconstitutional changes in government in Africa, seventy-eight of which took place between 1961 and 1997 (Mulikita 2010).

The pervasiveness of coup activity notwithstanding, one should not overlook the fact that seventeen of forty-eight countries (35.4 per cent) have so far avoided a military coup. These include countries as diverse as South Africa, Namibia, Mauritius, Eritrea, Cape Verde, Botswana, Malawi, Zimbabwe, Senegal, Djibouti, Angola, Mozambique, Cameroon, Tanzania, Kenya, Gabon, and Zambia (Lindemann 2011: 1).

This is a very significant number and raises the question of why some African countries like Zambia have proved immune to the seemingly inescapable 'coup epidemic' (loc. cit.).

In light of the foregoing, Zambia's record in maintaining civilian authority over the armed forces must therefore be lauded as perhaps the country's major political accomplishment in the first five decades of its existence as an independent state.

2. CIVIL–MILITARY RELATIONS IN THE COLONIAL ERA

In the colonial period, in the predecessor state/protectorate of Northern Rhodesia, civil political authorities used undemocratic coercive measures to maintain control over the military (Haantobolo 2008). This was characterized by the establishment of discriminatory and racist structures based on the principle of 'divide and rule' at legislative, executive, and judicial levels.

Haantobolo points out that this approach then made the colonial authorities create an army with two faces: one white and one black. In this environment, the essential role of the military was to protect the interests of the white settlers and the colonial regime and ensure the subordination and subservience of the indigenous African population. Haantobolo has further argued that the two-faced nature of the colonial army made its relations between the white political and military elite harmonious, and those between the military and the African population antagonistic. It is the antagonistic character of the relationship between the military forces and the African populations that Haantobolo points out, which may have contributed to mutinies staged by black non-commissioned personnel against their white officer corps in newly independent countries such as Democratic Republic of Congo (DRC) (1960) and Republic of Tanganyika in 1964 (Purcell 2012)

3. CIVIL–MILITARY RELATIONS IN THE FIRST REPUBLIC: 1964–1972

The current Zambian Defence Forces (ZDF) grew out of the Northern Rhodesia Regiment, which the British colonialists created in 1933 (Phiri 2001: 3). At the time of independence of the Republic of Zambia, the new state encompassed seventy-three different ethnic groups, with different cultures and origins. The composition of the military reflected the divisive racial and ethnic policies of the colonial regime in terms of which military forces were designed to be instruments of both imperial and colonial rule. In external terms, Zambia was in a dangerous position in that it was surrounded by hostile colonial states which resented its policy of providing bases to liberation movements fighting colonial or settler regimes in other countries in the region. Given this vulnerable political position, it is necessary to examine how democratic consensual measures in form of structural reforms of the military in the First Republic, and their—largely positive—effects on civil control of the military evolved in this period.

3.1 Constitutional measures to ensure civilian control over the Armed Forces during First Republic

Zambia's new parliament was largely democratically elected by means of universal adult suffrage. This included the five members nominated by the president. This was in line with Article 60 of the 1964 constitution which stated 'The president may appoint as nominated members of the National Assembly five persons as he considers desirable to obtain the service as a member of the Assembly, by reason of his/her special qualification . . . would be of special value as such a member' (GRZ 1964b: 48).

One of the new parliament's functions was to regularise the position and role of the military in post-independence Zambia, and its relationship with the government and citizenry. It did so by repealing all racist legislation related to the Zambian defence forces, and introducing a number of constitutional and other legislative reforms that had an important bearing on the nature and quality of civil control over the military.

The Republic of Zambia (Modification and Adaptation) (General) Order, 1964, Section 3(b) stipulated that from 24 October 1964 onwards, any reference in the existing laws to the governor of Northern Rhodesia was to be read and constructed as a reference to the president. This meant that all powers other than those specifically entrusted to military commanders were now vested in the president. Article 49(1) of the 1964 constitution stated that the supreme command of the armed forces of the republic shall vest in the president, and he shall hold the office of commander-in-chief (GRZ 1965: 63).

Article 49(2)(a) and (b) stated that the powers conferred on the president by subsection (1) of this section shall include (a) the power to determine the operational use of the armed forces, and (b) the power to appoint members of the armed forces, to make appointments on promotion to any office in the armed forces, and to dismiss any member of the armed forces (ibid.). Article

49(3) also stated that the President may, by direction in writing and subject to such conditions as he may think fit, delegate to any member of the armed forces any of the powers mentioned in subsection (2) of this section (ibid.). In line with this, responsibility for the appointments, promotions, and dismissals of warrant officers Class I and lower ranks was delegated to commanders and exercised in accordance with appropriate enlistment and service regulations.

Air force commanders were also given powers to approve the selection and appointments of officer cadets on the basis of the recommendations of officer selection boards. Army commanders were also given powers to select officer cadets for training courses overseas. After cadets had completed their training courses, their commissions had to be approved by the president. Besides this, the appointment of any officer other than a cadet could not be gazetted until the president had signed the certificate bearing his commission. These measures effectively placed the appointments of senior military officers under civil control.

The president also continued the practice of appointing elected or nominated members of Parliament as heads of the Ministry of Defence (Ministry of Defence Headquarters 1964e: 5). This also helped to ensure civil control of the military, in line with established practice in democratic polities. Parliamentary oversight over the presidential command of the armed forces and other functionaries was enabled by Article 49(4) of the 1964 constitution, which stated that 'Parliament may regulate the exercise of the powers conferred by or under this section' (GRZ 1965: 63). Within this framework, the government created important administrative and advisory institutions that facilitated civil control of the military in the First Republic—notably the Defence Council, and the Office of the Command Secretary. Another important step was the restructuring of military institutions in postcolonial Zambia.

3.2. The Defence Council

Phiri (2001: 2) states that the Defence Council was established in 1955, and its civilian oversight roles were adapted for the postcolonial situation after 1964. However, Haantobolo (2008) indicates that the Defence Council was established by the postcolonial government. Chapter 131 of the Laws of

Zambia, Number 45 of 1964, promulgated in Government Notice No. 497 of 1964, authorised the government to implement the provisions of the Defence Act. One of these provided for the establishment of the Defence Council, which was intended to play a key role in civil control of the military. Chapter 131, Section 8(1), (2), and (3) state that there shall be a Defence Council which shall advise the president on such matters of policy and matters affecting the command, discipline, and administration of the Defence Force and shall perform such other functions and duties as may be referred to it from time to time by the president. The members of the Defence Council shall be appointed by the president. The president shall have power to co-opt any other person as a member of the Defence Council from time to time as he may decide (GRZ 1964a: 18). In line with these provisions, the formation of the Defence Council was approved on Tuesday, 11 February 1964. Its first task was to examine the size and shape of the army and air wing (Ministry of Defence Headquarters 1964a: 4). The Defence Council met for the first time at Government House on Saturday, 7 March 1964. Since Northern Rhodesia was preparing for independence on 24 October 1964, K. D. Kaunda, then prime minister of Northern Rhodesia, attended and participated fully in the first meeting of the Defence Council (Ministry of Defence Headquarters 1964c: 1).

While the Ministry of Defence remained the main policymaking and executive body in respect of defence matters, the Defence Council was charged with advising the president on matters related to defence policy and command, discipline and administration of the defence force as stated in Chapter 131 Section 8(1), (2), and (3) above.

The composition of the Defence Council was aimed at ensuring the maintenance of civil control of the military. Minutes of a meeting of the Defence Committee in the Ministry of Defence dated 31 October 1964 state, 'the president's deputy, as chairman of the Defence Council, will be the vice president, and no other alternate will be appointed at this time' (Ministry of Defence Headquarters 1964e: 1). Other members of the Defence Council were the ministers of Defence, Works and Supply, Transport, and Finance and Development; service commanders; and co-opted officers, depending on the issue under consideration.

3.3. The restructuring of military institutions in postcolonial Zambia

The restructuring of the army in postcolonial Zambia was an important consensual measure that played a key role in cementing civil control of the military. The government reviewed the composition of the army as inherited from the colonial period, confirmed the retention of some units, and closed others. Officers in units that were not retained, such as Military Intelligence, were retired, and those serving in units that were retained had to demonstrate that they were loyal to the new government.

This decision was made because the Zambia Defence Force inherited British conditions of service for the officer corps, which was dominated by whites. Those officers were more loyal towards the Southern Rhodesian government than the Zambian government. In 1971, Zambia decided to fully support the liberation struggle in Southern Rhodesia. In order to avoid spying by remaining British officers, the government decided to Zambianize the officers' corps, which resulted in the retirement of British officers (Haantobolo 2008).

3.4. Establishment of Zambia Air Force

The government also decided to establish an air force base at Livingstone commanded by officers who had agreed to be transferred from the Royal Rhodesia Air Force based in Salisbury. Since it became difficult for the Air Force Command in Lusaka to direct operations from the Livingstone base, the government decided to build a new air wing base in Lusaka. The construction of this new base began in December 1964.

A total of GB £750,000 sterling was released for the purpose, based on GB£2 sterling per square foot (Ministry of Defence Headquarters 1963a). The location of the command units in Lusaka—the seat of civil government—facilitated civil control of the military authorities (Haantobolo 2008).

Most of the military personnel retained by the government had been recruited under the tribal and racial policies of the colonial government. Therefore, it is necessary to interrogate the new policies introduced by the post-independence government with regard to military recruitment, training, and the Zambianization of the defence force between 1964 and 1972—and their effect on civil control of the military.

3.5. Military recruitment and training and the Zambianization of the Defence Force

The post-independence government abolished all racial or ethnic discrimination in recruitment for the Zambia Defence Force—an important step that facilitated effective civil control of the military in the First Republic. The government was aware that ethnicity had played a major role in military intervention in domestic politics in the Congo, and a military mutiny in Tanzania.

As a result, it abandoned the use of race and tribe as a basis for military recruitment, and introduced the motto of 'One Zambia, one nation'. In terms of this approach, recruitment for the defence force was guided by Article 49 of the Constitution of Zambia, as quoted earlier, and the 1964 Defence Act Chapter 106 of the Laws of Zambia. CAP 106 provided for the creation and maintenance in Zambia of a Defence Force consisting of an army, comprising the Regular Force of the Army, the Territorial, Army Reserve, and Air Force comprising the Regular Force of the Air Force, the Auxiliary Air Force, the all Air Force Reserve, to provide for the conditions of discharge of the soldiers from the Regular Force and for their transfer to the Reserve Force when necessary in the public interest (GRZ 1964b: 5).

Accordingly, young men and women from all seventy-three ethnic groups in Zambia qualified for recruitment as officer cadets as well as lower ranks as long as they met the minimum entry and application qualifications. Recruitment took place in both urban and rural provinces. Rural resident secretaries were asked to report on the recruitment potential in their provinces. After selection by the Military Selection Board, recruits were subjected to the same medical check-ups used during the colonial days.

Thereafter, they were trained under the supervision of expatriate British military personnel brought into the country under the British government's loaned personnel agreement (Ministry of Defence Headquarters 1964a). This agreement required British military specialists to train Zambians for key posts in the Zambia Army Technical Corps and other specialist units. The recruits were trained in military drill, warfare, discipline, and all other aspects taught to recruits in the Northern Rhodesia Regiment.

After training, these soldiers were employed on a pensionable basis, and posted to various barracks under various commands. These measures ensured effective civil control of the military as no single ethnic group dominated the defence force, and the possibility of one ethnic group organising a successful military coup d'état—as had happened in Nigeria—was very remote (Olusoji, Seyi, and Oluwakemi 2012).

Appointments to senior command positions in the armed forces were calculated to ensure that no one single ethnic group would establish hegemonic control. Some commentators have also argued that the selection of Brig. Gen. Kingsley Chinkuli, an officer from a small ethnic group (Lenje), as first indigenous commander of the Zambia Army on 6 December 1970 prevented the growth of an ethnic oligarchy of officers from the country's bigger and more politically influential ethnic groups (Lindemann 2011: 16).

At the same time, military authorities were required to maintain standards in order to avoid a loss of efficiency in the defence force. Given the problem of the destabilizing influence of western military institutions, which was the main cause of President Kwame Nkrumah's overthrow in Ghana in 1966, President Kaunda frequently addressed the military. One of the most important of his speeches was delivered at a seminar for army and air force officers at Kalewa barracks in Ndola on 21 March 1967. In it, Kaunda warned against military seizure of political power. In his warning he asserted that the military is '*ill-equipped to rule*' and that consequently, the coup d'état is followed by '*an inevitable train of disaster and general chaos*' and by '*an inevitable return to the Dark Ages*'.

He then exhorted the officers to channel their energies into acquiring professional competence instead of planning or plotting to wrestle political power from the civilian authorities (Haantobolo 2008). Later, Kaunda was to introduce seminars to orient Defence Force officers to the national ideology of Zambian humanism.

The Zambian government further decided to diversify training for the Officer Corps. While it was important to maintain good relations with Sandhurst Military College in Britain, officers should also be trained at other institutions within and outside the Commonwealth. It was in this context that Zambia established military ties with Soviet-bloc countries, the People's Republic of China, and the Non-Aligned Movement (NAM) (ZIDIS 2014: 3).

In the interests of uniformity, Zambian military officers who had been trained elsewhere had to undergo further training and reorientation. Therefore, the government established a nine-month cadet course and other orientation courses at the School of Military Training at Kohima Barracks in Kabwe.

It was hoped that these policies would improve the relationship between the new government, the new officer corps, and the citizenry, and would gradually change the people's view of the military from that of an oppressive colonial instrument to that of a protector of the people. The government was also aware that post-independence Zambia was a member of both the Organization of African Unity (OAU) and the United Nations (UN). It was, therefore, important for the new government to have a viable army in order that it could make a useful contribution if the United Nations or a Commonwealth country sought assistance.

3.6. Formation of the Zambia National Service: A political army?

In 1971, the Zambian government decided to upgrade the Zambia Youth Service (ZYS) that had been introduced in 1964 into the Zambia National Service (ZNS). According to Lopa (2014), the publicly declared objective of the ZYS was to absorb the multitudes of unemployed youths who were involved in the struggle to liberate Zambia. A corollary objective that motivated the establishment of ZNS was to provide a national armed militia that could relieve the Zambia army and Zambia air force, which were overstretched in securing the country's frontiers from hostile military incursions from settler-ruled territories as they pursued liberation movements domiciled in Zambia. The Youth Service and its successor ZNS was used as a tool to win hearts and minds, thereby bringing the armed forces closer to the civilian population.

Lopa further adds that the introduction of the ZNS camps in all districts in Zambia improved relations between military forces and the civilian population in that civilians around camps benefited from the services which were provided by the camps such as medical facilities, transport, famer support programmes, and others. This point is further corroborated by Haantobolo who states, 'Moreover, the government's policy of dispersing ZNS camps throughout the country resulted in close ties between the military, the citizenry, and the government.'

Lopa also observes that the introduction of compulsory military training for school leavers in 1975 further improved relations among the military, the citizenry, and the civilian government. Indeed in his study on civil–military relations in Zambia, Lopa states that the fact that many school leavers and university students were exposed to the operations of the military made them understand and appreciate why Zambia needed armed forces and how these forces functioned, thereby boosting relations between the citizenry and the military forces.

However, the establishment of the ZNS effectively created a third wing of the Zambia Defence Force, also led to stiff competition over the sharing of resources and promotion prospects in the Ministry of Defence. According to Ambassador Lieutenant-General (retired) Francis Sibamba (Sibamba 2010) a former commander of the Zambia Army, even though the idea of establishing the Zambia National Service was good, not all stakeholders were happy with its establishment. Civilian bureaucrats viewed ZNS as an unnecessary organization and a drain on public resources. More ominously, the Zambia Army reportedly viewed ZNS as a *political army / praetorian guard* aimed at counterbalancing the regular army in case a cabal of army officers might plot to oust the civilian government (Sibamba 2010).

Evidence was available of African governments that had set up *presidential guards / praetorian armies* to counter the conspiracies of highly ambitious army officers. President Nyerere had not only disbanded the Tanganyika Rifles following the 1964 mutiny which almost toppled his government, but also introduced a parallel command chain of political commissars to monitor the army and ensure that army personnel were unquestionably loyal to him and his ruling Tanganyika African National Union (TANU) and its successor, the Chama Cha Mapinduzi (CCM). To augment the political commissar system, Nyerere created the highly ideologically indoctrinated Tanzania National Service (TNS) and the National Militia, which ensured a delicate balance of power among the country's military and quasi-military forces (Lupogo 2001; Ringquist 2011).

In Ghana, at the time of his overthrow in 1966, President Nkrumah was in the process of equipping his Soviet bloc backed and trained presidential guard, the President Own Guard Regiment (POGR) with superior weaponry that threatened the preeminent position of the Ghana Army. Some scholars have argued that it was the impending tilt in the balance of power between the regular army and POGR that triggered a cabal of army officers to overthrow Ghana's founding president in 1966 (Kraus 1966).

3.7. Intra-UNIP factionalism and the route to the one-party state

By 1971, even though prices of copper, Zambia's principal export commodity, were favourable, enabling the UNIP government to ensure that the armed forces were well supplied with military equipment and their welfare was of satisfactory standard, the ruling party had splintered into two major factions. The factionalism, as the turbulent UNIP General Conference in 1967 had demonstrated, had taken on regional/ethnic/tribal dimensions.

It was against this background that in 1971, former vice president Simon Kapwepwe and senior Bemba-speaking ministers in the government resigned from the government to form the United Progressive Party (UPP). Kaunda's response to this challenge to his authority was to take the political route that several founding African leaders had charted when faced by mounting opposition to their rule: constitutional reform to enact single-party states.

Hence, in 1972, Kaunda appointed a Constitutional Review Commission chaired by then vice president Mainza Chona to go around the country in order to come up with a constitutional framework to establish what Kaunda characterized as a one-party participatory democracy. Thus Zambia joined a growing list of African countries that had replaced independence era multiparty constitutions with new basic laws which declared ruling parties as sole legitimate political entities in their countries.

4. CIVIL–MILITARY RELATIONS IN THE SECOND REPUBLIC (1973–1991)

The constitution of the single-party state elevated the ruling United National Independence Party (UNIP) to a position of supremacy over all state institutions, including the Defence Forces. The president of the republic retained his position as commander-in-chief of the Armed Forces. The Central Committee of the ruling party established a Defence and Security Sub-Committee which oversaw both the civilian Ministry of Defence and the defence forces.

During the Second Republic, UNIP under its long-serving pro-Soviet-bloc secretary general, Alexander G. Zulu, strengthened political and security cooperation with allied political parties from Eastern-bloc countries as Zambia stepped up its support to the liberation movements fighting to overthrow settler colonial rule in Southern Africa (ZIDIS op. cit.: 3). Security cooperation with Soviet-bloc countries enabled the Zambian political class to study modalities and strategies used by Eastern-bloc regimes to maintain ideological control over their armed forces. The lessons learned were accordingly adapted to suit the Zambian scenario.

A number of strategies to reinforce civilian control over the armed forces were deployed during the Second Republic.

4.1. Co-optation of senior defence personnel into echelons of political leadership

Following the general elections of 1973, President Kaunda nominated the three heads of the armed services to Parliament and appointed all three of them ministers of state. Such a strategy of co-optation was maintained throughout the 1970s and 1980s, with many current or former army officers being appointed to the cabinet, the UNIP Central Committee, or as district governors. Former commanders of the armed forces were also appointed to prestigious diplomatic positions. A former army commander, Gen. Malimba Masheke (*Interview Lusaka* 2008), who was himself appointed prime minister during the 1980s, argued that the practice of co-optation helped to convince the military leadership 'that to arrive into a higher office, you do not need to take up arms'. Kaunda argued that the country's 'One Zambia, one nation' policy sought to eradicate the traditional fault line between the civilian leadership and the armed forces. The armed forces were not only expected to demonstrate loyalty to their civilian masters, but were actively encouraged to take part in implementing national development policies.

During the Second Republic, it was normal to see high visibility representation of the Defence Forces, Zambia Police, and Zambia Prison Service at meetings of the General Congress and National Council of the ruling United National Independence (UNIP) as well as at other party forums at provincial and district levels.

4.2. Regional/tribal balancing in senior command appointments

A close look at the regional affiliation of Zambian army commanders during the Second Republic reveals that members of all five major language groups were represented at the very top of the military hierarchy.

Distribution of Defence Services Commanders by Region, 1976–2008

	ZAMBIA NATIONAL DEFENCE FORCE (1976)	
	Gen. G. K. Chinkuli (Central)	
	Lt Gen. P. D. Zuze (Eastern)	
	Lt Gen. B. N. Mibenge (Luapula)	
	DE-UNIFIED COMMAND (1980)	

ZAMBIA AIR FORCE	ZAMBIA ARMY	ZAMBIA NATIONAL SERVICE
Maj. Gen. C. Kabwe (Northern)	Gen. M. Masheke (Western)	Brig. Gen. C. Nyirenda (Eastern)
Lt Gen. H. Lungu (Eastern)	Lt Gen. C. S. Tembo (Eastern)	Brig. Gen. F. S. Mulenga (Northern)
Maj. Gen. Simbule (Northern)	Lt Gen. G. Kalenge (Southern)	Maj. Gen. T. Fara (Central)
Lt Gen. H. Simutowe (Northern)	Lt Gen. F. G. Sibamba (Western)	
THIRD REPUBLIC		
Lt Gen. R. Shikapwasha (Central)	Lt Gen. N. Simbeye (Northern)	Lt. Gen. W. G. Funjika (North-Western)
Lt Gen. S. Kayumba (North-Western)	Lt. Gen. S. L. Mumbi (Eastern)	Maj. Gen. M. Mbao (Eastern)
Lt Gen. C. Singogo (Northern)	Lt Gen. G. R. Musengule (Central)	
Lt Gen. S. Mapala (Central)	Lt Gen. I. Chisuzi (Central)	Maj. Gen. R. Chisheta (Luapula)
Lt Gen. A. Sakala (Eastern)	Lt Gen. W. M. Lopa (Northern)	Maj. Gen. A. Yeta (Western)
Lt Gen. E. Chimese (Luapula)	Lt Gen. P. Mihova (North-Western)	Lt Gen. Gen N. Mulenga (Northern)

This did not change after the democratic transition of 1991. According to ambassador Dr Mbita Chitala, a member of the Defence Council under President Chiluba, ethnic balancing was continued at all levels of the army to ensure that the whole country was represented.

At the level of the rank and file, a quota system introduced in the First Republic was followed during the Second Republic. This system prescribed that army units were to be composed of soldiers from all provinces and districts—a system that ensured that the whole country had a stake in the army. Also, trained soldiers were purposefully posted outside their home areas to further ensure the national integration of the armed forces. Thus, the combination of a balanced government and army undermined the prospects of military intervention.

Zambia's military leadership had little inclination to engage in coup activity. First, as members of all groups felt represented in the ZDF officer corps, there was no serious ethnic discontent that could have become the basis of subversive action. Secondly, the broad-based nature of the ZDF officer corps meant that members of competing ethnic groups always kept an eye on each other, which made it extremely difficult to organize a serious military conspiracy without being detected and contained. Gen. Malimba Masheke, a long-serving army commander under Kaunda, identified this mechanism as the main driver behind the absence of military takeovers in Zambia (Lindemann 2011: 16).

4.3 Establishment of Zambia National Defence Force (ZNDF)

In 1976, President Kaunda announced the formation of the Zambia National Defence Force (ZNDF), which entailed combined command of Zambia's military forces, i.e. Army, ZAF, and ZNS. The rationale for introducing this administrative reform was allegedly to better position the armed forces vis-à-vis the escalating liberation struggle in Southern Africa at the time.

The commander of the Army, Maj. Gen. Kingsley Chinkuli, was made commander of the new ZNDF and was promoted to the rank of full general, while the commander of the Air Force, Air Commodore Peter D. Zuze, was made deputy commander of the ZNDF and promoted to lieutenant general (Ngoma and Lungu 2005: 319). The air force rank nomenclature that was identical to that of the British Royal Air Force was changed to that used by the army.

The symbolic change in uniform was, however, not well received by Zambia Air Force personnel, judging by the ultimate switch back to the traditional blue.

Nonetheless, there was seemingly a firm political decision to achieve a strongly unified military force. A general staff was created to oversee and coordinate operations of the ZNDF, and the army, air force, and ZNS were each headed by a chief of staff co-located in Arrakan Army barracks in Lusaka (Ngoma and Lungu op. cit.: 320).

According to Lopa (2014), ZNDF, which lasted from 1976 to 1980, brought out the best in how Civil-Military Relations were exercised. Lopa claims that according to an Expert Opinion survey he carried out (2014), both the civilians and the military during this period knew exactly how they were to function in the context of civilian–military relations. Lopa also reports that ZNDF served as a mechanism for civilian authorities to exercise control over the armed forces with increased coherence and efficiency (Lopa 2014: 99).

Regional commands were established in each province of Zambia—including where there were no military units. Members of the different services were cross-posted to units not necessarily of their original service. Some army officers were therefore posted to command air force units and vice versa. Even staff cars were cross-posted—including relatively new air force staff cars that were posted to the army and old ones from the army to the air force (Ngoma and Lungu op. cit.: 320).

Most senior appointments in the ZNDF were filled by army officers; a move that created resentment and rejection of the ZNDF by the air force and ZNS, which felt dominated by the army. The general feeling was that their identity was obscured and their professionalism interfered with. The extent to which the latter could be regarded as a reality is debatable. Nevertheless, the system created discomfort for the chiefs of staff, who felt overshadowed and over supervised. Consequently, the ZNDF was disbanded in 1980 and the defence force reverted to the command system inherited at independence (loc. cit.)

However, some value of the system appeared to have been identified clearly enough; in the immediate aftermath of the failed coup d'état 1990, Lt Gen. Hanania Lungu, then air commander, was appointed minister of defence in a unified command structure, reintroduced with some modifications. This time, the army, air force, and ZNS headquarters were at different locations. The services maintained their structures and autonomy but the commanders reported to the chief of general staff. In essence, a department of defence had been created. However, Lt Gen. Lungu—the new minister of defence—was also appointed chief of general staff to oversee the transition up to the eventual appointment of a chief of the Defence Forces (Sibamba 2010; Ngoma and Lungu op. cit.: 320).

4.4. Political control of the armed forces

During the Second Republic, the ruling United National Independence Party sought to infuse into the armed forces its left nationalist-socialist ideology called humanism through a commissar system. Every unit had a political commissar attached to it to conscientize both officers and rank-and-file soldiers in the ruling party's ideology to ensure that the party exercised command over the gun rather than vice versa. Party committees were established in all cantonments to ideologically sensitize military personnel as well as to watch for any signs of dissent, as Zambia's economy hit turbulent waters in the mid and late 1980s.

The ruling party regularly organized political education seminars for senior officers to sensitize them on the external causes of economic hardships that the country was going through and to urge them to resist the temptation to seize power that had plunged other African countries into a vicious cycle of coups and instability.

Political oversight over the armed forces was reinforced by an internal security czar, the state secretary for defence and security (SSDS), whose mandate was to coordinate the activities of the entire security sector, comprised of ministries of defence and home affairs, the armed forces, and all civilian security institutions in the country. The political sensitization work carried out by political commissars added to sustained intelligence gathering by both military and civilian intelligence operatives contributed to a considerable extent in discouraging any power-grab schemes during the Second Republic, as Zambia's socio-economic outlook worsened.

4.5. Materialistic pay-offs

Providing army leaders with generous pay-offs is one of the most obvious strategies to secure the loyalty of the military since material satisfaction can be expected to yield low propensities toward military intervention (Goldsworthy 1981; Decalo 1989; Feaver 1999). Pay-offs can be either direct or indirect in nature. Direct pay-offs may include high salaries and various other material privileges. Indirect pay-offs may result from the co-optation of army personnel into government, the civil service, or the parastatals. In Zambia, the Kaunda regime provided military leaders with generous pay-offs. As for direct pay-offs, the ZDF benefitted from growing defence budgets from the 1970s, which mainly reflected regional threats to national security. The defence budget as share of GDP and the defence budget per soldier increased dramatically during the 1970s and remained high throughout the 1980s (Lindemann 2011: 26).

As this growing military expenditure was no longer made public from 1970 onwards, the military leadership gained considerable discretion in the distribution of financial resources as well as control over personnel policy and defence planning. Also, the army was from the beginning granted further material privileges, including free access to mealie meal (the country's staple food) and subsidised prices for other foodstuffs and beer.

4.6. The Iraqi / Saddam Hussein connection

As Kaunda feared latent dissent as Zambia's economy experienced contraction in the late 1980s and as Western donors put pressure on his regime to implement a harsh economic austerity programme, Kaunda turned to his ideological comrade, the Iraqi leader Saddam Hussein.[1]

Kaunda's party UNIP and Saddam Hussein's Baath Party had established political ties originating from Kaunda and Saddam's participation in the Non-Aligned Movement (NAM), where they took congruent positions against the Israeli occupation of Palestinian territories and apartheid South Africa's destabilization policies against Zambia and the front-line states.

Apart from supplying Zambia with petroleum, when Zambia's foreign exchange reserves were in a parlous state, Saddam dispatched military supplies in the form of trucks, vehicles, boots, and even uniforms for the defence

---

1   See R. C. Longworth, 'Other Nations, Diplomats Will Try To Persuade Iraq', *Chicago Tribune*, 10 January 1991: 'Zambian President Kenneth Kaunda, a friend of Hussein's who earlier persuaded the Iraqi president to free a jailed British nurse, will go to Baghdad "very soon", a Zambian official said', http://articles.chicagotribune.com/1991-01-10/news/9101030462_1_arab-peace-efforts-iraqi-withdrawal-aziz, accessed 24 December 2014.

forces. Zambian officers were sent to Iraq on training missions, at a time Iraqi forces were fighting in the Iran/Iraq border war. Resources provided by oil-rich Iraq enabled Kaunda to continue buying off dissent among the armed forces. Further still, Zambian officers on training missions in Iraq used petro dollars they earned from their duty tours to acquire luxury goods, which was a disincentive for them to attempt a putsch against the single-party regime.

4.7. Coup attempts during the Second Republic

4.7.1. 1980 coup attempt

The coup attempt of 16 October 1980 arose in the context of Zambia's escalating economic crisis from the late 1970s and mainly involved influential businessmen who were alienated by UNIP's economic policies and therefore established contacts with a few disgruntled army officers (Larmer 2008: 114 ff.). Even though the majority of the conspirators belonged to the Bemba-speaking bloc, the broad-based character of government and army stood in the way of ethnically based mobilisation. As a result, the mutineers failed to build substantial support in the civilian and military hierarchy and were arrested after a brief gun battle.

4.7.2. 1990 coup attempt

A second coup attempt occurred on 30 June 1990, when Lt Mwamba Luchembe and a few followers took control of the national radio for several hours and announced that the army had taken over (Sibamba 2010). This coup attempt followed prolonged economic decline and food riots, which is why it received some spontaneous public support. Yet, the conspiracy again lacked an ethnic base, which hampered the prospects of mobilisation. Accordingly, the protagonists of the coup were junior officers who were isolated in the officer corps and therefore easily contained (Phiri 2001: 12). However, the political impact of this attempt was that it forced Kaunda to come to terms with the wind of democratization that was sweeping across Africa as a consequence of the collapse of Soviet-bloc single-party regimes in Eastern and Central Europe, which were political allies of the UNIP government (Mulikita 2003: 105). Kaunda eventually cut short his term and allowed general elections to take place in 1991 which ultimately swept UNIP from power and installed the Movement for Multiparty Democracy (MMD), led by trade unionist Frederick Chiluba.

5. CIVIL–MILITARY RELATIONS IN THE THIRD REPUBLIC (1991–2014)

5.1. Dismantling of unified command

With the reintroduction of a multiparty system of government in 1991 under a new political party—the Movement for Multiparty Democracy (MMD)— the unified command structure was abolished and the defence force structure reverted to that inherited at independence. Zambia has continued with this system, making the Zambia Defence Force unique in a region where all defence forces employ a unified command structure.

5.2. Delinking of armed forces from political party activities

During the Third Republic, the armed forces have been delinked from political party affiliations, and government policy is that the armed forces should be non-partisan and profess loyalty to the government of the day as demanded in a democratic polity.

In order to reorient the defence forces to their new role, in the post–Cold War era, a Defence Services Command and Staff College was established in 1994, to offer courses to both local and foreign defence personnel. Courses offered by the college receive considerable support from major Western powers such as the USA, UK, and other countries that were not ideologically close to the UNIP government during the Second Republic. The college has evolved into a centre of excellence and runs a Diploma in Defence and Security Studies in conjunction with the University of Zambia (UNZA) which, as a consequence, runs the Master of Arts in Defence and Security Studies. The college also runs courses that prepare Zambia's armed forces for UN and African Union peace support operations. Officers from neighbouring African countries have attended courses offered by the college since 1994.

5.3. New mechanisms for buying off dissent

In the Third Republic, high-ranking army officers have been heavily implicated in lucrative corruption scandals, evidenced by the fact that many of them were subsequently prosecuted and convicted (*Saturday Star* 2004; Agence France-Presse 2006; *Times of Zambia* 2009). President Levy Mwanawasa, who succeeded Chiluba in 2001, kept the army busy by sending large numbers of military officers to participate in peacekeeping missions. By 2008, the country was involved in a total of nine such missions worldwide whereby the number of Zambian well-paid observers has grown from 8 in 1994 to 108 in 2008 (Lindemann 2011: 23). Moreover, while all military officers who had been appointed to civilian positions under Kaunda were either retired or retrenched after 1991, the MMD regimes never fully abandoned the UNIP's strategy of appointing military personnel to high political office. Accordingly, two out of three vice presidents under Chiluba were of military background, namely Brig. Gen. G. Miyanda and late Lt Gen. C. Tembo. Even under Mwanawasa, former military officers like Lt. Gen. R. Shikapwasha (Minister of Home Affairs and Minister of Foreign Affairs) and Brig. Gen. Brian Chituwo (Minister of Health) occupied key cabinet positions, while many others were given lucrative posts as ambassadors.

5.4. The 1997 coup attempt

The last coup attempt took place on 28 October 1997, when Captain Lungu (alias Captain Solo) and a few comrades managed to gain control of Radio Zambia, claiming that they had assumed political power on behalf of the National Redemption Council, the alleged political wing of the army. This coup attempt appears to have been carried out by UNIP loyalists who were put off not only by their own dismissal from the army but also by a law that required presidential candidates to have Zambian parents, thus preventing former President Kaunda from opposing Chiluba in the 1996 elections (Haantobolo 2008: 203). Even though Nyanja speakers from Eastern Province—the only remaining UNIP stronghold in the country at the time—seem to have been prominently represented among the plotters, the broad-based character of the Chiluba administration again made ethnic mobilisation difficult. Tellingly, the conspiracy again originated among relatively junior officers who enjoyed only minimal support in the armed forces and were quickly arrested by loyalist forces.

All things considered, Zambia's armed forces have been loyal to all the post-one-party era governments of the Third Republic. The soldiers have adapted to the turbulent character of plural politics by maintaining a non-interventionist stance vis-à-vis multiparty politics. During periods of power transitions, the armed forces have not only facilitated democratic transfers of power from one government to its successor, but have also demonstrated unquestionable loyalty to the legitimately elected president.

6. CONCLUSION AND FORWARD LOOK

i.   In conclusion, it can be said that Zambia's armed forces have remained loyal to civilian authority, owing to a number of key variables. One key variable was the inclusive mode of recruitment into the armed forces that the first government of President Kaunda implemented shortly after attainment of independence in 1964. This made it impossible for any one ethnic group to establish overwhelming preponderance in the military forces. The practice of ethnic/regional balancing in senior command appointments augmented the inclusive mode of recruitment into the defence forces. Thus, the national character of the armed forces made it very difficult for ethnic-based mobilization to take place.

ii.   A second factor was the politicization of the armed forces, particularly during the Second Republic. The ideology of Zambian humanism placed supreme emphasis on national unity and encouraged the defence forces to embrace the 'One Zambia, one nation' motto. This ideological sensitization of the armed forces eliminated the dichotomy between the armed forces on the one hand, and the civilian leadership and the general population on the other. The establishment of the Zambia National Service also contributed to a fusion of the armed forces and the civilian population.

iii. The co-opting of defence forces personnel into senior party and government positions convinced military personnel that the armed forces were an integral part of the polity of the one-party state. General

Chinkuli, first commander of the Zambia Army and the Zambia National Defence Force, upon retirement from the military went on to serve as a Cabinet minister, General Malimba Masheke went on to serve as prime minister in the Second Republic. Other military personnel followed this career trajectory. The country's soldiers were therefore incentivized to remain unshakably loyal to the civilian authorities.

iv. Another explanatory variable for sustained civilian control of Zambia's armed forces since independence can be traced to the astute political instincts of Zambia's first President Kenneth Kaunda. When faced by challenges to his rule, Kaunda refrained from authorizing the death penalty, which is the mandatory punishment for high treason. Rather than brutally and ruthlessly eliminating coup plotters, Kaunda only detained them under Emergency regulations and released them when he felt the threat they posed to his regime had subsided. By exercising restraint and moderation towards coup plotters and other regime opponents, Kaunda promoted a spirit of tolerance and reconciliation in the polity's evolving democratic culture, a stance that all his successors have adopted in the management of civil-military relations.

v.   The UNIP government and its successors however were wise enough to realize that ideological sensitization was not proof against putsch plots. Civilian authorities endeavoured to improve comfort levels of the armed forces so their morale would not be dampened. Dissent had to be bought off by using material incentives such as subsidized consumer goods for the armed forces.

vi. In the ultimate analysis, the fact that Zambia's armed forces have stayed in the barracks for the last fifty years of Zambia's independence means military non-interventionism has become a key characteristic of Zambia's political culture. The soldiers have learned that their sacred duty is to protect the territorial integrity of the Zambian State, rather than dabbling in political governance. Military coups in other African countries have demonstrated that soldiers are not trained to govern but rather to faithfully execute the orders of constitutionally constituted civilian authority. Hopefully, Zambia's soldiers will remain steadfast on this non-interventionist path for the next 50 years.

References

Chulu, Kabanda (2014), 'Ex-ZAF boss convicted', https://www.daily-mail.co.zm/?p=6508 accessed 24 December 2014.

Decalo, Samuel (1989), 'Modalities of Civil–Military Stability in Africa', *Journal of Modern African Studies* 27/4: 547–578.

Feaver, Peter D. (1999), Civil–Military Relations. *Annual Review of Political Science*, 2: 211–241.

Goldsworthy, David (1981), 'Civilian Control of the Military in Black Africa', *African Affairs*, 80/318: 49–74.

Haantobolo, Godfrey (2008), *Civil Control of the Military in Zambia*, unpublished PhD thesis, Johannesburg: University of the Witwatersrand. http://mobile.wiredspace.wits.ac.za/bitstream/handle/10539/7129/haantobolo%20revised%20thesis%20with%20GCs%20comments%20-%20final.pdf?sequence=1

Huntington, Samuel (1957), *The Soldier and the State: The Theory and Politics of Civil–Military Relations* (Belknap Press S), paperback, 15 October 1981.

Kraus, John (1966), 'Ghana without Nkrumah: The Men In Charge', *Africa Report*, http://home.koranteng.com/writings/ghana-without-nkrumah-men-in-charge.html accessed 1 January 2015.

Larmer, Miles (2008), 'Enemies Within? Opposition to the Zambian One-Party State, 1972–1980', in Jan-Bart Gewald, Maria Hinfelaar, and Giacomo Macola (eds.) *One Zambia, Many Histories: Towards a History of Post-Colonial Zambia* (Leiden: Brill), 98–128.

Lindemann, Stefan (2010), 'Civilian control of the military in Tanzania and Zambia: Explaining persistent exceptionalism', *Crisis States Working Papers Series* No. 2, Crisis States Research Centre, September http://www.lse.ac.uk/.../research/crisis_States/download/.../wpSeries2/WP802.pd accessed 25 December 2014.

Lindemann, Stefan (2011), 'The Ethnic Politics of Coup Avoidance: Evidence from Zambia and Uganda', *Africa Spectrum* 2: 3–41 http://journals.sub.uni-hamburg.de/giga/afsp/article/download/460/458 accessed 22 December 2014.

Longworth, R. C. (1991), 'Other Nations, Diplomats Will Try To Persuade Iraq', *Chicago Tribune*, January 10 http://articles.chicagotribune.

com/1991-01-10/news/9101030462_1_arab-peace-efforts-iraqi-withdrawal-aziz accessed 24 December 2014.

Lopa, Wisdom M. (2014), An Assessment of Civil–Military Relations in Zambia, unpublished MA thesis, Dag Hammarskjöld Institute of Peace and Conflict Studies, Copperbelt University (CBU).

Lupogo, Herman. (2001), 'Civil–military Relations and Political Stability', *African Security Review* 10/1, http://www.issafrica.org/pubs/ASR/10No1/Lupogo.html

Mulikita, Njunga M. (2003), 'A False Dawn? Africa's Post-1990 Democratization Waves' *African Security Review*, http://www.issafrica.org/pubs/ASR/12No4/Mulikita.pdf

—— (2010), 'The AU Peace and Security Council and the Quest for Constitutional Democratic Governance in Africa—A Critical Assessment', *Africa Insight*, ISSN: 0256 2804.

Ngoma, Naison (2004), 'Civil–Military Relations: Searching for a Conceptual Framework with an African Bias', http://www.issafrica.org/uploads/CIVILNGOMA.PDF

Ngoma, Naison (2005), *Coups and Coup Attempts in Africa: Is there a missing link?* http://www.issafrica.org/pubs/asr/13no3/engoma.pdf

Ngoma, Naison and Lungu, Hanania (2005), *The Zambian military—trials, tribulations and hope* http://www.issafrica.org/pubs/Books/Evol_Revol%20Oct%2005/Chap12.pdf

Olusoji, George; Seyi, Shadare and Oluwakemi, Owoyemi (2012), 'Military Interventions in the Nigerian Politics: "A Timed Bomb" Waiting to Explode? The Avowal of a New Management Elites', *International Journal of Business, Humanities and Technology* 2/5, August, http://www.ijbhtnet.com/journals/Vol_2_No_5_August_2012/21.pdf

Phiri, B. J. (2003), 'Civil control of the Zambian military since independence and its implications for democracy', in R. Williams, G. Cawthra, and D. Abrahams (eds.) *Ourselves to Know: Civil–Military Relations and Defence Transformation in Southern Africa* (Pretoria: Institute for Security Studies) 3–16.

—— (2001), 'Civil Control of the Zambian Military since Independence: Implications for Democracy', *African Security Review* http://www.issafrica.org/pubs/ASR/10No4/Phiri.html

Purcell, Joseph Patrick (2012), *Decolonisation: Congo 1960–1961* http://www. eceme.ensino.eb.br/cihm/Arquivos/PDF%20Files/37.pdf accessed 23 December 2014.

Ringquist, John (2011) 'Political Parties, Praetorianism, and Politicization of the Tanzanian Military', http://www.usma.edu/nsc/SiteAssets/SitePages/ Publications/Political%20Parties,%20Praetorianism,%20and%20 Politicization%20of%20the%20Tanzanian%20Military.pdf accessed 1 January 2015.

Sibamba, Francis G. (2010), *The Zambia Army and I: My Personal Experience, The Autobiography of a Former Army Commander* (Ndola, Zambia: Mission Press).

Zambia Institute of Diplomacy and International Studies (ZIDIS) (2014), Report of the Roundtable to Commemorate Fifty Years of Zambian–Russia Bilateral Relations, 29 October.

Chapter 7

Zambia's Dependency Syndrome
Christabel Ngongola

SCOPE AND BACKGROUND

Looking at the establishment of Zambia as a nation, this author has nothing but gratitude for the nation's brave heroes that fought to make this country independent. Yet, five decades on into the existence of the independent state, the battle still rages for better living standards, quality education and access to proper health care, equality in terms of gender, reduction in income disparities, and lastly but definitely not the least, the battle against poverty. This is not to say the country has not made any progress, but maybe her achievements have mostly been in the creation of nationhood, the solidarity and peace that the country enjoys today. This peace cannot be taken for granted, especially considering how other resource-rich countries have descended into civil wars. But if the country on the other hand is to assess its economic progress and standards of living, it must be honest to say that its achievements have not been satisfactory. As a nation, Zambia still struggles to significantly reduce the high levels of poverty that its people face and rid herself of dependence, among other things, on factors that have rather slowed and perhaps even terminated progress in nation-building, both politically and socio-economically. It is therefore a matter of importance that as a nation, Zambia stands responsible and accountable for the progress she has made in the quest for development. Fifty years on, and many more to go, it is important that Zambians establish the country's true worth and forge on, without overlooking the numerous setbacks in her journey to socio-economic development. It will in this chapter be argued that Zambia's dependency on copper earnings was the beginning of the country's descent into dependency on foreign actors as well as neo-patrimonial politics. Economically, the heavy dependency on the extractive sector, among other things, has had heavy constraints on the rest of the economy and this led into a poverty circle that has become very hard to break out of, to date.

There is no precise definition in the economic sense of what the dependence syndrome actually is. However, this chapter adopts the definition of dependence as given by Todaro and Smith (2012: 122) to mean '*the reliance of developing countries on developed-country economic policies to stimulate their own economic growth*". It also extends dependence to mean that the developing countries adopt developed-country education systems, technology, economic, and political systems, attitudes, consumption patterns, dress, and sometimes even culture. Zambia's dependency syndrome will be looked at from two angles: one based on theories that support underdevelopment as an externally induced phenomena and the other, on the basis of theories that stipulate that underdevelopment is a much rather internally induced phenomena than an external one that cripples a nation's progress. More so, this chapter will articulate matters of Zambia's heavy dependence on the extractive industry and how that has worked to disadvantage rather than advantage the potential for growth. The chapter will explore the most cardinal types of dependence that have persisted in the post-independence era for Zambia. The chapter will also explore: (i) what might have been the strengths of the kind of models implemented by the governments at the time, and to consider how they miserably failed and (ii) what might have gone wrong in the nation-building models and henceforth suggest a way forward for measures to be taken in the present-day socio-economic stance to development. The analysis will take into consideration development indicators such as the Human Development Index (HDI) for growth. HDI is a summary measure for assessing long-term progress in three basic dimensions of human development: a long and healthy life, access to knowledge and a decent standard of living.

THE INTERNATIONAL DEPENDENCE REVOLUTION

The Neo-colonial Dependence Model

The neo-colonial dependence model grew especially out of developing country intellectuals as a result of disenchantment with the structural-change model. The main proposition of the model is that underdevelopment exists in developing countries because of continuing exploitative economic, political, and cultural policies of former colonial rulers towards less developed countries. This model is an indirect outgrowth of Marxist thinking and mostly attributes underdevelopment primarily to the historical evolution of a highly unequal international capitalist system of rich country–poor country relationships. According to this model, whether it is because rich nations are intentionally exploitative or unintentionally neglectful, there is coexistence of rich and poor nations in an international system that is dominated by such unequal power relationships. These relationships are manifest between the *centre* (the developed countries) and the *periphery* (the developing countries), rendering attempts by poor nations to be self-reliant and independent most difficult and sometimes even impossible (Baran 1975; Griffin and Gurley 1985).

In this model, it is believed that certain groups of elites in the developing countries enjoy high incomes, social status, and political power but constitute only a small exclusive ruling class whose principal interest is in the perpetuation of the international capitalist system of inequality and conformity in which they are rewarded. In short, the neo-Marxist, neocolonial view of underdevelopment attributes a large part of the developing world's continuing poverty to the existence and policies of the industrial capitalist countries of the northern hemisphere and their extensions in the form of small but powerful elites in the less developed countries (Leys 1975). The very fact that developing countries portrayed their dependence and vulnerability to key economic decisions made in the capitals of North America, Western Europe, or Japan and huge international institutions like the IMF and the World Bank forced these nations to recognize the importance of some of the insights of the international-dependence school (Todaro and Smith 2012). Further, there was a portrayal of an 'invisible umbilical cord' that ultimately tied the less developed economies to the former colonies as a representation of the dependency on the latter for key economic decisions.

The motive for nationalising state resources in the UNIP era stemmed from the background of reducing Western control over Zambia's mining resources under the umbrella of 'Zambia for Zambians'. The model might have failed for Zambia as result of continued intervention by the powerful international group of elites such as the World Bank and the IMF. According to this author, there is need to establish Zambia's stance in the entire interplay of dominance and dependence and investigate which side of the coin it falls on. Undoubtedly, Zambia is on the developing side of the coin. Literature on postcolonial Zambia has endeavoured to establish why a natural-resource-endowed country is not in a better economic position than it was at the time of independence. In fact, according to the UNDP's *Zambia Human Development Report* (1999/2000), Zambia is the only country in the world with data on the human development index available with lower human development indicators in 1997 than in 1975 (UNDP 2001: 1). Overall, poverty was measured at 72.9 per cent in 1998 with extreme poverty having risen to 57.9 per cent (ibid. 2001).

RESOURCE CURSE AND NEO-PATRIMONIALISM

Has Zambia's dependence on other countries or the dominance by other countries caused the catastrophically slow rate of economic growth or are there other factors at play? To what extent have Zambia's abundant natural resources been a curse rather than a blessing to economic transformation? Have the historical ideologies of nation-building of Zambia post-independence played any significance to the role in deterring the growth agenda of the country? To try and answer the above questions it is necessary to examine the 'resource curse' school of thought.

At the time of independence, Zambia was said to have '*the highest export value per head in Africa*' (MacPherson 1977: 72). This meant that Zambia's copper exports gave her a very healthy flow of money into the country. Essentially, the UNIP government agreed that it was very dangerous for a nation to be so dependent on copper as the world market for copper could easily change and further that the mineral was a diminishing resource which could adversely affect Zambia's development programme (ibid.). Between 1968 and 1971, the major parts of the Zambian economy were nationalised (Rakner 2003). There was a drastic shift of power from foreign ownership to public sector control and domination of the industries. As a result, Zambia was plagued by the 'resource curse'. The resource-curse phenomenon assumes that the state has a high degree of political control over the extractive sector and receives large amounts of revenue from the sector (Luong and Weinthal 2006: 242). The UNIP era showcased a strong example of this trend of national ownership and strict regulation of the extractive industry (Hallum 2011).

According to Hallum, neo-patrimonial politics is based on the assumption that political leaders will try to 'maximize' their time in office. Bratton and van de Walle (1997), among others, have depicted neo-patrimonialism as the institutional hallmark of African politics. Neo-patrimonialism means *there is a concentration of power by the president along with systematic clientelism and abuse of state resources* (ibid). Dominant postcolonial leaders often accumulated considerable private wealth in this scenario (a detailed explanation is given where postcolonial leaders are discussed individually later in the chapter depicting the element of neo-patrimonialism). However, in some cases the mechanism for generating and allocating rents was or is an elite cabal or a dominant organization (e.g. a political party). To the extent that under these arrangements there remains a blurring of the distinction between public wealth and the private wealth of the rulers, these types of regimes all fall under the standard definition of neo-patrimonialism (Bratton and van de Walle 1997: 61–96). The authors have argued that three stable, informal institutional structures have facilitated and strengthened the neo-patrimonial patterns of rule in post-independence African politics. These are the continued adherence to presidentialism, implying that regardless of regime form, large segments of political control remain located within the executive office; the continued presence of clientelism as a means for maintaining governmental power; and finally, the excessive employment of state resources for purposes of political gain.

The windfall that accrues to the state during a boom in the prices of natural resources lets the political leaders to rely on redistributive politics in order to secure support, rather than focusing on creating economic growth (Kolstad and Wiig 2009; Karl 1997). Consequently, resource-rich states 'do not need to formulate anything deserving the appellation of economic policy; all [they need] is an expenditure policy' (Rosser 2006: 16). In other words, the mechanics of running the country's policies is driven by economic gains made from (the Zambian case) the extractive industry. The end in this cycle is to drive the agenda of a few 'big men' forward rather than meet the needs of the majority poor of the nation. A clear indication of patronage is showcased as was the case for Zambia in 2003 with the soaring of copper prices on the world market. The winners of liberalisation were the few country elites that showed links to state capitalism in the 1970s through the processes of acquisition of small parastatals in the opaque processes of the Zambia Privatisation Agency (ZPA) (Larmer 2007). This was evidenced by the high levels of inequality and the lack of this wealth to have trickled down to the rest of the Zambians.

From the given explanation, it can be inferred that there is a causal relationship between neo-patrimonialism and the 'resource curse'. Let us consider that while the endowment of abundant natural resources is a large asset for economic development, it sometimes harbours a pitfall leading to economic retardation (Rosser 2006). This is the basis of the argument for neo-patrimonialism as the root cause of Africa's underdevelopment. The effect of too much government intervention in market mechanisms coupled with bad economic policies is essentially seen in this context as was the case for Zambia in the Kaunda era.

Further enlightenment on the effects of the resource-curse phenomena is given in brief under three different explanations according to Hallum (2011) in the case study for Zambia as presented below.

1. Neo-patrimonial politics and rent-seeking

Under this explanation, one has to understand that the framework of political decision-making is heavily altered by the mining revenues collected to necessitate redistributive neo-patrimonial politics (Karl 1997: 44). Rent-seeking activity increases, on the other hand, such as where domestic actors try to extract revenue from the state rather than engage in productive economic activity (Kolstad and Wiig 2009). Many problems arise as a result of such ill practices as unprecedented levels of corruption that have heavy repercussions on economic performance (Sala-i-Martin and Subramanian 2003). The nature of sudden and high levels of increased public spending tends to create inflationary pressures in the economy (ibid.; Karl 1997: 28). Lastly under this heading, massive public spending and redistributive policies tend to create unsustainable debts as public investments are financed on future earnings from the extractive sector (Karl 1997: 29–30; Auty 1993). The probable results of such high debt levels have both short- and long-term negative effects such as lowered productive entrepreneurial activity (Mehlum et al. 2006b: 1122)

2. Lack of personal taxation

According to Luong and Weinthal (2006), the reason why resource-rich countries have failed to develop is because of a weak (or non-existent) tax regime that is perhaps the most prevalent negative outcome of resource wealth. The explanation, according to Karl (2007: 259), is centred on the notion that 'the revenues a state collects, how it collects them, and the uses it puts them to define its very nature'. This trend of thought stems from Tilly's influential work on state-building (ibid: 260). Therefore, it is the case, according to this school of thought, that the modern states emerged in Europe because of pressures imposed on the state to self-finance. The results of this kind of tax regime were twofold. Firstly, it necessitated bargaining with the population as subjects were more likely to pay their taxes if they felt that the state had legitimacy, bringing about demands for representation in exchange for taxation, thereby helping in bringing about modern representative politics (Moore 2004: 302). Secondly, the demanding task of collecting tax made it necessary for the state to build a modern bureaucracy (ibid: 298).

According to the resource-curse literature, the effects of taxation are in contrast to the situation in resource-rich developing countries. The scenario here is taken to assume that because of the high degree of natural resource wealth, the states feel relieved from the burden of having to tax their own people (Karl 2007: 256). Failure to enter into bargaining with the population over their rights creates failed modern bureaucracies on one hand and instead creates centralised states as a result of entering into bargaining with foreign companies (Moore 2004: 313; Collier and Hoeffler 2007: 11; Karl 2007: 262–263). The biggest problem of the failure to enter into bargaining with the populace is that it leaves little room for public spending accountability. According to the resource-curse literature, the lack of accountability produces few checks and balances on the political system, which has been shown to be one of the most important institutional factors in determining whether resources become a curse or a blessing (Tornell and Lane 1999: 42; Collier and Hoeffler 2007).

3. State-led industrialisation

This is a concept adopted from the above mentioned explanations. According to Auty (1993) most developing countries adopted a statist approach in the 1950s and 1960s as a path to development. However, as Auty (1994) also demonstrates, resource-poor countries soon abandoned their statist approach policies in favour of more market-led and export-oriented policies much earlier than their resource-rich counterparts. He argues that the reason why resource-rich countries sustained their economically hurtful statist policies was the easy access to foreign exchanges from the extractive sector (Auty 1993: 257; Auty 1994: 24). The argument under this explanation not only focused on foreign reserves, but also on the state's revenue base adding that the easy access to *unearned income* (refer to Reinke's chapter 'Sovereignty and Democracy: Zambia's Challenges') in resource-rich countries make state-led industrialisation more plausible in these countries, to the detriment of long-term development (Karl 1997; Karl 2007).

The explanations given above provide a brief insight into the problems and effects of the resource curse from three different perspectives. The argument in all three is the establishment of whether natural resource wealth of a nation becomes a problem or not and what factors easily make that plausible in a resource-rich developing country.

Viewed from a different angle, the resource curse is also known as the Dutch disease. It is named after the experience of the Netherlands on its discovery of a rich natural gas deposit in the North Sea in the late 1950s (Hayami and Godo 2005: 120). Exploitation of this new resource base brought about a major improvement in the balance of trade for the Netherlands, but ironically resulted in declines in domestic industries with increased unemployment. Appreciation in the real rate of exchange for local currency, which resulted from increased trade surplus, undermined the international competitive position of agriculture and industry (Corden and Neary 1982). In general, the shrinkage in value added in the agricultural and manufacturing sectors in resource-rich economies due to the resource-export boom is more than compensated for by increased income in the extractive sector. However, because the mining of gas and oil as well as minerals is characterised by high capital intensity (Bairoch 1975), the increase in employment in the mining sector is not sufficient to absorb workers laid off from the agriculture and industrial sectors.

The danger for resource-rich economies is that the resource-export booms, such as those experienced in the first and the second oil crisis in 1973–75 and 1979–81 respectively, vastly increase export prices and earnings but are also abrupt and short-lived. Sharp appreciation in the exchange rate of the local currency in the boom period tends to seriously damage domestic agriculture and industry, resulting in an irreversible loss in fixed facilities, and labour and management skills for the production of non-resource tradables. As a result, it becomes difficult for these sectors to recover. Meanwhile, with the collapse of the resource boom, derived demand for non-tradables declines precipitously. A major economic slump with a high unemployment rate then becomes inevitable. If some key manufactures (or agriculture) having strategic complementarities with other industries are destroyed by the natural resource boom, the economy may not only be unable to return to the former development path but might even be trapped at a low-level equilibrium (Krugman 1987, 1991; Matsuyama 1991).

According to Hayami and Godo (2005), this pathology of the Dutch disease was typically observed in Nigeria. As a major oil exporter, this country benefited greatly from an export boom during the two oil crisis periods. Similar to other developing economies, the official exchange rate was fixed. However, because much of increased oil revenue was spent for conspicuous development projects and government consumption, excess effective demands were created that resulted in inflation. The real rate of exchange sharply appreciated under the fixed official exchange as the domestic price level increased faster than the international level. Consequently, the sectors producing non-oil tradables, especially agriculture, were severely damaged. Rural villages were deserted, and urban slums were infiltrated by migrants seeking employment in service sectors. This process was aggravated by the government's construction of modern large-scale, capital-intensive industries, based on large oil revenues and foreign credits attracted by high solvency of Nigeria in the expectation of continued high oil prices. After the collapse of the second oil boom in 1981, Nigeria was left with desolated rural villages and swarms of unemployed workers in cities—a situation resembling the low-equilibrium trap (Hayami and Godo 2005). This was proof that a rich endowment of natural resources is not necessarily a good support for economic development, but can instead be a stumbling block. It also clearly demonstrates that such a trap for resource-rich economies can be avoided with the application of appropriate policies (ibid.).

The Problem of Africa—The Case for Zambia

To narrow the perspective down to Zambia, development miserably failed to take off as the economic boom was short-lived and the high dependence of Zambia on copper proved more and more difficult to become the country's enabler of growth. According to Mills (2010), while some countries in Africa were undoubtedly plagued by an exaggeration of tribalism, violence, corruption, and patronage, Zambia seemed to have been spared of the extreme ends. In Zambia, by the 1980s, the Industrial Development Corporation (INDECO) was the largest company in the manufacturing sector, directly employing 30,000 people in three dozen subsidiaries including vehicle manufacturing, and a variety of engineering concerns (ibid. 2010). The questions Mills (2010) sought answers for were: Why did all these collapse? Why were they unable to compete internationally and transform into robust companies capable of standing alone without national subsidies and protectionism? The following part of the chapter attempts to answer these concerns.

According to Rakner (2003), it is a fact that copper played an immensely important role in the economy of Zambia. With the growth of copper mining in the 1930s, foreign capital and multinational corporations developed one of the largest mining complexes in the world on what was later to become Zambian territory. By the end of the Second World War, Northern Rhodesia was among the foremost producers of copper in the world. The growth of the mining industry led to the creation of urban centres, and by the time of independence, Zambia was one of the most industrialised and urbanised of

Africa's new nation-states. With a gross national product (GNP) of close to US$ 2 billion at independence in 1964, Zambia had one of the highest per capita incomes in independent Africa, and at the time, GNP was two times higher than South Korea's (World Bank 1991; MacPherson 1995). Two decades later Zambia was reduced to one of the poorest countries on the African continent. From 1975 to 1991, Zambia's average per capita income declined by 2.5 per cent per annum (MacPherson 1995). At the same time, the country's external debt rose from US$ 627 million in 1970 to a staggering US$ 7.2 billion in 1990 (ibid.).

The defining moment for Zambia's economic history was the collapse in copper export earnings *and* the government's response to this collapse. Rakner (2003) argues that it was the UNIP government's failure to adequately address the economic decline as it shifted its political project in line with the creation of a developmental state where the main economic element was the nationalisation of the main industries. The economic decline was the defining factor that triggered the political opposition leading to the 1991 political transition (ibid.: 44). The first independent constitution of Zambia provided for a unitary state with a strong chief executive and a cabinet selected from, but not responsible to, the National Assembly. The constitution further specifically named Kenneth Kaunda as the first president of Zambia. The struggle for national unity became from an early date the main political ambition of the new leadership, reflected in the rallying slogan adopted at the time of independence, 'One Zambia, one nation' (Gertzel et al. 1984).

Starting in April 1968, the UNIP government implemented the first of what proved to be a series of economic reforms by buying controlling shares in twenty-six major companies. In 1969 the state acquired a 51 per cent controlling share in the major copper-mining companies, Anglo-American Corporation and Roan Selection Trust, the two main pillars of the Zambian economy (Turok 1989: 42). From 1969 onwards, the government was the primary direct recipient of the revenues from the copper industry with the control of government investments vested in Zambia Industrial Mining Corporation (ZIMCO). Nationalisation effectively ended investments from abroad in Zambian industries (Burdette 1988: 89).

In theory, nationalisation was intended to shift power from foreign ownership to private *and* public Zambian interests. But the reforms of 1968 and 1969 marked a greater determination by the government to tilt the balance against the foreign private sector in favour of the public sector (Turok 1989; Beveridge and Oberschall 1979). Through state intervention in the economy, the parastatal system was established on a significant scale of organization and power, dominating all industries.

The nationalisation resulted in a rapid expansion of the public sector. The numbers of state employees grew from 22,500 in 1964 to 51,000 in 1969, and for each new job in the private sector, the state administration recruited four new employees (Pausewang and Hedlund 1986: 18). Through the major state industrial conglomerate, Industrial Development Corporation (INDECO), the government became both the leading supplier and competitor to private sector business, thereby imposing heavy constraints on private enterprises (Bates and Collier 1993; Taylor 1997). The magnitude of the state's involvement in the economy is illustrated by the fact that Zambia inherited 14 parastatals at independence, among them four agricultural marketing boards. After the major nationalisation effort was completed by the mid-1970s, 147 parastatals were in existence and 121 under a single holding company, ZIMCO (Callaghy 1990: 289). By 1971, most major industries were owned and controlled by the government and government companies. The process of nationalisation beginning with the Mulungushi reforms in 1968 resulted in 80 per cent of the Zambian economy being state-controlled by the conclusion of the nationalisation programme in the mid-1970s. The nationalisation of major sectors of the economy and the aim to promote Zambianization in all sectors of political and economic life brought interest groups representing labour, business, and agriculture into a close, albeit conflictual, relationship with the state (Rakner 2003: 46).

As a result of the UNIP government acquiring majority shares in all major industries, large public investments were made in power, transport, and roads by the state through the parastatal corporations. The parastatal sector created the infrastructure perceived as necessary for further growth. State intervention largely displaced foreign capital and personnel (Beveridge and Oberschall 1979: 273). The influence of the private business sector was further reduced by Zambia's dependence on and preoccupation with the mining industry. As copper accounted for 90 per cent of Zambia's export revenue, all other economic interests, public and private, were given secondary importance (Sklar 1975). This as it turned out was a huge mistake!

Government market control severely depressed the prices for agricultural produce as food prices were strictly controlled and kept largely below market levels. Producers were unable to find alternatives to the highly controlled domestic market since the kwacha was overvalued, making Zambian exports uncompetitive (Hawkins 1991).

During the first ten years after independence, the Zambian economy expanded fairly rapidly with GDP increasing at an average of 2.3 per cent annually in real terms (World Bank 1984). However, Zambia's modest luck ran out in 1974, and according to estimates, in the period between 1975 and 1990, Zambia experienced a 30 per cent decline in real per capita growth (World Bank 1990). After 1974, copper prices fell sharply on the world market. The fall in copper prices also coincided with an enormous increase in oil prices. Zambia's revenues fell sharply with the decline in the price of its major export. Diversification of the Zambian economy away from copper had been an expressed political goal since independence. Nevertheless, Zambia remained dependent upon copper for 90 per cent of its exports and 40 per cent of its GDP throughout the 1970s and 1980s (Rakner 2003). As argued by Burdette (1988: 95), 'In essence, the [Zambian] economy was always a house of cards balanced narrowly on the prosperity of the copper mines'.

Suffice it to say and specific to the Kaunda era, following the 1965 and 1969 economic reforms, the (UNIP) party and its government (aided by several units of the state) had complete control of the country's economy. They controlled and directed the economy through the bureaucratic coordination of its formerly independent corporate mining entities that was provided by the Industrial and Development Corporation (INDECO) and the Zambia Industrial and Mining Corporation (ZIMCO) set up from the reforms (Phiri 2001). At the time, President Kaunda was at the top of the pyramid (as chairman) of ultimate political control of the economy (ibid.). The First and Second Republic rule under Kaunda was a depiction of neo-patrimonial politics.

The SAP Debate and the Privatisation Agenda

The economic pressures on the Zambian economy were not immediately felt by the society as the government was able to continue social spending through domestic and foreign borrowing. Until copper-prices started to fall, the Zambian government had showed no interest in the IMF or in the loan programmes from the World Bank. However, from 1973 onwards, Zambia started drawing on IMF financial resources. The World Bank was initially slow to respond to the financial requests from Zambia, due to the country's high copper earnings (West 1989). However, in 1978 the World Bank declared Zambia eligible, i.e. poor enough, to qualify for International Development Association (IDA) funds, and pledged US$ 50 million per annum for the next five years at the first Consultative Group (CG) meeting it organised for Zambia (*EIU Country Report* 1978). Neither the World Bank nor the bilateral donors took active parts in policy discussions concerning Zambia until the early 1980s. In the 1970s, the IMF was the most important external advocate of liberal economic reforms in Zambia but its application of conditionality was weak. The first two IMF standby agreements (1973 and 1976) contained few conditions. Zambia utilised all the financial assistance offered in both the IMF programmes, yet the balance of payments was not restored to equilibrium.

Towards the end of the decade, it was becoming increasingly clear that the Zambian economy was unlikely to recover without developing new exports and more efficient import substitution. By the late 1970s, the Zambian economy was showing signs of deterioration and destabilisation. Attempting to refinance its way out of the growing external imbalances, Zambia had since the early 1970s turned to private creditors as well as the IMF. Thus, by 1978 Zambia's economic situation called for more substantial aid, and in return the conditions imposed by the IMF became more severe (Rakner 2003). The levels of debt were skyrocketing.

The unfortunate combination of an overwhelming dependence on one export product and the nature of the price fluctuations of this product were features which placed Zambia in a particular category when the economic problems started to make themselves felt. After implementing the single-party system, the president became the key economic player and patronage was an important mechanism employed in defence of Kaunda's and UNIP's continued rule (Gertzel et al. 1984). Whereas the rest of the world was blaming Kaunda and his ways of political governance, in reality however, the donor community also had a part to blame in the country's downfall. Zambia had very little choice but to follow the economic demands set forth by the IMF and the World Bank. In addition to two IMF standby agreements negotiated, the year 1983 also marked the introduction of the first World Bank Structural Adjustment Programme (SAP) in conjunction with the IMF stabilisation programme.

With the desperate failed attempts by the UNIP government to resuscitate the economy came the new Movement for Multiparty Democracy (MMD) government. The MMD government essentially inherited an economy that was on the brink of implosion. Emanating from strong roots in the powerful unions, the local business community also played a key role in the early years of the MMD movement, primarily as a source of finance for the MMD (Larmer 2006b: 296; Rakner 2003: 65).

Attention in this part of the chapter is drawn to establishing why the mines were privatised and liberalised. Why was this not a sustainable solution of a long-term plague of economic disarray? Following through will be an analysis of the dependency dynamics on development.

Hallum (2011) notes that while the MMD government used the economic reform momentum to challenge the power of the previously strong unions, the case was different in relations to the strong but inefficient bureaucracy inherited from the UNIP era. The donor community did try to push through reform of the bureaucracy and the government did include promises of modernising and downsizing of the bureaucracy, but little was done in this regard. The government adopted a World Bank programme intended to downsize and streamline the bureaucracy, which included a goal of laying off 25 per cent of public employees within three years (Rakner 2003: 71). Instead the civil service grew by 19 per cent between 1989 and 1994 (ibid.). The government had made plenty of foes with the economic reforms and was clearly not ready to alienate public employees and therefore decided against reforming the bureaucracy which meant that inefficiencies continued.

The donor community had the advantage that unlike the unions and business sector they could provide the one thing that government was most in need of, namely *hard cash*. According to the resource-curse literature, governments in resource-rich countries will look to the extractive sector to secure funds. But the copper sector was in a dismal state in the 1990s. Wages for the mining workers were being funded by government loans, while the mines were making a loss of approximately USD 1 million per day (Lungu 2008: 8).

The mining sector had lost its function as a cash cow and had instead become a burden on the state coffers. Therefore, the overriding objective of the government was to secure funds in order to stay in power. Of all actors involved in Zambian politics, only the donor community could provide this. Hence, a coalition was formed with donors. This explains to a large degree the fact that the economic reforms carried out in the 1990s essentially were the same that the IMF had pressed for during the 1980s. As has been pointed out, it was a policymaking process of 'aid for reform' (Rakner 2003: 134). The donor-state coalition meant that popular objections to reforms were put aside: 'the MMD was forced to choose between maintaining its popular support base and meeting donor conditions. It has consistently chosen the donors' (Larmer and Fraser 2007: 616).

The forced privatisation process of the late 1990s put the government in an unfavourable negotiation position. Copper prices were historically low, support for the government was at a low point, and the pressure from the donor community meant that the government was in a hurry to sell. Consequently, the so-called development agreements (DAs) outlining the conditions of investment were extremely favourable to the mines (Ratty 2008: 18).

While the state–donor coalition was relatively stable during the 1990s, the coalition came to a deadlock on the question of privatisation and liberalisation of the mines. In 1992 the idea of privatising the mining sector was floated by a minister in the MMD government. A public outcry followed immediately, not least from the unions (Rakner 2003: 95). Since then, the issue of privatisation of the mines was not pursued by the government.

The donors, however, insisted on the need to privatise the mines, and when the issue of debt relief came on the agenda in 1996, they were quick to link the two together through conditionality (Lungu 2008: 6). The crushing debt was perhaps the most important constraint on the Zambian economy. Faced with the hard choice of going against the wish of powerful domestic actors in Zambia, and the wish of the donors, the MMD government once again chose to please the donors (ibid.: 7). Throughout the period of 1997–2000, the mines were divided and sold to foreign investors.

For the donors, the need to privatise and liberalise the mines was not only necessary in terms of economic efficiency, it was also necessary in order to demonstrate Zambia's new development model. As one World Bank report on Zambia stated, the privatisation and liberalisation was necessary 'for providing a clear signal to investors of the government of Zambia's commitment to private enterprise' (quoted in Ratty 2008: 15).

Investments in the mining sector only materialised after 2003 when copper prices began to soar (Hallum 2011). However, from 2003 and onwards, investment soared and can be accredited with saving the mining industry in Zambia. While the mining sector was saved and resumed its former position as the most profitable and productive sector in the country, the boom left the state with little additional tax revenue. The table below shows the government's sources of income during the height of the boom.

Table: Taxes, grants, and budget balance 2006–2007, all numbers in per cent of GDP

	2006	2007
Mining taxes	0.6	1.4
Other taxes	16.1	17.9
Income taxes	7.5	8.4
Value added tax	4.6	4.9
Excise taxes	2.1	2.6
Customs duties	1.9	2
Non-tax	0.8	0.7
Grants	26	4.6
Projects and budget support	4.6	4.6

Debt reduction	21.4	0
Overall balance of budget		
Including grants	18.6	-0.2
Excluding grants	-7.4	-4.8

Source: IMF 2009: 17 (quoted in Hallum 2011: 61)

From the table above, it is most interesting to note the relative size of donor grants compared to mining taxes. In 2006 where debt relief was granted, donor funding was more than forty-three times larger than mining revenue. This shows how high the stakes were for the country in giving in to the demands of the donors in relation to debt relief. In 2007, after debt relief was delivered and thus a year when donor funding resumed its regular level, funding from donors was still more than three times the size of revenue from mining. At the same time it is clear from the table that the government's budget only barely balanced because of donor funding. Without these funds, there would have been a budget deficit of 4.8 per cent of GDP in 2007, at the height of the mining boom (Hallum 2011).

However, the dynamics of the boom spelled political trouble for the government and its reliance on donor interests. As prices soared, domestic discussion was on whether the country was getting a fair share from the copper exports surfaced (ibid.). The opposition parties, especially the Patriotic Front (PF), quickly sought to capitalise on this outrage. A testament to the unfairness of the DAs was the donors' change of stance during the boom. While the World Bank and IMF had pressed through the privatisation and liberalisation, they too began to argue that the DAs were too favourable to the investors (Lungu 2008: 9).

With the civil society, the opposition, the unions, and even donors arguing for a change in the tax regime surrounding the mines, it would seem that a new political course was a possibility in Zambia. With this also came the possibility for government to forge a new coalition, one that would bring more revenue to the Zambian state from mining and thereby break the flawed development model put in place in the 1990s.

The inception of the 2008 financial crisis came with threats from the mining companies and multinational corporations to pull out their investments and pursue legal action if the government decided to impose new tax regimes that would break the DAs (Lungu 2008: 12). The fact that the mines were granted concessions despite the immense pressure on the MMD government for higher taxes shows the degree of power and influence that the mines have over the government (Hallum 2011). The benefits for the mining corporations were clear, but what were not obvious in this case were the benefits of the government in terms of less regulation and higher profit margins. This was a contrast view of the resource-curse theory.

It is therefore held in speculation that there is pressure from the mining constituency coupled with the need to stay on good terms with the IMF that created the political need to water down the new tax system (ibid.: 64). However, the line between due and undue influence is thin, and judging by the large influence of the mining sector on government policy, it would seem relevant to describe the situation as outright state-capture by the mines.

State-capture describes the situation in which big corporations use their large influence on weak governments to influence the regulatory environment (Kaufmann and Hellman 2001). There is no doubt that the mining MNCs had a large degree of influence on the content of the DAs, thereby more or less writing their own regulation. As well, the government turnaround on taxes in 2008 also points to a large degree of influence from the mining sector on government policy. The fact that the government refuses to tax the mines more, despite the backing of the corporate-friendly World Bank and IMF arguably shows the large influence of the mines on the government (Hallum 2011). Zambian governments have a trend of in short-term goals for money, leading to another situation of state-capture. The argument here is that because of neo-patrimonialism, foreign investments have assumed more power by capitalising on the short-sightedness of the Zambian politics.

The presence of clientelism was evidenced in the Chiluba era from 1991 onwards. This regime tilted the scale from one end of complete government control (of Kaunda's era) to Zambia's economic liberalisation and privatisation of the extractive sector. This phase is widely recognized as having been disastrous as a result of the collapse of the manufacturing industry, a significant contraction of the economy from the soaring levels of unemployment, a severe pension crisis, and high inequality levels (Hallum 2011). In order to retain power, the MMD government under Chiluba was forced to choose between maintaining its popular support base and meeting donor conditionalities, it consistently chose the donors (ibid. 2011). Furthermore, to retain power, the MMD resorted to the suppression of the opposition, electoral rigging, and constitutional changes that enabled it to rule without majority electoral support (Larmer 2007). Marred with high levels of corruption and evidenced by the existing huge income inequality, the MMD regime and structural adjustments were believed to only benefit members of the party, their relatives and the multinational corporations (MNCs). According to Larmer (2007), 'the privatisation of the strategic Zambia Consolidated Copper Mines (ZCCM) between 1997 and 2000 epitomised the problems of liberalisation in a society with a weak domestic business class, a corrupt government negotiating team, and a lack of effective popular oversight. The sale of ZCCM in which the state held a 60.7 per cent share, was shaped by Zambia's *dependency* on the international financial institutions (IFIs) and the immediate need to attract investors for the mines'. As a result, mine privatisation breached legal requirements for transparency in the bidding processes, stakeholder consultation, and social and environmental impact. As the investors knew Zambia was dependent on the sales, the leverage was all on the investors' side (ibid. 2007).

Conclusion

Even though Zambia has done considerably well in the last ten years with GDP per capita growing at an average of 5.7 per cent per annum, this author believes that the state's potential to govern and rule has been heavily influenced and much to the detriment of the country, fallen under the tight (and sometimes even distant) control by the dominant countries. Zambia couldn't have sold the mines at a worse time—when the copper prices on the world market had fallen and under the DAs' conditions that essentially were a giveaway model at the enrichment of the West. The argument of the resource curse here was in contrast to the findings of the present-day Zambian economy.

Zambia seemed to have suffered from both the resource curse and heavy dependency on donor aid for the most part of her development. This is more evident in the first (post-independence era) and second boom of soaring copper prices on the world market (mostly 2003 onwards). The heavy interlinkages between politics and economic measures also pose a real threat to the country's future resource management and hence development. The period 2008 onwards is characterised mostly by control and influence of the government by mining MNCs. Depicting the Mwanawasa era where the effective introduction of windfall tax and later withdrawn is a clear example of this (Fraser and Larmer 2010: 19). Clearly, the MNCs have proved to be more powerful than the state and hence perpetuate a kind of dependency on Zambia.

According to van de Walle (2001), in terms of policy outcomes, African politics in general are embedded with a stronger aspect of neo-patrimonialism. This concept was birthed around politics that showed a strong interaction between the clientelistic needs of neo-patrimonial states, the extremely low capacity of these state structures, and the dominant economic ideas among policy elites in the 1960s and '70s. The political institutions established following decolonization were weak and endowed with little legitimacy. In its 1991 election campaign, MMD promised to reduce the power of the presidency by reducing the size of the Cabinet, enhancing the influence of the parliament, and further, to separate the powers of the party from those of the government. However, almost from their inception, these goals were disregarded. In order to reward the large number of people who had contributed to MMD's electoral victory in 1991, the size of the MMD Cabinet increased from the UNIP era. The Zambian case study suggests that political leaders manipulate formal institutions to their own advantage. Thus, the neo-patrimonial perspective is a useful reminder about assuming that political institutions will function in the same way independent of context (Hellman 1998; Roberts 1995; Gibson 1997; Schamis 1999).

The emerging research programme 'Africa Power and Politics Programme' provides great insight into how Africa can benefit from the development that has taken place in Asia while recognizing disadvantages present in Africa (Booth and Golooba-Mutebi 2011). One of the cases focused on is Rwanda, a country which has moved from the tragic genocide to a successful developmental state. The authors argue that there is need to recognize the presence of neo-patrimonialism. To avoid the devastating effects of rent-seeking, a government needs to ensure that the rents are centralized by the ruling party to avoid the free-for-all corruption practices often prevalent in Africa. The government must also work with a long time horizon and actually invest in infant industries. This has been the case in Rwanda where the ruling Rwandan Patriotic Front created their own holding company: Tri-Star Investments (ibid.: 8).

Following Rwanda's example, the long-term strategy for Zambia to follow at this stage when the economy is stable should be in alignment with the recognition and acceptance of the existence of neo-patrimonialism. Zambia could consider the path of developmental (neo-)patrimonialism that will avoid political party misuse of resources as a result of a short-lived tenure of rule.

Encouraging south-south trade could be encouraged but might also have high risks of leading the country back into a dependency as a result of the neo-patrimonialism and the state of underdevelopment of the country. Care and thought should be given into encouraging Chinese trade. Arguably, China definitely benefits in their relationship with Zambia by being a superior bargainer with a country where short-term gains tend to be more important than the long-term achievements. Zambia is still influenced by neo-patrimonialism and it can be critical for Zambia when China invests because of their lack of accountability in the deals that these countries strike.

The more sustainable way of avoiding the dependency burden altogether, in this author's opinion, would be emphasis on the building of a stronger human capital base, as in the case of Norway (with the highest HDI according to the UNDP 2013 report) where state resources are channelled into a fund for its citizens. It follows that the country exhibits strong HDI indicators as a result of state accountability to the populace that is heavily taxed.

REFERENCES

Auty, Richard. (1993), *Sustaining Development in Mineral Economies—The Resource Curse Thesis* (London: Routledge).
Auty, Richard (1994), 'Industrial Reform in Six Large Newly Industrializing Countries: The Resource Curse Thesis', *World Development* 22/1: 11–26.
Bairoch, P. (1975), *The Economic Development of the Third World since 1900*, trans. by C. Postan (London: Methuen).

Banerji, A. and Jain, S. (2007), 'Quality dualism', *Journal of Development Economics* 84: 234–250.

Baran, Paul (1975), *The Political Economy of Neo-Colonialism* (London: Heinemann).

Bates, R. and P. Collier (1993), 'The politics and economics of policy reform in Zambia', in Bates, R. and A. Krueger (eds.), *Political and Economic Interactions in Economic Policy Reform* (Oxford and Cambridge: Blackwell), 387–443.

Beveridge, A. and Oberschall, A. (1979), *African Businessmen and Development in Zambia* (Princeton: Princeton University Press).

Booth, D. and Golooba-Mutebi, F. (2011), *Developmental Patrimonialism—The Case of Rwanda* (London: Overseas Development Institute).

Bratton, M. (1994), 'Economic crisis and political realignment in Zambia', in Widner, J. (ed.), *Economic Change and Political Liberalization in Sub-Saharan Africa* (Baltimore: The Johns Hopkins Press).

—— (1992), 'Zambia Starts Over', *Journal of Democracy* 3/2: 81–94.

Bratton, M., Alderfer, P. and Simutanyi, N. (1997), *Political participation in Zambia 1991–1996: Trends, determinants and USAID program implications*. Zambia Democratic Governance Project, Special Study No. 5 (East Lansing: Michigan State University).

Bratton, M. and Posner, D. (1999), 'A First Look at Second Elections in Africa with Illustrations from Zambia', in Joseph, R. (ed.), *State, Conflict and Democracy in Africa* (Boulder: Lynne Rienner Publishers), 377–409.

Bratton, M. and van de Walle, N. (1997), *Democratic Experiments in Africa: Regime Transitions in Comparative Perspective* (Cambridge: Cambridge University Press).

—— (1992), 'Popular protest and reform in Africa', *Comparative Politics*, 24/4, July.

Burdette, M. (1988), *Zambia Between Two Worlds* (Boulder: Westview Press).

Callaghy, T. (1990), 'Lost between state and market. The politics of economic adjustment in Ghana, Zambia and Nigeria', in Nelson, J. M., *Economic Crisis and Policy Choice: The Politics of Adjustment in the Third World* (Princeton: Princeton University Press).

Corden, W. M., and Neary, P. J. (1982), 'Booming Sector and De-industrialization in a Small Open Economy', *Economic Journal* 92: 825–48, Dec.

Collier, P. and Hoeffler, A. (2007), 'Testing the Neocon Agenda: Democracy in Resource-Rich Societies', downloaded paper http://ideas.repec.org/a/eee/eecrev/v53y2009i3p293-308.html

Economist Intelligence Unit *EIU Country Report*: Zambia (1991–2002).

Fraser, A. and Larmer, M. (2010) *Zambia, Mining, and Neoliberalism—Boom and Bust on the Globalised Copperbelt* (New York: Palgrave Macmillan).

Gertzel, C. (ed.), Baylies, C., and Szeftel, M. (1984), *The Dynamics of the One-Party State in Zambia* (Manchester: Manchester University Press).

Gibson, E. (1997), 'The populist road to market reform: Policy and electoral coalitions in Mexico and Argentina', *World Politics* 49/3: 339–70, April.

Griffin, K. and Gurley, J. (1985), 'Radical analysis of Imperialism, the Third World, and the transition to Socialism: A survey article', *Journal of Economic Literature* 23: 1089–1143.

Hallum, C. (2011), *Privatisation and Liberalisation of the Extractive Sector in Zambia—Implications of the Resource Curse* (Aarhus: Aarhus University).

Hawkins, J. (1991), 'Understanding the failure of IMF reform: The Zambian case', *World Development* 19/7: 839–49.

Hayami, Y. and Godo, Y. (2005), *Development Economics—From the Poverty to the Wealth of Nations*, third edition (New York: Oxford University Press).

Hellman, J. S. (1998), 'Winners take all: The politics of partial reform in post-communist transitions', *World Politics*, 50/2: 203–35.

Karl, Lynn T. (1997), *The Paradox of Plenty—Oil Booms and Petro-States* (Berkeley: University of California Press).

—— (2007) 'Ensuring fairness: The case for a transparent fiscal social contract', in Macartan Humphreys, Jeffrey D. Sachs, and Joseph E. Stiglitz (eds.) *Escaping the Resource Curse* (New York: Columbia University Press).

Kaufmann, Daniel and Hellman, Joel (2001), 'Confronting the challenge of state capture in transition economies', *Finance & Development*, 38/3.

Kolstad, Ivar and Wiig, Arne (2009), 'It's the rents, stupid! The political economy of the resource curse', *Energy Policy* 37: 5317–5325.

Krugman, P. (1987), 'The Narrow Moving Band, the Dutch Disease and the Competitive Consequences of Mrs Thatcher', *Journal of Development Economics*, 27: 41–55, Oct.

—— (1991), 'History versus Expectations', *Quarterly Journal of Economics* 106: 651–67, May.

Royson Mukwena — page 188

Larmer, Miles (2006b), '"The Hour Has Come at the Pit": The Mineworkers' Union of Zambia and the Movement for Multi-party Democracy, 1982–1991', *Journal of Southern African Studies* 32/2: 293–312.
—— and Fraser, A. (2007), 'Of Cabbages and King Cobra: Interpreting the 2006 Zambian elections', *African Affairs*.
Lewellen, C. Ted (1995), *Dependency and Development: An Introduction to the Third World* Westport.
Leys, C. (1975) *Underdevelopment in Kenya: The Political Economy of Neo-Colonialism* (London: Heinemann).
Lungu, John (2008), 'The Politics of Reforming Zambia's Mining Tax Regime', paper presented at the *Mine Watch Zambia Conference: Politics, Economy, Society, Ecology and Investment in Zambia*.
Luong, Pauline Jones and Erika Weinthal (2006), 'Rethinking the Resource Curse: Ownership structure, institutional capacity, and domestic constraints', *Annual Review of Political Science* 9: 241–263.
MacPherson, M. F. (1995), 'The sequencing of economic reforms: Lessons from Zambia', *Development Discussion Paper* No. 516, Harvard Institute for International Development (HIID), November.
—— (1977), *Kwacha Ngwee—How the Zambian Nation Was Made* (Lusaka: Oxford University Press).
Matsuyama, K. (1991), 'Increasing Returns, Industrialization, and Indeterminacy of Equilibrium', *Quarterly Journal of Economics*, 106: 617–50, May.
Mehlum, Halvor, Karl Moene, and Ragner Torvik (2006b) 'Cursed by Resources or Institutions?', *The World Economy* 29/8: 1117–1131.
Mills, G. (2010) *Why Africa Is Poor: And what Africans can do about it* (Penguin Books SA).
Moore, Mick (2004), 'Revenues, State Formation, and the Quality of Governance in Developing Countries', *International Political Science Review*, 25/3: 297–319.
Pausewang, S. and Hedlund, H. (1986), *Zambia. Country Study and Norwegian Aid Review* (Bergen: Chr. Michelsen Institute).
Phiri, B. J. (2001) 'Colonial Legacy and the Role of Society in the creation and Demise of Autocracy in Zambia, 1964–1991', *Nordic Journal of African Studies* 10/2.

Rakner, L. (2003), *Political and Economic Liberalisation in Zambia 1991–2001* (Stockholm: Nordiska Afrikainstitutet).

Ratty, L. (2008), 'Mineworkers in Zambia: Meaningful democracy and the rise of the Patriotic Front', paper presented at the *Mine Watch Zambia Conference: Politics, Economy, Society, Ecology and Investment in Zambia.*

Roberts, K. M. (1995), 'Neoliberalism and the transformation of populism in Latin America. The Peruvian case', *World Politics* 48: 82–116, October.

Rosser, A. (2006), 'The Political Economy of the Resource Curse: A Literature Survey', *IDS Working Paper* No. 268.

Sala-I-Martin and Subramanian (2003), 'Addressing the natural resource curse: An illustration from Nigeria', *NBER Working Paper* No. 9804.

Schamis, H. (1999), 'Distributional Coalitions and the Politics of Economic Reform in Latin America', *World Politics* 51: 236–68.

Sen, A. (1999), *Development as Freedom* (New York: Knopf).

—— (1985), *Commodities and Capabilities* (Amsterdam: Elsevier).

Singer, W. Hans (1970), 'Dualism revisited: A new approach to the problems of dual societies in developing countries', *Journal of Development Studies* 7: 60–61.

Sklar, R. L. (1975), *Corporate Power in an African State: The Political Impact of Multinational Mining Companies in Zambia* (Berkeley: University of California Press).

Smith, Stephen C. (1991), *Industrial Policy in Developing Countries: Reconsidering the Real Sources of Expert-Led Growth* (Washington DC: Economic Policy Institute).

Taylor, S. (1997), 'Open for Business? Business Associations and the State in Zambia', Mimeo. paper prepared for the Business Associations and the State in Africa Project, February 6 (Washington DC: American University).

Temple, Jonathan and Ludger Woessmann (2006) 'Dualism and cross-country growth regressions', *Journal of Economic Growth*, 11/3: 187–228.

Todaro, Michael P. and Smith, Stephen C. (2012) *Economic Development*, 11th ed. (Pearson Education Inc.).

Tornell, A. and Lane, P. (1999), 'The Voracity Effect', *American Economic Review* 89/1: 22–46.

Turok, B. (1989), *Mixed Economy in Focus: Zambia* (London: Institute for African Alternatives).

United Nations Development Program (UNDP) (2001), *Human Development Report: Zambia* (Lusaka).

van de Walle, Nicolas (2001), *African Economies and the Politics of Permanent Crisis, 1979–1999* (Cambridge: Cambridge University Press).

West, T. (1989), 'The Politics of Hope: Zambia's Structural Adjustment Programme, 1985–1987', unpublished PhD dissertation, Yale University.

World Bank (1990), The Long-Term Perspective Study for Sub-Saharan Africa (Vol. 1–4). Washington DC: World Bank.

—— (1991), *World Bank Debt Tables 1990–91* (Washington DC: World Bank).

—— (1984), *Towards Sustained Development in Sub-Saharan Africa* (Washington DC: World Bank).

Zambian Eye (2014), 'Zambia–China bilateral relation and the visit of the Chinese VP', 24 June http://zambianeye.com/archives/21834 accessed on 28 September 2014.

Chapter 8

Employment Creation Through Micro, Small, and Medium Enterprises in Zambia

James Mulenga

1.0 Introduction

Employment creation has become top priority for governments around the world (Grimm 2013). Almost every country is looking for strategies of addressing the problem of unemployment—which has been described by many as a time bomb. World over, micro, small and medium enterprises (MSMEs) have been recognized as offering a viable solution to the problems of unemployment and poverty. According to a study by the International Finance Corporation or IFC (2010: 6), formal small and medium enterprise (SMEs) contribute up to 45 per cent of employment and up to 33 per cent of gross domestic product (GDP) in developing economies. These numbers are significantly higher when taking into account the estimated contribution of SMEs operating in the informal sector. In high-income countries, SMEs contribute nearly 64 per cent to the GDP and 62 per cent to employment (IFC 2010: 6). This signifies that smaller businesses are one of the world's most powerful economic forces, comprising the lion's share of employment and GDP. If well nurtured and backed by appropriate conditions and policies, the MSMEs can constitute key determinants for thriving, globally competitive industries, creating the large numbers of jobs needed to reduce poverty.

As is the case in many parts of the world, 'Micro, Small and Medium Enterprises cut across all sectors of Zambia's economy and provide one of the most prolific sources of employment and wealth creation and are a breeding ground for industries' (MCTI 2009: iv). Like many other governments have done, the government of the Republic of Zambia recognized the potential of MSMEs to economic growth, employment creation, and poverty reduction from as early as the 1980s. From this period, institutions such as the Village Industry Organisation (VIO), Small Industrial Development Organisation (SIDO), Development Bank of Zambia (DBZ), and the Zambia Development Agency (ZDA), among others, have been put in place to grow the sector. Despite this, the sector remained underdeveloped until the 1990s. In the last two decades there has been increasing recognition by politicians, policymakers, and cooperating partners of the significant role that MSMEs play in employment creation and in helping the marginalized and vulnerable groups to meet their basic needs. This recognition is highlighted in the African Entrepreneurship Sub-Saharan Report of 2012 (2012: 12) and the statement by the finance minister, Mr Alexander Chikwanda, on SMEs and employment creation (MoF website 2014).

The problem of unemployment has for some time been one of the major worrying challenges in Zambia as highlighted in the AfroBarometer Survey (2014: 3). According to the Labour Force Survey LFS (2012: 14), unemployment rate stands at 7.8 per cent, which is slightly above the global average of 6.0 per cent and higher than the average for sub-Saharan African (SSA) countries of 7.6 per cent (ILO 2014: 19). The Zambian government is alive to the fact that unemployment is one of the major problems facing the country's economy and has put in place a number of policies and strategies to curb the problem. In a number of policy documents, MSMEs have been seen as the solution to the huge problem of unemployment the country is facing. Examples of such policy documents include Vision 2030, the Zambia Decent Work Country Programme (Z-DWCP) 2007–2011 and 2012–2015, the Sixth National Development Plan (SNDP 2011–2015), the Private Sector Development (PSD) Reform Programme, the Strategy Paper on Industrialization and Job Creation, and the Micro and Small Enterprise Development (MSME) Policy. In view of the foregoing, this chapter sought to examine the contribution of MSMEs to employment creation in Zambia. It assesses the role of MSMEs as an alternative avenue for creating jobs in Zambia. The chapter attempts to answer the following questions:

- Do the MSMEs play a role in employment creation?
- How many jobs do they create?
- What types of jobs are provided/created by MSMEs?
- What factors influence how MSMEs contribute to employment creation?

To answer these questions, this chapter takes a review of the recent literature on MSMEs and employment creation from various countries in general and Zambia in particular. The information used in this chapter is based on a desk analysis of the past MSMEs' experiences in Zambia and other countries. The sources include the International Labour Organization (ILO), Global Entrepreneurship Monitor (GEM) Reports, World Bank, the latest Zambia Business Survey Report (2010), CAFOD/JCTR, Ministry of Commerce - Zambia, Central Statistical Office (CSO) Zambia, UNCTAD, OECD, and a number of peer-reviewed research papers and journals. The chapter explores the importance of MSMEs to the economy as a whole and to employment creation in particular. It further explores the major constraints facing the sector. It is worth noting that most of the studies reviewed exclude microenterprises and informal enterprises in their definitions. For the purpose of this study the acronyms 'SME' and 'MSME' will be used interchangeably.

2.0 Definitions of MSMEs

Micro, small, and medium-sized enterprises are a very heterogeneous group. They are found in a wide array of business activities, different markets and may be in the formal or the informal economy (OECD 2004: 10). There is no standard definition of what constitutes MSMEs. The statistical definitions of MSMEs vary from country to country and from institution to institution. Many countries and international organizations set their own guidelines for defining an MSME, often based on the number of employees, sales, or assets. However, the main criterion for defining small businesses is the number of employees (OECD 2004; EIG 2013; CAFOD 2011; IFC 2013; Ayyagari et al. 2005). This variable is commonly used because it is easy to collect and measure.

Although number of employees is a common measure, there are still variations in the definition of the upper and lower size limit of an MSME. Despite this variance, a large number of sources define an MSME to have a cut-off range of 0–250 employees. This is confirmed by the MSMEs Country Indicator (2010: 2) which observed that 46 out of 136 economies surveyed define MSMEs as those enterprises having up to 250 employees while other countries have different cut-offs.

The variations in the cut-off ranges can be seen by looking at the definitions in various countries. For example, in the United States of America, small businesses that are defined by the number of employees refers to those with fewer than 100 employees, while medium-sized business entities often refers to those with fewer than 500 employees (USITC 2010). In Germany an SME has a limit of 250 employees, while in Belgium it has a limit of 100 employees. In Ghana, small business enterprises are divided into micro, small, and medium enterprises. The microenterprises employ up to 5 employees, small enterprises are those employing between 6 and 29 employees, and medium enterprises employ between 30 and 99 (Agyapong 2010). In Malaysia, microenterprises across all sectors are those with less than 5 full-time employees, while small enterprises are defined as businesses with 5 to 74 employees in the manufacturing sector or 5 to 29 in the service and agricultural sectors and the medium enterprise is regarded as one with 75 to 200 employees and operating in the manufacturing sector while medium enterprises operating in the service sector should have 30 to 75 employees (NSDC 2013). Uganda defines a microenterprise as one employing up to 4 employees, a small enterprise as one employing up to 50 people and a medium one as that employing over 50 employees (UIA 2008: 6).

Moreover, multilateral institutions like the OECD, World Bank, IFC, and AfDB use the number of employees as a defining factor of the size of a business although there is still no consensus on the cut-off range. Table 1 below summarizes the definitions of MSMEs by multilateral institutions (World Bank, IFC) and the European Union.

Table 1: Definitions of Micro, Small, and Medium Enterprises—Global

Firm Size	World Bank Group		World Bank Enterprise Survey	IFC		EU	
	# of Employees	Annual Turnover	# of Employees	# of Employees	Total Assets	# of Employees	Annual Turnover
Micro	0–10	<$100,000	0–4	0–10	<$100,000	0–10	< €2 million
Small	10–49	$100,000 < $3 million	5–19	10–49	$100,000 < $3 million	10–49	< €10 million
Medium	50–299	$3 million < $15 million	20–99	50–299	$3 million < $15 million	50–249	< €50 million
Large	>300		>100	>300			

Source: IFC (2013) and Gagliardi et al. (2013)

In all economies around the world, a significant proportion of micro and, sometimes, small enterprises is found in the informal sector or the shadow economy (OECD 2004). The informal sector is composed of both informal firms and informal employment, the former being defined as all firms that are unregistered with the registration office, municipality, or tax authority, or owners and employers of microenterprises that employ few paid workers (Stein et al. 2012). Informal sector employment is defined as employment where the employed persons are not entitled to paid leave, not entitled to pension, gratuity, and social security, and working in an establishment employing five persons or fewer (CSO-LCMS 2010: 119). The size of the informal sector has important implications on the economy and employment creation as it is associated with low levels of economic development and can induce lower productivity levels and lower-quality jobs (IFC 2013).

Related to the concept of MSMEs is the concept of entrepreneurship, for which there is no universally accepted definition (Chigunta 2014: 14; Bonger 2014: 13). According to the Global Entrepreneurship Monitor (GEM) 1999 report, entrepreneurship is any attempt at new business or new venture creation, such as self-employment, a new business organization, or the expansion of an existing business, by an individual, a team of individuals, or an established business (GEM 1999). Much of the current drive for MSME development is being championed from an entrepreneurship development perspective (Bonger 2014). Most MSMEs owners are in fact entrepreneurs.

3.0 Significance of SMEs to the Economy: Global View

Small and medium-sized enterprises play an important role in the world economy and contribute substantially to income, output, and employment (Edinburg Group 2012: 4). World over, MSMEs are seen as catalysts or enablers of economic growth. Because of their labour-intensive nature, they also play a very important role in employment creation. It is envisaged that with more and more people being employed and earning a living wage, the MSMEs would contribute to poverty reduction. These entities also provide backward and forward linkages to larger businesses.

Economic Growth

Economic growth is one of the main macroeconomic objectives of every country around the world. Every country wants to grow and therefore puts in place various strategies to achieve economic growth. A widely celebrated role of MSMEs is that of their contribution to economic growth. Recent evidence show that one of the most important characteristics of a flourishing and growing economy is a booming small and medium enterprises sector (Ngek et al. 2013). This observation signifies the direct link between SMEs and economic growth. Being a dominant sector in almost every economy, SMEs have a direct effect on GDP through their aggregate output and value addition. In addition they enhance economic growth through their innovation and dynamism. Agyapong (2010) argues that innovation is not only key in developing new products or processes but also in stimulating investment interest in new ventures being created. This argument is in line with the views of the Dalberge report (2012) and Nkwe (2012: 35). Further, Matambanya (2000: 3) argues that on the whole, the economic role of SMEs in Southern African Development Community (SADC) economies can be predicated upon their contribution to the process of resource accumulation and allocation as well as to the structure and dynamics of the economies. SMEs are important for the utilization of local resources which would otherwise remain idle.

In almost all the countries around the world, MSMEs dominate economic activity and they are the majority enterprises in any particular economy. Of the total estimated 365 million to 445 million formal and informal MSMEs in developing countries, only 25 million to 30 million are formal SMEs—with 5 to 250 employees (Stein, Goland, and Schiff 2010). That is, less than 10 per cent of all enterprises are formal SMEs, while more than 90 per cent are micro or informal enterprises (Kushnir, Mirmulstein, and Ramalho 2010), contributing immensely to GDP in almost all the countries around the world. In Europe, according to the Annual Report on European SMEs 2012/2013, the SME sector as a whole delivered 57.6 per cent of the gross value added tax generated by the private, non-financial economy in Europe during 2012. In Asia, a joint study by the Asian Development Bank (ADB) and Organisation for Economic Co-operation and Development (OECD) titled Enhancing Financial Accessibility for SMEs (2014) revealed that MSMEs accounted for more than 90 per cent of total enterprises, contributed to 59.1 per cent of nominal gross domestic product (GDP) in Indonesia in 2012, and MSMEs in Thailand contributed up to 37.0 per cent of nominal GDP in 2012 while in Malaysia it was 32.7 per cent of real GDP in 2012 (ADB 2014). This study covered fourteen countries from the five ADB regions: (i) Kazakhstan (Central Asia); (ii) the People's Republic of China and the Republic of Korea (East Asia); (iii) Bangladesh, India, and Sri Lanka (South Asia); (iv) Cambodia, Indonesia, Malaysia, the Philippines, Thailand, and Vietnam (Southeast Asia); and (v) Papua New Guinea and Solomon Islands (the Pacific). The figures in these various countries show that MSMEs play a significant role in the economic growth of various countries in Asia. In South Africa, the estimated 91 per cent of the formal business entities in South Africa are SMEs and contribute 52–57 per cent to GDP while in Ghana, SMEs are even more prominent in the local economy, representing about 92 per cent of Ghanaian businesses and contributing about 70 per cent to Ghana's GDP (Abor and Quartey 2010 in Edinburg Group 2012). In Zambia, Mphuka (2014) estimates that MSMEs contribute 35 per cent to national turnover (contribution to GDP) per annum.

While SMEs play an important role in Africa's economies (GDP and employment creation), cross-country and micro-level research is not conclusive on the causal link between SMEs and economic development—in other words, growth depends on all type of firms equally, small and big (Kurokawa et al.

2008). Using a sample of sixty-two countries, Beck, Kunt, and Levine (2005: 25) found a strong association between the importance of SMEs and GDP per capita growth. This relationship, however, was not robust to controlling for simultaneity bias. Thus, while a large SME sector is a characteristic of successful economies, the data do not confidently support the conclusions that SMEs exert a causal impact on growth. These results are in agreement with those of Sveinung et al. (2010) who found that the number of SMEs in the economy does not necessarily say much about their contribution to the overall economy. Similarly, a study by Ayyagari et al. (2011) shows that while SMEs employ a large number of people and create more jobs than large firms, their contribution to productivity growth is not as high as that of large firms (Ayyagari et al. 2011).

Despite the conflicting views from literature, the importance of SMEs to economic growth cannot be ignored. This is evidenced from their contribution to GDP in various countries. In almost all the countries around the world, MSMEs dominate economic activity and are the majority enterprises in any particular economy (Kushnir, Mirmulstein, and Ramalho 2010; Gebremeskel 2014). This dominance signifies the important role they play in production, value addition, and exchange of various goods and services. Moreover, SMEs have played a major role in propelling the East Asian economies to their current status as global economic giants, and based on this evidence, many countries around the globe have initiated a range of policies and programmes to promote their growth and expansion (Fongwa et al. 2013). To get a clear picture of their contribution, studies should capture the informal MSMEs.

Employment Creation

An important contribution of small businesses to the national economy is that of employment creation. It is argued that MSMEs are more labour-intensive than large firms and are better placed to create jobs (Mphuka et al. 2014). Worldwide, jobs in SMEs account for more than half of all formal employment (IFC 2013: 11). Several studies (de Kok et al. 2011; Ayyagari et al. 2011) have found that SMEs create more jobs than large firms do, both in developed and developing countries. De Kok, Deijl, and Veldhuis-Van Essen (2013: 36) in their study titled 'Is Small Still Beautiful?' concluded that small is still beautiful. They noted that SME-size class may be considered to be the main job engine, not only for developed countries but also for emerging and developing countries. This is partly because of the positive employment effects of business dynamics (the processes of entry and exit).

According to Ayyagari et al. (2011) globally, small and medium firms (those with less than 250 workers) account for nearly 80 per cent of employment in the formal sector in low-income countries. If the micro and informal firms are included, the employment share of micro, small, and medium enterprises (MSMEs) in developing countries rises to an estimated 90 per cent of all workers (Page 2012). This implies that the share of employment provided by MSMEs is understated when data only on formal enterprises are used. It should be noted that the MSMEs' share of total employment varies from country to country. In Europe, they employ two thirds of total private employment and create about 80 per cent of new jobs (EC 2009: 6). Similarly, in Kenya 90 per cent of all enterprises are SMEs providing employment to over 60 per cent of the total employed population (Katua 2014). SMEs in South Africa are pivotal drivers of job creation, providing approximately 70 per cent of national employment (Dalberg 2014: 1). In Indonesia, the share of SME employees to total employment was 97.2 per cent in 2012 (ADB 2014).

Despite the general view that MSMEs play a significant role in job creation, it should be noted that not all small businesses create employment as some of them have no growth aspirations and most of them die before their fifth birthday. Most of the jobs created can be attributed to the high growth of SMEs also known as gazelles.

Poverty Reduction

Poverty is one of the major problems faced by most developing countries. The development of MSMEs is viewed as one of the sustainable ways of reducing the levels of poverty and improving the quality of life of households through wealth and job creation (MCTI 2009: 1). Matambalya (2000) argues that since production in MSMEs tends to be labour-intensive, they offer more employment opportunities at the given level of capital input and are thus significant for private-sector-driven poverty alleviation. De Kok, Deijl, and

Veldhuis-Van Essen (2013: 6) note that if SMEs are to play a major role in the reduction of poverty by creating new jobs, the creation of new jobs is in itself not sufficient: poverty will only be reduced to the extent that earnings are sufficient to cover basic necessities. However, various studies (de Kok, Deijl, and Veldhuis-Van Essen 2013; de Kok et al. 2011; Page and Soderbom 2015; Lawless, McCann, and Calder 2012; ZBS 2010) have observed that most MSMEs firms pay lower wages than large firms and sometimes do not pay wages at all. Therefore this revelation casts doubt on the ability of the MSMEs to reduce poverty in the developing world. Most of the workers in the informal sector, where most MSMEs are found, can be classified as the working poor because they do not earn enough wages to cover the basic necessities. The best panacea for addressing the scourge of poverty and improving the living standards of citizens is the creation and provision of decent jobs, and stable, secure, and good conditions.

Linkages

MSMEs help to absorb productive resources at all levels of the economy and add to the formation of flexible economic systems in which small and large firms are interlinked (Nkwe 2012). Such linkages are very crucial not only to the growth and sustenance of MSMEs but also to the attraction of foreign investment. As observed by Chisala (2008: 2) investors or large-scale firms, whether foreign or domestic, look at the reliability of the supporting industries before they make their investment decisions. MSMEs' units are supplementary and complementary to large- and medium-scale units as ancillary units. Therefore, the organization of these linkages is crucial both upstream with the suppliers and subcontractors, and downstream with the distribution and marketing channels (Kabaso 2013: 13).

4.0 MSMEs in Zambia

4.1 Definitions of MSMEs in the Zambian Context

In the Zambian context the MSMEs definition has evolved over time from a narrow definition to the current wider definition which captures the micro component and the following variables: total fixed investment, sales turnover, number of employees, and legal status. The current official definition is contained in the Micro, Small and Medium Enterprises Development Policy (2009: 5–6) according to Table 2 below. The capital investment category is delineated by whether the firm is engaged in manufacturing or if it is a trading/ services firm.

Table 2: Definitions of Micro, Small, and Medium Enterprises in Zambia

	Informal	Micro	Small	Medium
Registered with the Registrar of Companies	No	Yes	Yes	Yes
Total investments excluding land and buildings	K50,000	K80,000	K80,000–K200,000	K200,000–K500,000
Investment services and trading	K50,000	K80,000	K150,000	K151,000–K300,000
Turnover	Unspecified	K150,000	K150,000–K250,000	K300,000–K800,000
Employment	1–9 workers	1–10 workers	11–49 workers	50–100 workers

Source: The Micro, Small, and Medium Enterprise Development Policy, April 2009

4.2.1 The Configuration of MSMEs in Zambia

The MSMEs sector in Zambia is characterized by business activities of enterprises engaged in traditional economic sectors, primarily in the production of goods and services for domestic consumption. MSMEs are characterised by use of low technology, rely largely on social networks and inter-firm cooperation, and are oriented towards the local and less affluent segments of the market (MCTI 2009). Most SMEs and especially the micro-sized have the characteristics of household enterprises. They are operated mostly by a single person with or without the help of family members, and usually not licensed with a government agency (Mbuta 2007). Discussed below are the key features of MSMEs in Zambia.

- **Sectoral Distribution**

According to Chisala (2008: 7) the SMEs business activities are concentrated mainly in four sectors, namely manufacturing, trading, services, and mining, which are summarized in Table 3 below. Mphuka (2014) observes that the majority of enterprises engage in agriculture activities followed by wholesale and retail trading. His observations are in line with the ZBS (2010), which shows that most MSMES are in rural areas (81 per cent), and operate in agricultural production (70 per cent) or wholesale/retail trade (21 per cent). On the other hand, there are relatively few manufacturing MSMEs (only about 3 per cent of MSMEs), hotels or catering enterprises (2 per cent), or enterprises in other sectors (4 per cent). Mphuka (2014) however noted that entry of MSMEs is highest in the wholesale and retail trade sector. The GEM (2012) makes similar observations that retail, hotel and restaurant is the dominant sector with 63 per cent of total early-stage entrepreneurial activity (TEA) with the agriculture standing at 11.1 per cent (TEA is the key indicator of GEM and measures the percentage of adults—18 to 64 years—who are in the process of starting or who had just started a business enterprise).

Table 3: Distribution of MSMEs by Sector

Manufacturing	Trading
Textile products	Consumable products
Carpentry and other wood-based business	Industrial products
Light engineering and metal fabrication	Agricultural inputs
Food processing	Agricultural produce
Leather products, handicrafts, and ceramics	Printing
Processing of semi-precious stones	
Essential oils	
Services	**Mining**
Restaurants and food production	Small-scale mining
Hair salons and barbershops	Small-scale quarrying
Passenger and goods transport	
Telecommunication services	

Financial services	
Business centres	
Cleaning services	
Guest houses	
Building and construction	

Source: Chisala (2008: 7)

A noticeable feature from the distribution of the MSMEs is the missing middle phenomenon. 'Missing middle' refers to a shortage of middle-sized growth-oriented SMEs that could make an important contribution to development. This missing middle is generally attributed to hidden and largely inadvertent biases in the economic policies of these countries that militate against the gradual and organic growth of their enterprises. The lack of coherent SME development strategies, which take into account the three dimensions of enterprise evolution (i.e. start-up, survival, and growth) and the different needs of enterprises in their various stages of evolution, is another important contributory factor (UNCTAD 2005: iv). This gap can be filled through the allocation of more capital to SMEs than to large enterprises (LEs). The phenomenon is confirmed by Mphuka (2014) and ZBS (2010), who observe that the most dominant firms are microenterprises accounting for over 90 per cent of the total number of firms in the nation. The small- and medium-sized enterprises together make up only about 7 per cent of enterprises (ZBS 2010).

- **Ownership and characteristics of owners**

In Zambia, about 88 per cent of the entities under the MSMEs category are sole proprietors and the remaining 12 per cent are partnerships (ZBS 2010). Further, most of the MSMEs are owned by domestic investors, and only 0.5 per cent have foreign ownership (Mbuta 2007). In terms of age distribution, the activity of starting a business is more prevalent among those aged between 25 and 35 years and account for 50 per cent, the lowest group is of those aged between 18 and 24 with about 32 per cent (GEM 2012). Similarly, two thirds of MSME owners are aged between 25 and 49 years (ZBS 2010).

A number of studies have confirmed a strong and positive relationship between the level of education of the business owner and the growth performance of the business (ZBS 2010; Bonger 2013; Mbuta 2007). Primary education is one of the basic requirements and higher education is an efficiency enhancer. Among the innovation and entrepreneurship factors is entrepreneurship education and training (GEM 2012). In Zambia, however, the majority of small business owners have low levels of education—68 per cent primary education, 19 per cent secondary education, 11 per cent no formal education (GEM 2012)—explaining the poor performance of the majority of MSMEs. According to Mbuta (2007) and the ZBS (2010), the untrained dominated the microenterprises category while the trained dominated the medium enterprises category.

In terms of gender distribution, by far the vast majority of the MSME owners are male (Bonger 2013). This is also confirmed by Mbuta (2007) and the GEM (2012) report. According to the ZBS (2010), just under a third of MSMEs were headed by women, suggesting that about 1.3 million MSMEs in Zambia are headed by women. Many factors explain this phenomenon and these include stereotypes, cultural norms, and perceptions that impede on women to a greater extent than on men in obtaining credit, productive inputs, information, and other public services, which limit their entry into entrepreneurship (ZBS 2010). Their role in society is viewed to be that of child-rearing and home management (GEM 2012). Mbuta (2007) further argues that women-run enterprises tend to be smaller than for their male counterparts.

- **Nature of jobs**

The ZBS (2010) report highlights that most of the entities in this group are micro, survivalists with largely no paid up employees (mostly family members) and about one fifth have any employees that are paid up. Further, most of these enterprises are not formally registered and are called informal MSMEs. Before 2007, this category of enterprises accounted for almost 96 per cent of total firms in Zambia (Mbuta 2007). Informal enterprises are associated with informal jobs which cannot be classified as decent; the workers in these entities are actually regarded as working poor as they do not earn sufficient incomes to afford the basic necessities of life.

- **Categorisation**

The ZBS (2010) further survey categorises the MSMEs into three main segments using the Business Facilitation Measure (BFM analysis); these include:

I.   The BFM 1–4, which is made up of tiny, owner operator 'survivalists' that make up 77 per cent of the MSME market,

II. The BFM 5 includes 13 per cent of MSMEs and represents a sweet spot of high-potential enterprises that are not being provided with appropriate services. Although markedly more urban than their lower BFM counterparts, 60 per cent of BFM 5 businesses are in rural areas, and the last group,

III. The BFM 6–8, which comprises 16 per cent of MSMEs. This group is more urbanised, have better educated owners, and add value to their businesses.

The importance of the above classification is that it can help government and other stakeholders to come up with policies, strategies and support services to target specific segments of MSMEs. This would enhance the impact of services offered to MSMEs.

- **Productivity**

Both labour and capital productivity are very low in Zambia (ZBS 2010). Value added per dollar of capital is only 23 cents, which is very low in comparison to Tanzania, Uganda, and Kenya. The productivity of capital stock in Tanzania is almost twice as high while that in Uganda is three times higher (World Bank 2004: 42). Workers in manufacturing microenterprises produce about one ninth of the amount of their counterparts in large firms and one twelfth as much as in those in retail trade (ZBS 2010). The factors contributing to low productivity include, among others, informality, low education level, lack of management skills, lack of access to both soft and hard infrastructure, obsolete technology, and capital deficiency (ZBS 2010; Mbuta 2007; Bonger 2013; World Bank 2004). Low productivity amongst MSMEs in Zambia, has affected competitiveness, and this has in turn impacted aspects such as access to finance and ability to pay for services such as BDS (Bonger 2014:

19). Capital finance is therefore required if many microenterprises have to contribute significantly to economic growth and development (Mphuka et al. 2014).

- **Death rate and birth rate**

Being small is not of itself a virtue; it can be a symptom of failure and many small businesses are set up out of desperation as survival strategies (CAFOD 2011). Therefore, not all small businesses will be viable. According to the Global Entrepreneurship Monitor 2012 report, the death (closure) rate for Zambian enterprises stood at 20 per cent. This is higher than the average death rate for sub-Saharan Africa which stood at 16 per cent (GEM 2012). There are a number of reasons for discontinuing a business, most notable of which are: non-profitability (23 per cent), lack of capital (26 per cent), personal reasons (20 per cent), another job or business opportunity (11 per cent), and incident (11 per cent).

GEM recognizes that entrepreneurs have different motivations for starting businesses and classifies them into necessity-driven and opportunity-driven motives. Necessity-driven businesses arise when an individual needs a source of income, but has no other job options and is thus pushed into entrepreneurship because there is no choice. In this case, there is little or no analysis and/or preparation before starting the venture is done. The opportunity-driven motive is where an individual decides to pursue an opportunity, even if there are other employment options available. The entrepreneur may have done thorough analysis and planning before embarking on this new venture.

Necessity-driven is known to be prone to mortality and dismal patterns of productivity (Mphuka et al. 2014). According to the GEM 2012, Zambia has one of the highest business start-up rates in the world, standing at 43 per cent. Despite the high incidence of business start-ups, the number of established business owners (those in existence for more than three and a half years) is extremely low and stands at 4 per cent. This scenario stifles the potential contribution of MSMEs to job creation and begs for policy intervention to address the factors that affect and perpetuate enterprise failure. According to Mphuka et al. (2014), more MSMEs enter the wholesale and trade sectors than the agricultural sector despite the fact that the likelihood of surviving in the agricultural sector is higher than it is in the wholesale and retail trade sector.

4.3 Overview of the MSMEs in Zambia

It was not until the Third National Development Plan or TNDP (1979–1983) that the government recognized the important role that small-scale enterprises could play in industrial development. As observed in the Third National Development Plan:

> Small-scale industries, whether in the manufacturing sector, non-manufacturing sector or informal sector, generate more jobs per unit of investment than large firms. Their indirect employment impact is also greater because they draw more on domestic sources as against the larger capital-intensive firms, which rely heavily on imported inputs. In addition, small-scale industries are instrumental in encouraging local entrepreneurship. In view of the manifold advantages of small-scale industries and the appropriateness of the technology involved, establishment of these industries, particularly in the rural areas, was one of the priority objectives of TNDP. (GRZ 1979)

With this realization, the government started putting in place systems to coordinate the activities of MSMEs. Marketing and finance were identified as the two major challenges faced by small-scale industries, and government resolved to provide support in these areas. For this purpose, the government through the Small Industries Development (SID) Act of 1981 established the Small Industries Development Organisation (SIDO) in 1981, as the apex government institution that was given the task of fostering the development of small enterprises. Furthermore, other non-governmental institutions such as the Village Industry Services (VIS) and the Small Enterprise Promotion Limited (SIPL) were established to promote small-scale enterprises. Notwithstanding the support services put in place to support the MSMEs, emphasis was placed on collective enterprise rather than on individual ownership. This situation made it difficult for private enterprise to thrive and impeded entrepreneurship.

In 1991, after the election of a new government, there was a shift in economic policy from the commandist type to the market-driven economy. The new government fully implemented the World Bank–assisted Structural Adjustment Programme (SAP). Under the SAP, most of the state-owned enterprises (SOEs) were privatized and at the same time the economy was opened up to foreign competition. Most of the businesses closed down as a result of the intense competition and lack of protectionist policies. Consequently, many people were thrown into the streets and unemployment levels increased. In addition, subsidies on education and health services were removed and the majority of the people could not afford these services anymore. These developments prompted the unemployed Zambians to find alternative means of survival by engaging in self-employment activities mostly in the informal sector (Page 2012).

To encourage private enterprise, the new government undertook to encourage local governments to review their infrastructure services and licensing regulations so as to support small enterprises, legislation to support growth of the sector, decentralize business registration, and remove any impediments to the operations of the sector by formulating the MSMEs Development Policy. However, as noted by Chisala (2009: 8) these policies remained mere public pronouncements, with little effort to implement them. Moreover, most of these policies tended to favour the large-scale enterprises at the expense of the intended MSMEs.

In 1996, the government realised that the MSMEs were still facing challenges despite the various support institutions and mechanisms put in place. Because of this, the government decided to revise the SID Act with the Small Enterprises Development (SED) Act (MCTI 2009: 2). One of the major salient features of the SED Act was the provision of incentives to MSMEs to enhance their development. Most of the incentives were, however, never implemented partly because the systems for their implementation were never put in place (MCTI 2009: 2).

During the Fifth National Development Plan or FNDP (2006–2010), there was renewed interest in MSMEs as they were seen to constitute a critical component to the attainment of the broader national development goal of reducing unemployment, increasing participation of citizens in economic development, equitable wealth distribution, and value addition to local raw materials.

A number of developments took place during the period of the Fifth National Development Plan, which included:

- The establishment of the Zambia Development Agency and the MSME Development Policy. The Zambia Development Agency (ZDA) was established under the ZDA Act No. 11 of 2006. The SME Division at ZDA was charged with the responsibility of coordinating, promoting, and nurturing MSMEs in Zambia.
- The MSME Development Policy was developed in 2009 and was meant to provide the much-needed guidance and direction on all activities and development efforts related to MSMEs. The policy has seen the implementation of the BDS voucher (in 2008) and business incubators, among others.
- The enactment of the Citizenship Economic Empowerment Act in 2006 which saw the establishment of the Citizenship Economic Empowerment Commission. The commission was mandated to promote broad-based and equitable economic empowerment of citizens that are or have been marginalized or disadvantaged and whose access to economic resources has been constrained due to factors like race, sex, education, education background, status, and disability.
- National Credit Guarantee Scheme for Micro, Small and Medium Enterprises (MSMEs)
- The National Long Term Vision 2030 (Vision 2030) is Zambia's first ever written long-term plan, expressing Zambians' aspirations by the year 2030. It articulates possible long-term alternative development policy scenarios at different points which would contribute to the attainment of the desirable social economic indicators by the year 2030. The vision recognizes the importance of MSMEs towards economic growth, employment creation and poverty reduction.

Under the Sixth National Development Plan or SNDP (2011–2015), additional measures have been put in place to promote the growth of MSMEs:

The SNDP aims at increasing participation of indigenous Zambians in the manufacturing sector, promote entrepreneurship training and development at all levels of the education system, encourage innovation and technological skills development and on-farm agro-processing training, facilitate access to market opportunities and business development services, the establishment of business incubation centres and linking them to industrial parks, the establishment of business industrial clusters, facilitate business linkages between MSMEs and multinational corporations, create the Trade and Investment Fund targeted at MSMEs, and facilitate the establishment of Small Aggregation Initiative joint ventures among MSMEs. (GRZ 2011: 136)

Private Sector Initiatives

In addition to government support, the private sector and the donors have also initiated activities aimed at the development of the MSME sector. The private sector and donors that have initiated such activities include the Zambia Chamber of Small and Medium Business Associations (ZCSMBA), International Labour Organization, and USAID. These efforts though a good step in the right direction need to be coordinated, monitored, and channelled towards achievement of set national goals.

4.4 MSMEs and Employment in Zambia

The importance of MSMEs to employment creation in Zambia has been highlighted in various government policy documents. These include the Vision 2030, Zambia Decent Work Country Programme (Z-DWCP) 2007–2011 and 2012–2015, the Sixth National Development Plan (SNDP 2011–2015), the Private Sector Development (PSD) Reform Programme, the Strategy Paper on Industrialization and Job Creation, and the Micro and Small Enterprise Development (MSME) Policy. As stated earlier, the government of Zambia and cooperating partners attach great importance to MSMEs as evidenced in various policy documents. MSMEs are important in employment creation and improving the living standards of the vulnerable.

The Role of MSMEs in Employment Creation

To analyse the job creation ability of MSMEs, data is needed on new entrants in each category of enterprises, their survival and growth, numbers of business failures and job creation potential (de Kok et al. 2011). This important piece of information is provided by the Global Entrepreneurship Monitor country studies. As highlighted above, Zambia has a high incidence of business start-ups (43 per cent) and a high business closure rate (20 per cent) resulting in only 4 per cent of the newly born enterprises surviving after three and a half years and these rarely grow into bigger enterprises. This development implies that the contribution of MSMEs to employment creation is therefore hampered by the high discontinuance rates whereby a large number of jobs are created and then destroyed, even though the net number of these jobs remains quite small.

Despite the high death rate among MSMEs, the GEM report of 2012 established that 18 per cent of small businesses are run by individual entrepreneurs, while the remaining 82 per cent of businesses generate employment. Of those businesses that generate employment, the large majority are micro businesses (70 per cent) employing 1 to 5 people, while small businesses (employing 6 to 19 employees) account for 10 per cent. Only 2 per cent of businesses employ more than 20 persons (medium businesses). These findings are highly consistent with Shah (2012) and Mbuta (2007: 14). In the same vein, Shah (2012: 6) highlights that the MSME universe is comprised of 4.68 million workers which represents about 90 per cent of the workforce in Zambia. These findings are consistent with the 2012 Finscope MSMEs Survey report for Malawi which observed that there were 4.5 million MSMEs in Zambia owned by 3.9 million owners (FinScope 2012: 28). More than one third of firms are run by an owner alone; family firms comprise another one third of the total, 21 per cent of firms use a mix of paid and unpaid workers, while only 12 per cent of firms in the MSME sector operate with at least one paid employee, and no unpaid workers (Shah 2012). The fact that MSMEs employ the largest number of the workers implies that they play an important role in sustaining the lives of the owners as well as those employed in these entities.

It should be noted however that creating jobs through entrepreneurship is not a numbers game but about encouraging high-quality, high-growth companies to be founded (CAFOD 2011). It is these high-growth MSMEs that have the capability of bridging the missing middle and creating jobs. In terms of growth prospects, 81 per cent of the enterprises expect to create between one to five jobs in a period of five years (GEM 2012). It is these entities that need support to help realise their aspirations and ensure that they create formal and decent jobs.

Nature of Jobs Created by MSMEs

Most of the MSMEs in Zambia, particularly the micro and small enterprises, operate in the informal sector (Shah 2012; ZBS 2010; Mbuta 2007). The informal sector is marked by acute decent work deficits and a disproportionate share of the working poor (ILO 2014: 1). According to the Labour Force Survey (2012), 88.7 per cent of the labour force is in informal employment. In this category, most of the employees have little or no qualification or education and earn very low wages which are not sufficient to cover the basic needs of life. More than 90 per cent of firms are self-employed and not paying market wages to anyone (Shah 2012: 11). The low cash remuneration or payment in kind are indicators of poor working conditions. In addition, the levels of job stability and security and compliance to health standards are very low. Therefore, despite the fact that MSMEs provide a greater number of jobs in Zambia, these jobs cannot be classified as decent or quality jobs and as such bear little effect on addressing the scourge of poverty (ZCSMBA 2012). Hence, the majority of the people working in the MSMEs sector can be classified as working poor.

Challenges Facing MSMEs in Zambia

Firms of different sizes rank obstacles differently (Kushnir, Mirmulstein, and Ramalho 2010). Constraints that affect all types of businesses in general include access to hard infrastructure such as energy, transport, and water, soft infrastructure such as education or financial services as well as stable and predictable political and macroeconomic environment. Small firms are disproportionately handicapped by lack of finance but receive stronger boost in growth than large firms if financing is provided (Dalberg 2011: 10). Finance is regarded as the lifeblood of any business enterprise, without which business entities cannot start up, survive, or grow. Various studies rate inadequate access to finance as a major obstacle to the growth of business enterprises (World

Bank ES 2008; ZBS 2010; Stein 2010; Mbuta 2007; Chongo and Montgomery 2014). Moreover, non-availability of capital remains one of the major factors that perpetuate the missing middle phenomenon.

In addition to the above, lack of market for products ranks highly among the challenges faced by small businesses (Chongo and Montgomery 2014: 9). It is difficult for most of them to find customers for their products, especially customers who will pay a fair price. Another notable obstacle limiting the capacity of MSMEs is access to timely, current, relevant, and adequate information for informed decision-making (Banda et al. 2004: 99). Most of the MSMEs do not have access to relevant information to enhance their business performance. Regulatory burden and the red-tapism involved in registering a business is yet another inhibiting factor in the growth and productivity of MSMEs (IFC 2013: 36). It is also recognized that low-quality institutional framework hampers SMEs from growing into medium-sized and large companies, causing the 'missing middle' phenomenon (de Kok, Deijl, and Veldhuis-Van Essen 2013: 37). Existence of the missing middle implies missing jobs. The poor attitudes and work culture of Zambians, lack of financial discipline, focus, management skills, and self-confidence serve as further impediments to the growth of the MSMEs and subsequently to job creation (Chisala 2008). Most of these constraints arise because most of the MSMEs fall into the informal category, therefore cannot access the various services that would enhance their growth.

5.0 Conclusion and Recommendations

From the literature reviewed, the chapter concludes that MSMEs play a critical role in the area of employment creation in Zambia, although much more needs to be done to ensure that they contribute meaningfully to the creation of quality and decent jobs. The chapter suggests a holistic approach to addressing the challenges and needs of the MSMEs which includes first setting the preconditions to encourage new entrants and second putting in place strategies and policies that would nurture and enhance the growth of the existing ones.

The chapter has examined the significance of MSMEs for employment creation on the Zambian economy and world over. The problem of unemployment has been described by many as a time bomb which needs urgent attention. MSMEs have been recognized by various studies as a solution for tackling the problem of unemployment both in the developed world and the developing world. The study has also highlighted the fact that MSMEs play a crucial role in the economy not only through employment creation but also through their contribution to economic growth, poverty reduction, backward and forward linkages in industries, among others. In Zambia, the study found that 88 per cent of those in employment are employed by MSMEs, signifying their importance in the economy. However, despite the fact that MSMEs are the greatest employers in Zambia, most of the jobs they provide are informal and cannot be classified as decent. Therefore, there is a need to support this sector to ensure that they create formal and decent jobs which can contribute to the attainment of the Vision 2030.

Notwithstanding the significant contribution to employment and the economy as a whole, the MSMEs still face manifold challenges which impede them from contributing to their full potential. In order to address these challenges, meaningful strategies are required in order to unlock the full potential of MSMEs. This paper suggests the following as possible solutions:

- Setting specific preconditions for the growth of MSMEs such as favourable policies relating to physical and social infrastructure in order to encourage entry and organic growth of MSMEs enterprises and to create a stable political and macroeconomic/business environment. In addition, government should resolve market failures in financial markets, to enhance accessibility to finance as well as to reduce the cost of borrowing. The financial sector should also come up with tailored financial services for the MSMEs such as the venture capital funds and mutual funds. There is a need for the focus to shift from the available collateral in the business to the viability of the business and the ability of the entrepreneur. Such preconditions would also address the factors that perpetuate the 'missing middle' phenomenon, hence addressing the missing jobs.
- Formulating MSME development strategies and policies which take into account the three dimensions of enterprise evolution (i.e. start-up, survival, and growth) and the different needs of enterprises in their

various stages of evolution. The policies should not just target small and medium enterprises but also microenterprises because this is a significantly larger and potentially viable group. Moreover, high-growth MSMEs should be identified and given special support. This can be done by using the Business Facilitation Measure and information from the GEM studies.

- Formulating policies that would enable the MSMEs to establish backward and forward linkages with large-scale enterprises. The success of the Malaysian automobile industry, which was once regarded as an infant industry, lies in the linkages that were developed with the Bumiputra (indigenous) firms, mainly the SMEs (Chisala 2008: 22). The existence of MSMEs would also encourage the formation of large businesses.

- Provision of certain incentives such as tax exemptions, grants, business development services and others in order to encourage business formalization and hence create formal employment and decent employment.

- Developing and nurturing entrepreneurial skills—learning institutions and families should instil in children the values of work, hard work, ingenuity, self-reliance, and entrepreneurship. Entrepreneurship can also be raised through capacity building and awareness-raising programmes about the importance of MSMEs to individuals and the economy. The programmes should also focus on shifting the mindsets from survivalist entrepreneur to strategic enterprise.

- Formulation of strategies which would encourage women and youth participation in the MSMEs sector by taking into account the special needs of women and youths.

- Conducting research and collecting more data, particularly on the nature and characteristics of the informal sector and the microenterprises, would help in making informed decisions for the policymakers.

- Growth and increases in productivity require a policy focus on the potential obstacles, which range from lack of access to finance, the need for business training and literacy programs, as well as addressing other constraints such as taxes, regulations, and corruption, which are the focus of an active research agenda.

References

ADB (2014), ADB–OECD Study on Enhancing Financial Accessibility for SMEs (Philippines: Asian Development Bank).

Agyapong, P. (2010), Micro, Small and Medium Enterprises' Activities, Income Level and Poverty Reduction in Ghana—A Synthesis of Related Literature, *International Journal of Business and Management* 5/12.

Ayyagari, M., Beck, T., and Demirgüç-Kunt, A. (2005), *Small and Medium Enterprises across the Globe.*

—— Demirgüç-Kunt, A., and Maksimovic, V. (2011), 'Small vs. Young Firms Across the World', Policy Research Working Paper 5631, (Washington, DC: World Bank).

—— Beck, T., and Demirgüç-Kunt, A. (2003), Small and Medium Enterprises across the Globe: A New Database, World Bank Policy Research Working Paper 3127, World Bank. http://elibrary.worldbank.org/doi/pdf/10.1596/1813-9450-3127 Accessed on 16/02/14.

—— Beck, T., and Demirgüç-Kunt, A. (2011), Small vs. Young Firms across the World Contribution to Employment, Job Creation, and Growth, Policy Research Working Paper 5631, World Bank, accessed on 20/04/15

Banda, C., Mutula, S. M. and Grand, B. (2004), Information Needs Assessment for Small Scale Business Community in Zambia: Case Study of Chisokone Market, Kitwe, Malaysian Journal of Library & Information Science, 9/2: 95–108, December.

Beck, T., Demirguc-Kunt, A., and Levine, R. (2005), *SMEs, Growth, and Poverty-Cross-Country Evidence* (Washington, DC: World Bank). http://siteresources.worldbank.org/INTFR/Resources/SMEs Growth and Poverty Cross Country Evidence.pdf accessed 12/01/15.

Bonger, T. and Chileshe, C. (2014), The State of Business Practices and the Impact of BDS on MSMEs in Lusaka and Kabwe, Zambia, ICBE-RF Research Report No. 76/13 (Dakar).

CAFOD (2011), 'Thinking small: Why poor producers and small business owners may hold the key to a sustainable recovery', a CAFOD Policy Discussion Paper (London, UK).

Cheelo, C. et al. (2012), *Zambia Case Study On Economic Transformation African Centre For Economic Transformation* (Zambia).

Chigunta, F. (2014), 'Entrepreneurship In Zambia, Challenges and Opportunities', *Corporate Face* magazine (Zambia).

Chisala, C. (2008), *Unlocking the Potential of Zambian Micro, Small and Medium Enterprises 'Learning from the international best practices—the Southeast Asian Experience'*, IDE Discussion Paper No. 134, Japan http://www.ide.go.jp/English/Publish/Download/Dp/134.html

Chongo, G. and Montgomery, S. (2014), 'A Pro-poor Business Enabling Environment: The case of Zambia', The Jesuit Centre for Theological Reflection (JCTR) and the Catholic Agency for Overseas Development (CAFOD), Zambia http://www.jctr.org.zm/images/stories/pdf/Documents/A Pro Poor BEE - Zambia case study.pdf accessed 20/10/14.

CSO (2010), 'Living Conditions Monitoring Survey Report' Central Statistical Office, Lusaka, Zambia.

—— (2013), *Preliminary Results of the 2012 Labour Force Survey*, Republic of Zambia, Lusaka

Dalberge (2014), 'The Small and Medium Enterprise (SME) Catalyst for Growth Initiative in South Africa', (South Africa: JP Morgan).

—— (2011), Report on Support to SMEs in Developing Countries Through Financial Intermediaries, Geneva.

de Kok, J. et al. (2011), *Do SMEs create more and better jobs?* EIM Business & Policy Research, Zoetermeer, Netherlands, http://ec.europa.eu/enterprise/policies/sme/facts-figures-analysis/performance-review/files/supporting-documents/2012/do-smes-create-more-and-better-jobs en.pdf accessed 19/10/14.

—— Deijl, C., and Veldhuis-Van Essen, C. (2013), *Is Small Still Beautiful? Literature Review of Recent Empirical Evidence on the Contribution of SMEs to Employment Creation*, German Ministry for Economic Cooperation and Development and International Labour Organization, Department of Statistics, Geneva. http://www.ilo.org/wcmsp5/groups/public/---ed emp/---emp ent/---ifp seed/documents/publication/wcms 216909. pdf accessed 19/10/14.

EC (2009), Think Small First—Considering SME interests in policy-making including the application of an 'SME Test', Report of the Expert Group European Commission, Brussels, Belgium.

Edinburgh Group (2012), 'Growing the global economy through SMEs', http://www.edinburgh-group.org/media/2776/edinburgh group research growing the global economy through smes.pdf accessed 16/02/15.

Finmark Trust (2012), FinScope MSME Survey Malawi 2012, South Africa.

Fongwa, S. and Fohtung, G. N. (2013), Impact of Investment Climate Reforms on Growth and Development of SMES: Comparisons from South Africa, Nigeria and Cameroon, ICBE policy brief, Trust Africa, Dakar–Fann, Senegal.

Gagliardi, D. et al. (2013), Annual Report on European SMEs 2013—A Partial and Fragile Recovery, (Brussels, Belgium: European Commission).

Gebremeskel, Y. (2014), 'Determinants of Profit Variability among Micro and Small Enterprises (MSEs) in Zambia', *International Journal of Economics and Finance* vol. 6.

GEM (1999), Global Entrepreneurship Monitor, Executive Report, Kaufman Centre for Entrepreneurial Leadership.

—— (2012) African Entrepreneurship, Sub-Saharan Africa Report, IDRC.

—— (2013), Global Entrepreneurship Monitor 2013 Report: Fifteen Years of Assessing Entrepreneurship across the Globe.

Grimm, M. (2013), 'Interventions for employment creation in micro, small and medium-sized enterprises in low- and middle-income countries: A systematic review', University of Passau, Erasmus University Rotterdam, IZA *http://www.iza.org/conference files/worldb2013/grimm m4353.pdf* accessed 19/10/14.

GRZ (1966), *First National Development Plan, 1966–1971*, Office of National Planning and Development, Lusaka.

—— (1972), *Second National Development Plan, 1972–1976*, Office of National Planning and Development, Lusaka.

—— (1979), *Third National Development Plan, 1979–1983*, Office of National Planning and Development, Lusaka.

—— (1988), *Fourth National Development Plan, 1988–1993*, Office of National Planning and Development, Lusaka.

—— (2006), *Fifth National Development Plan (FNDP): 2006–2010*, Ministry of Finance.

—— (2011), *Sixth National Development Plan (SNDP): 2011–2015*, Ministry of Finance.

IEG (2013), 'Evaluation of the World Bank Group's Targeted Support for Small and Medium Enterprises'.

IFC (2010), *Scaling Up SME Access to Financial Services in the Developing World*, International Finance Corporation-World Bank, http://www.ifc.org/wps/wcm/connect/bd1b060049585ef29e5abf19583b6d16/ScalingUp.pdf?MOD=AJPERES accessed 18/10/14.

—— (2013), 'IFC Jobs Study: Assessing Private Sector Contributions to Job Creation and Poverty Reduction', International Finance Corporation–UKAID.

ILO (2014) *Transitioning from the Informal to the Formal Economy*, Report V(1), International Labour Office, Geneva, Switzerland, http://www.ilo.org/wcmsp5/groups/public/---ed_norm/---relconf/documents/meetingdocument/wcms_218128.pdf accessed 13/01/15.

Kabaso, Nicholas (2013), 'The Voice of the Private Sector', *The ZACCI Journal*, 2/2 (Lusaka).

Katua, N. T. (2014), 'The Role of SMEs in Employment Creation and Economic Growth in Selected Countries', *International Journal of Education and Research* 2/12.

Kurokawa, K., Tembo, F., and Velde, D. W. (2008), Donor support to private sector development in sub-Saharan Africa, Understanding the Japanese OVOP programme, Working Paper 290, Japan International Cooperation Agency, Japan.

Kushnir, K., Mirmulstein, M. L., and Ramalho, R. (2010), 'Micro, Small and Medium Enterprises Country Indicators', IFC/World Bank.

Matambalya, F. A. S. T. (2000), *Profile of Small and Medium Scale Enterprises (SMEs) in the SADC Economies*, Center for Development Research, Bonn University, Bonn, http://www.wipo.int/export/sites/www/about-ip/en/studies/pdf/study_f_matambalya.pdf accessed 11/11/14.

Mbuta, W. S. (2007), Small and Medium Enterprises Survey 2003–2004, MCTI, Lusaka.

MCTI (2004), *Private Sector Development Reform Programme*, Lusaka: Government of the Republic of Zambia, Ministry of Commerce, Trade, and Industry.

—— (2009), *The Micro, Small and Medium Enterprises Development Policy of 2009*, Republic of Zambia, Lusaka.

MoF (Ministry of Finance) www.mofn.zm accessed on 11/12/2014.

Mphuka, C., Simumba, J., and Banda, B. (2014), Switching Costs, Relationship Banking and MSMEs Formal Bank Credit in Zambia, ZIPAR, Working Paper No. 20.

Mujenja, F. (2014), 'The Employment Status of Zambians: Official Definitions versus Citizen Perceptions', Afrobarometer Briefing Paper No. 135.

Ngek, N. B. and Smit, A. A. (2013), 'Will promoting more typical SME start-ups increase job creation in South Africa?', *African Journal of Business Management* 7/31.

Nkwe, N. (2012), 'Role of SMES in Botswana', *American International Journal of Contemporary Research*, 2/8 *http://www.aijcrnet.com/journals/ Vol 2 No 8 August 2012/3.pdf* accessed 19/10/14.

NSDC (2013), Guideline for New SME Definition, National SME Development Council, Malaysia.

Ntundo, C. (2009), *Developing a Diversified Zambian Economy Small Business Opportunities for Zambian Entrepreneurs*, CilTax International Trade Compliance Expert, Winnipeg, Manitoba, Canada, http://www.ciltax. com/docs/sbdofze.pdf accessed 15/11/14.

OECD (2004), *Promoting Entrepreneurship and Innovative SMEs in a Global Economy: Towards a More Responsible and Inclusive Globalisation*, (Istanbul, Turkey: OECD Publications) http://www.oecd.org/cfe/smes/31919590. pdf accessed 18/10/14.

Page, J. (2012), 'Aid, the Private Sector and Structural Transformation in Africa', UNU-WIDER Working Paper, 2012/21 (Helsinki: UNU-WIDER).

—— and Söderbom, M. (2012), 'Is Small Beautiful? Small Enterprise, Aid and Employment in Africa', UNU-WIDER Working Paper, 2012/94 (Helsinki: UNU-WIDER).

Shah, M. K. (2011), 'The informal Sector in Zambia: Should it disappear? Can it disappear?' Working Paper 12/0425, International Growth Centre, London, http://bit.ly/1kPmzxW accessed 19/10/14.

Stein, P., Goland, T., and Schiff, R. (2010), 'Two trillion and counting: Assessing the credit gap for micro, small, and medium-size enterprises in the developing world', IFC and McKinsey & Company, http://www.ifc. org/ifcext/media.nsf/Content IFC_McKinsey_SMEs

Stein, P., Ardic, O. P., and Holmes, M. (2013), 'Closing the Credit Gap for Formal and Informal Micro, Small, and Medium Enterprises', IFC Advisory Services, Washington DC.

Sveinung, Fjose, et al. (2010), *SMEs and growth in sub-Saharan Africa: Identifying SME roles and obstacles to SME growth*, MENON-publication no. 14/2010, Oslo, http://www.norfund.no/getfile.php/Documents/ Homepage/Reports%20and%20presentations/Studies%20for%20 Norfund/SME%20and%20growth%20MENON%20%5BFINAL%5D. pdf accessed 19/10/14.

UIA (2008), Small and Medium Enterprises (SME) Business Guide, Uganda Investment Authority, Uganda.

UNCTAD (1997a), *Growing Micro and Small Enterprises in LDCs The "missing middle" in LDCs: why micro and small enterprises are not growing*, UNCTAD/ITE/TEB/5, Geneva, http://unctad.org/en/docs/poitetebd5. en.pdf accessed 18/10/14.

USITC (2010), Small and Medium-Sized Enterprises: Characteristics and Performance, USITC Publication 4189, United States International Trade Commission Washington DC.

Wiggins and Higgins (2008), 'Pro-poor growth and development: Linking economic growth and poverty reduction', ODI Briefing Paper 33, ODI, London. http://bit.ly/1pdPh0U accessed 18/10/14.

World Bank (2004), Zambia, An Assessment of the Investment Climate, Report No. 29741-ZM, World Bank/RPED.

—— (2008), Country Assistance Strategy for the Republic of Zambia, Country Management Unit, Zambia.

—— (2013), 'Zambia's Job Challenge, Realities on the Ground', Zambia Economic Brief, Issue 2, Africa Region, Lusaka (Washington, DC 20433, USA) http://bit.ly/1kPrW08 accessed 20/10/14.

ZBS (2010), *The profile and productivity of Zambian businesses*, Lusaka: FinMark Trust, ZBF, PSD, WB.

ZCSMBA (2012), *Small Business and Employment*, Lusaka, Zambia http:// www.zcsmba.org/index.php? accessed 08/02/15.

—— (2012), *Strategic Plan 2009–2013*, Lusaka, Zambia http://www.zcsmba. org/index.php? accessed 08/02/15.

Chapter 9

The Evolution of Marketing Systems in Zambia

Maimbolwa Sepo Imasiku

Introduction

A marketing system is a community of buyers, sellers and consumers trading in a good or service. Trading has been taking place in Zambia from way back, before it even became Zambia. In the past, before the white settlers brought money as a medium of exchange, communities used the barter system.

This chapter will focus on how marketing has evolved in Zambia, from pre-independence to the present day. How was the end user able to acquire products pre-independence and how was it done after independence, and now fifty years down the line, what has changed? Is the change for better or for worse? We have seen from previous chapters the political history of Zambia and how Zambia got its independence. Zambia's independence meant a lot in terms of changing the way consumers' needs were satisfied.

Generally, marketing is 'an organization function and a set of processes for creating, communicating, and delivering value to customers, and for managing customer relationships in ways that benefit the organization and its stake-holders' (American Marketing Association as quoted by Czinkota and Ronkainen 2007). Therefore marketing may mean one thing to one person/ business and something else to another. One business entity may be concerned about the price at which a product is being sold, whilst another may not necessarily care about price but availability/delivery of the product.

Depending on where one goes to either buy a product or service, customer services vary from business to business and town to town. Most multinational corporations (MNCs) have brought in more efficient and effective ways to serve customers. However, most local businesses have been slow in adopting new ways to serve customers. Others have adapted and changed to suit changing times and changing needs of consumers. A walk along Cairo Road in Lusaka clearly tells you that something has changed. An easy example is the services provided by different business houses now, compared to the late '70s, '80s and '90s.

Marketing in Zambia before independence

Before independence, dating back as far as 1947, the British who settled in Southern and Central Africa traded with each other and goods came mainly from Britain and later from India as well (*The Northern News* 1947). Basic food commodities were either grown/made locally but clothing items, shoes and jewellery came from Great Britain. Traders advertised their products through the local newspapers and customers were notified of any major shipments due to arrive.

The major challenge for black Northern Rhodesians was that they were only allowed to purchase basic goods which they did through shop windows. All shops were either owned by whites or Indians and this trend continued until in the late 1950s. All butcheries and bakeries were owned by whites, no black African was allowed to own or trade in this line of business. From an early stage, as Northern Rhodesians we experienced stigmatisation; it was not an option for a black person to own or buy certain goods/services. Modern marketing trends only existed for whites at the time. Black Africans were never considered; they were never the target audience of any marketing strategies that were carried out.

By 1961 there was a bit of change in the way marketing of goods was conducted. The target market began to include natives, as they were called. This was a great opportunity for businesses as the market had suddenly grown for their products. And so, slowly things began to change as the natives were now able to shop from inside shops; however, they were still not allowed to enter butcheries. They could only buy from windows as buying from inside was reserved for the white settlers (author's observation from the *African Eagle* advertisements prior to 1961 and after 1961).

At this stage some products were only targeted at the natives whilst other products were targeted at the white settlers. Still segregation and stigmatisation continued. An example of such a product is Chibuku (an opaque beer brewed from a mixture of sorghum and maize). Chibuku was targeted at natives whilst fine spirits like gin, whisky, and Castle lager were targeted at the white settlers (*The African Eagle* 1961). By this time there was not much variety in terms of the different types of products available; therefore, advertisements were meant to alert the public about the availability of a product and its use, rather than advertising for competitive purposes as is currently the case the world over.

Promotional strategies seemed to be aimed at informing and educating the public, other than competitive type of advertising. By this time, a number of Northern Rhodesians had been to school and were able to read at least in their native language. Papers like the *African Eagle* would carry advertisements in Bemba for certain products that would mostly only be used by the natives, for example, storm lanterns used as torches which were used with paraffin. As most of the natives lived in non-electrified homes it was new technology at the time, from the Koloboi, which was previously used to light up a room (*The African Eagle* 1961). A Koloboi is a modern-day kerosene lamp.

By this time not a lot of research had been carried out to ascertain the benefits of certain products. For example, sugar was advertised as a healthy energy boosting product which everyone could consume on a daily basis. Health risks associated with products were not an issue as products like cigarettes were widely advertised to the public. Opportunities came in terms of new products being introduced onto the Northern Rhodesian market and this came with opportunities for trade. The new products also began to make life easier in terms of product variety and advancement.

The independent Zambian customer after 1964

At independence in 1964, Dr Kaunda insisted that all Zambians should be allowed to enter shops to buy the products they needed. By this time Zambia was actively trading with Salisbury, Bulawayo, and Johannesburg. A lot of new products became accessible and Zambia began to produce a lot of consumer products locally. This brought about variety for the Zambian consumer in certain products, for example, soaps, drinks, spreads for bread, and also clothes and shoes. As Zambians preferred to consume British-made products to locally made products, this trend continued.

The *Central African Mail* (1965) ran a competition 'why we must buy Zambian' and this competition was won by a Mr Kasapatu, then a student at Munali Secondary School. He argued that if Zambia is setting up industries and people are continuously buying foreign products, this would not help the local industries as they will not get any support. Therefore jobs would be lost as the industries would be forced to close down.

By 1966 Zambians were becoming more and more educated and being exposed to the outside world. Dr Kaunda's government was one to be reckoned with, and producers of products knew this was a country they could surely sell their products in. Some stayed until the '80s and some closed down and left after independence. One of the British companies that stayed after independence was KEES, which was later taken over by the government and turned into Zambia Consumer Buying Corporation (ZCBC). This provided an opportunity for the country to manage operations of parastatals, thereby securing employment opportunities for citizens.

Airlines marketed not only the destinations but how comfortable and convenient their airplanes were. Airlines today focus more on the cost and destination; emphasis is no longer about convenience. Strategies were more inclined to use illustrations, advertisements were more detailed, and a lot of shops sold goods on credit. By 1965 most advertisements were also placed in local languages.

In 1964, Zambia Airways, a subsidiary of Central African Airways, broke away to be operated on its own as the first Zambian airline. This flew to Salisbury,

Blantyre, Lagos, and Johannesburg, amongst some of its destinations, and locally it flew to Fort Jameson (now Chipata). Zambia Airways began to increase its fleet and increased its destinations including the UK, USA, Italy, Nairobi, Monrovia, Bombay, and Amsterdam, to name a few. The world was now becoming smaller for the once-British colony. This obviously meant that trade with these nations was present because people travelled to and from these destinations.

Fifty years later

Fifty years down the line, a walk through major supermarkets shows evidence of foreign products on the shelves compared to Zambian products. This continues to be a challenge for businesses trying to manufacture and market local products. The country continues to import basic products such as orange juice, cooking oil, and milk products which can be locally manufactured. Could this be because of the country's past? Were Zambians spoilt by the British settlers who brought their good-quality products and have not been weaned from wanting only the best products? Could this be the cause of Zambia's limping manufacturing sector?

This can all be changed by citizens supporting local products. What does this mean? This means buying locally grown fruit and vegetables, buying locally manufactured products first, over foreign products. By preferring local over foreign products, Zambians will be promoting local industries which the country needs in order to create more and more jobs. The more a country manufactures, the less it imports for its consumption and the less the demand for foreign currencies such as the US dollar. It is therefore imperative that Zambians support local producers and manufacturers and demand that shops carry more Zambian products than foreign products. The opportunities in the manufacturing industry are endless for Zambia.

The Modern Marketing System

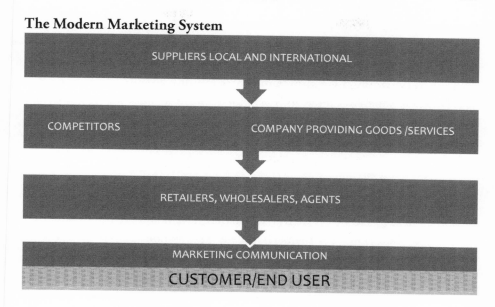

From the diagram above, it can be observed that both the company and competitors, whether through an intermediary, aim to serve the end user. Modern marketing systems lessen the channels a product takes to get to an end user. Therefore customers expect to get quality products and services. However, there are some unseen aspects of people's lives that have highly influenced the way they do business and respond to certain products/services.

Modern marketing systems demand that products and services be advertised with a certain sense of ethics. Therefore certain products have to tell the user the potential harmful effects that may arise from the consumption of a particular product, for example, the consumption of alcohol or cigarettes. It is normal to find a disclosure telling the consumer the side effects or after-effects of consuming a particular product. There are certain aspects of marketing that have changed the way marketing is currently done in Zambia.

The modernised Zambian customer service

A customer can be a client or a person paying for a good or service. Customer service 'describes the assistance provided to help a customer with the purchase or use of a product' (Bearden, Ingram, and LaForge 2004: 194).

How is a customer relevant to your organization? A paying customer brings money into the business. A paying customer provides employment. Most Zambian businesses treat a customer like they are doing the customer a favour. This is a very common trend in Zambia. Are Zambians used to the colonial days of when a native wanted to buy from a shop they had to line up by the window and the whites would pretend they did not need the natives' money by pretending that they were doing the natives a favour? Who is favouring who here? Businesses need to get their facts right as society is now in the twenty-first century, not in the colonial days. But because as Zambians, this is the life the nation's grandparents knew and these are the lives the people have grown up with, they tend to accept being treated like they have no choice but to buy from the window. This is still a challenge in the marketing industry getting customer service right the first time. Bartley and Minor (1999) noted that it is cardinal for businesses to be strategic in the way they market their businesses because serving a customer is not about chance but about getting it right with your customer.

It is not uncommon to walk into a bank and not get greeted by a bank teller or a customer assistant and sometimes they actually look like they are being forced to be there. What are businesses doing about this? Changing the way our customers/clients are being looked after is very important in the business world. Sometimes you walk into a Zambian boutique and you can walk out with not even a hallo. Are people still being forced to buy from windows? Is the way people were treated in the colonial days still rubbing off on them or are they never going to stop trading through the windows?

Organizations need to train their employees on the importance of customer service. Banks in overseas countries literally fight for customers because there are so many banks and outlets they scramble for customers. In Zambia, some towns still have one or two banks at most; others have none. Therefore customers in such areas are unable to demand for better services. Not having options should not mean poor services. That does not mean that these customers do not deserve better service than what they get because the business is enjoying being a monopoly. Regardless of how many banks or any other businesses there are in an area, residents deserve the best quality service because they are paying customers and hence deserve the best service.

How far has Zambia come in terms of customer service? It is impressive to see, especially, some of the foreign companies/franchises (locally) emphasizing on customer service. Certain business houses when visited clearly greet customers with a smile and offer to help. Proper customer service involves being there for your customer and serving them to their satisfaction. Whether the customer buys today or tomorrow should not be the reason why they should be given substandard service. Customers are there to keep the business going, hence they need to be given the attention they deserve.

There is need for staff who deal directly with customers (front-line staff) to be continuously trained in proper customer service procedures, grooming, and dealing with aggressive customers. This can help Zambia as a country to move forward in terms of customer service levels and continue to improve the way we do business in general. Staff cannot be inducted once and left to figure the rest on their own; they need guidance and continuous reminders through training on how the customers should be treated. Fifty years down the line, customers will always be *king*. The fact that a customer gets their money to pay for a product/service means that your business can keep going simply because the customer is paying for it.

E-marketing and the Zambian buyer

Traditional marketing has seen an evolution in the way marketing is done. Sellers are now using more advanced ways in which to approach the buyer with a means to making a sale. E-marketing is simply marketing done using the Internet as a medium of communication. The use of this form of medium is meant to attract the buyer to view the product, buy the product, and get quick feedback (Egan 2007: 297).

Chivhanga (2000), in a study about the increased number of Internet users in Africa, found that Zambia was one of those countries with a very high number of Internet users. This goes to show that the country is truly embracing the use of online media.

Technology has brought with it social media. Any organization that has not embraced social media is lagging behind as social media has been embraced by a lot of Zambians both in the formal and informal sectors. Most Zambians young and old are using Facebook, Twitter, Whatsapp messaging, and Viber, to mention a few, at least once a day, meaning that social media has become a platform for selling and promoting of goods and services and also as a sales medium.

The use of the Internet gives users two very important features:

1. It enables genuine two-way communication
2. It enables information resources to be acquired or processed with relatively equal ease, (Sandelands 1997: 7).

Countless numbers of products are now sold online via youths who have decided to take advantage of social media to sell goods and services. The more likes a page gets, the more exposure about the goods or services being offered. Social media is proving to be one of the cheapest ways to market products and a lot of Zambians local and abroad have embraced it. E-business continues to provide countless opportunities for the youth who have decided to make a job out of selling products via social media. The challenge with social media is that some unscrupulous individuals decide to use it as a way in which to steal money from unsuspecting individuals. This creates a challenge because not everyone might be willing to buy online for fear of being swindled.

In summary, fifty years down the road, Zambians are able to buy goods and pay for services all over the world by the click of a button. One does not have to travel the world; one may do this via the Internet. With the coming of fibre in Zambia, and the improvement of Internet connectivity, the Zambian customer will continue to enjoy buying of goods and services by the click of a button. Eventually, Zambian customers shall be able to pay for most services online, reducing the number of queues at ATMs, in banks, and utility bill payment outlets.

Culture and lifestyles

Trompenaars and Hampden-Turner (2003: 20) look at the meaning of culture in the following way: 'a fish only discovers its need for water when it is no longer in it. A community's culture is like water to a fish. It sustains the community. A community lives and breathes through it. What one culture may regard as essential, a certain level of material wealth for example, may not be so vital to other cultures.' Zambians need to understand what is vital to them as Zambians and push towards becoming self-sufficient in all aspects of our lives.

When one looks around the country, it is clear that Zambians have changed the way they live in all aspects of their lives. They have learnt to find ways to sustain themselves and this has influenced the way they do business, the way manufacturers are advertising their products, and the people's consumption of these products. As a country, the people of Zambia have grown up with strong norms and values which resulted from beliefs passed on from their forefathers. Each society develops certain norms, values, and behaviours which influence how its people solve certain dilemmas. Like other societies, Zambians have been influenced by how their great-grandparents and parents lived fifty-plus years ago. Culture also influences our day-to-day purchase decisions (Lado, Martínez-Ros, and Valenzuela 2004: 574).

The main staple food was nshima as far back as pre-independence and is still the staple food to date. With the integration of other cultures into the society, Zambians have learnt to embrace other foods from other cultures. These foods include rice, bread, potatoes, noodles, pasta and naan bread or chapatti. Zambians have embraced other cultures and foods coming from other parts of the world. The opportunity here is the acceptance of other foods, relieving pressure and the need to purchase mealie meal, which is and has been a staple food for years.

Nshima still remains the dominant staple food consumed in every Zambian household. The integration of other cultures in the Zambian culture has caused a change in Lifestyles.

Zambians are learning the importance of owning a home. This has increased the need for certain things, including land and building materials. The need for land has meant that people are now building further and further away from CBDs (central business districts). By doing so, people are requiring transport to get to work and pick up schoolchildren and for just general errands. This has therefore increased the need for motor vehicles. The building of homes has created a boom in the construction industry, thus creating jobs.

The need for motor vehicles has evolved from the buying of brand-new cars in the 1970s and 1980s to buying second-hand cars in the late 1990s to date. The increase in the number of car companies selling brand-new cars symbolises that there is a niche for brand-new cars. Therefore the Zambian consumer has seen the importance of owning a brand-new car and has reverted to buying brand new. This simply shows that Zambians have more choices now to enhance their lifestyles than before. This has created an opportunity for new vehicle manufacturers to set up industries in Zambia, even though the cost of a brand-new car is one to be reckoned with, as the majority of Zambians are still unable to afford a brand-new car.

Culture and lifestyle has played a huge role in changing the Zambian consumers' behaviour. Zambian consumers want more variety. Their shopping baskets no longer contain bare necessities. They have learnt to consume already prepared meals, therefore creating an increase in takeaways, restaurants, and other eateries. This in turn has created more business opportunities and employment in a sector that was small in the olden days.

Globalisation and its impact on the Zambian consumer

The change in lifestyle has been necessitated by globalisation. Owning a car has become as easy as buying a mobile phone (except more costly) and car sellers in Japan, Singapore, and now the UK are realizing the importance of not just the African market but the Zambian market in particular. This is evident from the foreign advertisements, collaborations, and outlets being run by foreign car companies in Zambia.

Ball, McCulloch, Frantz, Geringer, and Minor (2004: 9) define globalization as 'the international integration of goods, technology, labour, and capital; that is, firms implement global strategies that link and coordinate their international activities on a worldwide basis'. When you look at globalisation, it has made the world smaller; you can be in one part of the world today and in another part of the world tomorrow. Manufacturers of technological products have learnt the concept very fast by identifying Africa as the next big thing in terms of a marketplace for their products.

The Zambian consumer now has the latest gadgets, latest cars, and other technology. Producers of these products have identified that Africa has become a big user and consumer of the latest products and gadgets. *African Business Review* (2014) carried an article where Samsung targeted Africa as a potential growth market. International companies are quickly setting up base in African markets for they have seen the potential of these markets. This can be observed by the number of outlets selling international products. Companies such as Samsung have set up several outlets in the country to give the Zambian buyer an original product.

The number of Zambians working in foreign countries has increased over the last fifty years. It is probably at its highest now than ever before. The opportunity here is lessening the number of job seekers in the economy. Zambians can be found in all five continents working and living in these foreign countries. Zambia has enjoyed cordial relationships with all its neighbours and other foreign countries and so most are able to travel with or without visas depending on the entry requirements. This has ensured a continued flow of various resources from different countries all over the world (Deacon et al. 2011). This in turn has exposed a lot of Zambians to different living standards which has also been a contributing factor to the change in needs of the Zambian consumer. The major challenge in human capital migration is the brain drain on the country where citizens emigrate from. The fact that Zambia has a number of professors, doctors, and other qualified specialists living and working abroad creates a gap in the economy.

The world has become small for the Zambian consumers as they are able to have access to products from anywhere in the world, be it goods, capital, or labour. Trade has continued to soar with other countries. Below is a diagram showing the total trade balance. It is evident that Zambia is heading in the right direction in terms of importing less and exporting more. The only sad part is that the majority of the exports are coming from the mining industry (ECZ 2001). This means that the country is not producing enough of other products to export. This has been covered in other chapters of this book.

Zambia's import/export statistics

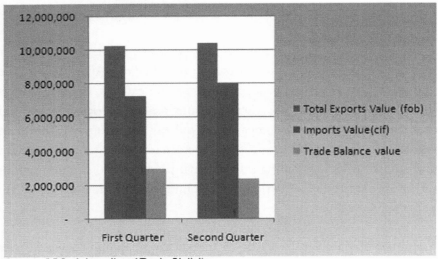

Source: CSO - International Trade Statistics

Diagram 1

A simple way in which consumption affects production

Production is described by Perreault and McCarthy (2003: 5) as 'actually making goods or performing services'. Therefore production goes hand in hand with marketing. Without the production of a product there will be no product. Businesses produce a product, promote it, and sell it to the consumer. Without the paying customer there is no business.

A Zambian will rarely walk into a supermarket and ask the fruit and vegetable attendant where the bananas being sold are coming from. Why is this important? By buying locally produced products, the money spent stays within the Zambian borders and therefore makes the Zambian kwacha stronger. Why do Zambians buy imported bananas, do they cost less than locally grown ones? Are they cheaper than locally grown ones? If so, what is making imported products cost less than locally grown bananas? Are Zambian bananas overpriced? By buying foreign-grown bananas, the money does not stay within the country's borders but is sent back to pay the grower in a foreign country. This example applies to any other product that can either be manufactured or grown locally in Zambia.

Most people tend to argue that locally produced goods are not well packaged or presented. The cry here is for Zambian growers and producers to learn to present their products to make them more appealing to the buyer. Emphasizing on quality and grading products so that quality is maintained is an important part of production. By emphasizing on the quality, local products will be able to compete with foreign products any day, therefore keeping the money within the borders of Zambia. The challenge the country faces is the lack of manufacturing companies, whether small scale or large, manufacturing products needed in the economy. The key word here is 'needed'. The idea behind production is to produce a product that is needed, one that will solve the customers' problem. It is not a matter of producing just about anything.

After attaining fifty years of independence, Zambia is still not producing enough to cater for the entire population. She is still importing products which can either be manufactured locally or at least be grown locally. It is therefore to the country's advantage to embrace locally produced products in order to boost the national economy. Local producers must also learn how foreign manufacturers present their products so that the Zambian consumer can appreciate local products. That being said, the Zambian paying customer must be encouraged to buy locally made produce, in order to support local businesses. Zambia needs to identify opportunities in this sector, make the most of it by carrying out marketing research and identifying the needs of the people.

The Evolution of the Zambian Consumer

Consumer behaviour 'can be defined as the mental and emotional processes and the physical activities that people engage in when they select, purchase, use, and dispose of products or services to satisfy particular needs and desires' (Bearden, Ingram, and LaForge 2004: 75). Consumers the world over are now becoming more health-conscious than they were fifty years ago. This applies to Zambians who have also seen the downside of being overweight or obese.

The Zambian consumer has become more conscious about what they eat. For example, roller meal is no longer the poor man's mealie meal. A lot of households just prefer to eat roller meal because it is healthier. Even brown bread (wholemeal bread) is now on demand as more and more citizens are learning the importance of eating less refined foods. Most consumers are also substituting sugar with honey as honey is a natural product compared to sugar, which is refined.

A healthy nation is a wealthy nation. The fact that a healthy nation puts less strain on the health system of a country is why governments should always be focused on citizens leading healthy lives. Therefore selecting healthy choices should be a must in this day and age.

It goes without saying that sometimes we get irritated by how phone companies can send to or call you even up to five times per day with promotional information. It can be both stressful and annoying to hear your phone ring and run off to pick it up only to notice it is your phone provider calling you about the latest promotional campaign. In most cases people will either leave it on, pay no attention to what is being said, or simply cancel the call. Phone providers have realized that most Zambians are quite tolerant and therefore will complain about something but will never get up to actually act upon it. The Zambian consumer is a tolerant consumer and sometimes may not be aware that they have rights as a paying customer.

How many times have you purchased a wrong product and simply just used as it is and not gone back to the shop to complain about it? Shops overseas will resolve an issue with an angry customer quickly, because of stiff competition; even if a customer is wrong, they will solve the problem to avoid making a scene. Marketing in Zambia is somehow not taken seriously by a lot of organizations. Marketing encompasses a lot of aspects, including selling and sales, customer service, marketing research, and aftersales service. How many companies will sell a highly priced product and actually call a customer to ask them how they feel about their purchase and whether or not they are happy with their purchase? Very few. Most of them will not even bother. Businesses should always remember that the customer is king, and if they are not treated well today, they may not come back tomorrow.

Making a courtesy call is vital in ensuring a lasting relationship with your customers. Calling your customers to find out from them how your product is performing not only shows the customer that you care about them. This will ensure customers recommend your business to friends and relatives. The Zambian consumer is the best marketing tool any organization can ever use to market its product. Word of mouth has proven to be one of the best ways to market a product and still is the world's cheapest marketing tool to date.

It is still a challenge for most businesses to identify the needs of the Zambian consumer. The Zambian consumer has evolved over the years, hence their needs have changed, their purchasing power has changed, and their lifestyles have changed. As a marketer, one has to identify the various needs and provide goods and services suitable for those needs.

Conclusion

In conclusion, it is evident that there has been change in the marketing systems in Zambia. This has been made possible by global and regional integration, technological advancement, and trade with other countries as well as a shift in Zambian culture. Zambians are renowned for being very tolerant to foreigners and in most cases easily adopt other people's cultures changing the way they live.

Organizations have seen the importance of marketing due to high levels of competition they experience because the Zambian customer now has a choice. The Zambian consumer does not have to queue for cooking oil anymore because there are so many varieties, both local and foreign. A Zambian consumer finally has a choice.

For most of the country, change is needed in creating more Zambian-owned manufacturing businesses and giving these businesses support by buying locally made products. This in turn may increase the people's standard of living by creating more job opportunities.

Businesses ought to change their marketing styles to suit world standards, including advertising, customer service, customer relationship management, and brand quality.

To sum up, this chapter reviewed marketing before independence, after independence, and examined the strides marketing has made over the last fifty years. The chapter also looked at some of the different aspects that have enabled this evolution and some of the challenges and opportunities brought about with time. It has also shown that marketing systems in Zambia will not remain the same but will keep changing because of globalization, technology, and integration with other countries.

References

African Business Review (2014), Available http://africanbusinessreview.co.za/marketing/1294/Samsung-target-Africa-expansion retrieved 15 August 2014.

Ball, D. A. et al. (2004), *International Business: The Challenge of Global Competition* 9th edition (New York: McGraw Hill Irwin).

Bartley, D. L, and, Minor, M. S. (1999), 'Small business consulting on a shoestring: an example from Zambia', *CrossCultural Management: An International Journal*, 6/2: 3–7 (Online, Emerald).

Bearden, W. O., Ingram, T. N., and LaForge, R. W. (2004), *Marketing Principles and Perspectives* (New York: McGraw Hill Irwin).

Chivhanga, B. M. (2000), 'An evaluation of the impact of the Internet in Africa', *Aslib Proceedings,* 52/10: 373–383, (Online, Emerald).

COMESA (2014), Available http://about.comesa.int/index.php?option=com_content&view=section&id=12&Itemid=112 retrieved 21 August 2014.

Czinkota, M. R. and Ronkainen, I. A. (2007), *International Marketing*, 8th edition (Mason, USA: Thompson South-Western).

Deacon, B., De Lombaerde, P., Macovei, M. C., and Schröder, S. (2011), 'Globalisation and the emerging regional governance of labour rights', *International Journal of Manpower* 32/3: 334–365, (Online, Emerald).

ECZ (2001), *State of Environment in Zambia 2000*, (Lusaka, Zambia).

Egan, J. (2007), *Marketing Communications* (London: Thompson Learning).

Greenley, G. E. (1989), 'An Understanding of Marketing Strategy' *European Journal of Marketing*, 23/8: 45–5, (Online, Emerald).

Hill, M. E., McGinnis, J., and Cromartie, J. (2007), 'A marketing paradox', *Marketing Intelligence & Planning*, 25/7: 652–661 (Online, Emerald).

Hrbek, I. (1992), *Africa from the seventh to the eleventh century* (Musica Britannica, James Currey Publishers).

Lado, N., Martínez-Ros, E., and Valenzuela, A. (2004), 'Identifying successful marketing strategies by export regional destination', *International Marketing Review*, 21/6: 573–597 (Online, Emerald).

MCTI (2014), Available http://www.mcti.gov.zm/index.php/statistics 2014 retrieved 24 August 2014.

Perreault, W. D. and McCarthy, E. J. (2003), *Essentials of Marketing* (New York: McGraw Hill Irwin).

Sandelands, E. (1997), 'Utilizing the Internet for marketing success', *Pricing Strategy and Practice*, 5/1: 7–12 (Online, Emerald).

The African Eagle (1961), 30 May.

The Central African Mail (1965), issue no. 256, 15 January.

The Central African Mail (1965), 'Why must we buy Zambian', issue no. 255, 8 January.

The Northern News (1947), 2 January.

Trompenaars, F. and Hamped-Turner, C. (2003). *Riding the waves of culture: Understanding cultural diversity in business*, 2nd edition (Maine, USA: Nicholas Brealy Publishing).

WTO (2014), Available http://www.wto.org/english/thewto e/countries e/zambia e.htm retrieved 22 August 2014.

Chapter 10

Harnessing Library and Information Services for Economic and National Development in Zambia: a Fifty-Year Retrospective Overview
Paul Zulu

1. Introduction

Library and information services can be harnessed and utilised to enhance economic and national development in Zambia. Libraries and other information institutions all over the world aim at providing opportunities to all people for free and equitable access to information and knowledge available in different formats and media. They play a significant role in bridging the information and knowledge divide between the poor and the rich. They are inclusive in that they build bridges between individuals at both the local and the global levels of knowledge (Krolak 2005). The IFLA/UNESCO Public Library Manifesto (1994) states that freedom, prosperity, and the development of society and of individuals are fundamental human values which can only be attained through the ability of well-informed citizens to exercise their democratic rights and to play an active role in society. Constructive participation, good governance, and the development of democracy depend on satisfactory education and unlimited access to knowledge, thought, culture, and information. Access to information and knowledge is essential in enabling people make rational decisions in their day-to-day efforts aimed at uplifting their socio-economic status.

Following Zambia's celebration of fifty years political independence on 24 October 2014, it is important to reflect on the contribution library and information services have made in promoting access to information and knowledge. To ensure the realisation of an informed citizenry, libraries and other information institutions should aim at providing relevant, timely, and up-to-date services and products. Their advocacy, marketing strategies, and collections should be diverse and all-inclusive to cater for different social, economic, cultural, and educational backgrounds of people. This chapter provides a brief historical development of library and information services in Zambia and attempts to demonstrate how these services have performed fifty years since independence. Special reference is given to the development of public libraries among other types for it is upon them that the obligation of serving the public lies.

Currently, there is a lot of information and knowledge being generated every day through modern technologies, yet many people in Zambia still do not access this information and knowledge. Furthermore, public library and information service providers also seem not to have done much to provide their services for the benefit of all.

2. Library and information services defined

The *Harrod's Librarians' Glossary and Reference Book* (1984: 458) defines library service as 'the facilities provided by a library for the use of books and the dissemination of information'. The glossary (1984: 379) also defines information service respectively as 'a service provided by or for a special library which draws attention to information possessed in the library or information department in anticipation of demand; which is done by preparing and circulating news sheets, literature surveys, reading lists, abstracts, particulars of articles in current periodicals, etc. which it is anticipated will be of interest to potential users of the service'. In this chapter, the terms 'library service' and 'information service' are combined and used simultaneously as 'library and information services' to refer to facilities and activities in a library or any other information institution provided and undertaken for the dissemination of information and knowledge.

A library is a collection or group of collections of books and/or other print or non-print materials including computer programs or data files, music, films, photographs, and other visual non-book materials organized and maintained for reading, consultation, study, research, etc. (*Online Dictionary for Library and Information Science* 2014; *Harrod's Librarians' Glossary* 1984). It is an organized collection of sources of information and knowledge for either reference or borrowing. A modern library may be a building or virtual space or both which provides physical or digital access to information and knowledge (*New Encyclopaedia Britannica* 2003). Based on the foregoing definitions, this chapter shall consider a library as being any systematic collection of information and knowledge resources, available in either a building or virtual space, or both, capable of providing timely access to information and knowledge in print or electronic form. The purpose of providing library and information services is primarily aimed at linking information users to the library collections to ensure a constant flow of information and knowledge that would benefit the users as soon as it is generated. Thus libraries and other information institutions need to develop measures to enhance levels of user awareness of the services they provide.

Traditionally, most library and information services were responsive rather than proactive, designed to guide the users to the materials and locations where the information they sought was likely to be found. The staff in the libraries would sit and wait to be approached by the users before they could act to render a service. In the present times, however, new trends are dynamic and are not only confined to lending or inter-lending of materials but also to identifying users and their needs, thus ensuring that all citizens are able to access and use the information they need all the time it is available (Krolak 2005; Fourie 2001; Ryynänen 1999). For a library or any other information institution to provide a satisfactory service, it is important that it develops a strategy that takes into account both traditional and new trends of information delivery.

In this vein, libraries and other information institutions need to embrace a combination of both print and electronic resources which are now referred to as 'hybrid approach to digital libraries' (Eastwood and Thompson 2001). This approach is a practical and workable solution that can address the information needs of the traditional users who still depend on print materials, as well as the millennial generation who are addicted to using new technologies such as the Internet and other electronic resources (Chanakira and Shiweda 2014).

Common services in libraries and information institutions which collectively address both traditional and new trends include the following:

(i) **Lending services**

Lending services are offered by libraries and other information institutions to enable users to borrow materials from the library. In public libraries, lending services are usually free, and members of the public are welcome to join membership to enable them to borrow books, CDs, DVDs, magazines, and other information materials. The members of staff in the library are always available to provide expert guidance to the users as they select the materials they seek to borrow. Lending services are important as they bring the users closer to the library and build relationships that allow free exchange of views and ideas expressing the information needs of the users. Lending services also include the lending of materials between libraries. Materials which are not available in one library and are stocked in another may be borrowed by the seeking library on behalf of the users.

(ii) **Reference services**

Reference services are all the functions performed by a trained librarian employed in the reference section of a library to meet the information needs of patrons (*Online Dictionary for Library and Information Science* 2014). The reference section of a library is responsible for providing users with direction to library resources, giving advice on library collections and services, and offering a variety of information from different sources. The reference section of a library should have a rich collection of bibliographic and reference tools such as bibliographies, indexes, abstracts, dictionaries, encyclopedias, thesauri, etc. Referral services are also offered by the reference section. Referral services are transactions in which users with information needs are directed to reputable persons or agencies outside the library, better qualified to offer specific information which could be free or at a fee. In some libraries an index of referral agencies or resources with contact information is maintained. Reference services are important to library users for they are intended to assist the users to make maximum use of the available information resources a library can offer. The members of staff at the reference section are intermediaries between the users and library materials and thus should be well-qualified librarians who should be friendly as they guide users to the resources and interpret what is contained in them.

(iii) Indexing and abstracting services

Indexing and abstracting services in libraries and information institutions entail the preparation of indexes, abstracts, and bibliographies to assist users to easily locate the information they need. Indexing and abstracting services are aimed at enabling users to locate information in a document, and also have essential facts of theories or opinions presented in it. Indexing and abstracting services augment cataloguing services, which in contrast are aimed at assisting users to locate specific documents in a collection of library resources. These services are important because they allow good bibliographic control over publications, making it possible to minimize the challenges of retrieval and management of information and knowledge in a constantly increasing information environment. Indexes and bibliographies enable quick retrieval of information, while abstracts enable quick perusal of the information contents of documents. All important disciplines of knowledge may have one or more indexes, bibliographies, or abstracts which a library or information institution can prepare. Libraries need to stock these in order to retrieve information quickly and keep track of what information is being or has been published in various disciplines of knowledge.

(iv) Current awareness services

Current awareness services (CAS) are provided usually in form of publications in order to keep the users abreast with the latest developments in their disciplines. The term is sometimes used synonymously with selective dissemination of information (SDI), another form of CAS which targets a specific user group, for instance by subject, profession, gender, etc. CAS aim at promptly informing the users about the availability of new information as soon as it has been published in primary sources and before it is absorbed into comprehensive secondary sources. According to Fourie (2001), CAS were at first based on manual methods such as accession lists and indexing or abstracting bulletins, but now various CAS based on the use of computers such as SDI service are also in use. CAS are offered through different methods which include the following:

- Book displays
- Accession lists
- Preparation and distribution of CAS bulletins
- SDI service
- Circulation of contents page
- Telephoning individuals
- E-mails to individuals
- Publications on the Internet.

(v) Electronic services

Electronic services involve management of resources with a computer; the ability to link the information provider with the seeker via electronic channels; the ability for staff to intervene in the electronic transaction when requested by the information seeker; and the ability to store, organize, and transmit information to the information seeker via electronic channels (Eastwood and Thompson 2001). Electronic services are in other words services offered using computer and telecommunication facilities such as provision of access to OPACs, electronic databases, electronic information resources on the Internet and other networks or media. Electronic services have made transactions in libraries and other information institutions easy, faster, and more reliable than before. For instance, data can be stored on strong highly resistant compact discs, CD-ROM, with a lot of capacity to contain data of more than 300,000 pages when printed on A4-size paper. Moreover, online search, also an electronic service, makes it possible for information located on a host computer in a distant place to be accessed through a computer in another place.

(vi) **Photocopying services**

Reproduction of library materials is necessary in order to expedite the transmission of knowledge and to improve library resources and services. Copying and duplicating documents and other materials is usually done for purposes of permanent preservation. The processes of copying and duplicating documents and other materials are sometimes collectively referred to as reprography (*Harrod's Librarians' Glossary* 1984). Users are also allowed to photocopy small parts of texts from publications without violating copyright regulations. Many countries world over conform to the principles of the Berne Convention (1979) for the protection of literary and artistic works. Under this protocol, copying for research and reference purposes or sharing of publications among information institutions may not amount to violation of copyright rules as long as this is done in accordance with the stipulations of individual countries' copyright laws.

3. Role of library and information services in society

Libraries and other information institutions play a fundamental role in society as they take the information, knowledge, and heritage of the past and present, and lay them down for the future. They add value to the information, knowledge, and heritage by cataloguing, classifying, and describing them to assure timely access by the users (Reding 2005). In simple terms it can be stated that the role of public libraries is to acquire, organize, and disseminate information. Libraries arrange and organize their information materials in a systematic manner to enable timely retrieval of information and knowledge to satisfy user requests, demands, and needs. In the words of Clarke (2001: 72), 'a traditional assumption in the design of information and retrieval systems is that users will want to find all and only relevant items, in response to a particular query. Similarly, with alerting services, only wanted items should be routed through to the user'.

Libraries are a vital part of the community: they provide a neutral space for community engagement; they share vital information relevant to the development of the community; they provide a space for recreational activities such as play grounds, art festival, and cultural games for the community's children and the youth; and they promote community culture by collecting and preserving cultural information as well as providing a space for cultural activities (Radijeng 2013). Libraries are also agents of social change and development, and hence they can be utilized by government to attain its various activities, programmes, and above all economic and national development. The Australian Library and Information Association (ALIA 2009) states that public libraries create a vibrant, productive local economy; assist people to improve their life chances and businesses to become more competitive; and help people develop the skills companies need.

A vibrant library and information service can be said to be an integral part and engine of a country's general progress without which the future of the people and their destinies could be bleak. According to Nyangoni (1981) a library and information service is one of the most efficient means of acquiring, organizing, and making available, on a democratic basis, information and educational materials. This is particularly applicable to a nation the population of which has had little or no formal educational opportunity, for these are the people who, to a large degree, must make their new governments work and must understand and control the great social and technological changes taking place so rapidly. Library and information services are aimed at enabling people to have free access to information and knowledge; they can assist the less privileged in society to keep abreast with information of national interest by providing current and up-to-date information. Information is a strategic asset that must be managed in order to help organizations improve their productivity, competitiveness, and overall performance, hence the need for current, reliable indications of the types of information required by knowledge workers in organizations (Sykes 2001).

Libraries and information services provide opportunities and a conducive atmosphere for people of all age groups as well as the less privileged in society to access information and knowledge either free of charge or at affordable charges. Public libraries for instance are places where both children and adults are free to mingle with friends and peers to discuss the information and knowledge derived from books or other resources and share a common understanding. ALIA (2009) states that public libraries add an extra dimension to education and learning throughout childhood and teenage years, reaching reluctant learners as well as star pupils and giving them a better start in life. In fact universal elementary education and public libraries are complementary to one another so much that without the existence of either of them, the other one is bound to fail (Singh 1960). For young adults, libraries support both academic and vocational training, helping to create opportunities for young people and enabling them to achieve economic independence.

Libraries play an important role in terms of offering a neutral welcoming community space, holding large stocks of material and access to IT facilities, providing a venue for a wide range of services, such as supporting literacy through adult education or children's activities and providing the services of trained librarians who can help members of the public find the information or resources they need (ALIA 2009; Macdonald 2011). Furthermore, according to Mnkeni-Saurombe (2010) public libraries are also essential during economic recessions, and countries striving to address challenges such as illiteracy, poor education, unemployment, housing, poverty, health, and other socio-economic issues can rely on them to a certain extent as they contribute to community development by helping people to cope or adapt to their different predicaments.

4. Historical development of library and information services worldwide

Libraries can be said to have existed for almost as long as records have been kept, spanning through the ancient world, Middle Ages, the nineteenth century, and through to modern times, and in the earliest times there was no distinction between a record room (or archive) and a library (*New Encyclopaedia Britannica* 2003). According to Bashirudidin (1968), the story of the library as it developed over the centuries can best be spread over three periods, namely ancient, medieval, and modern.

Early libraries were connected to palaces and temples, and were mostly used to keep official records. Records were kept on different media ranging from clay tablets, papyrus, and other forms. One of the world's first written languages was cuneiform, which was written on clay tablets and was common among the Sumerians in Mesopotamia (*Chambers Encyclopaedia* 1973). Hieroglyphics was the written language on papyrus and was commonly used in ancient

Egypt. Similarly libraries gradually developed in other parts of the world. In the seventeenth and eighteenth centuries, book collecting everywhere became more widespread. The nineteenth century saw libraries increasing in size because of the growing numbers of books collected.

As libraries increased in size, their growth became haphazard; administration became weak, with standards of service almost non-existent; and funds for acquisition tended to be inadequate. In the twentieth century the paradigm for libraries and librarianship shifted radically with the advent of new information technologies (*New Encyclopaedia Britannica* 2003). Over time, different types of libraries, including national libraries, university libraries, public libraries, special libraries, school libraries, and subscription libraries developed to be what they are today. Archives, which are collections of papers, documents, photographs, and other materials that are preserved for historical value, also developed alongside libraries.

5. Historical development of library and information services in Zambia

The development of public library services in Zambia began way back before the country attained independence in 1964. Among other reasons, the discovery of copper and the subsequent expansion of the colonial administration which saw an influx of white settlers coming to work in the mines and government while others settled as farmers contributed to the development of public library services. According to Kantumoya (1987), the historical development of library services in the country, like that of many other former colonies, is closely related to the country's colonial history, and it can be traced back to the penetration of the territory by European settlers towards the end of the nineteenth century.

In urban areas, public libraries began in the early years of the twentieth century as subscription libraries for Europeans and social welfare libraries for the African employees of mines and other large companies (Msadabwe s.d.). These libraries were gradually taken over by local authorities in the towns where they existed, including Livingstone, Lusaka, Kabwe Ndola, Kitwe, Mufulira, Chingola, Luanshya, Kalulushi, and Chililabombwe. In the present times a number of local authority libraries have been closed and a few were adopted by Zambia Library Service (ZLS) (Zambia, Ministry of Education 2012). For the rural areas, the colonial administration established a welfare fund, part of which was used to establish the Northern Rhodesia Publications Bureau (NRPB), which was given the responsibility of promoting African authorship and encouraging Africans to read by distributing books (Kantumoya 1987).

Since at that time there were very few literate Africans, the NRPB failed to realize its initial goal of commercializing the book distribution, but instead ended up spearheading library development in Northern Rhodesia (Asplun cited in Kantumoya 1987). By 1959 the NRPB had introduced a system of book boxes throughout the country which were distributed to hospitals, schools, and community centres from which the white settlers and the few literate Africans could borrow books.

The greatest contribution to the development of public library services was made by the Ford Foundation of the United States of America which gave a grant of US$43,000 for the establishment of the Northern Rhodesia Library Service (NRLS) in 1962 after successful negotiations by the director of the NRPB (Kantumoya 1987; Zambia, Ministry of Education 2012). The NRLS was established as a department in the Ministry of African Education, and immediately took the role of the NRPB regarding the distribution of books. The NRLS changed its name to ZLS soon after Zambia got independence on 24 October 1964.

Apart from public libraries, other types of libraries, namely academic libraries, school libraries, and special libraries also developed as time went by to cater for different categories of users. Academic libraries are libraries falling under academic institutions such as universities and colleges and are funded and supported by their institutions; school libraries fall under different schools at both primary and secondary schools; and special libraries are those that are attached to different organizations, private, governmental, and non-governmental.

Regardless of the types, functions of libraries in general can be summarised as follows (RIN and RLUK 2011; ALIA 2009; Krolak 2005; IFLA/UNESCO 1994):

- **Information provision:** Libraries are places where parents, grandparents, carers, young people, and children can share the excitement of discovery through books, the internet and other activities. Their purpose is to meet information needs for all through collection, storage, organization, and dissemination of information contained in the various library resources.

- **Education:** Libraries support educational activities at various levels by providing the requisite information resources to both the learner and the one imparting knowledge. Libraries assist in finding, using, and interpreting appropriate information that opens up opportunities for lifelong learning, literacy enhancement, creative imagination, and critical thinking.

- **Research:** Libraries provide information resources which facilitates research. They help researchers to keep abreast of progress in the fields of knowledge of their interests. By developing and sustaining their collections, libraries can provide high-quality information and knowledge resources that can be useful to researchers. They can help researchers with information that can win grants and contracts and also exploit new technologies and new models of scholarly communication.

- **Preservation and transmission of culture:** Libraries serve as repositories of knowledge and experiences upon which the past and the present are based. Libraries organise knowledge in books and other resources and make it available for the future.

- **Recreation, entertainment, and leisure:** Libraries provide resources that result in personal happiness, enjoyment, and social well-being. They encourage wholesome recreation and constructive use of leisure time.

Of particular note and attention, having identified the existence of different types of libraries, is the absence of a national library in Zambia. A national library is a library with books and other information resources usually for reference use, wholly funded by government and serving the nation as a whole

(*Harrod's Librarians' Glossary* 1984). A national library also serves as a legal depository in line with appropriate legislation existing in a country. A national library is a strategic information institution whose functions are so cardinal for a country to create an environment and opportunities for access to information, knowledge, and heritage of national importance.

According to IFLA and Lor (1997: 13–15), functions of a national library service include:

(i)   acquisition and preservation of the complete collection of publications of the country;
(ii) acquisition of library material for constituent and affiliated libraries of the service;
(iii) serving as a national preservation library;
(iv) serving as the national bibliographic agency;
(v)   national collection management and availability of publications through inter-lending systems;
(vi) serving as a national reference library;
(vii) providing professional and technological leadership and consultancy service to individual libraries and institutions;
(viii) undertaking research and development relating to the development of the service;
(ix) assisting other libraries and information agencies such as archives, documentation centres, museums, etc. in the country in heritage promotion;
(x)   promotion of literacy, information literacy, and other information awareness activities.

Despite the absence of a national library, there are a few individual institutions in Zambia that perform, by default, some of its functions, but their level of delivery is unsatisfactory. These institutions include ZLS, which provides public library services on a national scale; University of Zambia Library serving as a national reference library for Zambia; the National Archives of Zambia (NAZ) mandated to serve as a legal depository for printed publications; and the National Institute for Industrial and Scientific Research (NISIR) for science and technology information.

6. State of library facilities and services in Zambia

Having defined library and information services, and discussed their role in society, the question that remains to be asked is 'Have libraries and information institutions in Zambia been able to provide adequate and satisfactory services to foster economic and national development fifty years since independence?'

Libraries, especially public libraries in Zambia, have failed to exhibit the vibrancy required for service delivery that would foster economic and national development. The provision of library and information services in Zambia has been described as poor and uncoordinated, and hence failing to meet the needs of the users (Lumpa and Moyo 2012; Zambia, Ministry of Education 1996; Chiwaura 1993; Longwe 1988; Lundu 1988; Lungu 1988). The general picture depicted of libraries in Zambia, especially public libraries, is gloomy. Collections in public libraries have been described as being irrelevant and outdated, their facilities and buildings as dilapidated, unsuitable, not purposive, and inadequate while their services as being traditional and not proactive (Msadabwe s.d.; Walusiku 1997).

The staffing in these public libraries has not only been insufficient but more so unqualified and inexperienced. Furthermore, public libraries are difficult to be accessed by underprivileged people in far-flung areas because of distance as most of these libraries are situated in administrative centres such as cities and towns as opposed to remote outskirts and rural places. Electronic facilities such as computers and other ICTs are non-existent in most public libraries under government responsibility, and above all, these libraries do not provide extension and outreach services (interviews with senior library staff at Zambia Library Service, Lusaka City Council Library, and Kabwe Municipal Council Library, 23 January 2015).

In many instances, the public libraries are housed in buildings not purposely built, such as local council buildings and abandoned school classrooms or storerooms. Where the libraries are housed in planned buildings, many of such buildings happen to have been constructed many years ago, usually with seating arrangement capacities of less than eighty persons, and the space for shelves was designed to accommodate books hardly exceeding 10,000 volumes (interviews with senior library staff at Zambia Library Service, Lusaka City Council Library, and Kabwe Municipal Council Library, 23 January

2015). The construction of these buildings was done without consideration of the growing population of potential library users and the increase in the introduction of new services and facilities.

Apart from a few public libraries that have been run by foreign missions/organizations and local nongovernmental organizations (NGOs), most of these libraries have been administered and funded by government. Unfortunately, senior government officials responsible for planning and budgeting for these libraries have over the years portrayed an attitude of little or non-appreciation and recognition of the role played by public libraries towards national development, thereby resulting in poor support for libraries from government. This state of affairs has in turn created a situation where retention of qualified and experienced staff in public libraries has been a pipe dream.

The Zambia Education Policy (Zambia, Ministry of Education 1996: 86) also acknowledges that library facilities in Zambia are scarce, at both institutional and public levels, and outlines the general situation as follows:

- although almost all primary schools have recently received small book collections, there are no libraries in government primary schools;

- approximately 800 schools have collections of 250 library books loaned by Zambia Library Service, each collection serving 500 to 100 pupils and 12 to 20 teachers;

- most secondary schools have no libraries, and very few have trained librarians;

- libraries in teacher training colleges are stocked with inappropriate books and are not well organized;

- there are six Zambia Library Service provincial libraries with at least 10,000 books each; and

- sixteen Zambia Library Service branch libraries, each with at least 3,000 books, have been established in district council offices, secondary school library buildings, or other premises.

In spite of the shortfalls highlighted above in the provision of library and information services, some achievements in the development of library services in general can also be pointed out as including the following:

- The development of fairly effective academic libraries, embracing a combination of both print and electronic resources, in some universities and colleges which support research and academic programmes and provide reference services to the general public. Examples of fairly effective academic libraries include the University of Zambia, Copperbelt University, Mulungushi University, Evelyn Hone College, and the National Institute of Public Administration (interviews with some librarians at University of Zambia Library, 23 January 2015; Mulungushi University Library, 22 January 2015; and National Institute of Public Administration Library, 23 January 2015).

- Some bibliographic control activities, namely legal deposit and the publication of the National Bibliography of Zambia, are being undertaken at the National Archives of Zambia, which continues to provide resources for research to the government and the public (interviews with the director and senior archivist at the National Archives of Zambia, 23 January 2015). The latest publication of the National Bibliography of Zambia was for 2013. The national bibliography is ideally an annual publication, but because of the low output of new publications from publishers, some years have been combined in single volumes covering a number of years. For instance, before the 2013 publication the last two publications covered the years 2006 to 2008 and 2009 to 2012 respectively.

- A number of libraries attached to research institutions have been established and these continue to provide vital services to their parent institutions and the general public. Such institutions include Mount Makulu Agricultural Research Library for agricultural research, NISIR Documentation and Scientific Information Centre for scientific and technological information, and Tropical Diseases Research Centre (TDRC) Library for medical research.

- The ZLS has continued to provide rural public library services and support to school libraries throughout the country. The ZLS also serves as a centre for sourcing of library materials from donor agencies and distributing them to both private and public institutions.

- Several organisations, both governmental and non-governmental, have established libraries which offer various services to the public.

- Development of libraries for the disadvantaged such as the visually impaired.

7. Library policies and legislation in Zambia

At present (2014) there is neither a specific library policy nor is there library legislation to address nationwide library activities in Zambia. Regarding library policy, nationwide library activities are covered as administrative guidelines in the National Policy on Education (Zambia, Ministry of Education 1996). Under this policy, libraries are covered as essential supports for educational provision, and are recognized as institutions that hold information resources that can help everybody to improve their lives. Libraries are also acknowledged as containing information and knowledge that is important in the lives of individuals and organisations, opening up new horizons and developing imagination and creative powers of individuals. The education policy however does not cover specific issues about library activities in the country and is biased towards education and learning activities, which it covers in detail.

Efforts to fill this lacuna have been underway through the draft National Library Policy, which was first submitted in 2000 to the Ministry of Education for action through the ZLS. Realising that no action was taken by the Ministry of Education, the ZLS revised the document in 2012, and currently (2014) several stakeholders and the library fraternity are being involved to polish up the document before resubmitting it (interview with chief librarian at Zambia Library Service, 23 January 2015).

As regards library legislation, the Zambia Library Association (ZLA), now Library and Information Association of Zambia (LIAZ), submitted library legislation bills in 1976 and 1977 respectively which were both rejected by government (Kantumoya 1987). In both instances the government advanced the same reasons for the rejection, stating that the bill sought to transform ZLS into a parastatal organization for which government was not ready then as it did not have funds available for that. Although emphasis for the rejection of the bill was put on lack of funds, the library fraternity, however, thought that the reason given for the rejection was not a good reason. Instead, they felt that the bill was not sufficiently understood by government (Lungu 1988). This led to the submission of the revised Zambia Library and Information Service (ZLIS) Bill in 1998, which reached Cabinet but was returned after noting that it lacked the backing of a policy document. It was then that the ZLS was tasked by the Ministry of Education to prepare a national library policy.

Despite the absence of a comprehensive library act in Zambia, some library activities have been undertaken under the umbrella of other legislation. Some pieces of legislation which cover library and information activities in Zambia include the following:

- **Local Government Act (CAP 281) no. 22 of 1995 of the Laws of Zambia:** Under this act, libraries are mentioned in section 61, which stipulates, 'Subject to the provisions of the Act, a Council may discharge all or any of the functions set out in the Second Schedule'. In the Second Schedule, libraries are covered under function 36 which states, 'to establish and maintain art galleries, libraries, museum and film services'.

- Clearly, this piece of legislation is not mandatory and not specific to library development. This explains why in most councils in Zambia, libraries are non-existent. Even in some councils where they existed, libraries were either closed or handed over to the ZLS.

- **The Higher Education Act (CAP 136) no. 4 of 2013:** This Act states, 'There shall be a Librarian for a higher education institution appointed by the Council, on such terms and conditions as the Council may determine, and who shall, under the direction of the Vice-Chancellor, be responsible for the development, control, management, and coordination of library services in the higher education institution'.

- **University Act (CAP 136) no. 26 of 1992 of the Laws of Zambia:** Under this act, section 11 stipulates, 'There shall be a Librarian for each public university appointed by the Council, on such terms and conditions as the Council may determine and who shall, under the direction of the Vice-Chancellor, be responsible for the development, control, management and coordination of all library services in a university'. University libraries, as already mentioned, have been fairly effective.

- **Printed Publications Act (CAP 161) no. 44 of 1969 of the Laws of Zambia:** This act stipulates, 'The publisher of every book published in Zambia shall, within two months of the publication, deliver at his/her own expense a copy of the book to the Director [of the National Archives] at Lusaka, who shall give a written receipt for every copy received by him/her'. The act further states, 'No person shall print or publish, or cause to be printed or published, any newspaper until there has been registration at the office of the Director at Lusaka the full and correct title thereof and the full and correct names and places of abode of every person who is or is intended to be the proprietor, editor, printer or publisher of such newspaper, and the description of the premises where the same is to be published'.

Apart from the legal deposit function, this act does not mention any other function of a national library service.

- **National Council for Scientific Research Act (CAP 140) no. 13 of 1994 of the Laws of Zambia, repealed following the issuance of Statutory Instrument No. 73 of July 1998:** Under this Instrument, the National Institute for Scientific and Industrial Research (NISIR), as it is now called, is empowered to compile an inventory of scientific resources; call for reports on research work being carried out by any organization anywhere in Zambia; and publish from time to time such scientific and technical information as it may deem necessary.

To accomplish these tasks, the NISIR maintains a Documentation and Scientific Information Centre which serves as the national reference library for scientific and technological information.

- **National Museums Act (CAP 174) no. 13 of 1994 of the Laws of Zambia:** Museums are themselves also a kind of information institution as they collect and maintain objects which contain information and knowledge. According to the *Online Dictionary for Library and Information Science* (2014) a museum is 'a publicly or privately funded non-profit institution whose primary function is the preservation and display of collections of physical artefacts and specimens for the purposes of education, scholarship, and enjoyment. Since books and bindings are physical artefacts, some museums include them in their collections, for example, the illuminated manuscripts and treasure bindings exhibited by the Metropolitan Museum in New York City. Other items found in museums and of interest to librarians include inscriptions, clay tablets, papyrus scrolls, rare maps, letters, diaries, etc. Many museums maintain a library on the premises containing books and other reference materials pertinent to their collections and activities'. This act fully provides for the establishment, control, management and development of National Museums and for matters incidental or connected to museums.

The Zambia Library Service, which runs public libraries and is responsible for school libraries in both urban and rural areas throughout the country, is only covered in the National Education Policy, and is only governed by the terms of reference it adopted when it was first established in 1962 as the Northern Rhodesia Library Service (NRLS). The original terms of reference have been adapted into what are referred to as ZLS objectives.

The current ZLS objectives are as follows (Zambia, Ministry of Education 2014):

(i) To provide timely and relevant information in various formats, including ICTs;
(ii) To facilitate the establishment of and coordination of libraries in schools, colleges, and teacher resource centres in Zambia;

(iii) To establish and manage a public library network in Zambia;

(iv) To assist other organizations or institutions providing library and information services to the public in Zambia;

(v) To offer training in basic library skills; and

(vi) To conduct workshops and seminars to keep abreast of latest developments in librarianship.

There is no legislation in Zambia under which the ZLS is covered. The ZLS Annual Report (1997) cites low funding, lack of transport, and lack of general support by government as some of the problems the ZLS was facing; as a result of these problems, the service was accorded low esteem from the public. It is hoped that with legislation in place, i.e. if it will ever be passed, some of the problems the ZLS is facing may be lessened. According to Kantumoya (1987: 47) a country needs library legislation for it to provide adequate and appropriate public library services which would meet the information needs of society.

8. Harnessing library and information services for economic and national development

Before understanding how library and information services can be harnessed for national and economic development, it is necessary to first define the term 'development'. Development can be defined as growth that accommodates new and better ways of living, and responds to the changes that come with new technologies (United Kingdom, Department of Communities and Local Government 2012). The *Oxford Advanced Leaner's Dictionary* (2006) defines development as 'the gradual growth of something so that it becomes more advanced or strong'. Bellù (2011) gives different perspectives of development as follows:

- **Economic development**: i.e. improvement of the way endowments and goods and services are used within (or by) the system to generate new goods and services in order to provide additional consumption and/or investment possibilities to the members of the system

- **Human development**: people-centred development, where the focus is put on the improvement of the various dimensions affecting the well-being of individuals and their relationships with the society (health, education, entitlements, capabilities, empowerment, etc.)

- **Sustainable development**: development which considers the long-term perspectives of the socio-economic system, to ensure that improvements occurring in the short term will not be detrimental to the future status or development potential of the system, i.e. development will be sustainable on environmental, social, financial, and other grounds

- **Territorial development**: development of a specific region (space) achievable by exploiting the specific socio-economic, environmental, and institutional potential of the area, and its relationships with external subjects

In this chapter, development refers to all forms of positive growth and changes that include aspects of economic development, human development, sustainable development, and territorial or national development.

Harnessing library and information services for economic and national development requires that libraries and other information institutions are able to provide information that is up to date, relevant, and useful for the development of both individuals and society in general. It requires that library staff must possess appropriate qualifications, skills, and experiences to effectively and efficiently manage library activities, and market their services to raise user awareness. Harnessing library and information services is user focused, and requires that library collections should be both responsive and proactive to user needs, demands, or requirements. Above all, harnessing library and information services requires the support of government and all stakeholders to be achieved.

Human endeavour of many kinds, including education, research, invention, business, and leisure, has always depended to some extent on access to information, and libraries have been reservoirs of information and knowledge (Pearson 2007).

Information for economic and national development includes inter alia information on:

(i) **Health**

A healthy citizenry is an obvious prerequisite in all processes of production of goods and services and consequently the creation of wealth for a nation. Health information enables the prevention and management of various diseases and infections, and thus making it possible for people to remain alive and healthy, and actively participate in community activities aimed at poverty reduction. For instance people require clinical information on HIV/AIDS, tuberculosis, malaria, and other diseases; how these diseases can be prevented and treated; and above all information on accessibility to different opportunities for treatment. This information can be accessed and effectively utilized by members of the public from well-stocked and properly equipped libraries and information institutions.

(ii) **Education**

The need for information on education facilities and the availability of opportunities in a given community is important to all. For instance, knowledge about a nation's education system, which comprises both the public and private sector ranging from preschools, primary schools, secondary schools, colleges, and universities provide options that parents can choose from for the education of their children. Zambia's education policy (Zambia, Ministry of Education 1996) stipulates that every individual in Zambia has a right to education and that access to, and participation in the education system be available to all. Libraries and information institutions can provide such information through their various resources aimed at meeting the needs and demands of the users.

(iii) **Agriculture**

The United Nations Economic Commission for Africa (UNECA 2012: 103) reports, 'African economies have grown impressively over the past decade, but the sources of growth have been mainly agriculture and natural resources.' It can be presumed that the majority of the people contributing to this growth live in rural areas where most of them are small-scale farmers who still use simple traditional methods of farming such as the use of a hoe, while a few who have animals like cattle and donkeys use ploughs to cultivate their land. To sell their produce, they largely depend on government, otherwise they fall prey to unscrupulous traders who end up exploiting them by dictating prices which are usually lower than the real value of the products. Agricultural information such as fertility of land, appropriate soils, sustainable agricultural practices, and markets where farmers can sell their produce is key to the enhancement of management and production practices of crops and livestock. Libraries and other information institutions, when spread to these areas, can play an important role in providing relevant information that can educate people on such issues and accordingly raise their awareness.

(iv) **Water and sanitation**

It is a truism to say 'water is life', and indeed it is, but depending on the source from which it is obtained, water can also be dangerous and detrimental to human life. Yes, in its pure form water is everything and can only be compared with the air we breathe in. When contaminated, water can act as a conduit to fatal diseases like cholera, dysentery, and typhoid, which are associated with poverty and poor sanitation. According to UNECA (2008), human progress has depended on access to clean water and on the ability of societies to harness the potential of water as a productive resource.

The scarcity and erratic availability of clean water is a common phenomenon in rural communities in Zambia and other underdeveloped countries. This situation is exacerbated by the prevalence of ignorance in many adults living in these communities who lack information on the importance of treating water, such as boiling it or applying chemical disinfectants like chlorine before the water can be consumed. Information on general hygiene and sanitation is in many instances also lacking in these communities. Libraries and other information institutions can provide facilities and services to enable people to have access to information that would deter the occurrence, recurrence, and spread of preventable waterborne diseases.

(v) **Environment and natural resources**

Information on the importance of a clean environment and preservation and prudent utilization of natural resources is in the present times a must and a contemporary issue to any society. Climate change, deforestation, soil degradation, pollution, and indiscreet fishing practices are issues that negatively and adversely affect the environment and natural resources. For instance, traditional practices involving the cutting and burning of trees to fertilize the soil (known as chitemene system in Zambia) can deplete plant resources and be a cause of soil erosion, poorly planned for emissions of industrial fumes and disposal of waste material can be some of the causative factors to climate change, and similarly indiscreet fishing that does not take into account the breeding and rebreeding of fish can cause the depletion and extinction of fish species.

In communities where well-stocked and properly equipped libraries and information institutions are available, the probability of people having access to information that highlights the dangers of activities which can be destructive to the environment and natural resources is likely to be higher than in those communities where library facilities and services are lacking. Moreover, such information can easily be shared among members of the community and utilised for rational decision-making.

(vi) **Politics and governance**

The impact of politics and governance on the daily lives of people cannot be overemphasized. The general citizenry of a nation need to understand and keep abreast with the political and governance structure of their country. A good understanding of the politics and governance system can enable people to effectively participate in the running of the affairs that directly affect them. In democracies, for instance, people through their representatives at various stages from branch, ward, and constituency levels can submit their contributions which can then be presented and debated upon in parliament. The United Nations Economic Commission for Africa (UNECA 2012: 105) states, 'democratic participation becomes meaningful only when citizens, through their respective popular organizations, take an active part in shaping public policy, and hold their government and elected representatives accountable'. Parliament for instance is a strategic link between ordinary members of society and decision makers in government. The representation of members of parliament calls for constant contributions from ordinary members of society regarding the various issues that affect their lives. Information on politics and governance, like any other information, can also be accessed from libraries and other information institutions.

For library and information services to be harnessed for economic and national development in Zambia, libraries especially public libraries must be well stocked with up-to-date and relevant resources of high-quality information content on health, education, agriculture, water and sanitation, environment and natural resources, and politics and governance, among other information and knowledge. To the contrary, in Zambia public libraries have proved, as stated earlier, not to have achieved a lot in realising their call of providing information for economic and national development.

9. Conclusion

Generally and collectively, libraries and other information institutions are an ideal facility that can be conducive for harnessing services that would enhance economic and national development. However, libraries, especially public libraries in Zambia, have failed to exhibit the vibrancy required for service delivery that would foster economic and national development. The provision of library and information services in Zambia is poor and uncoordinated, and hence failing to meet the needs of the users. The collections in most public libraries are irrelevant and outdated. Their buildings and other facilities are dilapidated, unsuitable, not purposive, and inadequate, while electronic facilities and services to cater for new trends in the provision of library and information services are lacking. Compounding these challenges is the lack of a library policy or legislation to address nationwide library activities in Zambia.

Library and information services aim at providing opportunities to all people for free and equitable access to information and knowledge available in different formats and media. Library and information services, being facilities and activities in libraries or any other information institution, play a significant role in bridging the information and knowledge divide between the poor and the rich. The purpose of providing library and information services is aimed at linking information users to the library collections to ensure a constant flow of information and knowledge that would benefit the users as soon as it is generated. To achieve this, libraries and other information institutions need to embrace a combination of both print and electronic resources to address the needs of the traditional users who still depend on print resources, as well as the millennial generation who are addicted to using new technologies.

Hence, harnessing library and information services for economic and national development requires libraries and information institutions to have the ability of satisfying the information needs of the users. It is therefore incumbent upon librarians in Zambia to seriously take up the responsibility of addressing these challenges and ensure that possible solutions are arrived at and employed immediately. There is also need for librarians and other stakeholders to see to it that a library policy and subsequent legislation are put in place to address the numerous challenges libraries are currently facing.

References

ALIA (2009), *The little book of public libraries*. Available on http://www.alia. org.au/sites/default/files/documents/advocacy/ALIA.Little.Book .of . Public.Libraries pdf.for .web .pdf (Accessed 10 July 2014).

Bashiruddin, S. (1968), 'The story of the library over the century', in *Foundations of Library Science,* edited by N. N. Gidwani (Bombay: Hans).

Bellù, L. G. (2011), 'Development and Development Paradigms: A (reasoned) review of visions', *Resources for policy making, module 1102.* FAO. Available on http://www.fao.org/docs/up/easypol/882/ defining development paradigms 102en.pdf (Accessed 20 July 2014).

Berne Convention (1979), Berne Convention for the Protection of Literary and Artistic Works, September 1979. *WIPO Database of Intellectual Property Legislative Texts,* available on http://www.wipo.int/export/sites/www/ treaties/en/ip/berne/pdf/trtdocs wo001.pdf (Accessed 20 July 2014).

Chambers Encyclopaedia (1973), Vol. IV. (London: International Learning Systems).

Chanakira, T. W. and Shiweda, T. (2014), Paradox of harmonising learning commons with the learning habits of the millennial client using innovative librarianship. Paper presented at the 48th general conference of the Zimbabwe Library Association, Zambezi River Lodge, Victoria Falls, Zimbabwe, 24–27 June 2014.

Chiwaura, Y. M. (1993), *The development of public libraries in Zambia: problems and constraints*, MA dissertation (Loughborough: Loughborough University of Technology).

Clarke, S. G. D. (2001), 'Organizing access to information by subject', in *Handbook of Information Management*, edited by A. Scammell (London: Aslib) 72–110.

Eastwood, E. J. and Thompson, S. R. (2001), 'The use of the Internet in special librarianship', in *Handbook of information management*, edited by A. Scammell (London: Aslib) 1–142.

Fourie, I. (2001), Current awareness services in an electronic age—the whole picture, in *Handbook of information management*, edited by A. Scammell (London: Aslib) 274–306.

Harrod, L. M. (1984), *Harrod's librarians' glossary of terms used in librarianship, documentation and the book crafts and reference book* (Vermont: Gower).

IFLA and Lor, P. J. (1997), Guidelines for legislation for national library services. *IFLANET.* Available on http://www.abinia.org/foro/ifla.pdf (Accessed 22 February 2014).

IFLA/UNESCO (1994), *Public Library Manifesto* (Paris: UNESCO).

—— (2001), *The Public Library Service: IFLA/UNESCO guidelines for development*, prepared by a working group chaired by Philip Gill et al. on behalf of the section of public libraries (Müchen: Saur).

Interview with chief librarian at Zambia Library Service, 23 January 2015.

Interviews with the director and senior archivist at the National Archives of Zambia, 23 January 2015.

Interviews with senior library staff at Zambia Library Service, Lusaka City Council Library, and Kabwe Municipal Council Library, 23 January 2015.

Interviews with some librarians at Mulungushi University Library, 22 January 2015.

Interviews with some librarians at National Institute of Public Administration Library, 23 January 2015.

Interviews with some librarians at University of Zambia Library, 23 January 2015.

Kantumoya, A. (1987), *Public library legislation for Zambia*, MA LIB dissertation (Sheffield: Sheffield University).

Krolak, C. (2005), 'The role of libraries in the creation of literate environments', Background paper prepared for the Education for All Global Monitoring Report 2006: Literacy for Life (Paris: UNESCO).

Lumpa, M. and Moyo, J. (2012), 'The need for library legislation in Zambia', *The Post*, 18 October.

Lundu, M. C. (1988), National Information Policy for Zambia: a discussion paper. *Proceedings of two seminars called to specifically discuss the question of a national information policy for Zambia, 1st seminar: 9–13 September 1985; 2nd seminar: 23–24 February 1987*, Lundu, M. C. and Lungu C. B. M. (eds.), Lusaka: Zambia Library Association: 113–133, available on http://unesdoc.unesco.org/images/0007/000799/079904eb.pdf (Accessed 09 July 2014).

Lungu, C. B. M. (1988), Library legislation for Zambia. *Proceedings of two seminars called to specifically discuss the question of a national information policy for Zambia, 1st seminar: 9–13 September 1985; 2nd seminar: 23–24 February 1987*, Lundu, M. C. and Lungu C. B. M. (eds.), Lusaka: Zambia Library Association: 21–31, available on http://unesdoc.unesco.org/images/0007/000799/079904eb.pdf (Accessed 09 July 2014).

Macdonald, L. (2011), *Public libraries*, briefing paper (Dunfermline: Carnegie UK Trust).

Mnkeni-Saurombe, N. (2010), 'Impact of the 2009 economic recession on public/community library services in South Africa: perceptions of librarians from the metropolitan municipality of Tshwane', *Mousaion* 28/1: 89–105, available on http://0reference.sabinet.co.za.oasis.unisa.ac.za/webx/access/electronic_journals/mousaion/mousaion_v28_n1_a6.pdf (Accessed 20 July 2014).

Msadabwe s.d. *Libraries in Zambia*, Afran Study and Research Institute, available on http://www.afran.info/modules/publisher/item.php?itemid=442 (Accessed 05 August 2014).

Nyangoni, C. K. (1981), 'Libraries for national development: the Zimbabwe case', *Zambezia* IX/i: 49–58.

The New Encyclopaedia Britannica (2003), vol. 22 (Chicago).

Oxford Advanced Leaner's Dictionary (2006), 7ᵗʰ ed. (Oxford: Oxford University Press).

Pearson, D. (2007), *Libraries as history: the importance of libraries beyond their texts*, available on http://eprints.rclis.org/10700/1/pearson_07_libraries_as_history.pdf (Accessed 20 July 2014).

Radijeng, K. (2013), 'The role of public libraries in the attainment of Botswana's vision 2016', Paper submitted to IFLA World Library Congress 2013, available on http://library.ifla.org/258/1/201-radijeng-en.pdf (Accessed 06 July 2014).

Reding, V. (2005), The role of libraries in the information society. Speech delivered at CENL Conference, 29 September 2005, Luxembourg, available on europa.eu/rapid/press-release_SPEECH-05-566_en.pdf (Accessed 05 August 2014).

Reitz, J. M. (2014), *Online Dictionary for Library and Information Science*, available on http://www.abc-clio.com/ODLIS/odlis_l.aspx (Accessed 06 July 2014).

RIN and RLUK report (2011), 'The value of libraries for research and researchers', available on http://www.rluk.ac.uk/wp-content/uploads/2014/02/Value-of-Libraries-report.pdf (Accessed 20 January 2015).

Ryynänen, M. (1999), *The role of libraries in modern society*, 7ᵗʰ Catalan Congress on Documentation, 5 November 1999, available on http://www.cobdc.org/jornades/7JCD/ryynanen.pdf (Accessed 06 July 2014).

Singh, S. (1960), 'Library legislation', Regional seminar on library development in South Asia (Delhi, India: UNESCO) October.

Sykes, J. (2001), 'Organizing access to information by subject', in *Handbook of information management*, edited by A. Scammell (London: Aslib) 111–127.

United Kingdom, Department of Communities and Local Government (2012) *National Planning Policy Framework*, available on https://www.gov.uk/government/uploads/system/uploads/attachment_data/file/6077/2116950.pdf (Accessed 20 July 2014).

United Nations Economic Commission for Africa (2012), *Economic Report on Africa*, Unleashing Africa's potential as a pole of global growth (Addis Ababa: United Nations Economic Commission for Africa).

United Nations Economic Commission for Africa, Sustainable Development Report on Africa (2008) *Five-year review of the implementation of the world summit on sustainable development outcomes in Africa*, available on http://www.uneca.org/eca_resources/Publications/books/sdra/index.htm (Accessed 23 July 2014).

Walusiku, L. (1997), 'Rural library services in Zambia: their development and prospects', (Cape Town: University of Cape Town).

Zambia, Ministry of Education (1996), *Educating our Future: National Policy on Education*, Lusaka.

Zambia, Ministry of Education (2012), *Draft National Library Policy*. Lusaka.

Zambia, Ministry of Education (2014), *ZLS brochure*. Lusaka.

Chapter 11

Labour in Zambia Since 1964

Fanuel K. M. Sumaili

Introduction

This chapter addresses the issues of labour as important factors in any nation's growth or development and therefore, factors that need to be properly harnessed and nurtured through basic training and continuous professional development. It discusses the word 'labour' not in the usual sense of referring to human capital needed for development, though this is important, but rather labour as 'organization for production'. In this sense, the chapter uses the word in its widest sense, ranging from its relationship with the International Labour Organization's use of the International Labour Standards (ILS), to its use by governmental regulators in the sense of labour administration, including the organizations that represent the employers and the workers.

At the outset, it must be stated that the story is often told that at the time of Zambia's independence in 1964, the country could boast of only one hundred university degree graduates but fifty years down the line, in 2014, one university alone, the Copperbelt University, graduated a total of 1,196 degree holders at its graduation ceremony held on 23 and 24 July 2014. The basic drawback, however, has been that Zambia has had no tertiary-level institution that was charged with producing qualified manpower in the area of labour administration specifically. This is not because the importance of this kind and level of training was not recognized by our political leaders. To the contrary, the need to build a labour college was recognized in the mid-1960s when a decision was made to establish such a college. When funds became available, the said structures for the labour college were erected at the current Mulungushi University. But as we shall see later, the opportunity was lost when the newly built college was redesignated the President Citizenship College (PCC). Thus the country lost the opportunity to produce expertise in this area. It took the government of the late President Levy Mwanawasa to rekindle the idea of tertiary training in labour studies when it decided, forty-four years after independence, to set up a completely new university where the former PCC had operated from. In setting up its schools and faculties, the new university decided to rekindle the idea of labour studies by setting up a Centre for Labour Studies as one of the academic units.

The decision to set up the Centre for Labour Studies as a key academic unit of the university is very important in addressing concerns in the area of labour. It is expected to provide skills and carry out research in areas of need in the labour market and in issues relating to productivity, industrial relations, and legal framework, both international and domestic, governing the world of work.

In terms of the law, Zambia moved quickly to replace colonial legislation with a number of statutes aimed at concretizing Zambia's march into independence. In the fifty years of independence, the country has enacted a large number of labour laws, namely the *Employment Act* Cap 268, *Employment (Special Provisions) Act* Cap 270, *Industrial and Labour Relations Act* Cap 269, the *Minimum Wages and Conditions of Employment Act* Cap 276, the *Employment of Young Persons and Children Act* Cap 274, the *Factories Act* Cap 441, the *Occupational Health and Safety Act of 2010*, the *Public Service Act No. 35 of 1996*, the *National Pension Scheme Act No. 40 of 1996*, the *Local Authorities Superannuation Act* Cap 284, and the *Workers' Compensation Act No. 10 of 1999*. This large number of labour laws has engendered its own problems ranging from lack of coherence in provisions from one act to another to poor or lack of coordination in the enforcement of the acts because some acts sit in the Ministry of Labour and Social Security while others sit in other ministries such as Mines and Mineral Development. The government has recognized these challenges, and to this end, in 2012, it appointed a team of consultants to undertake a review of all the labour laws under the Labour Law Reform Project. It is expected that when the reforms are completed, the country shall have a more coherent labour law regime which will positively impact on productivity and hence, the economy.

To the extent that this discussion addresses the route travelled in the area of labour, reference will be made to the political history, especially to the fact that in these past fifty years, the country has been led by three different political parties whose political agendas, though largely similar when it came to labour, have had nuanced differences in emphasis and implementation, which differences impacted the development of the world of work.

Labour and the International Community in Zambia

Zambia joined the community of international states at independence in October 1964. It signalled its internationalist stance by selecting 24 October, the United Nations Day, as its independence day. With it, it also joined the oldest of the United Nations specialist organs, the International Labour Organization (ILO), which according to Beaudonnet (2010: 7) seeks to promote social justice and human rights at work, and is the world's only multilateral institution with a tripartite structure representing governments, employers, and the employees. Its principal function being to draw up International Labour Standards (ILS) in the form of conventions, recommendations, protocols, and declarations which help to establish the minimum conditions of protection at work and to ensure their implementation.

The ILO also provides technical assistance to member states and disseminates best practices, runs training programmes and communication campaigns, and publicizes many works documents. Its various actions are coordinated around four strategic objectives:

(a) To promote and implement standards, principles, and fundamental rights at work;

(b) To increase the opportunities for women and men to obtain decent work and income;

(c) To increase the extent and effectiveness of social protection for all;

(d) To reinforce *tripartism* and social dialogue (Beaudonnet 2010: 7).

But in order to better appreciate the above and some of the things we shall discuss below concerning the work of the International Labour Organization, it is necessary to make a very brief presentation of the organization's origins as well as its structure.

The International Labour Organization (ILO) was founded in 1919 under the Treaty of Versailles, which brought an end to the First World War and reflected the belief that universal and lasting peace can be accomplished only if it is based on social justice. According to the preamble to its constitution, the High Contracting Parties were 'moved by the sentiments of justice and humanity as well as by the desire to secure the permanent peace of the World'. Aware that workers were heavily exploited in the industrialized economies of the time, the parties to the Treaty of Versailles appreciated the importance of social justice in securing peace. Further, because of the increasing interdependence between national economies, the major trading nations understood that it was in their interest to cooperate to ensure that workers did not have to endure inhumane working conditions and that they could avoid certain negative forms of international competition (Beaudonnet 2010: 7). All this thinking was reflected in the preamble to the ILO constitution which says:

> Whereas universal and lasting peace can be established only if it is based upon social justice;
>
> And whereas conditions of labour exist involving such injustice hardship and privation to large numbers of people as to produce unrest so great that peace and harmony of the world are imperiled; and an improvement of those conditions is urgently required;
>
> Whereas also the failure of any nation to adopt human conditions of labour is an obstacle in the way of other nations which desire to improve the conditions in their own countries

In terms of structure, the ILO has three main bodies: a general assembly (the International Labour Conference, an executive body (the governing body), and a permanent secretariat (the International Labour Office). The first two are comprised of representatives of governments, employers, and workers.

The International Labour Conference meets annually in June and each member state is represented by two government representatives, an employer representative, and a worker representative, assisted by technical advisers where necessary. The representatives of the employers and workers are appointed in agreement with the most representative employers' and workers' organizations. Each delegate has the same rights and total freedom of voting irrespective of the vote cast by the other members of the delegation.

The main functions of the conference are:

(a) To adopt international labour standards in the form of conventions, recommendations, protocols, and declarations and it plays an important role in supervising their implementation;
(b) It is also the place where social and labour issues that are of a global importance are freely discussed;
(c) It adopts resolutions that form guiding principles for the organization's general policy and activities;
(d) It adopts the ILO's programme and votes on the budget;
(e) It elects the members of the governing body;
(f) It decides whether to accept new member states (unless it is a case of automatic acceptance in the event of a formal application from United Nations member states). (Beaudonnet 2010: 8)

The governing body of the ILO meets three times a year in March, June, and November at the ILO headquarters in Geneva. Its membership is comprised of fifty-six full members, twenty-six representing governments, fourteen representing employers, and fourteen representing workers. Ten of the government seats are permanently held by the most industrialized states namely Germany, Brazil, China, the United States of America, the Russian Federation, France, India, Italy, Japan, and the United Kingdom. The other government members are elected by the government delegates to the conference every three years, taking geographical distribution into account. Employers and workers representatives are elected by their respective delegates to the conference and are chosen according to their capacity to represent employers and workers of the organization as a whole.

The main functions of the governing body are

(a) To make decisions on ILO policy
(b) To decide on the agenda of the conference
(c) To establish the programme and the budget, which it then submits to the conference for adoption;
(d) To elect the director general of the International Labour Office
(e) To run the office's activities and
(f) To play an important role in supervising the implementation of international labour standards. (Beaudonnet 2010: 8)

The International Labour Office, situated in Geneva, is the permanent secretariat of the International Labour Organization. It is at the centre of every activity undertaken by the ILO. Its main functions include the preparation of the ILO's activities which it prepares under the scrutiny of the governing body and under the leadership of a director general. The office prepares the documents and reports which form the essential basic material for ILO conference and meetings and manage technical cooperation programmes throughout the world in support, especially, of the organization's standard-setting activities. It also has a research and documentation centre that publishes a range of specialist publications and journals addressing social and employment issues (Beaudonnet 2010: 9).

The structure of the office also includes a number of field offices around the world, such as the ILO country office in Lusaka that covers Zambia, Mozambique, and Malawi. It is through such field offices that the ILO maintains direct contacts with governments, workers, and employers.

For instance, the ILO country office in Zambia has been at the centre of studies aimed at fostering the Decent Work Agenda in the country and is involved in the ongoing Labour Law Reforms. The ILO, through the work of the Committee of Experts on the Application of Conventions and Recommendations (CEACR), is also continuously engaged with government on the application of the International Labour Standards (ILS). According to NOMLEX, the ILO's database on International Labour Standards, the Zambian government annually reports on Direct Requests and Observations on Labour Conventions to the ILO.

The International Labour Standards (ILS)

Up until June 2014, Zambia had ratified forty-eight conventions, including all the eight fundamental labour conventions and all the four governance (priority) conventions.

The eight fundamental conventions which aim to ensure the observance of the International Labour Standards (ILS) are Convention No. 29 'Forced Labour Convention, 1930', Convention No. 87: 'Freedom of Association and Protection of the Right to Organize Convention, 1948', Convention No. 98: 'The Right to Organize and Collective Bargaining Convention, 1949', Convention No. 100: 'The Equal Remuneration Convention, 1951', Convention No. 105: 'Abolition of Forced Labour Convention, 1957', Convention No. 111: 'Discrimination (Employment and Occupation) Convention, 1958', Convention, No. 138: 'Minimum Age for Admission to Employment Convention, 1973', and Convention 182: 'Worst Forms of Child Labour Convention, 1999'. These standards aim to achieve the Decent Work Agenda.

The Decent Work Agenda is a globally recognized framework for reducing poverty and balancing development. In doing so, it works around four objectives:

1. **Job Creation**—this refers to the building of an economy that fosters investment, entrepreneurship, skills development, and sustainable livelihoods
2. **Rights**—this refers to ensuring recognition and respect for the rights of all workers and employers
3. **Social protection**—this ensures a safe and healthy workplace, an adequate work–life balance, income protection, and access to healthcare for all

4. **Social dialogue**—this refers to strong and independent workers and employers organizations to avoid disputes and build harmonious and productive workplaces. (ILO, Measuring Decent Work in Zambia: The Decent Work Country profile at a Glance 2014)

The principle of Decent Work is also contained in the Millennium Development Goals (MDGs) where the four indicators are presented as:

1. Labour productivity growth rate;
2. Employment-to-population ratio;
3. Working poverty rate and
4. Vulnerable employment rate. (ILO, Measuring Decent work in Zambia: The Decent Work Country Profile at a Glance 2014)

The International Labour Organization, using the above Decent Work Agenda Criteria, produced Zambia's Decent Work Country Profile in a document entitled *Measuring Decent Work in Zambia* in which they covered the years between 1998 and 2008. Those findings gave a fairly unflattering picture of the Zambian labour situation. The study summarized the picture as follows:

- Agriculture is the main employer, accounting for 71 per cent of total employment, although the mining sector has been the main driver of economic growth. Most of this growth is based on extractives, principally copper. There has been little sectoral diversification, making the economy vulnerable to global crises.
- Working poverty and HIV/AIDS levels among the working age group remain high at 66.4 per cent and 14.3 per cent respectively.
- Net school enrolment rate improved significantly from 86 per cent in 2000 to 96 per cent in 2006. However, because of the limited space available, only half of the primary school graduates can be enrolled in secondary level. This situation is further aggravated by the lack of places at tertiary level for the eligible group.
- Youth and urban unemployment rates were found to be high at 14 per cent and 18 per cent respectively in 2008. Informal employment was very high and remained constant at 90 per cent. Vulnerable

employment represented 81 per cent of the population in 2008, with a much higher proportion in rural areas.

- The working poverty rate indicated that two thirds of Zambian workers in regular employment remain in relative poverty due to low levels of pay. The working poverty rate is higher in rural areas at 79.5 per cent compared to 22.9 per cent in urban areas (2008).

- Women are still earning less compared to their male counterparts, which is partly due to the concentration of more women in low-status jobs.

- Casualization of the labour force has contributed to the deterioration of conditions of work. Increasingly, parts of the private sector are replacing secure long-term employment contracts with casual short-term staff who tend to provide cheaper labour.

- Domestic workers are among those who work long hours for little pay, some work for a total of sixty-six hours a week, instead of the forty-eight hours allowed by law.

- Legislation explicitly places family responsibilities disproportionately more on women than men, e.g. only women can go on leave to nurse a hospitalized child.

- The HIV/AIDS pandemic has increased the number of orphans who have no choice but to resort to child labour for their livelihoods. Although the number of children in employment decreased from 45.8 per cent to 33.7 per cent between 2005 and 2008, this figure remains high.

- Women's share of the labour force rose from 45.9 per cent in 1998 to 48.7 per cent in 2008. Women continue to have difficulty accessing employment opportunities, because of low educational standards and barriers in pursuing higher education. Employment of people with disabilities remains a serious challenge as the majority of establishments lack disability-friendly premises.

- The biggest challenge to maintaining a safe work environment lies in the inadequacies of the institutions tasked to enforce regulations, as they are severely constrained by insufficient funding and lack of support infrastructure.

- The National Pension Scheme Authority (NAPSA) is the largest social security scheme in force, yet it has an estimated coverage of only 8 per cent of the labour force. Further, this coverage is limited to the formal sector. So the majority of the population does not have access to any form of social security since they earn their living from informal employment.

- Membership of the employers' organization rose consistently after 2000, while membership of the trade unions declined between 2006 and 2010. Trends towards casualization and the exemption of some professional groups from forming unions effectively reduced the number of trade union members, and this has had a debilitating effect on the labour movement in the country.

As stated earlier, the specific mechanisms that the ILO uses to set the International Labour Standards (ILS) are conventions and recommendations. Conventions are instruments which on ratification create legal obligations on the ratifying state. Recommendations on the other hand are not open to ratification, but give guidance as to the policy, legislation, and practice. Both kinds of instruments are adopted by the International Labour Conference under Article 19 of the Constitution.

Kalula and Zulu (2009: 27) noted the Zambian Constitution does not give any guidance on the status of international law in Zambia outside of ordinary rules of interpretation. But as a dualist state, international law ordinarily requires domestication before it may be relied upon by the courts, otherwise international law remains only as a source for inspiration. This is unlike in the monist countries, such as the French-speaking African countries where a ratified treaty has immediate equal value to that of ordinary law or may even be accorded higher status. To illustrate this, we may take Convention 158 on Termination of Employment (1982) which Zambia ratified on 9 February 1990. Despite the ratification, the provisions of this convention had no legal force in Zambia until the convention was domesticated through an amendment to the law in 1997. What this means is that for Zambia to adhere to its international obligations with the ILO, for instance, it is not enough to merely ratify a convention; it needs to move a step further by having the ratified convention domesticated. This way, the obligation it has acceded to at international level acquires domestic legal standing and may be relied upon as a source of legal authority.

In other words, Zambia has not fully benefited from the large number of conventions that it has ratified because of the slow pace at which the conventions are domesticated. It therefore ought to be emphasized that ratification may not always be enough, especially for a dualist country like Zambia. Emphasis ought to be put on ensuring that all the ratified conventions are domesticated in order to accord this legal force of implementation. To do this, the country would need an effective, well-manned, and adequately funded Ministry of Labour and Social Security, to which we now turn.

Labour Administration

The International Labour Organization needs a strong local partner with whom or through which it may bring its expertise to the local scene. In Zambia, this partner is principally the Ministry of Labour and Social Security. Through this ministry, the workers, the employers, and partners such as the ILO find a body to galvanize them and around which body they coalesce.

At independence in 1964, this was one of the fourteen ministries created, and at that time, it combined the mines portfolio. It was considered a key ministry. To this extent, in 1963, before the attainment of independence, the outgoing government had decided to build an adult labour college (Naumann 2011). The original site was to have been in Luanshya. But with the dawn of independence, this project seemed to have disappeared from the radar. When it surfaced and funding was sourced from the Friedrich Ebert stiftung, a German labour non-governmental organization (NGO), the site was moved to the current site where Mulungushi University sits (Naumann 2011). At its inception, the place was conceived as an adult education institute for trade union leaders. When construction was completed in 1974, the then government had a change of mind. Instead of having it as a labour college, it was named the President Citizenship College, ostensibly to help Zambians to better appreciate the newly declared one-party state dispensation. With that decision, the prospects for training high-level skilled manpower to man or organize the world of work was lost. It would be picked up again twenty-four years later when in 2008, the government of the late President Levy Mwanawasa decided to turn the National College of Management and Development, as it then had become, into a fully fledged university and management decided to include labour studies as one of its teaching units. The result of the earlier decision to abandon the idea of a labour college had also meant that for much of the fifty years of our independence, Zambia has not produced its own expertise in the area of labour studies. The nearest the country has come to producing a labour expert is through the human resource management programmes, which in essence have concentrated on personnel work—recruitment, training, compensation, industrial relations—and little or no coverage of the Zambian labour laws, social security, health and safety issues, collective bargaining and dispute resolution issues, productivity, and ILO International Labour Standards (ILS). The result of this neglect of an important area in our country's development has been that while other ministries—Health, Agriculture, Education, Finance, Works and Supply, et cetera—have been building up a core of institutions aimed at manning these departments at the highest levels, Labour and Social Security have had to be content with what others cannot use. This is manifested in the recruitment guideline for employment of university graduates which simply require anyone with a bachelor's degree in the humanities and social sciences (Ministry of Labour and Social Security job description document). In this age and era, this is obviously inadequate. But the situation is made worse by the fact that the Ministry of Labour and Social Security has no budget line to enable such officers pursue either short-term training or venture into enrolling for academic courses at universities in the areas of labour studies. In an attempt to redress this, in 2012 the ministry requested the Centre for Labour Studies to design short-term courses to be offered to serving officers of the ministry. These were designed following discussions with ministry officials, and the courses were approved. But no training has yet taken place because there are no funds in the ministry to undertake the training.

This position is supported by the fact that the Ministry of Labour and Social Security's share of the budget from parliament has remained the lowest of all the ministries for many years. Table 1 below shows budgetary figures allocated by parliament to all ministries between 2007 and 2011. The share allocated to the Ministry of Labour and Social Security is, in comparative terms, pitiable given the fact that this is the ministry responsible for the production of wealth and is supposed to have a presence in every district in the country as there are supposed to be employers and employees in every district. Its annual budgetary allocation has continued to be low, and for a number of years, it has received the least allocation as illustrated by the said table below. Notwithstanding the fact that it was one of the fourteen ministries at independence, it has been unable to obtain its fair share of the resources it needs to properly manage the world of work for production. It has been argued that the main challenge faced in the implementation of the Zambia Decent Work Country Programme was the 'lack of appreciation of labour issues by several ministries in the government, in particular the Ministry of Finance and National Planning' (GRZ, Draft Zambia Decent Work Country Programme 2012–2015: 19).

Table 1: MINISTERIAL BUDGETARY ALLOCATION

MINISTRY	2007	2008	2009	2010	2011
AGRICULTURE	1,019,063,951,992	786,652,085,160	1,074,393,173,160	875,292,933,911	985,221,496,496
LANDS	24,283,533,138	22,240,983,414	22956,159,297	34,712,481,423	36,229,196,739
EDUCATION	1,885,094,406,427	2,151,264,712,528	2,777,571,479,070	3,250,450,878,876	3,791573,847,495
DEFENCE	809,606,035,597	981,993,629,583	1,067,259,617,403	1,344,080,814,560	1,502,512,496,519
SPORT, YOUTH AND CHILD DEVELOPMENT	59,953,379,203	60,771,453,586	22,860,190,713	31,338,014,299	40,827,131,451
TOURISM, ENVIRONMENT AND NATURAL RESOURCES	171,096,728,631	123,227,689,352	165,825,196,256	215,888,767,185	172,541,094,124
SCIENCE, TECHNOLOGY AND VOCATIONAL TRAINING	130,858,901,651	135,610,621,478	120,182,978,027	111,494,205,547	140,568,950,127
WORKS AND SUPPLY	260,999,237,515	293,871,479,335	332,623,882,240	139,986,370,175	151,183,109,618
COMMUNICATIONS AND TRANSPORT	73,498,886,263	110,516,850,609	105,120,779,122	94,975,403,410	102,811,810,471
HEALTH	1,218,289,707,432	1,512,340,942,914	1,804,792,357,570	1,371,692,096,274	1,758,952,077,757
COMMUNITY DEVELOPMENT AND SOCIAL SERVICES	72,158,830,429	67,136,144,896	62,761,381,224	76,556,649,274	133,460,366,536
LABOUR AND SOCIAL SECURITY	**16,375,818,658**	**19,735,244,588**	**16,657,299,740**	**18,091,129,278**	**25,305,952,284**
FINANCE AND NATIONAL PLANNING	1,075,213,046,089	1,329,135,480,736	866,546,539,375	966,439,566,849	836,006,665,219
COMMERCE, TRADE AND INDUSTRY	73,325,949,084	78,106,839,728	52,988,211,524	41,590,710,579	65,364,771,850
JUSTICE	260,232,070,124	375,636,736,743	294,261,721,084	316,463,152,148	278,822,407,611

LOCAL GOVERNMENT AND HOUSING	172,100,414,558	217,670,098,576	256,850,684,836	298,509,774,488	320,797,867,421
INFORMATION AND BROADCASTING	26,366,395,376	31,948,528,690	30,100,685,981	31,717,087,749	48,287,685,11
FOREIGN AFFAIRS	166,846,203,279	194,303,671,231	245,496,685,366	283,952,206,795	356,178,852,615
HOME AFFAIRS	140,634,746,311	182,11,775,731	188,473,886,609	247,856,741,144	209,097,136,276
MINES AND MINERALS DEVELOPMENT	140,634,746,311	182,11,775,731	29,823,220,257	24,484,817,871	25,727,996,933
ENERGY AND WATER DEVELOPMENT	26,223,746,311	42,193,263,246	139,266,071,011	297,280,814,889	386,718,658,099
LIVESTOCK AND FISHERIES	-	-	-	258,236,015,213	261,748,495,587

Source: National Assembly Budget Allocation Records

This is a damning indictment of the government ministries, particularly of the Ministry of Finance. But as true as this indictment is, because it is really true, we feel that this is only a symptom of the problem. We believe that the problem lies mainly with the fact the technocrats in the Ministry of Labour and Social Security have not been assisted by the nation in the way others have been. They lack the basic training to be able to more fully articulate these issues at inter-ministerial fora where the national cake may be distributed. It is a well-known fact that for one to be employed as a graduate by the Ministry of Labour and Social Security, one only needs to possess a social science degree. The result is that the ministry is full of educationists, human resource graduates, lawyers, social workers, sociologists, et cetera. The point of this is that none of these would be fully conversant with labour issues per se. The situation is compounded by the fact that the officers themselves are aware of their need for training in labour matters but the ministry never seems to have an adequate training budget (GRZ/ILO 2011: 15).

This is very discouraging to young people who may want to make a career working in the area of labour administration. This is very much unlike other ministries such as Education, Health, Agriculture, and even Finance itself, where continuous professional training is budgeted for, encouraged, and rewarded. It is perhaps worth noting that despite the fact that Mulungushi University's Centre for Labour Studies now has students in their fourth year of study, not a single student has been sponsored by the Ministry of Labour and

Social Security, the parent ministry, to pursue studies in labour. Naturally, such a situation does not render itself to being able to more fully and comprehensively articulate labour issues to others, especially when one needs to convince others with passion why a certain budget allocation must go to labour issues and not to another equally needy area elsewhere. Further, the fact that until the setting up of the Centre for Labour Studies at Mulungushi University, there was no institution in the country that offered training in this area, means that the Ministry of Labour officials would need to convince colleagues who themselves do not have any understanding of, or usefulness of labour issues in the national economy. This is a pretty daunting task for anyone, let alone for someone who has not been adequately schooled or trained in the area.

The result of this historical failure to provide for this ministry is that it is not adequately prepared to undertake its labour administration functions. For instance, when it comes to policing issues of health and safety of the work environment, we find the same challenges of inadequacies of the institutions tasked to enforce regulations. They all tend to be severely constrained by inadequate funding, coordination, and support infrastructure (ILO 2012). According to the ILO's report *Measuring Decent Work in Zambia*, occupational injuries rose to 1, 388 in 2006 yet the number of inspectors per 10,000 employees has remained a woeful 0.8 inspectors by 2009. The inherent weakness within the ministry have resulted in failure to realize the benefits from the existence of legislation aimed at protecting workers; the employers can afford to ignore the legal provisions fully aware that the ministry responsible has no capacity to enforce them.

In order to summarize where Zambia stands in matters relating to labour, we have chosen to look at the four ILO strategic objectives with which we began the discussion and which form the bases for examining the concept of Decent Work, and therefore, the general labour situation in the country.

Objective 1: To promote and implement standards, principles, and fundamental rights at work

We have noted that Zambia has ratified several ILO conventions but that implementation of these conventions has left much to be desired, largely because of the slow pace of domestication of these instruments and the funding and structural challenges at the Ministry of Labour and Social Security. Discussing the above objective, the Zambian government and the International Labour Organization have noted in their report *Country Context and Priorities for 2012–2015: Zambia Decent Work Programme* that there are about 1–2 million children aged between 7 and 14 years that are economically active, especially in family agriculture, and further noted that children's involvement in hazardous work was found to have been widespread, with 1–4 million children between the ages of 5 and 17 years exposed to loud noise, dust, fumes, gas, dangerous tools, heavy loads, or extreme temperatures in 2005.

The report further notes that the weak labour administration system in the country has also affected the effective promotion of fundamental principles and rights at work. It further notes that the Ministry of Labour and Social Security has 23 district offices around the country out of the nearly 100 districts (GRZ/ILO 2011: 9). This means that the larger part is not covered by labour inspections at all.

The above limitations notwithstanding, the ministry has worked out plans for enhancing administration capabilities and public services which include the following:

- Obtaining additional financing from the national budget to enhance the ministry's ability to deliver on its mandate;
- Intensification of labour and factory inspections through the recruitment, training and deployment of labour officers;
- The resuscitation of the Public Employment Exchange Services (PEES) to facilitate employment creation targeting semi, low skilled workers and youths; and
- The establishment of internship and placement mechanisms to enable young men and women to acquire the necessary work experience and skills for the labour market. (GRZ/ILO, *Measuring Decent Work in Zambia: The Decent Work Country Profile at a Glance*: 8–9)

Objective 2: To promote opportunities for women and men to obtain decent work and income

Zambia has witnessed relatively high rates of economic growth averaging 6.1 per cent during 2006–2009. But inexplicably, the poverty levels have remained the same, at about 64 per cent. Formal employment figures have averaged around 500,000 jobs with the majority either unemployed or working in the informal economy (GRZ/ILO *Draft Country Context and priorities for the 2012–2015 Zambia Decent Work Country Programme* 2011: 9).

According to the 2008 labour force survey, male employment in the formal economy accounted for 72.3 per cent compared to only 27.7 per cent for females (ILO 2011: 10). Regarding the informal economy, 50.6 per cent of the workers were female while 49.4 per cent were male. In 2008 the Southern Africa Federation for Persons with Disabilities estimated that 93 per cent of persons with disabilities in Zambia were living below the poverty datum line of US$0.93 per day because of limited access to education and training which reduces their opportunities to access the employment market (ILO 2011: 10).

Generation of employment in Zambia has tended to be hampered by the fact that the large enterprises tend to source their supplies from outside, while the micro, small, and medium enterprise sector continues to suffer from limited markers, finance, technology, and management skills.

There is therefore a need to build a conducive environment for the establishment and operation of formal MSMEs in order to kick-start the diversification of the economy as well as to generate more decent jobs.

Further, it has been argued that unemployment in Zambia can also been attributed to low productivity, especially in agriculture, where most farmers practice subsistence farming. In addition, there is also the notion that Zambia does not have a very strong work ethic or an enterprise/entrepreneurial culture (ILO 2011: 10). This is an area in which the Productivity Department in the Ministry of Labour and Social Security should take a keen interest.

Objective 3: To increase the extent and effectiveness of social protection for all

Zambia is a poor country. The statistics we have given about the employment levels among the youth, for instance, lay bare the fact that poverty has seriously undermined the economic development of many citizens.

In terms of social protection, the country has three national schemes, namely the National Pension Scheme Authority (NAPSA,) the Public-Service Pension Fund (PSPF), and the Local Authority Superannuation Fund (LASF). The drawback is that all these schemes put together cover only very few people, amounting to less than 10 per cent of the workers and their families. Worse still, they are only available to those individuals who are in formal employment; nearly 80 per cent of the workers in Zambia work in the informal economy. These major social protection schemes leave much to be desired.

According to the *Zambia Country Decent Work Country Programme*, the country had 28,340 individuals in eight districts on cash transfer schemes. Although there are plans to scale up these cash transfer schemes to a further seven districts by 2015, this is woefully inadequate, especially when one is faced with Zambia's poverty levels, which stand at over 60 per cent (GRZ/ILO 2011: 11). What is important, however, is that a meaningful start has been made.

In 2011 the government adopted three statutory instruments, namely Statutory Instrument no. 1 for shop workers, Statutory Instrument no. 2 for general workers, and Statutory Instrument no. 3 for domestic workers, aimed at providing some protection to the lowest workers in the country. For the first time, domestic workers were brought within the ambit of the law. In 2012, the new government of the Patriotic Front raised the minimum wage for a domestic worker from K268 to K419. This is a significant step, even though the money may not be sufficient. The recognition that domestic workers deserve a legal cover must be applauded.

In terms of working hours, the maximum weekly working hours is forty-eight hours (GRZ/ILO 2011: 12). Records show that since 2005 the percentage of workers working more than forty-eight hours per week had declined from 16.48 per cent to 12.84 in 2008 (GRZ/ILO 2011: 12). The female workers are allowed twelve weeks maternity leave under the Employment Act, upon completion of two years continuous service. However, the statutory instruments (S.1) issued in terms of the act provide for four months' maternity leave, hence introducing an element of confusion as to whether the employer should enforce the twelve weeks under the *Employment Act* [Section 15A(1)] as the principal piece of legislation or choose to follow the S.1 under Article 7(1) of the General Order; Article 7(1) of the Shop Workers and Article 10(1) of the Domestic Workers Order even though it is subordinate legislation. The real problem, however, is that while the general order expressly provides for paid maternity leave, the shop workers' and domestic workers' orders do not provide for pay. We think all this needs to be clarified. It also needs to be said that maternity leave has caused further concern because it is currently borne entirely by the employers, while in the earlier times, this cost was shared between the employer and the social security scheme. The law does not provide for paternity leave but some establishments do avail their male workers with this leave facility anyway. It is possible that going forward, the ongoing Labour Law Reforms will legalise this.

As regards safety at the workplace, the responsibility lies with the Ministry of Labour and Social Security, while the Mines Safety department in the Ministry of Mines and Mineral Development is responsible for safety standards in the mines. In terms of workplace accidents, the *Workers Compensation Act* (GRZ, Workers Compensation Act No. 10 of 1999) provides for compensation for such and for diseases suffered during the course of employment. The main challenge as has been stated above is that the Ministry of Labour and Social Security is large and poorly resourced, and as such, it is unable to perform its statutory functions. In terms of the law, there are two main acts which regulate occupational safety and health in Zambia and these are the *Factories Act* and the *Occupational Health and Safety Act*. There are also other acts which regulate specific aspects of occupational safety and health such as the *Environmental Protection and Pollution Control Act*, the *Public Health Act*, and the *Mines and Minerals Act*. (The key acts are the Factories Act cap 441 of the Laws of Zambia, Occupational Health and Safety Act No. 36 of 2010).

According to the *Factories Act*, the word 'factory' means any premises in which, or within the close or cartilage or precincts of which, persons are employed in manual labour in any process or incidental to any of the following purposes

(a) the making or assembling of any article
(b) the altering, repairing, ornamenting, finishing, cleaning, or washing or the breaking-up or demolition of any article; or
(c) the adapting for sale of any article. [Section 2(1) of the Factories Act]

The above notwithstanding, the act excludes the mining sector and explosives manufacturing and assembling, which are covered by other acts. Despite the relatively wide definition of what a factory is, the provisions leave out from its coverage huge areas of the Zambian labour force such as those in the agricultural or service sectors, or those in the informal sector.

The *Occupational Health and Safety Act* applies to all workplaces as it defines a workplace as 'any place where the employees work or are likely to work' [Occupational Health and Safety Act No. 36 section 2(1)]. The act makes possible the establishment of occupational safety and health institutions with power to set and enforce standards through a system of inspections and penalties. The act also provides for the establishment of workplace health and safety committees and sets out the rights and duties of employers and employees in terms of occupational safety and health. The main drawback is that these acts are administered from different ministries with little or no coordination. The Mines Safety department is responsible for the administration of OHS matters in the mines and the applications of the Mines and Development Act while the Factories Act is enforced by the Occupational Safety and Health Services department in the Ministry of Labour. Some mechanism ought to be found to bring all the occupational safety and health legislation under one ministry, or to at least create an authority through which coordination may be effected. Indeed, Kalula (2013: 117) has argued that the ILO has emphasized the establishment of a central body as an effective mechanism for the overall coordination and cooperation in occupational health matters. This may help resolve some of the legislative overlaps, ambiguities, and inconsistencies, for instance, which exist between schedules of occupational diseases, where the Workers' Compensation Act lists forty-two occupational diseases while the

Factories Act lists only fifteen (Kalula 2013: 117). The *Country Context and Priorities for 2012–2015* report says HIV and AIDS are still a major factor in the Zambian labour market with a national prevalence rate of 14.3 per cent among those aged between 15 and 49 years (ILO 2011: 13). Its effects were specifically identified and addressed in government's policies such as *National HIV and Aids Strategic Frameworks 2000–2010 and 2011–2015.*

Objective 4: To reinforce tripartism and social dialogue

Tripartism is the principal social dialogue tool used by the International Labour Organization in all its structures. In Zambia, tripartite partners are the Ministry of Labour and Social Security, the two national centres, namely the Zambia Congress of Trade Unions (ZCTU) and the Federation of Free Trade Unions of Zambia (FFTUZ) as well as the Zambia Federation of Employers (ZFE).

As partners, the members of this tripartite body are very weak in that they have no real capacity. The vagaries of Zambia's economy have prevented the unions and ZFE from recruiting members that would enable them attain financial independence and sustainability. Indeed, as for the workers organizations, only 259,294 were members of unions out of a total of 619,000 employees in the formal sector (GRZ/ILO 2011: 14). This must give the trade union movement in the country some concern. They must explain why they are unable to attract more than half of the workforce available for union membership.

The Tripartite Consultative Labour Council (TCLC) set up under section 79 of the *Industrial and Labour Relations Act cap 269*, remains the principal institution for social dialogue. Although the act gives this institution a very broad mandate to 'advise the government on all issues relating to labour matters, manpower development and utilization, and any other matter referred to the Council by the Government', in reality, the TCLC is a toothless bulldog. It does not meet regularly, and it is not unusual for it to meet only once in a year. It has no research capacity of its own; it has no secretariat and no resources of its own to speak of. When you add to all this the structure and financial weakness of the parent ministry, the size and the dwindling number of trade union members, and the weakness of the ZFE members, who are largely

MSMEs, one understands its failure to carry out its mandate. But it cannot be left in this state and be effective. The TCLC needs to be strengthened if it is to perform its statutory functions. As it has been argued, the TCLC is supposed to function more like a parliament, where all issues concerning the world of work are debated. One cannot have a parliament that hardly meets (Sumaili 2011: 43).

In the Labour Law Reform documents, there have been discussions suggesting the need to increase both the representation of government in the TCLC as well as bringing into the fold some professional and non-governmental organizations. But given its mandate, this would have to be accompanied by a significant restructuring of the institution as well as a huge inflow of financial and other resources.

The Zambian Worker on the March

As has been stated above, the labour movement is only one of the key social partners in the world of work. But we would like to devote a short section to it alone because in the minds of most people, 'labour' conjures up images of organized workers into big strong and powerful unions. In general, where the labour movement has been strong, the general outcome has been that the workers (labour) have felt that their well-being was better taken care of or protected. Conversely, where the labour movement was weak or perceived to be weak, the general outcome has been that the workers have seen themselves as worse off.

During the run-up to independence, the Northern Rhodesia Trade Union Congress (TUC) that had been formed in 1951 and was the premier union in the country broke up into two factions in 1959 when, after conflicts and cleavages within the organization, Lawrence Katilungu, their leader, expelled the leaders who attempted to oust him from the leadership. And as Mulenga (2011: 4) has written, those so-expelled leaders formed a rival congress, the Reformed Trade Union Congress (RTUC) in 1960 which was aligned to the United National Independence Party (UNIP). The Northern Rhodesia (African) Trade Union Congress (TUC) was led by Simon Katilungu while the radical breakaway Reformed Trade Union Congress was led by Jonathan Chivunga and others.

The two congresses, the Trade Union Congress (TUC) and the Reformed Trade Union Congress (RTUC), merged into one congress in 1961 and formed the United Trade Union Congress (UTUC). By many accounts, the unity of the workers in this form was seen in positive light, especially as the congress was expected to collaborate in the fight for independence. But when there was another break-up in the congress in 1963, when some unions broke away to form the Zambia Trade Union Congress (ZTUC), there was much consternation in the African nationalist movement. The political leaders wanted to see a united African trade union movement. They saw this as a great aid to their fight for independence. Despite the many attempts to unite these two factions, success was elusive until at the dawn of Zambia's independence when in July 1964, Simon Kapwepwe, who was then Minister of African Agriculture, managed to persuade the main protagonists, John Chisata and Jonathan Chivunga. They were asked to choose between serving in government as junior ministers and leaving the trade union movement or resigning their parliamentary seats and continuing to serve their unions. Both chose to remain in government and served as junior ministers. The other protagonist was Wilson Chakulya. He remained an ordinary Member of Parliament but later Kaunda appointed him consul general to Lubumbashi in the Democratic Republic of the Congo.

Having absorbed into government structures all the major workers' leaders, the United National Independence Party (UNIP) enjoyed unrivalled popularity and influence among the people. There were no other major trade union leaders to speak of. To this extent we can say that at the time of independence in 1964 there was no separate strong trade union movement in the country. But the fact that a strong trade union movement could pose a threat or act as an alternative pole of power from the political leaders remained. What seemed to have been seen as a greater threat was the fear of disunity, the fear that the trade union movement might be used by detractors to sow seeds of disunity by creating many smaller unions that could be used to destabilize the new nation.

To prevent this, the new government moved quickly when in 1965 it enacted the *Trade Unions and Trade Disputes Ordinance*, which was aimed at strengthening the trade union movement by enabling them to conduct their affairs more freely. According to the Minister of Labour, Justin Chimba, a former trade unionist himself, the bill was to protect the trade union movement from disruptive outside influences and the receipt of outside material assistance from any non-Zambian organization without his approval (Northern Rhodesia Hansard No. 1: 10 March–20 March 1964). Further, Zambia adopted a policy of 'one union, one industry' hence creating a 'closed shop' scenario by law. To this effect, the Zambia Congress of Trade Unions was formed in 1965. When a new *Industrial Relations Act* was enacted in 1971, it entrenched the position of the Zambia Congress of Trade Unions (ZCTU) as the only national centre to which all unions in the country had to be affiliated [Industrial Relations Act of 1971 section 15 (1) (b)].

What is clear from the discussions above is that both the 1965 *Trade Union and Trade Disputes Ordinance* and the 1971 *Industrial Relations Act* were meant to produce trade union leaders and/or a labour movement that was subservient to the political leadership. And as long as the labour leadership or the trade unions movement remained subservient to the political leadership, the latter saw no wrong with the trade unions or their leaders. Further, as long as the Zambian economy was doing reasonably well, a serious challenge to the political elites led by Dr Kenneth Kaunda by the only other African-organized body, the unions, was unthinkable. But by 1985, twenty years after the enactment of the *Trade Unions and Trade Disputes Ordinance*, Zambia's economy had fallen and was on its knees. In late 1985 the Zambian currency, the kwacha, was auctioned, an act that devalued Zambia's currency substantially and Zambians did not know what had hit them. The devaluation of the kwacha and the consequent depression in the economy resulted in widespread disenchantment in the country. Indeed, between 1985 and 1990 many educated Zambians preferred to leave the country to ply their trades abroad and even overseas because Zambia had become an unbearable place to live.

These economic vagaries continued to weaken the political structure of the one-party state as they increased the sense of disenchantment among the workers.

The labour movement, on the other hand, continued to enjoy growth and popularity in the country. The 1971 *Industrial Relations Act* had confirmed the Zambia Congress of Trade Unions (ZCTU) as the only mother body to which all trade unions had to belong in order to enjoy legal standing. The 'one union in one industry' policy also meant that trade unions were key organizations to which all eligible workers had to belong. Failure to do so jeopardized one's chances for employment. This 'closed shop' system bolstered the ranks of the ZCTU with members and organizational funds. This was further augmented by the existence, within the ZCTU, of a trio of highly committed and respected leaders of the workers movement, namely Frederick Chiluba, Newstead Zimba, and Chitalu Sampa.

Chiluba in particular, because of his oratory and charisma, was seen as a real threat to the one-party state structure that several attempts were made to bring him and his lieutenants into the fold of the UNIP's central committee. Chiluba and his lieutenant Newstead Zimba were appointed to the then all-important and powerful central committee of UNIP. According to Mulenga (2011: 8) when Chiluba rebuffed these overtures, attempts were to weaken the trade union movement by repealing the 1971 Act, which compelled trade union affiliation to the ZCTU. When this failed, further attempts were made to suspend Chiluba from the National Union of Buildings and Engineering and General Workers (NUBEGW), where he was national chairman so that he could be disqualified from contesting the presidency (chairmanship) of the ZCTU. Workers in NUBEGW, where Chiluba was chairman, were organized to suspend him. He was only saved by being adopted by ZNUT and ZUFIAW; otherwise he would have been disqualified to stand for the presidency of the ZCTU. This is a variation of what happened to Rayford Mbulu prior to the ZCTU quadri-annual conference which preceded the 2011 tripartite general elections. His employers, Chambishi Mines, decided to fire him and he consequently could not qualify to contest the presidency of the ZCTU because the government was uncomfortable with him. In the case of Chiluba, the Zambia National Union of Teachers (ZNUT) and the Zambian Union of Financial and Allied Workers (ZUFIAW) gave him senior positions in their unions, positions which qualified him to contest for the ZCTU chairmanship in 1990, which he won. With the triumph of Chiluba over every machination to undermine his power, influence, and authority, machination that were perceived to have been hatched by or supported by Kaunda and the UNIP, Chiluba's stock increased while that of Kaunda and UNIP was much diminished so that when, in 1990, the Movement for Multiparty Democracy (MMD) was formed to challenge the rule of Kaunda and UNIP, Chiluba and his labour movement had established themselves as an alternative to Kaunda. The ZCTU was seen as the only well-organized and funded organization capable of competing with UNIP and defeating it. So when in 1990 the ZCTU formally decided to throw their weight behind the MMD, the die was cast.

The defeat of UNIP by the MMD in the October 1991 general elections was perhaps the proudest moment for the Zambian labour movement. It was the crowning moment. The labour movement, using its organisation and national structure had overpowered a colossus by the name of UNIP, which had stood over Zambia's political landscape for twenty-seven years. That labour movement had supplied some of the senior national leaders, including the president, the Zambian workers could not have been more proud. In 1991 the labour movement even organized victory marches in Lusaka and in other parts of the country. In the words of Charles Dickens, it was a time of 'great expectations' for the Zambian workers. This sense of euphoria was short-lived. A special correspondent writing in the *Sunday Times of Zambia* of 4 September 1994 noted that

> Trade unionism is facing another crisis. Not since the specter of one-party politics threatened to whittle the power of the unions has the (labour) movement looked defeat in the face. The difference this time is that its demise is largely a result of a harsh economic environment which has reduced membership drastically. The coming of the third republic will be remembered for the fall of its strongest proponent—the trade unions. (*Sunday Times* 2011: 3–18)

True, the trade union movement has been in decline from its zenith in 1990/91. But this cannot be explained merely by considering the economic environment. To fully appreciate what has happened it is necessary to look at the power of the economic environment, the desire by the new political leadership to adhere to the International Labour Standards, the standards of which run counter to the 'one union in one industry' policy. As we have indicated earlier, this is a policy from which the ZCTU benefited immensely by the fact that it engendered unity in the labour movement, as well as the age-old desire of human beings, especially those in political power, to want to control everything and everyone around them.

There is no doubt that trade unions need a reasonably thriving economy for them to get stronger. Their strength is measured by the number of workers in (formal) employment and able to pay union dues to their unions, which in turn pay affiliation fees to national centres. The table below shows that the employment trend has been on the decline from 1992, and this has come with the decline of union membership.

"Measuring Decent Work in Zambia: the Decent Work Country Profile at a Glance" (ILO: 2012) the International Labour Organisation (ILO) observed that the unemployment rates increased despite an increase in the GDP of between 5 and 6 per cent in the 2000s. This was bad for the unions as it meant low union density which has translated into weaker unions.

This trend has continued unabated well into the twenty-first century. The weakening of the Kaunda regime occasioned by the deterioration of the economy and hyperinflation was not lost on the new MMD leadership. They were well aware that their popularity, especially of the labour movement, grew exponentially as that of UNIP waned as a result of the deteriorating economy. Like Kaunda before him, the new leader, Frederick Chiluba, turned to the World Bank and the International Monetary Fund for assistance. He embraced the policy of privatization which culminated into the enactment of the *Privatization Act No. 21 of 1992* and the creation of the Zambian Privatization Agency (ZPA). The agency targeted the privatization of 280 parastatal companies and as a measure of its speed, it had privatized 257 companies by 2001 (Mulenga 2011: 11). Further, the government had also embraced the Public Service Reform Programme that was aimed at reducing the public service. As Mulenga (2011: 11) noted, in three years, from 1997 to 2000, the public service was reduced from 139,000 to 101,000, a reduction of about 27 per cent. Zambians were stunned. Even their president saw the negative effect but believed it was the only solution. He once said:

> I don't like the structural adjustment programme but I kiss
> it and will continue doing so. In this respect I can declare
> that I don't care losing the coming presidential elections if
> people hate me because of the programme. Even when I lose,
> I will go a happy man because I have so far managed to

change people's minds from perpetual borrowing to fend for
themselves. (Mulenga 2011: 10)

It is unclear what his take would be with the current government's borrowing
beginning with the Eurobond floatation. But what appears to be clear is that
he was aware that a crumbling economy was a recipe for worker revolt against
his government. He had to ensure that the labour movement did not remain
strong for fear that going forward, the movement might come to be seen as an
alternative government, very much in the way that the ZCTU had begun to
be seen in the late 1980s. But these were early days yet.

The first real attempt to put its own stamp on the regulatory framework in respect
to labour came with the *Industrial and Labour Relations Act, 1993.* But given the
fact that the trade unions had been a major supporter and collaborator in the
formation of the MMD and the ushering in of the Third Republic, the governing
party was understandably reluctant to tinker with part II of the act, which
dealt with trade unions. Instead, the new act left issues of rights, formation and
organization of trade unions in almost the exact place they had been under the
1990 amendment act promulgated by UNIP. Fully cognizant of the role the trade
unions had played by lending the new political party its national organization
and structure, financial and material support, the new leaders attempted to
return the favour. To this end, they amended section 22 of the 1990 Act to
add a completely new provision which empowered the minister, by statutory
instrument, to order an employer to deduct at the end of each month, from wages
of an eligible employee, the subscription prescribed by the constitution of the
union. Obviously, this was meant to help with unions' finances.

This cosy relationship between the labour movement and the political party
in power remained undisturbed for five years until 1996 when the government
decided to ratify Convention 87, the *Freedom of Association and Protection of
the Right to Organise Convention.*

The first two articles of that convention illustrate its import in the balance of
power between the labour movement and the political party in power.

Article 1

Each member of the International Labour Organization (ILO) for which this Convention is in force undertakes to give effect to the following provisions.

Article 2

Workers and employers, without distinction whatsoever, shall have the right to establish and subject only to the rules of the organisation concerned, to join organisations of their own choosing without previous authorisation.

What this meant is that the power of unions could no longer be artificially protected through such policies as 'one union in one industry' as workers now had a right without distinction whatever, to establish, join organizations of their own choosing without previous authorization. No doubt the MMD must have found international support for this new view from the English case of *Young, James and Webster versus UK* (1981) (Pitt, Gweyneth Employment Law 2001: 313) where the European Court of Human Rights ruled against the United Kingdom government, which at the time allowed the practice of the closed shop. This allowed a situation where for one to get a job in a place where a trade union was in existence, one had to join the trade union or agree to join that trade union soon after. In the instant case, the three plaintiffs refused to join the existing trade union and were fired. When the English court ruled against them, they took the matter on appeal to the European Court of Human Rights. The court held by a majority that Article 11 of the European Court of Human Rights was contravened by English law, which permitted the practice of the closed shop at the time because employees risked being dismissed if they did not join the union, as was the case here. The majority view was that compulsion to join one union restricted freedom of association because it prevented workers from forming or joining another. In other words, the freedom to associate also necessarily means the freedom not to associate.

The country's ratification of Convention 87 and the amendments effected through Act No. 30 of 1997 of the *Industrial and Labour Relations Act* meant that the law now permitted more than one union in the same industry because the reverse would result in infringing both Convention 87 and the country's constitution, which guaranteed individuals the right to freedom of association. The result was that whereas the long title of Act No. 27 of 1993 said, 'An Act to revise the law relating to trade unions, the Zambia Congress of Trade Unions . . .' Act No. 30 of 1997 avoided the use of the name Zambia Congress of Trade Unions altogether and instead simply stated that this was an 'Act to revise the law relating to the formation of trade unions and employers' representative organisations, including the formulation of federation of trade unions and federation of employers organisations'. This meant that at the apex, the ZCTU would no longer enjoy monopoly, that there would be other federations of trade unions envisaged. The act further introduced an amendment to section 17(1)(d) to permit two or more registered unions which were not affiliated to the Congress or Federation of Trade Unions to form, in accordance with their constitutions, establish or form a federation of trade unions of their choice and have the same registered under this act.

The effect of all these legal changes was to fragment the once-mighty ZTCU into two; there are now two national centres with the formation of the Federation of the Free Trade Unions of Zambia (FFTUZ). The law signalled the abandonment of the 'one union in one industry' policy. Perhaps the most well-known manifestation of the union fragmentation and hence the weakening of the powers of the unions, was seen in the case of *Attorney General and Labour Commissioner v Fabian Zulu Amadeus G. Kawambawamba, Sitenge Mundia Mutanga and others* (Supreme Court Judgment No. 26 of 1995).

In this matter, the respondents, whom we shall refer to as plaintiffs, as they were in the high court, had applied to the labour commissioner, on behalf of the secondary school teachers to have a separate union called the Secondary School Teachers Union registered. The labour commissioner rejected their application on the grounds that secondary school teachers were already represented by the Zambian National Union of Teachers (ZNUT). The plaintiff took the matter to the high court for a declaration that their constitutional rights had been infringed upon by the denial to have their own union registered.

In the court of first instance, the court commissioner declared that the labour commissioner's refusal constituted a denial of the plaintiffs' enjoyment of their constitutional rights as articulated in article 21(1), which said:

> Except with his own consent, no person shall be hindered in
> the enjoyment of his freedom of assembly and association, that
> is to say his right to assemble freely and associate with other
> persons and in particular to form or belong to any political
> party, trade union or other association for the protection of
> his interests.

He further ruled that the provisions of 9(8)(c) of the *Industrial and Labour Relations Act*, which prohibits the registration of a trade union if it purports to represent a class or classes of employees already represented by an existing trade union were inconsistent with the provisions and the constitution of Zambia and that the said section was, therefore, invalid. But on appeal, the Supreme Court ruled that section 9(8)(c) of the *Industrial and Labour Relations Act* No. 27 of 1993 was not ultra vires the constitution (Supreme Court of Zambia Judgment No. 26 of 1995). The court stated that the above section allowed the registration of a separate union for secondary school teachers and that the proposed secondary school teachers union comprised a specific category, different from other teachers. It concluded that this category of teachers qualified to form a trade union of their own in accordance with the *Industrial and Labour Relations Act*, especially as it found that this category of teachers were not adequately represented by any other union. The import of this ruling can be seen in the proliferation of unions that have since been formed in the educational, financial, and other sectors, further fragmenting an already small formal workforce into even smaller organised units. This in turn has had the effect of further weakening both the bargaining power and the financial base of the unions.

The Industrial and Labour Relations Act

In addition, the government took further steps to weaken and control the labour movement by drastically amending the *Industrial and Labour Relations Act* especially through Amendment Act No. 8 of 2008. This act has literally brought the organized labour movement to its knees.

This act, even before the enactment of the amendments, had provisions such as section 2 of the act, which excluded from organized labour the Zambia Defence Force, Zambia Police Service, Zambia Prison Service, Zambia Security

Intelligence Service, and judges, registrars of the court, magistrates, and local court justices. In a country where the number of employees in formal employment and therefore eligible for unionization is barely 600,000 the exclusion of such a large number from eligibility is devastating for union membership. Section 18(i) (g) lays down the criteria for disqualification from election or appointment as officer of a trade union. Subsection (g) says, 'No person shall be qualified for election or appointment as an officer of a trade union or trade union secretariat who is not employed outside the trade union or trade union secretariat.' In short, one had to be in the employ of another in order to contest a union position. This means that even for those union members who get elected to full-time positions such as union secretary general or president, they too need to prove that they are on the employ of another employer. This obviously makes no sense but it was meant to ensure that government still had some control over such full-time union officers in that as government, they could lean heavily on the outside employer to terminate the employment of such an aspiring candidate and thus disqualify him/her from contesting a union position.

During the Kaunda era, a variation of this tactic was used to try to stop Chiluba from contesting the presidency of the ZCTU. According to Mulenga (2011: 6), it is alleged that UNIP tried to persuade the NUBEGW, of which Chiluba was chairman, to have him suspended on grounds that he was pursuing interests different from those of the workers he led. The aim was to disqualify him from standing for election as a ZCTU official, which was open only to those who held a post in an affiliated union. Chiluba was only saved when ZNUT and ZUFIAW gave him senior positions in their unions.

Having learned this lesson earlier, the MMD leaders who were now in government fashioned an amendment to the law that required such an aspirant to be in employment outside the trade union. When the need arose for the government to block the former Mineworkers' Union of Zambia (MUZ) president from contesting the ZCTU president, the government leaned on his employer, Chambeshi Copper Mines, to terminate his employment and thus ended his candidature. Mr Rayford Mbulu was president of the Mineworkers' Union of Zambia (MUZ) and was vying for the presidency of the ZCTU when the party in power, the MMD, leaned on his employers, Chambishi Mines, to dismiss him because he was an active member of the opposition, the Patriotic Front. His dismissal ended his possible candidature.

Section 21 was amended to give power to the labour commissioner to recommend the removal of a trade union member or dissolution of the board, as the case may be, to the Tripartite Consultative Labour Council. This is oblivious to the provisions of Convention 87, which says, 'Workers and employers' organization shall not be liable to be dissolved or suspended by administrative authority.' In an attempt to control the labour movement the government abrogated a fundamental tenet of such organization, which is that being organizations freely established by members, any suspension, removal, or dissolution must be a result of a decision of members themselves, acting freely, or as a result of a judicial decision.

Section 65(A) gives the labour commissioner absolute power to terminate a recognition agreement at the instance of a party to the recognition agreement. This is yet another attempt to control the unions by administrative fiat. Section 78 imposes arbitration at the instance of one party where there is a conflict over collective agreements, a practice which negates the principle of voluntary negotiation of collective agreements. It further restricts the period the workers can go on a legal strike to fourteen days, by imposing an automatic referral of any dispute to court if the dispute is not solved fourteen days following a strike, thus taking away from the workers the use of their ultimate weapon. All these and other amendments made to the *Industrial and Labour Relations Act* have had the effect of further weakening the labour movement in the country.

It is therefore, very important that this particular piece of legislation is reviewed and amended to enable the labour movement take up its place as an independent powerful actor in the work place.

The Labour Law Reforms

The 2011 general elections ushered into government a new government under the Patriotic Front (PF). On the labour front, the new government's priority has been the drive to reform the Zambian labour laws. To this extent the government, through the Ministry of Labour and Social Security, sought the services of a consultancy firm from the Institute of Development and Labour Law of the University of Cape Town to produce an *issues paper* on which the discussion would be based. The presentation of the final issues paper to stakeholders took place on 31 May 2013 at Pamodzi Hotel. In September 2014, this author received an appointment letter from the Ministry of Labour and Social Security to sit on the task force to review the Employment Act. As at 24 October 2014, this task force was yet to meet. It is possible this route has been abandoned. But it is also worrisome that what is being discussed now is reviewing the Employment Act and not the labour laws in their entirety.

The expectation is that the labour law reform process will take on board all the areas of concern and not merely the purely legal areas. It is expected for instance that it will provide guidance regarding the key officers and their functions in the ministry as well as the requisite structure; that the final reform documents will ensure that the various structures are fully funded and operationalized. But as we have indicated earlier, it is crucial that the ministry itself prioritizes education and continuous professional training and comes up with a reward system to both encourage staff to better themselves and a structure that will encourage such pursuits and in all this, the Centre for Labour Studies at Mulungushi University should be supported to play its role. While it is important for the Ministry of Finance and National Planning to begin to put a premium on funding the ministry, and to obtain the support from other ministries for this effort, we feel that it is only the professional cadre of the ministry who will carry the burden to articulate their needs and the place of those needs and the ministry and in the overall development process of the nation. For them to succeed, they will need the support of the nation to raise their own levels of expertise in matters related to labour.

Conclusion

This chapter has taken a historical view of the development of labour from the time of independence in 1964. It has attempted to explore key developments in both domestic labour law and international labour law. In this regard, the chapter has noted the numerous statutes that are classified as labour laws which have necessarily introduced ambiguities and inconsistencies within and among the various statutes. The chapter has, however, noted the government's attempts to resolve both the large number of statutes and the seeming ambiguities and inconsistencies by deciding to undertake labour law reforms. To this end the government appointed a consultant from Cape Town University to undertake a study and produce an issues paper on which the reforms would be based. The consultant produced the issues paper in May 2013. But sadly, there has been no significant movement yet to address the issues that were identified and the task force that was appointed by the minister in September 2014 was tasked to review only the Employment Act, and it was yet to meet since appointment.

On the international labour law front, the chapter has observed that Zambia has ratified forty-eight of the ILO conventions, including all the eight ILO fundamental conventions. But despite this, the process of domestication of the conventions has been very slow indeed, and when this has happened, the domestication has only been partial where some of the articles in the conventions have not been domesticated. This means that the country has not been able to fully benefit from the conventions ratified and so domesticated. As a dualist country, Zambia needs to domesticate the conventions before they can receive the full legal force of the law in the country.

The above notwithstanding, Zambia's membership in the ILO has been very helpful in that the country has benefited first from the financial and technical expertise of the ILO as well as by embracing the ILO Decent Work Country Programme and its four strategic objectives. These objectives emphasize job creation, workers' rights, social protection for the workers, and social dialogue between and among the social partners. With the assistance of the ILO, the government has used these strategic objectives to plan as well as assess the country's progress as regards to the ILO International Labour Standards (ILS).

In using this standard to evaluate the country's progress, the paper has noted several challenges that have mitigated against the government's attainment of the set goals in the Decent Work Country programmes. These have ranged from lack of budgetary support from the national budget to raise the necessary finances and other resources to meet the mandate thrust upon the Ministry of Labour and Social Security to the ministry's own internal weaknesses due to lack of qualified staff in the fields of labour and employment relations and the absence of a continuing professional development programme for the staff.

To mitigate this, the chapter has noted the establishment of the Centre for Labour Studies at Mulungushi University. The centre should help in producing highly qualified staff in this area so that the ministry is put on the same footing with other ministries that have had training institutions at tertiary level in the country from independence or soon after. But for this to make a difference, the ministry itself must want to utilise the institution by sending its staff for training. Six years after its establishment, Mulungushi University has yet to receive a single student sponsored by the Ministry of Labour and Social Security to study there.

Politically, the chapter has recognized the important role that labour—meaning the workers—played in the country's fight for independence as well as in the re-introduction of multiparty democracy in 1991.

On balance, the country has made some progress in the area of labour but a lot more needs to be done.

References

Attorney General, Labour Commissioner versus Fabian Zulu, Amadeus Kamukwamba, Sitenge Mundia Mutanga and Others (Supreme Court of Zambia Judgment No. 26 of 1995).

Beaudonnet, X. (ed.) (2010), *International Law and Domestic Law* (Geneva: International Labour Office).

CSO (2008), *Zambia Labour Force Survey* (Lusaka).

GRZ (2004), *National Employment and Labour Market Policy* (Lusaka).

—— (2006), *Vision 2030* (Lusaka).

GRZ/ILO (2011) *Country Context and Priorities for 2012–2015: Zambia Decent Work Programme*, draft (Lusaka).

ILO (2009), *Constitution of the International Labour Organization and Selected Texts* (Geneva: International Labour Office).

—— (2012), *Decent Work Country Profile: Zambia* (Geneva).

—— (2007), *The ILO at a Glance* (Geneva: International Labour Office).

—— (2012), 'Measuring Decent Work in Zambia', unpublished document.

Kalula, E., Pamhidzai, H., and Bamu (2013), *Zambia Labour Law Reform* issues paper, May 2013, unpublished document.

—— and Zulu, Dennis (2009), 'Zambia', *International Encyclopedia of Laws* pp. 1–64, Kluwer Law International.

Mulenga, F. E. (2011), 'Crises and Successes of the Labour Movement in Zambia: A Historical Perspective', *The Labour Movement in Zambia*, pp. 2–18.

Naumann, Heiner (2011), Speech delivered at the opening of a colloquium for labour movement experts on the 'Future of the Labour Movement in Zambia' held at Mulungushi University from 16 to 17 March 2011.

Sumaili, Fanuel (2011), 'The Legal Framework for the Operation of Trade Unions in Zambia', *The Labour Movement in Zambia*, pp. 35–45.

Northern Rhodesia Hansard No. 1: *Official Verbatim Report of the Debates of the First Session of the First Legislative Assembly*, 10–20 March 1964.

Attorney General Labour Commissioner v Fabian Zulu, Amadeus G. Kamukwamba, Sitenge Mundia Mutanga and others (Supreme Court Judgment No. 26 of 1995)

Sunday Times of Zambia, 4 September 1994.

Young, James and Webster v UK (1981) in Pitt, G., *Employment Law* seventh edition (London: Sweet and Maxwell).

Chapter 12

The Evolution of the Civil Service in Zambia: Precolonial Period to Third Republic
Rabecca Banda-Shula

Introduction

Zambia attained independence on 24 October 1964 and hence commemorated fifty years of independence or the golden jubilee in 2014. The commemoration was not only a momentous one filled with unprecedented jubilation but also a time for sober reflection to account for strides attained by the nation thus far. One area of concern is the civil service. Therefore, the event provided an opportunity for introspection to highlight major achievements and weaknesses experienced in the civil service in order to draw significant lessons as the nation journeys on to prosperity. The reflection is significant because largely, the civil service has a mammoth responsibility of providing public goods and services to the citizenry.

Subsequently, the chapter is a reflection of how the civil service in Zambia has evolved from the precolonial period to the Third Republic. It focuses on reviewing the trajectory it has treaded during this period and highlighting salient features, strengths, and setbacks. Before proceeding, it is noteworthy to acknowledge that there is already existing literature by renowned scholars on the subject matter such as Dresang (1975), Tordoff (1980), and Chibaye and Bwalya (in Subramaniam 1990). However, the literature does not address the trajectory of the civil service from precolonial to the Third Republic era in a systematic manner, thereby creating a gap the chapter intends to fill. Moreover, the literature by the scholars is useful but dated, hence the need to rejuvenate it through current discourse.

The chapter seeks to answer three major questions as follows: firstly, what changes have been experienced by the Zambian civil service from the precolonial period to the contemporary time? Secondly, what were the major successes and weaknesses? Lastly, are there any lessons to be drawn from the experiences of the civil service under each phase? Before taking stock of the Zambian civil service, it is important to appreciate, in general, the meaning and role of civil service.

Meaning and Role of Civil Service

Civil service is a device through which government realistically meets various needs of the public, either directly or indirectly. Ultimately, it drives the developmental agenda of the nation by striving to meet developmental goals. Therefore the civil service is the hub of government functions and activities. However, civil service is not synonymous with government as the latter is broader and is essentially an institution or an agency created to enforce rules of conduct and ensure obedience. Through the government machinery, people with a common purpose, occupying a definite territory, are regulated through the common rules of the land. In addition, it is a device which determines common policies and collective decisions. It also regulates public affairs and advances public interest (Chand and Kapur 1996). This exemplifies the significant role the government plays in the lives of its citizens and the general public at large. To carry out its role effectively and balance powers, the government is systematically structured in various components and interacts with various non-state actors thereby creating a subsystem.

Generally, government consists of three major wings, namely legislature, executive, and judiciary. The main function of the legislature is to make laws, the executive enforces laws, whereas the judiciary interprets and settles disputes arising from the enforcement. 'The term *executive*, in its broadest sense, includes not only the Head of the State, but also the entire body of administrative officials, high and low' (Chand and Kapur 1996: 595–596). As the practice is in many countries, the administrative wing of government or public service comprise of non-elective employees recruited on merit. According to a World Bank report (2008), the civil service is comprised of employees of central government assigned to perform administrative tasks. This definition excludes the military, teachers, health workers, and adjudicators. Therefore, civil servants constitute employees appointed and promoted on merit who are not political or judicial in orientation.

The importance of the civil service cannot be overemphasized. It is the nexus of the state and supports and upholds the entire system of governance to the extent that performance of government is largely determined by its civil service, notwithstanding other factors such as political systems that influence government performance. To promote performance orientation, the civil service is characterised by fundamental principles that underlie its operations, namely 'merit, competence, continuity, political insulation, and accountability' (Bekke, Perry, and Toonen 1996: 92). These principles are significant because they enhance professionalism. As Schick (1999: 12–13) noted, 'merit, competence, continuity, and political insulation give considerable power to civil servants'. Therefore, the principles protect the civil service from political interference which would otherwise compromise its operations and ultimately inhibit professionalism in meeting the public interest.

As for internal structures, the civil service undertakes its activities through an administrative unit called secretariat. The secretariat controls all administrative functions of the civil service such as recruitment and selection, promotion, wage administration, discipline, separation, and many more. The secretariat discharges some of its functions through the Public Service Commission. The latter is a specialised agency which coordinates and controls the activities of the civil service and ensures that various personnel functions such as recruitment, selection, promotion, transfers, and disciplinary matters are undertaken impartially and professionally. Generally, it acts as an advisory body on personnel matters. Besides, it is generally mandatory that a public service commission should have a statutory existence and powers (Kapur 1996). Usually, members of the Public Service Commission are appointed under special term of tenure, and are protected from removal of office unless under circumstances such as wrongful commissions. This enhances the integrity and independence of its members and operations.

Furthermore, the secretariat is usually divided into 'ministries or departments among which various subjects of government activity are distributed according to administrative convenience. A department is the basic unit of an organisation in which the administrative branch as a whole is under the chief executive' (Basu 2006: 228). Authority to organize departments may vary from country to country and is often vested in the constitution, the parliament, or the executive. It is also common that in departments or ministries there is at least one junior minister whose task is to assist the minister in administrative and parliamentary duties. Besides the political heads, departments or ministries are headed by Permanent Secretaries, whose role epitomises very high responsibility and importance. They help the political head to promote efficiency and effectiveness in the operations of the ministry in conformity with the policy of the government. Ministers have no experience in the art of administration and hence depend heavily on Permanent Secretaries. Besides the Permanent Secretary, there are a number of permanent officials and clerical staff to carry out the routine work of departments (Kapur 1996: 595–596). Concisely that is what characterizes the internal structure of the civil service. The structure facilitates the smooth operations of the civil service and enhances accountability to politicians and the public through the minister in charge of the department.

The civil service in Zambia identifies with the salient features of the administrative machinery in the foregoing description thereby putting the discourse into context as the focus shifts to the Zambian civil service during the precolonial period.

Traces of the Civil Service in the Precolonial Period

The metamorphosis of the civil service in Zambia can be traced as far back as the precolonial period. Before the colonial regime was instituted, Zambia like other African countries was ruled through traditional authority. During this period, authority was mainly based on tribal lines and territories were divided into chiefdoms or kingdoms. A family was a fundamental social unit of traditional authority. Consequently, people lived in territories that were divided on the basis of ethnicity (Roberts 1976). Besides, traditional authority was mainly exercised by kings, chiefs, deputy chiefs, headmen, and military men. The nature of traditional authority is hereditary and hence ascribed on birth. The implication is that authority in the precolonial period was passed from generation to generation to members of the same family or clan.

Other than being hereditary, traditional authority was assumed and expanded through military power such as wars of conquest. The conquerors subjugated the conquered, converted them into servants or slaves, and extended the authority to their territories. Ultimately the conquered were assimilated into the conquerors' society. The nature of traditional authority was authoritative, and unquestionable obedience was expected of subjects. Disloyalty was regarded as a serious offence attracting grave punishment. In some instances it was regarded as a treasonable offence and punishable by death (Chibaye and Bwalya in Subramaniam 1990). Subsequently, administration was regarded as a mere instrument to carry out directives of those in authority. Autonomy and professionalism was conspicuously missing in administration under this era.

With regards to functions, kings and chiefs exercised legislative, executive, and judicial functions through formulation and enforcement of laws, and settlement of disputes among subjects. Besides, they were responsible for protecting their territories and subjects against external aggression and internal disloyalty. They ensured that every subject observed customary laws and traditions (Roberts 1976). Customary laws and traditions formed the foundation of society and defined its existence. Failing to uphold customs and traditions entailed loss of identity and authority. As a result they were to be held in high esteem and protected diligently.

The other key function of traditional leaders was exercising spiritual powers, thereby assuming the role of priests. As priests, they encouraged the worship of ancestral spirits based on the belief that dead relatives had supernatural powers and controlled nature and all spheres of human life like rainfall patterns, drought, harvests, safety, prosperity, and many other related things (Chibaye and Bwalya in Subramaniam 1990). In addition, revenue collection was instituted, and as such, all chiefs levied tribute on beer, labour, local craftwork, food, and crops (Fagan 1966). As noted, revenue collection is not a modern invention in the Zambian public service. Traditional authorities understood the significance of revenue in the operation of the administrative system. The main difference is that whereas the modern trend is to collect the revenue in monetary terms, in the traditional setting, paying in kind was accepted.

Moreover, the chiefs' assistants or personnel performed various functions related to administration. Fagan (1966) notes that hierarchical societies had bureaucracies to carry out certain functions such as collecting taxes, supervising ceremonies, entertaining dignitaries, and compelling people to do the rulers' bidding. In addition, they organized rituals of kingship and determined the succession both to the throne (Roberts 1976). This is similar to what is obtaining in the contemporary Zambian civil service as government ministries and departments are in charge of various functions such as revenue collection and traditional affairs.

In terms of hierarchy, chiefs and deputy chiefs appointed various categories of people such as 'kapasus' to assist them in discharging various duties and ensure execution of orders. Kapasus can be likened to contemporary messengers in the public service. Further, chiefs had various unclassified workers such as slaves who were owned and used at will. This demonstrates that early administration was organized along a hierarchical structure through which traditional authority flowed from the chief to the lowest person, being either a servant or slave as dictated by the circumstance. The traditional structure was centralized because power was increasingly concentrated within a small circle of the chief's close relations. For example among the Bemba kingdom, a group of hereditary councillors called Bakabilo formed a core of the then administration (Chikulo 1981). The existence of the hierarchy, from the chief to the assistants signifies that ideas of organizing administration existed well before the establishment of the colonial regime. The traditional setting was well organized and the assistants or administration did not have a separate structure; they were simply at the lowest level of the hierarchy. This explains their unquestionable obedience to the ruler's orders.

Consequently, there are several features that are associated with the administrative machinery under this era. One of the outstanding features is that administration was organized on a self-rule basis where traditional authority administered its affairs without external interference as long as it was not challenged and overcome by external aggression. This entailed that administration lasted as long as traditional authority was not disrupted by external enemies. As soon as the chiefdom or kingdom was conquered, the administrative setting was equally disrupted. The other feature is that administration under this period was organized on the basis of patronage. This implies that appointment of administrative officers, army leaders, chiefs' advisers, spiritual leaders, and other related officials was mainly based on kinship, descent, ascription and patronage. The implication is that personnel functions such as recruitment, training, promotion, retention, and other rewards were based on ascription and loyalty rather than merit or achievement. Moreover, such personnel rewards were considered a privilege and to serve the chief was a symbol of honour (Fagan 1966). Subsequently, loyalty was seen as a duty arising from inter-web relations within the clan. This is in contrast with the contemporary Zambian civil service, which is organized on the basis of merit. Subsequently, personnel functions such as recruitment, development, wage administration, promotion are essentially based on merit in the modern setting.

In addition, as a result of the patronage-based administrative system, the chiefs' servants, advisers, military men, and other types of workers enjoyed life careers as long as loyalty was observed. Therefore the personnel under the traditional administrative setting constituted the chiefs' appointed officials who enjoyed life tenures and served in different capacities such as administrative officers and army leaders (Chibaye and Bwalya in Subramaniam 1990). Contrary to the life tenure, the contemporary Zambian Civil Service has a limited tenure where people have to retire from serving at some point in time. Moreover, there is a new trend of short-term employment contracts in the public service particularly at the higher echelons of the administrative structure.

Additionally, the traditional authority was authoritative and highly centralized. Subsequently, the personnel demonstrated a high level of discipline and loyalty in executing orders. In fact training in loyalty was initiated during childhood in preparation for administrative tasks (Chibaye and Bwalya in Subramaniam 1990: 290). As a result, the values of loyalty and discipline were passed on from generation to generation through training young generations.

Having looked at the key features of administration during this period, several strengths, weaknesses, and lessons can be identified. In terms of strengths, the chief's assistants and servants were essentially disciplined and exhibited a high degree of loyalty in the execution of orders. The lesson drawn here is that obedience and loyalty among administrators is very important even in the modern setting. In the absence of that, public policies cannot be implemented effectively and government's programmes can be thwarted and sabotaged. Discipline and diligence are cardinal in the civil service if it has to be performance oriented and achieve results and intended goals. This entails that top civil servants are expected to be highly disciplined as far as ensuring the performance of their respective ministries and departments is concerned. They should set explicit targets and put in place monitoring mechanism to deter and eradicate inertia generally associated with the public workforce.

Moreover, the top civil servants are expected to be loyal to the political heads in the context of professionalism and that of serving the public interest. This entails that they should be sufficiently tactful to harmonise political interests and professionalism. In a democratic country, loyalty to political heads is justified by the principle of representative government, where the interest of the public is largely assumed to be represented by those voted in authoritative offices. Once a culture of high discipline and diligence is exhibited by the top officers, it will diffuse to lower echelons of the administrative hierarchies and the public interest is likely to be met and not compromised. Ultimately, attaining national developmental goals would not be a far-fetched dream.

The second strength is that personnel enjoyed lifelong careers which promoted stability and continuity. Stability among administrative officers is a significant benefit as it creates a sense of security and commitment among workers. This principle is particularly critical in a democratic political setting because politicians are less stable because of limited tenure of office. Administrative officers therefore facilitate the much-needed stability and continuity of government to avoid disruption of policy implementation.

Thirdly, the authoritative nature of traditional chiefs and the subsequent obedience without questioning made the traditional chiefs establish strong kingdoms (Roberts 1976). This may appear to be a disadvantage at face value. However, decision-making and execution of orders was quick because of the concentration of power in few people, thereby making administrative systems efficient and reliable. Subsequently, the salient lesson is that there is need to balance between centralization and decentralization in order to maximize the benefits from both trends. This is because over-centralization of power is inconsistent with administrative systems that exist in a democratic political system, but caution should be taken against over decentralization because it tends to create coordination problems.

Despite the foregoing strengths, the administrative system had several inherent weaknesses. The first weakness relates to appointments based on patronage and ascription rather on merit (Fagan 1966). The practice was discriminatory in nature as it meant that subjects without close kinship ties to the royal clan would not benefit from the ensuing rewards. Moreover, it deprived the system the benefits that are associated with the merit-based administration such as fairness and superior performance. Moreover patronage-based reward systems tend to demoralise hard-working personnel and ultimately result in poor work outputs.

Furthermore, a scenario where traditional rulers wielded unlimited power made servants carry out orders even at the expense of ordinary people. The implication is that the traditional society was largely vulnerable to chiefs because servants and the administrative machinery became instruments of cruelty. Moreover, servants were not obliged to serve the public; rather, their allegiance was to the chief and had to serve him unconditionally. Serving the public interest was therefore nonexistence as far as administrative officers were concerned as the administrative machinery largely depended on the personality and whims of the chief (Mulinge and Lesetedi 1998). In the modern setting, the civil service is a device for meeting public interest and cannot be used as an instrument of cruelty by those in power. Moreover, in a democratic political environment, the civil service and government at large are often moderated by different stakeholders such as the civil society to compel them where necessary to act in public interest.

On the overall, despite the shortcomings of the administrative system in the precolonial period, certain successes stand out such as well-organized societies, and high level of loyalty and discipline. However, like other African countries, traditional authority was undermined with the introduction of colonial regime

(Mulinge and Lesetedi 1998). Therefore, it would be interesting to consider how the administrative machinery was organized under the colonial government.

The Civil Service in the Colonial Era: The British South Africa Company Administration

The foregoing administrative system was organized on the basis of self-rule by the traditional authority. This changed with the arrival of the British South Africa Company (BSA). The company was granted a royal charter by the British government to administer the territory allocated south and north of Zambezi River. The territory was named Rhodesia in honour of the owner of the company, Cecil Rhodes. The establishment of the company rule marked the beginning of colonial rule and the administrative system had to be organized on that basis. This signalled the advent of the evolution of the administrative machinery, from self-rule tribal-based administration to a colonially dominated system (Chibaye and Bwalya in Subramaniam 1990). Moreover, because of its vastness and for administrative convenience, the territory was divided into two parts, North-Western Rhodesia and North-Eastern Rhodesia. The colonization of Northern Rhodesia can be divided into two broad phases, namely the BSA Company rule and the British colonial government. The BSA Company rule began in the 1890s and ended in 1924, marking the first phase of colonialism. The second and final phase was ushered in when the BSA Company surrendered the rule of the territory to the British colonial government in 1924 and the latter assumed full responsibility of ruling the territory until in 1964 when Zambia attained political independence (Tordoff 1980). The two phases of colonialism had implications on the administrative machinery thereby contributing to the development of the civil service in Zambia.

The BSA Company began to administer North-Eastern Rhodesia and Nyasaland, and North-Western Rhodesia in 1891 and 1897 respectively. The territories were administered as two separate entities, namely North-Western Rhodesia and North-Eastern Rhodesia. Inevitably the British government had to grant two different charters to the company to cater for each territory. The provisions of the charters gave monopolistic commercial rights to the BSA Company and charged it with the responsibility of administering the area in the name of the Crown' (Dresang 1975: 15). However, in 1911, the two territories were amalgamated into one, called Northern Rhodesia. The main rationale for amalgamation was to create a large pool of economic resources (Lungu 1975). Also it was easier to coordinate administrative affairs in a unified territory than a divided one, thereby promoting efficiency in operations.

One of the salient features of the BSA Company rule was the embracing of a direct-rule policy in administering the territories. Under this policy, the British government controlled the administration of Northern Rhodesia directly through a team of officials headed by the BSA Company's administrator. The implication of direct rule was that even though administrative decisions were made directly by the British government from home, it was a team of company officers which was visibly involved in running the administrative affairs of the colonial territory (Cabinet Office 1967). This administrative outlook was necessary to enable the BSA Company take charge of the operations of the territory and realise its profit interest because its decision to rule the territory was profit motivated. Subsequently, the BSA Company instituted a prefectoral system of administration with some discretionary powers exercised by field officers. 'A prefectoral system of administration utilizes an officer of government to supervise implementation of programmes at the local level and to exercise general control over subnational government. Although designed to control from the centre, these systems often develop in ways that allow local governments to have substantial influence in the centre' (Peters 2001: 11963–11965). As much as the BSA Company controlled the administrative machinery from the centre, the discretionary powers exercised by field officers provided significant influence at the centre because the latter exercised delegated powers by taking care of administrative affairs at the local level. Besides, traditional rulers were incorporated in the traditional administration of civil service to represent indigenous people (Mulikita 1996). In practice, Robert E. Codrington, the first administrator of North-East Rhodesia organized an administrative team comprising of company officers, chiefs, kapasus, and court of messengers. This team formed a government network which acted as a central point of service (Cabinet Office 1967). Despite the inclusion of the locals in the administrative team, they had no significant influence in decision-making. They merely carried out orders of the BSA Company.

Another outstanding feature to be derived from this era is the domination of foreign rule as opposed to the native or self-rule. The implication on the administrative machinery was that it was run on the basis of racial discrimination. Subsequently, many decisions and actions such as racially differentiated wage plans were implemented to reinforce the distinction and discrimination between the two classes of workers consisting of Europeans and Africans. Furthermore, indigenous people were not only alienated from administrative authority, but also from political power and economic wealth, thereby occupying a lower social status in every sphere of life. As Dresang (1975: 14) argues, 'the establishment of rule by an alien group over an indigenous population results in a society in which a culturally distinct minority holds a preponderance of political power, economic wealth, and social status. Access to power is restricted to members of the culturally distinct ruling minority and the subjugated majority are relegated to a low position in all dimensions of social organisation'. Consequently, the ruling minority in Northern Rhodesia comprised of Europeans from various occupational backgrounds such as bureaucrats, missionaries, farmers, and miners (Cabinet Office 1967). The varied background implied that their interests would be in conflict with one another. However, there was a basic solidarity among these groups for the purpose of preserving their identity over the majority indigenous black population (Chibaye and Bwalya in Subramaniam 1990: 292). One important decision taken to reinforce racism in the administrative machinery was related to Codrington, the first administrator's demand that the qualification to be met by those recruited to serve in administration of the territory should be as follows: 'young men from England with a good physique, middle-class background, university education, and preferably, some teaching experience' (Dresang 1975: 13). His justification for such an array of personal attributes of potential employees was to command prestige and respect among the indigenous black people. As such, he 'argued that if the deference of colonised Africans could not be secured through the use of born rulers from a superior civilisation, then colonial presence could only be maintained through expensive military force' (Gann 1964: 96). This is similar to what Dresang (1975) noted in the following assertion:

> The imperatives for bureaucratic recruitment in Northern
> Rhodesia were to restrict to Europeans the access to positions

of any significant status or responsibility in order to maintain the myth of European racial and cultural superiority, it was essential to follow Codrington's advice and employ Europeans who possessed leadership ability and characterised the alleged best of European culture. This was especially important for positions where there would be the most contact with Africans. (Dresang 1975: 14–16)

Likewise, it is worth noting that 'the primary objective of colonialism in Northern Rhodesia was to pacify the country to allow exploitation of the Country's raw minerals. Subsequently, the early personnel recruited to administer the country were military men' (Subramanian 1990: 290). Subsequently, the prevalence of military personnel under the BSA Company rule produced an authoritative cadre of administrators with a firm control of things to ensure the company's profit-motivated interests were preserved. Dresang (1975: 17–18) notes that

In spite of Codrington's desire to recruit athletic, middle-class Englishmen with a university degree, not all the company's employees matched that criterion. In addition to the university graduates, the soldier adventurers who spearheaded the initial extension of company rule over the area north of the Zambezi were prominent in the ranks of provincial administration. Many of these were veterans of the pacification battles waged in South Africa and Southern Rhodesia, as well as Northern Rhodesia.

This shows that the administrative machinery under the colonial administration was not intended to spearhead development of the territory. Rather, it was a tool of oppression by the European settlers whose agendum was not development administration, but maintenance of minority interests. The implication on recruitment was that the upper echelon of the bureaucratic structure had to be filled by Europeans. Such a disposition exemplifies a value system embedded in a colonial society whereby there was an advancement of superiority complexities of the rulers over the ruled. Consequently, racial discrimination was predominant during the BSA Company rule administration.

Moreover, 'when the BSA Company began administering the North-Eastern and North-Western Rhodesia, it hired all personnel on a renewable contract basis but no provision was made for grading staff positions and enabling officers to calculate for promotions and opportunities for a full career' (Dresang 1975: 16). Therefore, short-term employment was what characterised the initial civil service personnel of the BSA Company. This is in contrast with life tenures enjoyed by personnel under the precolonial period. Nevertheless, 'in 1901, Codrington changed this and initiated a graded civil service that promised a full career. Based upon the higher frequency of resignations and level of discontent among officials in North-Western Rhodesia, the advantages of having a civil service were judged to outweigh the costs' (Dresang 1975: 16). The full career service continued even after the company had surrendered the territory to the colonial office. Subsequently, a full career civil service is one of Codrington's landmark contributions to the development of the civil service in Zambia. As indicated earlier, as much as there were traces of the administrative machinery, in the precolonial period, personnel were not graded until the establishment of the BSA Company rule. Moreover, they were not formally recognized as personnel; rather, the term has been imputed as they served traditional rulers in various endeavours.

Another administrative feature under this period can be identified in the context of administrative behaviour. The BSA Company's form of administration skewed towards the attainment, consolidation, and maintenance of British colonial policies to ensure control (Cabinet Office 1967). As noted by Chibaye and Bwalya (in Subramaniam 1990: 290) 'the administrative style involved directing, ordering, and forcing the indigenous people to undertake various tasks such as paying poll and hut tax to raise revenue for administration. This led to the increase of duties and responsibilities of the administration of Northern Rhodesia by the BSA Company.' Poll tax was charged on an individual as a requirement to participate in voting and hut tax was charged on a household basis. Through taxes, indigenous people were contributing to income generation to facilitate operations of the administrative machinery. Moreover, the BSA Company was profit oriented and hence collection of revenue to expand the local revenue base was taken seriously. It is important to note that both under the precolonial period and the BSA Company rule, revenue collection was a significant aspect of administration. The main difference bordered on the nature of sources of revenue. For example, poll tax and hut tax were the major source of revenue during the colonial period, whereas such taxes did not apply to the precolonial era. Moreover, both periods adopted forceful administrative styles. For example during the traditional administrative setting, servants served according to the dictates of chiefs and kings, and under the BSA Company rule, the style was militant in nature.

However, in the long run, the BSA Company realised that the amalgamation of North-Eastern Rhodesia and North-Western Rhodesia into Northern Rhodesia was not a profitable undertaking as it did not result in a surplus of income over expenditure. 'Between 1914 and 1924 the company had to absorb losses averaging £130,000 a year and by 1924 the company had accumulated a deficit of £1.5 million. Faced with such costs and without any immediate prospect of a favourable alteration to the situation, the company understandably sought to rid itself of administrative responsibility for Northern Rhodesia (Dresang 1975: 16). The foregoing loss was a big setback for a profit-making company and hence the decision to give up responsibility over the territory. Moreover, soon after the First World War, the company made plans to charge income tax on white settlers. Subsequently, the white settlers were also eager to see the company rule come to an end. 'This prompted the settlers to petition the company and the British government to reform the system of administration in Northern Rhodesia so that taxpayers could be certain their money was being used with care and discretion and was not being collected in order to show a big profit margin for a commercial company' (Bradley 1961: 446–452). In 1921 negotiations between the company and the British government began culminating in creation of the Northern Rhodesia Order in Council of 1924. The agreement declared the territory a British protectorate, followed by the establishment of a Crown Colony form of government to administer it (Chibaye and Bwalya in Subramaniam 1990) hence the next focus of the discourse.

The Administrative Machinery under the Colonial Office Rule

The beginning of the second phase of the colonial administration is marked by the British government's decision to take over the rule of Northern Rhodesia from the BSA Company. Consequently, a policy shift from direct rule to indirect rule was ushered in by the passing of the Whitehall policy in 1930 which abolished the former (Cabinet Office 1967). The implication of indirect rule was that the administrative affairs of Northern Rhodesia would be administered through the already instituted traditional leaders. Subsequently, local authorities were to be incorporated into the colonial administration to administer local affairs according to existing structures, customs, and laws. The main justification of indirect rule was to involve traditional leaders in local administration and the colonial government was to work at arm's length and not visibly (Cabinet Office 1967). In terms of the evolution of the civil service, the shift from direct to indirect was a significant feature as it entailed indigenous traditional authority would play a much more active role in administering local affairs. Therefore native authorities were established, and 'some local chiefs who accepted the British rule were appointed to serve authorities in advisory capacities' (Chibaye and Bwalya in Subramaniam 1990: 292). These traditional leaders were expected to interpret administrative regulations to indigenous people. Subsequently, the colonial administration exhibited a dual system, one for natives and another for whites. The dual administrative system presupposed that on one hand, it would cater for the natives while on the other hand, it would take care of the white minority groups that were settled along the Line of Rail (Mulikita 1996). As noted by Lungu (1982) indirect rule was an attempt to delegate administrative authority to Africans through their indigenous institutions comprised of chiefs and village headmen. It was expected that the foregoing administrative arrangement would benefit the local people.

However, in reality, indirect-rule policy did not promote participation of the local people. Rather the intention of the policy was merely to make the colonial government accepted to the natives. This is in line with Chibaye and Bwalya's argument in Subramaniam (1990: 292) that 'the rationale behind indirect rule was for the colonial administration to gain legitimacy as it ruled through local leaders'. Therefore, the local chiefs acted in the interest of the colonial and government and not for the benefit of the local people. Further, Chibaye and Bwalya (in Subramaniam 1990) noted that 'the colonial administration could exert pressure on local chiefs to ensure compliance with the wishes of the administration'. Moreover, Lungu (1982) argued that the incorporation of traditional leaders into administrative systems was not intended to widen discretionary powers over their communities but merely to employ them as tools for administrative efficiency and convenience. Moreover, Chikulo (1981) in the assertion below brought out something noteworthy:

> Indirect rule was a type of rule which involved running side by side of the European colonial administration with traditional authority. It was organised by either incorporating weak chiefs or creating illegitimate ones and putting them under the native affairs department to administer the affairs of the local people. This was done by taking traditional structures and transforming them into Native Authorities. Therefore, chiefs were given power and jurisdiction over traditional affairs and where there were no chiefs, the colonial government appointed some. (Chikulo 1981)

The foregoing assertion implies that colonial rule created rivalry relationships among local chiefs because some were perceived to be more favoured than others. In the context of administration, it entails that chiefs who cooperated with the colonial government would have more presence in the administrative machinery than the non-cooperative ones. Besides, the dual administrative system encouraged perpetration of racism experienced under the BSA Company rule. The other rationale of indirect rule was that it was 'cheaper to administer the area through chiefs than it would have been through direct rule' (Chibaye and Bwalya in Subramaniam 1990: 290). Therefore, it can be deduced that indirect rule was also a cost-saving measure, thereby making local chiefs and local people sources of cheap labour. The colonial government might have learnt a lesson on saving costs from the BSA Company's direct policy because the latter ultimately became quite expensive to run, leading to the transfer of the territory to the former.

Another prominent feature of the administrative system arising from indirect rule is a decentralised structure. 'The colonial administration was much decentralized and effective control was in the hands of the district commissioner and his small staff. The district commissioner and his staff had extensive operational responsibilities and performed a wide range of legislative, administrative, and judicial tasks' (Chibaye and Bwalya in Subramaniam 1990: 292). Subsequently, Northern Rhodesia was divided into administrative units consisting of provinces and districts and appointed provincial administrative heads called provincial commissioners and district commissioners respectively (Mukwena 2001). The provincial commissioner was answerable to the governor, who in turn was answerable to the colonial secretary based in London. In 1953, the amalgamation of Northern and Southern Rhodesia and Nyasaland ushered in the federation. Politically, the positions of governor general and executive prime minister were introduced. Provincial administration personnel's primary responsibility was to maintain order and subservience among the indigenous population (Cabinet Office 1967). The decentralized administration under the colonial office rule is a significant feature of the evolution of the civil service as it marked the departure from the relatively centralised or prefectoral system under the BSA Company's direct-rule policy and the precolonial period.

As for racism, the colonial government perpetrated it from the BSA Company administration. However, early efforts to establish a merit-based or professional civil service in the colonial administration were attempted in 1945 though its composition comprised of expatriate officers appointed from Britain (Cabinet Office 1967). The implication of such appointments was that the colonial civil service was dominated by foreigners rather than indigenous people, thereby making racial discrimination entrenched in the civil service as noted below:

> The Fitzgerald report which was published in 1947 reinforced the racial division as it came up with different recommendations and conditions of service for African and European staff. The pattern of separating European and African staff conditions continued with the Follows Report in 1952 which was presented in separate parts to deal with each sector. Additionally, in 1956 the Harragin Report affected super scale salaries which meant that only the expatriates would benefit from the system. (Cabinet Office 1967: 22)

All these efforts resulted in a two-tier structured racially divided civil service consisting of European and African workers as indicated below:

> The Northern Rhodesian African Civil Service was divided into a Junior Service and a Senior Service. There were no

minimum education requirements that had to be met for
admittance into the junior service, although preference was
given to those literate in English or, at least, in one of the
local languages. Of the 4705 members of this service in 1957
most were guards, district messengers and clerks. However
the racial divisions were not as prominent in the pay system
and civil service conditions of services as in the administrative
responsibility. The fact that only members of the European
Civil Service were eligible for the higher positions in the
administrative system meant that the benefits of authority and
status attached to these positions were the exclusive property of
the culturally distinct, ruling minority in Northern Rhodesia.
(Dresang 1975: 28–31)

The persistent discriminatory policies were meant to impoverish African
workers because poor wages negatively affected their families and the local
community at large. All these factors negatively affected the civil service,
thereby making it dysfunctional and irresponsive to local development.

Apart from establishment of indirect rule and the consequential creation
of a dual administrative system, the major factor that could be attributed
to the evolution of the civil service during the colonial rule was an attempt
to abolish formal racial divisions in the Northern Rhodesia administrative
system. However, in reality, the Whitehall policy did not completely abolish
direct rule as the influence of the BSA Company on administration signified
by the presence of former BSA Company employees persisted until 1945. This
scenario deprived the administration of the professional civil service that could
spearhead the administrative affairs of Northern Rhodesia as the officers were
essentially military in nature (Chibaye and Bwalya in Subramaniam 1990). As
Dresang (1975: 17) states, the colonial office retained the basic administrative
structure that had been established by the company and invited employees of
the company to become civil servants of the British Crown. As such, former
company employees became the core of administrative staff in the early years of
colonial administration or office rule. Moreover, a circular issued by the chief
secretary of the civil service was issued on 18 August 1955 stating the shift in
policy. Subsequently, all positions in the administration were open on equal

terms to all suitably qualified inhabitants of Northern Rhodesia, regardless of race, colour, or creed (Cabinet Office 1967). However, in reality the statement was merely rhetoric because there was perpetration of racial discrimination against Africans in the civil service. Since racism became an entrenched culture with persistent value systems which resisted alteration, its beneficiaries tended to endeavour to maintain it (Cabinet Office 1967). However, 'the pressures felt by the increasing strength of the independence movement in Northern Rhodesia and Nyasaland and by the steps towards decolonization that were taking place throughout the British empire combined to prompt the government to take a further step to eliminate the formal racial divisions in the structure of the civil service. Moreover, 'in 1959, it was announced that a single and unified civil service would be organized to replace the existing African and European civil services' (Dresang 1975: 38). The announcement must have been a relief to the local people because it created an opportunity to seek career advanced prospects in the civil service.

Nevertheless, 'it was not until November 1961 that a local civil service was established on a non-racial basis, making possible the implementation of what was an accepted policy of African advancement. The implication is that the civil service became unified. Consequently, 'conditions of service were worked out for locally based officers, although this could not and did not do away with the continued and continuing existence of expatriate officers who served on conditions of service separate to them' (Cabinet Office 1967: 22). The colonial government expected that many of the European civil servants, as well as Africans, would transfer to local conditions of service. However, by October 1961, when the details of the local service were made public, the future of an independent Zambia under majority rule was slowly becoming a reality. The Europeans were quite apprehensive about working for an independent African civil service as signified by the small number of Europeans transferring to local conditions. Moreover, the financial benefits that were available from remaining on expatriate terms of service were sufficient for most to desist from accepting local conditions (Dresang 1975). Therefore, the foregoing financial compensation partly acted as a deterrent to Europeans as far as joining the civil service was concerned.

Although the formal racial divisions were eliminated in the reorganization of the civil service, there was little alteration to the European predominance in the senior positions and the African predominance in the junior ranks. In October 1963, one year before independence, all positions in divisions III and IV were filled by Africans. To amplify the persistence of racial divisions in the civil service, the composition of divisions I and II was as follows:

Figure 1

	Europeans	Africans	Others	Totals
Division I	1,256	39	3	1,298
Division II	2,692	1,882	11	4,585
Total	3,948	1,921	14	5,883

Source: Dresang 1975: 39

With regards to strengths, the administrative system under the colonial regime had its own inherent good practices worth of emulation. First and foremost, 'the colonial administrative systems had been successful in consolidating British rule, pacifying conquered areas, maintaining law and order, and promoting the development of commercial mining and to some extent agricultural activities' (Chibaye and Bwalya in Subramaniam 1990: 232). This is a merit, at least on the part of the colonial government. The administrative system strengthened the colonial regime in Northern Rhodesia and enhanced its stability until the time of independence. If the civil service was weak, colonialism would not have been sustained that long, from the 1890s to 1964. The sustainability of the colonial government contributed to Northern Rhodesia's territorial stability as it was difficult for external forces to disrupt it. The assumption is that without the establishment of the colonial government, the Northern Rhodesia territory would not have existed. This is because, traditionally, territories were based on tribal lines. The implication is that without colonial administration, Zambia would not have been born as a nation; instead, the territory would have continued to be organized as chiefdoms and kingdoms, and tribal wars would have persisted. Therefore, despite the ills associated with the colonial administration, it acted to a large extent as a unifying factor of diverse tribes and ultimately was a predecessor of the Zambian nation. Therefore, the structure of the Zambian society owes much to the colonial legacy. Without colonialism, nation-building could have been an insurmountable challenge or indeed non-existent.

Another strength is that the colonial administration acted as a pace setter in terms of building modern institutions. It left an administrative system in place such that upon attaining independence, the Zambian government did not have to reinvent the wheel. The government inherited the administrative structure as designed by the colonial government. Moreover, the administrative machinery was not imposed on the Zambian government but a decision was made to inherit it without significant modifications. Although the structure was not responsive to development, there were principles and civil service ethos that were inherited. The implication is that civil culture in terms of administrative behaviour and ethos were passed from colonial civil servants to their Zambian counterparts. The argument is that the passing of the civil service culture from the colonial to the new administration was a positive contribution. Whether the culture was functional or dysfunctional is not the concern for now.

In addition, industrial harmony and teamwork were exhibited by the colonial administrators as far as working relationships among themselves, and with the British government, were concerned. It is difficult to come across documented industrial unrest among European workers. Of course one may argue that there was no need for such eventualities since European personnel had a better official status and conditions of service than their local counterparts. Nevertheless, the loyal disposition and commitment demonstrated by colonial administrators to the appointing authority and perpetration of colonialism is worthy of emulation by the Zambian public servants. For example, they could send timely and confidential reports to the Home government to perpetrate its rule (Cabinet Office 1967). Without high degree of loyalty among them, Zambia could have attained independence much earlier.

Another merit worth emulation is that the Europeans officers had an entrepreneurial spirit in the way they operated. This was essentially driven by 'paternalistic motivations and aspirations to erect personal monuments to their presence, officers saw that roads were built, bridges erected, irrigation systems developed, cash agriculture begun, and other small-scale projects completed. Of course, not all initiatives by colonial officers were development-oriented' (Dresang 1975: 14). This entails that the personnel were generally intrinsically motivated and had a desire to personally leave some landmark over which to act as memorial.

However, the administrative system under the colonial regime had numerous pitfalls. The main weakness of the colonial administration was the practice of racism manifested in the establishment of a two-tier racially divided civil service with separate conditions of service for African and European workers, resulting in ethically unjustifiable disparities in terms of recruitment and rewards. The scenario was demonstrated by racially based employment practices where indigenous people were employed in very low civil administrative ranks, thereby denying them participation in decision-making. Subsequently, the civil service skewed towards meeting only the interests of European workers at the expense of their African counterparts. However, racial discrimination in the administrative machinery and society in general became a subtle catalyst of independence as it created political awareness, unity, and desire for attaining freedom from the colonial regime. Without it, indigenous people probably would have been content under the colonial regime for a long time and would not have put up a spirited fight resulting in delays in attaining independence.

The other weakness was that 'the cultural eliticism and political authority possessed by the colonial administration created the image of the civil service as a reservoir of social status and political power. Natives aspired to positions of responsibility in the civil service both for personal gain and for chance to improve the general welfare of the locals in Northern Rhodesia. These aspirations were frustrated, however, as the civil service was the property of Europeans' (Dresang 1975: 32). Moreover, in terms of administrative behaviour, the European administrators exhibited a bossy attitude when relating to the indigenous people. Consequently, they did not link so much with the grass roots, thereby creating a wide gap between civil servants and ordinary citizens (Dresang 1975). Interestingly, this disposition seems to be a colonial legacy in the modern civil service, where the civil servants have formed middle-class elite which does not necessarily link with the masses. Such a disposition is detrimental and dysfunctional to socio-economic development.

Furthermore, the bureaucratic machinery under the colonial regime was essentially characterised by 'a power-laden hierarchy pursuing activities oriented to the routine tasks of maintaining public records, collecting revenue, and preserving order' (Dresang 1975: 1). As such, the administrative machinery was not oriented towards development and this partly explains why the colonial regime did not leave significant developmental traces in Northern Rhodesia. As much as administration was fragmented, control and decision-making were highly centralised, thereby making the local stakeholders like chiefs, mere colonial instruments for executing routine orders as earlier noted.

Likewise, the legacy of a racial-based recruitment system left a severe shortage of skilled labour for the newly independent Zambian government and the civil service in particular. Dresang (1975: 14) noted that 'separate institutions were established for European and African civil servants and only the most menial and insignificant of tasks were filled by members of the African civil service. It was not until the last few years of the colonial period that the barriers to African advancement in the public service were removed'. Of course, the foregoing practice was deliberate and intended to perpetrate the colonial rule.

Additionally, the British government's policy of indirect rule was dysfunctional on local administration in certain respects. It negatively influenced traditional leaders by making them compromise the application of traditional authority. Nkhrumah in Mulinge and Lesetedi (1998: 22) argues, 'Precolonial chiefs had limited and controlled powers. However, with the coming of the colonial regime, they were manipulated in the way local affairs were administered.' According to Leonard in Mulinge and Lesetedi (1998: 22) the colonial government expected colonial chiefs 'to be authoritarian figures who could make quick and final decisions and commanding respect and even fear. Chiefs were not notable for their respect of the niceties of law and or due process, they were known instead for their decisiveness, courage, presence, and ability to hold the crowd'. Therefore, the support given to chiefs by colonial government made the chiefs well established at the expense of being popular among the subjects and legitimacy of the chief was measured in terms of their strengthened position.

Further, since civil servants were appointed by the colonial government, loyalty was ascribed to the appointing authorities whose priority was not to serve the natives' interests but to seek the advancement of the colonial government. The focus was to use the civil service to enhance order and control to prevent any potential insurgency from the natives. Moreover, European officials under the British government could be deployed at any time to other colonies. This created a degree of disloyalty to serving local interests and undermined a sense of belonging and stability among them. This negatively affected the performance of the civil service (Cabinet Office 1967). These weaknesses indicate the colonial civil service was neither to develop Northern Rhodesia nor to meet interests of the local people.

Despite the numerous inherent weaknesses of the colonial regime, there are salient lessons that can be emulated by the contemporary civil service. Firstly, the colonial administration was focused on its main goal of consolidating the rule of the colonial government. Likewise, if the contemporary Zambian civil service became focused and committed to attaining developmental goals, it would not be very long before significant results begin to manifest. Related to this is a lesson on loyalty and diligence exhibited by the colonial personnel thereby producing an efficient administrative system from a perspective of meeting the interests of the white minority. The lesson is that the Zambian public servants should be loyal and committed to meeting the public interest. For example, it should emulate the colonial regime in efficient record-keeping and generating reports to the departmental and ministerial political supervisors in a meticulous and timely manner to enable them to take charge of ministerial and national affairs in a diligent manner. Therefore, performance management through setting and monitoring explicit performance targets and standards should be implemented in reality throughout the civil service hierarchy to enhance performance.

Moreover, the colonial government identified means for reducing administrative operational costs such as the indirect-rule policy, where traditional leaders were involved in administering local affairs. Likewise, the government through the civil service should explore feasible ways of reducing operational costs and enhancing performance. Apart from performance management, it is necessary to reorient a 'wage culture and mindset' prevalent among workers in Zambia. This statement is not meant to be against good conditions of service or indeed the good works of trade unions. However, there is a seemingly negative culture or imbalance of emphasizing on good wages without a commensurate passion for commitment, hard work and serving public interest, and producing tangible performance results. This tends to be unhealthy and often leads to an inefficient and non-responsive public service.

Therefore, the main recommendation on the foregoing is that the government should strengthen its partnership with trade unions by involving them in national and local strategic decision-making processes and monitoring of performance of their members. Besides, the new trend of public management signified by public–private partnerships (PPPs) and out-contracting in and out of services through public tendering need close and effective monitoring, failure to which may result in the provision of low-quality public goods and services and corrupt tendencies.

Another lesson from this era is that the colonial administration embarked on revenue collection in a meticulous manner. Likewise, Zambia should explore innovative ways of collecting revenue to expand the revenue base and direct the collected revenue to intended purposes or key developmental undertakings such as job creation directly or indirectly. One way this can be done is creating a formal and strong link with the think tank. Through this, viable ideas bordering on resolving various challenges facing the civil service and government at large can be generated.

On the overall, the evolution of the civil service under the colonial office administration can be summarised as follows:

- The creation of a dual administrative system to cater for African and European affairs
- An attempt to eradicate racial discrimination and the ultimate abolition of a two-tier racially discriminated civil service
- Appearance of a professional civil service
- An initial attempt to establish a unified civil service

With regards to the main contrast of the experience of administration under the precolonial and colonial era, the former was entrenched on patronage and ascription, resulting in discrimination of the indigenous people by the indigenous people, while the latter with its racially divided civil service led to the discrimination of the indigenous people by the foreigners. Which one between the two is a lesser evil is not the concern of this discourse.

The Civil Service in the Postcolonial Era: First Republic

The civil service under the postcolonial era has been reviewed under three major dispensations as follows: the First, Second, and Third Republic. An attempt has been made to bring salient features under each republic. Soon after independence, the civil service started experiencing various notable changes such as personnel reforms through the indigenization policy. However, it should be pointed out that the changes were generally applied in a gradual rather than drastic manner. The chapter will now focus on the First Republic.

The attainment of Zambia's political independence in 1964 under Kenneth Kaunda's United National Independence Party (UNIP) ushered in the First Republic of Zambia. Politically, this period was characterised by plural politics and continued until 1972. Subsequently, the civil service was reorganized according to the aspiration of the new government. Immediately after independence, one of government's preoccupations was to eradicate racial discrimination from the civil service. This is because racial discrimination continued throughout the colonial period despite several attempts to address it. Consequently, it was necessary to address it to pave way for accelerated development and deal with inbuilt emotions and frustrations resulting from the discrimination of indigenous people from socio-economic privileges. Therefore, one of the earliest notable changes relates to the establishment of a unified civil service in which African and European workers were to be treated on an equal basis. Subsequently, with the advent of independence and on the basis of the Hadow Commission Report of 1964, the Zambian civil service was apparently born a unified service (Cabinet Office 1967: 4). This change was considered to be urgent and significant to allow Zambians take charge of administrative affairs.

Additionally, another pressing task for the government was to transform the inherited fragmented 'structure of provincial administration which was the focal point of the colonial system of government into instruments of economic development because at independence Zambia inherited a fragmented civil service not suitable for attaining socio-economic goals' (Tordoff 1980: 185). Subsequently, the old system of provincial and district government which was arranged to coordinate and implement government policies could not provide a useful link between government and the new structure of party power

(Tordoff 1980). The new administrative machinery had to be reorganized and some of the native authorities' functions such as responsibility for agriculture, conservation, and primary education were transferred to central government (Mukwena (2001: 37). The change of hierarchy from a decentralized form under the colonial regime to a centralized one after the attainment of independence denotes a significant feature of evolution of the civil service under this dispensation. Moreover, in 1969, Kaunda appointed a cabinet minister for each province (Chibaye and Bwalya in Subramaniam 1990). The change from a fragmented or decentralised administrative structure to a relatively centralised one was meant to spearhead the much-needed socio-economic development in the newly independent state because Zambia inherited a bureaucracy with a high social status and substantial political authority. The initial design of the civil service was to preserve order and stability. Subsequently, the civil service was not suited as an engine of propelling development. Besides, the government was of the view that the civil service should not adopt slavish norms of past traditions and practices as the single basis for its development. As much as it was acknowledged that there were good features to be taken from the Whitehall type of civil service under the colonial government, it was not entirely appropriate to the requirements of a country with an agendum of urgent nation-building and economic development (Cabinet Office 1967). As much as order and stability was still important, it was inevitable to expand the role of the civil service to embrace nation-building and economic development.

In addition, personnel had to be reorganized because under the colonial regime, European workers dominated the civil service in terms of numbers, ranks, and conditions of service, as noted under the colonial era. After the unified civil service was established which focused on the eradication of racial discrimination, the government's priority was to replace Europeans with Zambians through a policy of indigenization commonly referred to as Zambianization. The government took cognisance that the change would take time due to shortage of skills; nevertheless, the process was initiated (Cabinet Office 1967). Therefore, apart from the unification and centralization of the civil service, Zambianization is another significant feature of the Civil Service under the First Republic. Zambianization is a landmark in personnel reforms because it indicates the initial efforts to change the personnel outlook of the Civil Service.

There are many factors that can account for the policy of Zambianization. At the outset, it should be noted that during the immediate post-independence period, the government saw the need to develop a civil service spirit based on national government and national pride. These sentiments were influenced by a nationalist spirit sweeping across newly independent states such as Zambia. Therefore, this period was characterised by a nationalist movement manifested by high levels of emotions, aspirations, and expectations by the people from the newly constituted government (Chibaye and Bwalya in Subramaniam 1990). The foregoing can be attributed partly to oppression and marginalisation experienced b the indigenous people during the Colonial Regime.

Moreover, nationalism was perceived to be vital to nation-building because Zambia inherited a legacy where traditional authority played an active role in administrative affairs as noted in the precolonial and colonial periods. Since traditional authority was organized on the basis of tribal lines, it became a basis for people's identity. Moreover, the colonial government largely maintained these groupings. As a result, the ramification on the new state was that people lacked a sense of belonging with regards to national identity, thereby threatening the government's legitimacy and stability. Therefore it was imperative to unite people under a national identity by embracing the spirit of nationalism and nation-building as one of the important goals tenaciously pursued by the UNIP government partly through Zambianization (Dresang 1975). Furthermore, there was need to build national identity and define the accepted parameters and process for selecting governmental officials and making authoritative policy become institutionalised (Lungu 1981). Therefore, the government's desire to enhance legitimacy paved a way for Zambianization. Besides, the need for enhanced legitimacy put demand on the government to improve the material welfare of its citizens. This demand was generated by the style of comfortable and luxurious living enjoyed by European administrators in Northern Rhodesia signifying the value of employment in the Civil Service (Pye 1966). Civil service positions were valued because of their relatively high salaries, status, and authority accompanying them. Subsequently, positive responses by the government to these pressures precipitated a policy of rapid Zambianization (Tordof 1980).

Another justification for Zambianization was to accelerate the attainment of socio-economic development goals. Freedom fighters made promises to the natives during the struggle for independence, thereby creating a high level of expectancy by the citizens from the newly formed government (Chibaye and Bwalya in Subramaniam 1990). Understandably, it was a payback period because for a long time the natives were deprived of many privileges due to the colonial regime's racial discrimination policy. Likewise, the policy was in line with the philosophy of Zambian humanism introduced by Kaunda which emphasized among other things the dignity of human beings. The philosophy coupled with the nationalist spirit called for rapid development and provision of social services to the Zambian people to create ownership and a sense of belonging. Kaunda emphasized the need to embrace the ideals of humanism and nationalism in the civil service and argued that policy implementation required an administrative cadre that would be loyal and faithful (Chibaye and Bwalya in Subramaniam 1990). As a result, the government worked towards attaining a goal of a civil service which was national in outlook and the expatriate was the last option particularly where there was a critical shortage of staff (Gertzel 1972). This is because a colonially oriented workforce was perceived unsuitable to execute a challenging task of accelerating social and economic development for Zambia. As a result, the Zambianization policy was assumed to be an appropriate intervention.

Furthermore, Zambianization was be justified by government's desire to seize control of the civil service given that it is a critical machinery of government and controlling it entails controlling the government as a whole. Initially, the focus was to Zambianize senior positions such as generalist administrators since their role was to direct and coordinate the activities of technical specialists. Moreover, the administrator was the point of contact between government and the people, during the colonial regime, thus, it was politically necessary after independence to Zambianize administrative posts (Dresang 1975: 45). As a result, there was an attempt to primarily Zambianize the most visible administrative and executive posts. Accordingly, the most visible positions in the civil service were Permanent Secretaries and District Secretaries. 'In 1968, all but two former Permanent Secretaries were Zambians and only one of the latter was not a Zambian; by 1970 all these officers were Zambians' (Dresang 1975: 45). In some way, Zambianizing the recruitment function provided an opportunity for career advancement for Zambians.

However, Zambianization suffered a setback of shortage of requisite skills among Zambians. As a result, the continued presence of expatriates was as important and compelling because they still occupied not only technical and professional positions but also top jobs (Chibaye and Bwalya in Subramaniam 1990). Therefore, attempts to fill technical and professional positions with indigenous people were made on the basis of meeting requisite qualifications through training. In spite of European workers being viewed as a threat to the source of political tension, their contribution to the civil service was vital and that is why such concerns were overlooked. Resultantly, expatriates were pronounced in the middle-level and technical positions because they required high-level expertise. Inevitably, those positions remained mainly dominated by expatriates (Tordoff 1980), as noted by Dresang:

> In 1968, 42 per cent of the super-scale personnel were expatriates and, importantly, 67.4 per cent of the departments and agencies, who were of super-scale rank, were expatriates. It is evident that Zambia has relied heavily on external sources of expertise to staff her administrative system. The presence of expatriates in important decision-making positions was no longer due to myths of racial superiority, or to the efforts of a racial group to preserve its position of predominance. Rather, expatriates were employed because of the severe shortage of skilled and experienced Zambian personnel. (Dresang 1975: 45)

The shortage of staff among Zambians could be attributed to the gap in requisite educational and professional qualifications mainly ascribed to restricted access to higher education, due to the colonial regime's racial discrimination policy. This created a critical shortage of local manpower with the necessary skills at the time of independence thereby creating a challenge in establishing a merit-based indigenized civil service. Furthermore, 'Zambianization was not simply a matter of replacing departing colonial officials but also coping with rapid growth under the impact of the first two development plans and the unexpectedly sharp increases in public revenues arising from favourable copper prices. Between 1963–1964 and 1969, the service more than doubled in size from 22,561 to 51,497 at a time when severe shortages of experienced personnel made it difficult to maintain existing levels of operation let alone assume new commitments'

(Tordoff 1980: 71). Moreover, UNIP's post-independence commitment to the expansion of the administrative machinery and a remarkable increase in its functionality put pressure on merit Zambianization. Additionally, workers were needed to sustain the main economic sectors still dominated by expatriate skills such as agriculture, commerce and manufacturing, and mining. 'Yet in 1964, there were only 109 Africans with university degrees and just over 1,200 with secondary school certificates. In 1965, 40 per cent of the established posts in the Civil Service were vacant; and of the occupied positions in Divisions I and II (clerical officer and above), only 38 per cent were held by Zambian citizens' (Tordoff 1980: 68). Subsequently, the main basis for filling top ranks with Zambians was not strictly on the basis of professional qualification and experience. Rather, recruitment was as mainly based on patronage and political expediency to enhance the legitimacy of the government. It was often used as a means of rewarding loyal party service, particularly during the struggle for independence (Chibaye and Bwalya in Subramaniam 1990). The foregoing are among the major weaknesses of setbacks associated with the First Republic.

However, the main strength of this dispensation is that Zambianization placed Zambians in influential positions, thereby enabling them to take charge of the civil service. This move was necessary to enable the government to assert the new state's political identity and economic independence and secure its integrity (Tordoff 1980). The other merit is that there was an attempt to establish a relatively professional Career Service where, generally, top civil servants had an opportunity to rise through the ranks. In terms of structure, the civil service was divided into various ministries and each was headed by a Permanent Secretary. Moreover, there was remarkable separation between politics and administration in terms of politician–officer relationship. This implies that formally, the party and government were distinct and the civil service was relatively autonomous from undue political influence.

The main lesson to be drawn from this period is that indigenization should be the basis for public service recruitment except where requisite skills cannot be found locally. This is important in promoting employability among locals and subsequently reducing unemployment levels and human capital flight. The First Republic continued until the end of 1972. Thereafter, another political dispensation began, hence the next discourse.

The Civil Service in the Postcolonial Era: Second Republic

The Second Republic was introduced on 13 December 1972 when the political system changed from plural to single-party politics. The main feature of the civil service under this dispensation was that it was largely politicized. Besides, the process of Zambianization continued into this period. Therefore, the politicization of the civil service signifies its evolution from the First Republic into the Second Republic.

Under this era, central and local government were merged and the party became a supreme organ of administration and government (Chibaye and Bwalya in Subramaniam 1990). Here, party politics were elevated above the government. To emphasize its supremacy, Kaunda could refer to the relationship between the party and the government machinery as 'the party and its government'. The major implication of the politicization of the civil service was that senior civil servants were politically appointed as opposed to allowing a career civil service. The government's assumption for this policy was that to efficiently and effectively carry out instructions of the political masters with loyalty, civil servants needed to be sympathisers of UNIP. For that reason, the president controlled the civil service, and politicians were appointed to hold various posts in the civil service. As indicated below:

> President Kaunda issued the following statement to justify his action: civil servants are required to implement decisions which are taken by the Party that believes and works for the establishment of a humanist society. How do we expect civil servants to follow humanistic principles if we exclude them from politics? Unless they are helped to understand and appreciate why the Party works for the establishment of a humanist society, they are bound to follow different lines of action. (Chibaye and Bwalya in Subramaniam 1990: 296)

Therefore, the connotation of merging politics and administration was Kaunda's belief that civil servants needed to be members of the party to implement policies of the ruling party faithfully and effectively. The assumption was that party membership would instil unquestioned loyalty in civil servants when implementing the government's decisions. As a result, Permanent Secretaries were appointed mainly on the basis of political allegiance and professional qualification was a secondary criterion. The Permanent Secretary needed to be a member of the party and was expected to act both politically and professionally (Chibaye and Bwalya in Subramaniam 1990). The trend of politicizing appointments was not restricted to Permanent Secretaries. Generally, any potential employee of the civil service needed to be a party card holder.

As this dispensation experienced the supremacy of politics over the government, party cadres were appointed to take positions in the civil service. From political administration, political secretaries were appointed to be in charge of administration in 1974 and later in 1976 Kaunda appointed members of Central Committee. Both positions were superior to provincial cabinet ministers, denoting the supremacy of party politics. At district level, the governor as a political appointee was in charge of the district assisted by another political appointee, the district regional secretary. Besides, the district secretary was a technocrat, appointed on the basis of professional qualifications (Mukwena 2001). This trend was strictly adhered to by the UNIP government.

Blending of politics was considered to be a suitable model for the civil service under the Second Republic. As a result of the party supremacy, the government was subordinated to the Central Committee. The implication was that cabinet ministers in charge of civil servants in their respective ministries were answerable to Central Committee members (Tordoff 1980). 'The basic assumption was that control could be achieved by establishing an additional layer of politicians in a supervisory role external to the ministries; and, there was an attempt to control decision-making by setting up supervisory party committees within the ministries' (Tordoff 1980: 152). Subsequently, politicization of the civil service was quite heavy during this dispensation. Moreover, the philosophy of humanism flourished to the extent that civil servants and politicians had to undergo political education to ensure indoctrination. Politicization of senior civil servants was easily embarked on because the head of state was and is still empowered to create and abolish offices in the public service as long as the decision is according to constitutional provisions. This implies that the head of state enjoys powers to appoint and dismiss personnel even without seeking the advice of the Public Service Commission (Tordoff 1980). Generally, the politicization of the civil service created uncertainty and fear because officers were treated according to the whims of politicians.

The main merit of supremacy of party politics over administration is that it created an atmosphere of unquestioned loyalty to the party, resulting in rigorous execution of government policies and other political decisions. Subsequently, implementation of party and government programmes was adhered to, because the civil servants understood the value systems of the ruling party in relation to the civil service. As a result the civil service became the main engine to propel national development. This might partly be the underlying reason for the massive infrastructure development during Kaunda's era. He might have succeeded in moulding a civil service cadre which was committed to the ideals of the party. The merging of party and politics also encouraged a relatively stable environment in terms of the politics–administration relationship. This is conducive for promoting harmony and the smooth running of the civil service.

Hypothetically, the common perceived weakness of a politicised civil service is that it is likely to be used as a tool to oppress perceived political opponents, thereby defeating its core purpose of serving public interest. In case of the Second Republic, because of the merging of the party and government, the civil service was essentially responsive and accountable to party structures rather than to the public and acting in the interest of the public was rather secondary. Moreover, the politicization of the public service was often associated with patronage where appointments were based on informal networks rather than formal qualifications. During this era, merit or professional qualification were not sufficient benchmarks for public service appointments as potential employees needed to demonstrate membership to the party (Tordoff 1980). This made the civil service become not only more autocratic and devoid of accountability, transparency, and the rule of law, but also irresponsible (Mulinge and Lesetedi 1998: 22). Consequently, the realisation of a neutral and merit-based civil service was far-fetched under such circumstances because the civil service became an extension of a political system.

Another weakness is that both the First and Second Republic periods witnessed the growth of the public sector resulting in a bloated civil service. For example, in 1969, Kaunda appointed a cabinet minister for each of the eight provinces.

Moreover, the British government handed down to Zambia a legacy of 5,853 civil servants immediately after independence. However, after five years of self-rule, in 1969, this figure rose to 51,497. The growth could be attributed to the policy of Zambianization, and the rising copper earnings during this period enabled the government to expand the size of the bureaucracy (Dresang 1975). Bloated civil services are usually associated with huge public debts, poor service delivery, and discontentment among the citizens.

The main lesson to draw from this dispensation is that politicization of the civil service should be avoided as it tends to challenge professionalism. Moreover, the susceptibility to corruption among public offices tends to increase. Further, it weakens the disposition of the civil service, thereby depriving it of the capacity to scrutinise directives from politicians and, ultimately, undermining its role of serving public interest. However, there is need to have a healthy balanced relationship between the civil service and the politicians. Moreover, politicians need to assume responsibility over the supervision of the civil service in an efficient and effective manner while allowing for its autonomy. This is because the autonomy of the civil service is a condition for professionalism but it should be exercised in the context of loyalty of the running government.

The Second Republic came to an end on 17 December 1990 when Kaunda reintroduced plural politics, leading us to the final period under discussion, the Third Republic.

The Civil Service in the Postcolonial Era: Third Republic

Politically, 1991 is a landmark in Zambian politics because it marked the first change of government, in the postcolonial dispensation, from the UNIP to the Movement for Multiparty Democracy (MMD) government under the leadership of Frederick Chiluba. He defeated UNIP's Kaunda in a landslide presidential election victory. The defeat was mainly attributed to the discontentment of the general citizens with service delivery during the UNIP government as suggested below:

> The limited ability of the bureaucracy to provide for rapid
> economic development can influence political change. Despite

the contribution made by massive bureaucratic efforts, the anticipations for economic development in the immediate postcolonial years are likely to be higher than the capacity for the administration to meet them. Yet, general, voluntaristic support for the incumbent regime and for the emerging political order is based on part in government's ability to improve the material welfare of its citizens. Any disparity between expectations and accomplishments is likely to contribute to political discontent. (Dresang 1975)

The main features characterizing this epoch can be identified as relative de-politicization of the public service by delinking the party from the government in general and the civil service in particular, and the undertaking of market-related reforms leading to the reorganization of government departments. The first reform that the MMD government implemented was to delink the party structure from the government, to enhance the autonomy of the civil service. However, unlike allowing for a career civil service where top civil servants would rise through the ranks, political appointments persisted from the Second Republic (Mulikita 1996). Besides, the MMD government embraced a capitalist policy which guided the nature of civil service reforms. This was a radical policy shift from UNIP's socialist orientation based on welfare economics. Essentially, the capitalist or market-based policies were driven externally by the Breton Woods institutions, namely the World Bank and the International Monetary Fund (IMF). As Mulikita (2000) notes, the MMD entirely embraced the Structural Adjustment Programme (SAP) as designed and given by the Breton Woods institutions. The market-oriented policies came as a set of conditions to receive foreign aid from the donor community.

The prescribed conditions, among other things, demanded the shrinking of the public sector in terms of size and scope of functions to make it efficient. Subsequently the government embarked on a massive privatisation programme which saw most of the public enterprises sold into private arms. Upon assuming office, the MMD government set up the Zambian Privatisation Agency (ZPA) and mandated it to privatise the huge parastatal sector which had experienced a prolific growth in the single-party era which the previous socialist-inclined government had opposed (Chibaye and Bwalya in Subramaniam 1990). Also the Public Service Reform Programme (PSRP) was introduced in 1993 in an attempt to restructure the public service and make it as efficient as possible.

The Public Service Reform Programme (PSRP)

The PSRP was introduced in 1993 by the MMD government and was motivated by the rationale to remove inefficiencies associated with the bloated civil service. Soon after attainment of independence, there was a tendency among new states such as Zambia to practice politics of appeasement to please freedom fighters and the general citizenry. This often resulted in massive recruitment based on patronage (Chibaye and Bwalya in Subramaniam 1990) as already pointed out. In addition, these states pursued socialist-oriented policies which often resulted in increased public expenditure resulting from blown-up civil services. Subsequently, huge debts, inefficiency, and discontentment of citizens were among prominent features of the Second Republic, and the MMD attempted to resolve these ills with market-oriented interventions.

From the economic thought point of view, it is assumed that the policy intervention to these public sector malaises entails allowing the market forces to determine the demand and supply of public goods and services. For the public sector, employing the market sector policies implies undertaking various programmes and strategies earmarked at promoting efficiency by creating value for money. One of the strategies implemented by the MMD government to cure the malaise of the civil service was the adoption and implementation of the PSRP. According to Mukwena (2001) and Mulikita (2000) the key components of the PSRP were as follows:

- A retrenchment programme to make the public service leaner so that the costs of running it can be made efficient,
- Employing performance-related incentives for a smaller and better remunerated workforce to enhance motivation of human resources, and
- Embarking on decentralization by devolving administrative power and resources away from central ministries to local levels' structures.

The general aim of the programme was to improve performance and cost-effectiveness in the public sector through the marketization strategy.

There are several factors that can account for driving the PSRP in new states such as Zambia. 'Most authors agree that the factors that have driven reform in developing and transition countries include one or more of the following: fiscal crisis and excess staffing, dissatisfaction with government services, declining confidence in government and citizens, demand for changes in the government, growing international competition, the presence of new reform ideas, revolutionary developments in information technology, concern with patronage and corruption, low qualifications of personnel, low salaries, and weak management systems' (Bresse-Pereira, Carlos, and Spink 1999: 12–13). Verhijen and Kotchegura (2000) in World Bank (2008: 41) state that studies of transition countries confirm the obvious pressure for reform created by the collapse of authoritarian regimes starting in 1989. According to a World Bank report (2008), external pressures from donors, especially in Africa, should be added to the causes of the reform programme and Zambia identifies with the aforementioned causes of public service reform. This is because Zambia's reforms were driven by the Breton Wood institutions, making the reform alien rather than indigenous.

Furthermore, the phenomenal growth of public administration in Zambia was paralleled by a proliferation of state-owned enterprises (SOEs) whose main function was to implement the government's economic policies whilst paying due regard to social justice. Like other developing countries, Zambia was in a hurry to improve the living standards of the majority. This resulted in a fast-growing public sector (Dresang 1975). The growth of the public sector was in line with the socialist policy pursued by the UNIP government from 1964 to 1990. During this period, the orientation of the public service was to promote a welfare state.

In terms of sustainability, the dramatic growth of public administration and the state-owned enterprise (SOE) sector in Zambia, in the context of ensuring basic needs satisfaction to all parts of the country, was by and large made possible by the availability of enormous foreign exchange due to favourable world market prices for Zambian base metals, namely copper, zinc, and cobalt in the 1960s and 1970s (Chibaye and Bwalya in Subramaniam 1990). Consequently, huge public expenditure was justified as long as social justice was the goal. However, when copper prices dropped, sustaining the public sector became a challenge. The socialist policy orientation 'not only led to a steep rise in the number of employees hired by the public sector but made the task of efficiently managing the expanding sector increasingly unwieldy' (Bresse-Pereira and Spink 1999: 13). The foregoing indicates that socialist-oriented policies were blamed for the civil service malaise. Whether the market-oriented policies were a panacea to these ills or not is another puzzle.

As noted by several scholars such as Mulikita (2006), PSRP in Zambia was implemented rapidly such that by 1993, most ministries and provincial administration had been restructured. However, this did not necessarily result in an efficient public service, as signified by the government's continuous borrowing of finances to supplement the national budget. In addition, the civil service did not become leaner because recruitment of staff was a permanent feature. 'Scholars agree that civil service reform efforts in developing and transition countries over the last twenty years have been difficult to implement and sustain over the time. Some reasons are related to the political process behind reform implementation' (Schneider and Heredia 2003 in a World Bank report 2008: 42). Generally, political regimes of new independent states were very powerful. Therefore, 'civil service and administrative reform threatened the status quo and alters the balance of power within society. The difficulty arises from the perceived loss of power and influence politicians face as they move from discretionary to merit-based management' (Schneider and Heredia 2003 in a World Bank report 2008: 42). Besides, administrative reforms require a workforce with technical and administrative capacities to tackle complexities of reforms. In many developing countries including Zambia, civil servants did not have sufficient technical and managerial capacity to undertake the reform process. On the contrary, reform 'interventions assumed that both the capacity and organisational arrangements were already in place' (Ozgediz 1983 in World Bank 2008: 42). It follows that the donor community did not pay attention to prominent structural features in the developing country's public service before prescribing PSRP as a cure for its inefficiencies.

Therefore, PSRP in Zambia did not perform as expected as far as meeting the core objectives is concerned. As indicated in the diagram below, the wage bill of civil service significantly grew instead of reducing, thereby challenging the goal efficiency. The increase of the wage bill can be partly ascribed to the civil service payroll, which moved district-health-level agencies to the civil service payroll (Repucci 2012). This creates a scenario wherein trying to solve one problem, another is created. Table 1 below shows civil service employment and wages between 1991 and 2000.

Table 1: Civil Service Employment and Wages

Employment	1991–1995	1996–2000
Civilian Central Government	21 000	40 720
	0.81 (% of population)	0.41 (% of population)
Wages		
Total Central Government Wage Bill (for all public workers)	4.7 (% of GDP)	5.2 (% of GDP)

Source: UN report (2004: 4)

However, there was an attempt to tackle this problem. 'To bring the wage bill back to sustainable limits, reductions were necessary throughout the civil service, which in turn required substantial separation payments mandated by strong trade unions. Furthermore, because the government could not meet the requirements for separation payments mandated but was already streamlining staff, it sent people home while they continued to receive pay' (Repucci 2012: 14). This scenario confirms that there was lack of adequate preparation before embarking on the PSRP.

Moreover, the speedy implementation of the PSRP in Zambia caused several unintended consequences as the main outcomes. For example, instead of enhancing economic costs in the public service, the converse was the case as indicated by the increased wage bill in table 1 above. Expectedly, 'scholars argue that implementation and lack of sustainability of civil service reform interventions in developing countries arise from reform designs. Designs that either use a single template to address highly heterogeneous institutional settings or introduce recent Organization for Economic Cooperation and Development

(OECD) managerial models that may not be suitable' (Shepherd 2003: 3). Hughes (2003) notes that in countries where patronage and informality are still predominant, managerialism may not be the best policy intervention. Managerialism entails applying the concepts of efficiency and economy to the public sector as though it was the private sector. It involves implementation of market-oriented reforms in the public sector. However, the requisite conditions of such policies include the existence of strong institutions to regulate private-sector-driven activities. Gaebler's viewpoint (Schneider and Heredia 2003: 8) is 'you have to invent government before you reinvent it'. This shows that extensive and comprehensive market policy interventions in the civil service became a fad rather than a cure for its challenges. Furthermore, the PSRP seems to have been implemented largely to impress the Breton Woods institutions so that Zambia, among other developing countries, could enlist more resources from the donor community within the framework of the country's socially painful economic programme. Therefore, it appears that the more ethically intended reform, with the vision of an efficient, well-remunerated, and morally upright civil service was quietly abandoned in favour of satisfying the fiscal cut benchmark promulgated by the IMF and World Bank.

Moreover, PSRP was associated with massive retrenchments as indicated by one of its goals. Retrenchment has brought a sense of insecurity among the remnant staff, particularly those serving on short contracts. Moreover, most of the retrenched workers and their families experienced socio-economic challenges because they were not psychologically prepared before the programme was undertaken. Further, the programme is related to the rise of casualization of jobs, resulting from the shrinking job opportunities. Besides, reforms brought market concepts such as user fees which undermine the core ethos of the public sector like equity and social justice in accessing public goods and services.

Despite the preceding weaknesses, the public service market policy interventions have enhanced participation of the private sector and other stakeholders in the delivery of the public service good. Some of the interventions include public–private partnerships (PPPs) and compulsory public tendering. These trends often enhance competition and, generally, translate into high-quality goods and affordable prices, thereby enhancing consumer satisfaction (Hughes 2003). Moreover, public–private partnerships give the government access to critical human and financial capital necessary to undertake certain specialised infrastructure projects. This is crucial in cases where the government is limited in such resources.

Besides, as the public sector shares the responsibility of providing public goods and services with the private sector, operational costs in the public sector are likely to reduce. Moreover, public choice has been enhanced in the provision of goods and services due to plural institutional delivery such as the involvement of the private sector (Hughes 2003). This gives consumers value for money, as goods can be packaged according to their purchasing power and preferences, for example, the concept of user fees such as fee-paying medical services in public hospitals and prepaid electricity metres.

Further, market policies tend to stress performance management. The implication on human resources is that short-term performance employment contracts are encouraged (Hughes 2003). This helps to arrest the challenge of ghost workers and excess of staff because accountability of employees is clearly spelt out. Under this practice, only necessary personnel in terms of numbers and skills are employed, because staffing is strictly linked to organizational objectives. In addition, short-term contracts tend to make workers perform highly to achieve targets for fear of losing jobs. Moreover, performance management emphasizes setting of explicit performance targets, and standards make it relatively easier to put in place monitoring mechanisms. After the MMD was removed from power, the Patriotic Front under Michael Chilufya Sata formed government. Under his reign, there was no remarkable departure in terms of party ideology, particularly where the administration of the civil service is concerned. The main remarkable feature was an attempt to push for more decentralization. This was signified by the creation of new districts such as Ngabwe in Central Province (Sardanis 2014). Other than that, there was no definite policy direction whether it be towards capitalism or socialism. Therefore, the market-oriented reforms introduced in the early 1990s mark the main experience of the civil service under the Third Republic.

Conclusion

In conclusion, the civil service in Zambia has evolved over a period of time, from the precolonial period to the Third Republic. The main features of evolution are as follows: The administrative machinery was organized on tribal lines under the precolonial period to a foreign, racially dominated one under the colonial period. Within the colonial regime, there was a shift from the BSA Company administrative system based on direct rule and dominated by company employees, to the one based on indirect rule resulting into a dual civil service and in which native authorities played an active role in administration. The transition from the colonial to the postcolonial era introduced the indigenization recruitment policy in the First Republic which continued to the Second Republic, and the politicization of the Civil Service in the Second Republic. Further, the evolution from the Second to the Third Republic brought in the depoliticization of the civil service where there was an attempt to delink the Civil Service from Party politics. Each stage experienced unique opportunities and weaknesses. Some of the salient lessons drawn are as follows: the need for civil servants to exhibit loyalty and obedience as noted in the precolonial period. In addition, there is need for the civil service to demonstrate discipline and hard work, maintenance of law and order, and inclusion of grass roots in administration as pointed out in the colonial administration.

Moreover, the implementation of the indigenization recruitment policy or Zambianization as stressed in the First and Second republics promoted loyalty and a nationalist spirit among Zambian civil servants.

Furthermore, the stress on the civil service professionalism and application of an efficient and responsive market-oriented intervention in the Third Republic, intended to avert the inefficiencies noted in the First and Second Republics, was a necessary reform strategy. The main challenge was that the reform was not applied selectively and gradually.

It has been deduced from the study that the various dispensations in the development of the civil service in Zambia have brought out rich experiences from which contemporary scholars and practitioners can learn to strive for a more efficient, more effective, and more responsive civil service.

The main recommendation is that the Zambian government should strengthen links and collaboration with local think-tanks such as universities, with regards to improving public sector management, among endeavours to enable the generation of appropriate and innovative interventions aimed at enhancing responsive service delivery. Subsequently, there is need for the government to invest in research on public sector management because of its critical role in running national affairs.

References

Basu, R. (2006), *Public Administration: Concepts and Theories* (New Delhi: Sterling).

Bekke, H. A. G. M., Perry, J. L., and Toonen, T. A. J. (eds.) (1996), *Civil Service Systems in Comparative Perspective* (Bloomington: Indiana University Press).

Bradley, K. (1961), 'Company Days: The Rule of the British South Africa Company in Northern Rhodesia', *Northern Rhodesia Journal* V, incomplete.

Bresse-Pereira, Carlos L. and Spink, P. (eds.) (1999), *Reforming the State: Managerial Public Administration in Latin America* (Boulder, CO: Lynne Rienner Publishers).

Cabinet Office, Zambia (1967), *A Hand-book for the Zambian civil servant* (Lusaka: Government Printers).

Chikulo, B. C. (1981), 'The Zambian Administrative Reforms: An Alternative View', *Public Administration and Development* I/I: 55–65.

Dresang, L. D. (1975), *The Zambia Civil Service* (Nairobi: African Publishing House).

Evans, A. (2008), *Civil Service Reform Thematic Paper* (Washington: World Bank).

Fagan, B. (1966), *A Short History of Zambia—From Earliest Until 1890* (London: Oxford Press).

Gann, L. H. (1958), *The Birth of a Plural Society South African Company* (Manchester: Manchester University Press).

Gertzel, C. J. (1972), *The Political Process in Zambia: Documents and Readings* (Lusaka: University of Zambia).

Hughes, E. O. (2003), *Public Management and Administration* (New York: Palgrave Macmillan).

Kapur, C. A. (1996), *Principles of Political Science* (New Delhi: S. Chand and Company Ltd).

Lungu, G. F. (1982), *Problems of Administrative Discretion in a Post-Colonial State: Lessons for Zambia* (Lusaka: Institute of African Studies, University of Zambia).

—— (1985), *Administrative Decentralization in Zambian Bureaucracy: An Analysis of Environmental Constraints* (Lusaka: Institute of African Studies, University of Zambia).

—— (1986), *Mission Impossible: Integrating Central and Local Administration in Zambia: Planning and Administration* (Lusaka: Institute of African Studies, University of Zambia).

Mukwena, R. M. (1992), 'Zambia's Local Administration Act 1980: An Examination of the Integration Objective', *Public Administration and Development* 12/3: 237–247.

—— (2001), 'Situating Decentralization in Zambia in a Political Context', *African Administrative Studies*, 57: 35–50.

Mulikita, N. M. (1996), *The Zambian Civil Service Reform Program (PSRP): Facing an Uncertain Future*, seminar paper, OSSREA Local Seminar on Zambia's Development Concerns Beyond 1996, 5 July 1996, Fairview Hotel, Lusaka.

—— (2000), 'Reform and the Crisis in Zambia's Public Administration: A Critical Appraisal', *African Peer Review Mechanism* Unpan025710. pdf

Mulinge, M. and Lesetedi, N. G. (1998), 'Interrogating Our Past: Colonialism and Corruption in Sub-Saharan Africa', *Afr. Political Science* 13/2: 15–28.

Peter, B. G. (2001), 'The Prefectoral Government', *International Encyclopaedia of the Social and Behavioural Sciences*, pp. 11962–11965.

Pye, L. W. (1966), *Aspects of Political Development* (City of Publication: Little Brown).

Repucci, S. (2012), 'Civil Service Reform', *UNU-Wider* 2012/90: 1–21.

Roberts, A. (1976), *A History of Zambia* (London: Heinemann).

Subramaniam, V. (ed.) (1990), *Public Administration in the Third World: An International Handbook* (Connecticut: Greenwood Press).

Tordoff, W. (ed.) (1980), *Administration in Zambia* (Manchester: University Press).

Chapter 13

History of Social Welfare in Zambia: Social Welfare Services and Social Work Education and Training

Chilala S. Kafula

Introduction

At independence in 1964, Zambia was the economic powerhouse of the region (Mtetesha 2013). This was mainly due to the thriving copper mining industry which comprised the country's largest export. With its rich mineral deposits, the country's economy had hit peak performance, rated as one of the highest GDP per capita in Africa. To that effect, Mtetesha (2013) indicates that the strength of the Zambian currency was at one point at par with the US dollar such that one Zambian kwacha could be traded for one dollar. However, despite the high economic performance, Zambia inherited a weak social service profile characterised by inequalities and poor human conditions for indigenous people (Noyoo 2000). As at the fiftieth anniversary, in spite of the efforts made to improve the living standards of the Zambian people, about 63 per cent are still living on less than $1.25 per day (BAA 2011). Since independence, the country has undergone rigorous transformation which has seen it through to the current status. Given this background, there is ample evidence to suggest that some ideological and policy changes the country has experienced since independence have had a huge bearing on the current social and economic status of Zambia.

This chapter therefore attempts to document these changes from independence to date—with particular focus on the impact of these changes on social services in the country. The chapter also reiterates the role of social work in socio-economic development. The chapter consists of three main parts. The first part focuses on early approaches to social welfare in Northern Rhodesia—today Zambia. The second part is about the trend of economic and social services in postcolonial Zambia—in three periodical terms. Part three focuses on the evolution of social welfare and social work in Zambia. Given the fragile economic and social conditions in the country, emphasis is placed on reviewing the focus of the profession—with a bias on empowerment as a solution to the prevailing situation. Finally, the conclusion is drawn on what has been discussed.

Meaning of Social Welfare

Social welfare exists mainly because of the nature of man. Man is a social being who depends on the cooperation and assistance from others to meet his own needs. In some cases, welfare is implicated in traditional virtues such as friendship, fairness, and justice. As such, people are expected to live in harmony with others in society. Initially, social welfare services were provided in an informal way. When need arose, relatives, friends, religious, and voluntary organizations provided welfare services to the needy. Gradually, the changes that occurred in society such as social patterns and networks, economic base, technology, and general lifestyles necessitated the involvement of government, the private sector, and other organizations in providing social services to help meet human needs and solve social problems. The rapidly changing society has become a breeding ground for complex social problems such as high levels of unemployment, moral decay, substance abuse, crime, violence, diseases, and mass poverty especially among the vulnerable. In response to this desperate situation, the idea of organized social welfare emerged to address social problems and meet human needs. It is therefore the business of social welfare to find solutions to these problems.

Social welfare is concerned with meeting people's needs, both rich and poor. The goal is to meet the basic needs of individuals, families, groups, and communities. Social welfare is about providing services to people in conditions of vulnerability including sickness, disability, childhood, and old age. It also targets some disadvantaged groups of people such as children, women, and the youth. Social welfare, therefore, involves rehabilitating drug addicts, providing counselling to emotionally affected individuals and families, fighting against discrimination of various disadvantaged groups, and advocating for the rights of people with special needs in a given society. According to Patel (2005), social welfare programmes and policies aim at promoting social inclusion, social cohesion, and integration in society. From this perspective, social welfare can thus be defined as:

> A nation's system of programmes, benefits, and services that help people meet those social, economic, education, and health needs that are fundamental to the maintenance of society (Zastraw in Patel 2005: 19)

This definition provides a yardstick by which a given society can measure how well it is meeting the needs of its people, as well as what people can expect from society (Patel 2005). Social welfare is more or less the same as a state of human well-being.

Social welfare is an ambiguous term. 'In an interconnected and interdependent global world, the nature and meaning of social welfare continues to be contested' (Patel 2005: 19). Thus, social welfare may be looked at from either a narrow or broad perspective. From the narrow perspective, social welfare emphasizes interventions by charitable and voluntary organizations. In this sense, social welfare is perceived as a drain on societal resources and has been viewed as promoting a dependency syndrome on the part of the recipients. On the other hand, the broader perspective views social welfare as *an integrated system of social policies, social services, benefits, programmes, and social security to promote social development, social justice and social functioning in a caring and enabling environment* (Patel 2005: 20). Patel suggests that the goal of welfare policies and programmes is to meet the needs of people, manage social problems, maximize opportunities, and promote human empowerment and social inclusion.

Early Approaches to Social Welfare in Zambia

In the precolonial era, the welfare needs of people were met by individual families, communities, and the wider society. Both material and emotional support in times of need were provided by the family. Communities believed in communal living, cooperation, mutual aid, and the extended family comprised of uncles, aunts, cousins, nephews and nieces, and grandparents. Thus, all vulnerable groups like orphans, widows, the aged, and other vulnerable people were looked after by their relatives, communities, and societies at large. People in precolonial Zambia survived by gathering wild fruits, hunting, and agriculture (both growing crops and keeping livestock) mainly on subsistence basis. However, these traditional modes of social living and provision were not favoured by the social relationships or networks that developed during the colonial period (Noyoo 2000). Like in other African countries, colonialism disrupted the traditional forms of social welfare services provision in Zambia—Northern Rhodesia then. As such, colonialism shaped the nature and direction of social welfare policy in the country.

Zambia was a British protectorate from 1924 to October 1964, when she attained political independence. At that time, the British government assumed direct responsibility over the territory. Colonial masters adapted both social and economic activities of the territory to their own interests, especially after the discovery of mineral deposits at Broken Hill—Kabwe today—around 1902, as well as on the Copperbelt. In this regard, Patel (2005: 66) argues, 'Indigenous inhabitants in the colonies had to adapt their technology, methods of production, forms of social organisation, culture, political, legal, and welfare systems to meet the demands and world view of the colonial powers.' The colonial masters considered themselves superior to indigenous people. This perception manifested itself in the expression of racial and social supremacy as well as in the judgement of indigenous people, their customs, and their tradition of subsistence and communal living to be inferior and barbaric. This view, as mentioned earlier, had significant influence in the shaping of social welfare programmes and policies during the colonial era. In colonial Zambia, social welfare services were defined in racial terms and Africans were accorded minimal services. For instance, Noyoo (2000) argues that though Africans were in the majority demographically, less money was spent on social services to meet their needs. He further gives an example where, in 1936 when the African population numbered 1,370,000 and that of Europeans was around 10,588 European education took up 29,934 pounds sterling from the colonial development fund, whilst Africans were allotted 24,484 pounds sterling (7 Year Book and Guide of the Rhodesians and Nyasaland, with Biographic 1938: 482 in Noyoo 2000).

According to Patel (2005: 67), colonialism imposed enormous social changes on traditional societies, but no responsibility was taken for the social costs of such large-scale social disruptions. The discovery of mineral deposits of copper at Chief Chipepo's area which was later renamed Broken Hill, now Kabwe, in 1902 (Noyoo 2000) and on the Copperbelt marked the beginning of the process of industrialisation in Northern Rhodesia. This process facilitated the transformation of indigenous social and economic structures from agrarian to industrial societies. The new mining industry needed a large labour force to carry out mining activities. As such, thousands of Africans, particularly young males and other able-bodied people were employed on the mines. Initially, Africans were not willing to work for the colonial masters as they were used to a subsistence lifestyle. Nevertheless, Africans were forced into wage labour upon introduction of African tax and passing of the decree that Africans could only pay tax in monetary form and not in kind as the case used to be. Noyoo (2000) indicates that tax defaulters were severely punished, imprisoned, or indeed forced into labour gangs. Thus, Africans had no choice but to move to town to seek employment to enable them raise the money that was required for tax. As a result, only women, children, the old, the sick, and the disabled remained in rural areas. This drift did not only affect productivity in these areas, but it also shook the very traditional systems as well as the rich values of the extended family and mutual-aid system.

These mineworkers were not allowed to bring their families to town as their stay in town was considered temporal. The mine labourers lived in small houses and were subjected to poor living conditions. They also worked under poor conditions and were given low wages for their labour, hence the argument that the colonial masters made profits at the expense of the indigenous population. Furthermore, Noyoo observes that Africans were being used to raise profits from minerals to fund Britain's social welfare system. Some of the profits also went to improve workers' conditions in Britain. Thus the British South Africa Company (BSAC) which owned the mines was more interested in reaping profits than in developing the areas it occupied. Consequently, no tangible infrastructure with respect to the broader community was erected by the company (Noyoo 2000). The wealth from economic activities was not shared equally between the white settler community and the Africans. As a result, the colonial masters tended to benefit more than Africans.

In Northern Rhodesia, unlike Africans, whites had a highly organized social welfare system compared to that of blacks. This was because it was assumed that African miners did not necessarily need an organized social welfare system as their needs would be met through the traditional extended family and kinship groups. However, the mass exodus of able-bodied young men to urban areas in search of employment negatively affected productivity in rural areas. This development had implications on the traditional mutual-aid system in rural areas, and thus, exposed Africans to heightened poverty. It can therefore be deduced that colonialism, and indeed the industrialisation process, resulted in high levels of poverty and other associated problems particularly among Africans, amid appalling inequalities especially in urban areas.

Welfare Associations in Zambia

In colonial Zambia, the country pursued a residual model of social welfare, although services provided benefited the white population more than it did Africans. However, high levels of poverty and inequality, mass exploitation of indigenous African people, and colonial domination in general resulted in increased African political consciousness which eventually led to the first ever African workers' strike in 1935 (Noyoo 2000).

These ills also resulted in the formation of welfare associations particularly among urban dwellers residing along the Line of Rail. According to Hinfelaar (1993), the first welfare association in Northern Province was founded at Mwenzo Mission station in 1912 under the leadership of Donald Siwale. Siwale together with Hezekiya Nkonjera Kawosa, Peter Sinkala, and David Kaunda (the father to Zambia's first president) organized the first formal meeting in the same year. The aim of the association was to advance the political, economic,

as well as social problems affecting all Africans and to bring to the attention
of the authorities certain injustices and to suggest ways of improving life in the
country (Hinfelaar 1993). In 1946, various welfare associations were united and
formed the Federation of African Welfare Societies (Noyoo 2000). However,
this movement was later transformed into the first political party known as
Northern Rhodesian African National Congress in 1948 under the leadership
of Godwin Mbikusita Lewanika. It was later reconstituted into the African
National Congress (ANC) and Godwin Mbikusita Lewanika was replaced by
Harry Mwaanga Nkumbula. Later on, the mineworkers' union was formed in
the same year to advance mineworkers' labour concerns (Noyoo 2000).

It can be argued that the pressure from the welfare associations forced the
colonial government to consider the introduction of welfare services for the
Africans, especially in urban areas where the pressure was coming from. It
also became necessary to introduce social welfare services for Africans as a
way of stabilising labour in order to ensure continuous flow of copper from the
region. However, the first organized welfare services in Zambia (particularly
for Africans) began when Archibald H. Ewell was appointed as the first welfare
officer, whose duty revolved around health, recreation, and education (Noyoo
2000). It can be observed that most welfare programmes for Africans centred
on delinquency, nutritional services, as well as recreation including football
matches and film shows. This was evidenced by the welfare halls built in
the post-independence period. Other welfare services included care of the
handicapped, education, health, and aftercare services. At this point, social
welfare activities in the rural areas were minimal with only missionaries and
voluntary associations providing needed services in such areas.

The first coordinated response to the meeting of welfare needs in colonial
Zambia was in the form of a policy framework for social welfare around 1945.
This marked the beginning of state intervention in social welfare activities
in Zambia. It can be argued that this was due to pressure from the welfare
associations. Despite the challenges experienced at that time, this development
constituted a great achievement for Africans as it provided an opportunity
for them to access the much-needed social welfare services. Thus, politics
and social welfare concerns have a symbiotic link in Zambian history. This is
evidenced by the formation of welfare associations which did not only advance

welfare concerns but also advocated economic and political concerns. To that effect, welfare associations were the first organizations that tried to bring African social and economic advancements into clear perspectives (Noyoo 2000). In fact, Rotberg and Gray (1990) and Cook in Hinfelaar (1993) describe them as 'embryonic political organisations' and 'indigenous nationalism'. They are also argued as to have marked the emergence of a new social group in African society.

Welfare Programmes for Ex-combatants in Zambia

At the end of the world wars, Zambian soldiers who participated as part of the British land forces returned to Zambia. Upon their return, the soldiers were demobilised and went to their places of residence in Zambia. However, Mibenge (2005) indicates that these soldiers struggled to adapt to civilian life, which negatively affected their ability to sustain themselves and their families economically. He suggested that the soldiers were perhaps not prepared for their demobilisation from the sheltered life they had enjoyed in the barracks. The other reason for the failure to adapt may have been a narrow employment base to which they were now exposed. The situation was exacerbated by high illiteracy levels, not only among civilians but also in the military circles. This was due to poor education as schools were rare in the country, and also a general colonial policy of segregation in terms of the indigenous locals. However, despite high illiteracy levels among the indigenous people, the military men and women were taught to write their names. This resulted in a general perception that soldiers were an 'illiterate lot' who could only write their names (Mibenge 2005). However, this is no longer the case in the military as the minimum entry qualifications have since been revised.

Given this scenario, retraining and upgrading of skills for ex-servicemen and women was essential for their successful integration in the challenging and competitive civil employment sector. Notwithstanding the importance of skills training in development, Lamb (2013) also suggests that the presence of a large group of unemployed and dissatisfied individuals with military training posed a potential security threat to the nation. As a result, government put certain measures in place to try and provide social welfare services to the ex-servicemen and women. To that effect, a pension fund was introduced for ex-combatants.

Although unsustainable, Mibenge (2005) indicates that ex-soldiers received one-off or monthly pensions for the remainder of their lives.

Apart from cash payments, training centres were also established in the country. For instance, a training school was established in Mazabuka prior to independence. The aim was to provide training for, among others, the unskilled former combatants in survival skills to enhance their success in meeting their family needs. Emphasis was put on reading and arithmetic. Training, it was assumed, would broaden their employment base in order to engage them in productive activities and give them an opportunity to contribute towards national development.

Despite the efforts, reintegration programmes for ex-soldiers had limited success in addressing the problems (Lamb 2013), perhaps because the training was based on a top-down approach. The programmes were initiated by the government and, hence, did not take into consideration the views of the beneficiaries. Lamb (2013) suggested that such training was often not linked to market dynamics nor did it consistently address the specific and realistic career aspirations of the servicemen and women. In addition, training was provided by government-affiliated institutions which were generally ill-suited to prepare ex-soldiers for income-generating options in the non-military private sector (Lamb 2013). It may also be assumed that the cash payments were not being saved or invested on income-generating activities but were spent on some immediate family needs, thereby making the program unsustainable.

Trends of Social Services in Postcolonial Zambia

Zambia attained political independence on 24 October 1964. Since then, the country's policy regime, and thus, the provision of social services can be divided into three major epochs. Each of these phases is characterised by a different political ideological direction which has significant influence on the type of national social policies adopted, as this impacts on the provision of social services in the country. In this regard, the first phase constitutes the period between 1964 and 1991, the second phase constitutes the period between 1991 and 2011, while the third phase constitutes the period between 2011 and 2014.

1964–1991 Period

This period may be referred to as the Kaunda regime (Kaunda is the first president of the Republic of Zambia). Since independence, it can be noted that Zambia experienced both great and hard times. Mtetesha (2013) argues that at independence, Zambia was the economic powerhouse of the region because of its rich copper mines which comprised the country's largest export. Despite the country's excellent economic performance then, in comparative terms, Zambia inherited a weak social service profile characterised by inequalities largely to the disadvantage of the indigenous people, who were previously stratified as inferior. However, despite some challenges, the new government, the United National Independence Party (UNIP) under the leadership of Dr Kenneth Kaunda was determined to deal with these ills in an effort to improve the living conditions of the Zambian people.

As expected at independence, Zambia had a critical shortage of qualified manpower to run the government. This state of affairs had a negative impact on the provision of social services. For instance, there were only a handful of education institutions and only a total of about 100 graduates and 1,000 others that had completed secondary school (Noyoo 2008). There were only 2 medical doctors, 1 engineer, 3 lawyers, no architect, no economists serving either government or private enterprise in that capacity, and only 33 graduate teachers (Lungwangwa 1999). As such, the country largely depended on foreign expertise. Further, there was a severe shortage of social institutions like housing, schools and hospitals.

The prevailing situation then demanded radical reforms in the political as well as the socio-economic sectors. Therefore, in an effort to meet the high demand for social services as well as the expectations of the people in a newly independent country, the first post-independence government (UNIP) embarked upon an aggressive programme and established a universal free social service system. As a measure of redressing the political and socio-economic ills and general inequalities that were inherited from the colonial government, the government of the day embarked on a plan to ensure all Zambians had equal access to the much-needed social services. Thus, social services were not associated with any specific group or class of people, but were provided to everyone regardless of race, class, and indeed background. This was also in line with the tenets of humanism as the guiding ideology at the time. To achieve this ambitious plan, like other newly independent African countries (Tanzania and Ghana among others), the UNIP government adopted the socialist ideology of humanism, which places man or human beings at the centre of all the activities in the country. The focus was on poverty reduction especially among indigenous Zambians in a bid to uplift the living standards of all. Arguably, Zambians comprised the most vulnerable group compared with other races, mainly because the local people were excluded from productive socio-economic activities in the period prior to independence. In this view, and also influenced by the president's religious background, the humanism ideology guided the national policies and subsequent provision of social services during this period.

Policies were also oriented towards socio-economic development and empowerment of the citizens, hence the need for diversification, job creation, and industrialisation. Mtetesha (2013) argues that many policies adopted in this era included import substitute industrialisation, Zambianization, and massive infrastructural development. Zambianization was the popular policy in which indigenous Zambians were to take over jobs, industries, and national administrative roles from foreign expertise in a bid to provide jobs for ordinary Zambians and to empower them despite the fact that most of them lacked training and/or experience to take over these jobs. Mtetesha also observes that this period saw mass investment in infrastructure such as schools, roads, hospitals as well as expansion of the public service to increase opportunities of employment for Zambians. Efforts at import substitution industries were made as well as the creation of new industries.

As indicated earlier, the humanism ideology entails that human life is precious regardless of race, tribe, creed, status, or ability of the individual. Thus, in line with the tenets of humanism as the country's guiding ideology then, social welfare services, particularly the basic needs of life, such as food, health, and education, were made universal. This was for the purpose of benefiting everyone. Universal access to social services policy was justified considering the prevailing situation then and also because the economy could afford it. As indicated earlier, at independence, Zambia was a middle-income country with a per capita gross domestic product (GDP) of US$650. Thus, the AFRODAD

(2007) report indicates that in the early years, Zambia was self-sufficient and could finance its budget.

In 1972, a decision was made to introduce the one-party state after a constitutional amendment. This, it was argued, was in the best interest of the nation as multiparty system was perceived to have promoted divisions in the country. Thus, this period was characterised by the one-party state in which UNIP was the only legal political party at that time. With the limited involvement of the private sector and NGOs in policymaking and provision of social services, government became increasingly centralised. In this regard, the process of policymaking and the provision of social services became the preserve of the government. The central government, the Ministry of Finance and National Planning in particular, dominated the process of policy formulation and implementation. However, the policy increased access to social services but also created problems of heavy dependence on government for social services. The situation was worsened by the poor economic performance of the country. It should be acknowledged that in the 1970s, Zambia's economic performance was not as good as in the years just after independence. During this period, the country experienced economic problems from mid-1970s to the 1990s, mainly due to the fall of copper prices at the international market, the oil crisis, the liberation wars in the neighbouring countries, and the Structural Adjustment Programmes (SAP). These developments negatively affected the provision of social services in the country.

At that time, the economy could not sustain universal provision of social services, resulting in heavy borrowing by government to finance the civil service employees' salaries as well as subsidies on other social services. Mtetesha (2013) argues that this borrowing was done in the hope that the copper prices would soon improve and the government would be able to repay the debts. However, this was not to be the case as the burden was increasing, and in the process, prices for commodities also increased. This was a particularly challenging period for Zambia as the country also suffered a critical shortage of essential commodities including fuel, mealie meal, and sugar, among others. In 1973, Zambia negotiated the first standby credit facility (SAPs) from IMF and World Bank to cover the perceived short-term shortfall in revenue, but the conditions attached were minimal (Noyoo 2008). However, the SAPs were abandoned as they had negative impact on the Zambian people. This negatively affected the future of the ruling party, and as a result, the new opposition political party (the Movement for Multiparty Democracy—MMD) was formed.

It is the case, therefore, that the 1964–1991 period constituted a transformative phase—during which the country recorded both positive and negative experiences. During this period, the new government embarked on a strategic plan to improve the welfare of the indigenous people. The government prioritised infrastructure development and education as tools for achieving this objective. During this phase, as indicated above, the Zambian government introduced a state-led provision of welfare services. In addition, the social services were provided on a universal basis, and the government had assumed the role of a provider in this regard. This was a sign of positive growth. Mtetesha (2013) also argues that this phase experienced an increase in social opportunities, political freedom, and economic liberty. It also increased human freedoms, rights and liberties, and upward social mobility of people, particularly those from poor backgrounds. Thus, this period saw improvement in the living standards of people, particularly Zambian citizens.

However, despite the positive advances presented above, this phase also recorded some challenges. For instance, nationalisation, introduction of subsidies, increased spending on social sectors such as health, education, and social welfare, the oil shocks of 1970s, the rise in copper production costs as well as the fall in copper prices at the international market negatively affected government operations (Mtetesha 2013). As a result, the government resorted to substantial borrowing and the eventual adoption of the Structural Adjustment Programmes (SAPs). The conditions attached to these SAPs brought about severe poverty and untold human misery, especially among the vulnerable groups like the unemployed.

1991–2010 Period

This phase was characterised by economic and social transformation in which Zambia experienced change of government from the United National Independence Party (UNIP) to the Movement for Multiparty Democracy (MMD) in 1991 under the leadership of Frederick T. J. Chiluba. As reported by AFRODAD (2007), the new government came into office on the platform of political and economic reorientation which involved a departure from the socialist agenda that the country had pursued since 1964. It should be noted that the MMD government inherited huge debts from the UNIP regime due to considerable borrowing as a result of the poor economic performance as well as high social expenditure around the 1970s. However, over the years, Zambia's economic condition deteriorated further, culminating in the Adjustment Programmes of 1992. In order to begin addressing the some of the challenges, the MMD government embraced a free-market economy and liberal democratic system. The new government negotiated with the IMF and World Bank a comprehensive Structural Adjustment Package for the 1992 SAPs.

The AFRODAD (2007) report indicates that in comparison with the SAPs of 1973 and the years that followed, the Adjustment Programme of 1992 carried the most comprehensive and most severe conditions, which included the liberalisation of the economy and the privatisation of all state-owned enterprises. Noyoo (2008) also notes that the government implemented the conditions completely, sometimes without regard to the prevailing social and economic conditions in the country.

As a condition for the package, the Zambian government was compelled to embark upon a radical privatisation programme which involved selling most of the state- or public-owned enterprises. Therefore, the strong industrial base that had been created through the public sector was destroyed. At the same time, there was massive disinvestment leading to massive job losses as a result of privatisation, downsizing of public service, and liquidation of enterprises thereby increasing the already high levels of poverty in the country (Mtetesha 2013). Liberalisation also meant that the government was assuming the role of facilitator and not necessarily provider in the field of social services. The adoption of a liberal approach saw the involvement of the private sector in the provision of social services such as health, education, housing, and social welfare. This aspect, in addition to massive loss of employment, exposed a lot of people to severe poverty, as employment in Zambia is regarded as the main qualification for social security. As such, the country recorded a decline with regard to the indicators of human development such as life expectancy and mortality rate, among others.

During the same period, notable increases were recorded in the cost of food and services such as health and education. AFRODAD (2007) reported that the high cost of food items resulted in multiple health-related problems such as malnutrition, compromised immunity in people, stunted growth, and death. At the same time, access to education and healthcare for ordinary people was reduced because of the introduction of cost-sharing amid cuts in social spending. The SAPs also saw the commercialisation of water and sewerage in urban centres, high cost of electricity, the dilapidation of infrastructure, zero economic growth, and mass migrations of public employees to neighbouring countries such as Botswana, South Africa, and Zimbabwe for greener pastures. It was thus noted that the 1992 SAPs resulted in unprecedented corruption, malnutrition, diseases, death, and illiteracy (AFRODAD 2007).

In view of the above, it can be argued that the SAPs facilitated the widening of income gaps between the poor and the rich, basically due to individual ownership of property. As a result, it may be assumed that poverty was affecting certain groups of people and not necessarily everyone, hence the need for welfare services only for those groups perceived as poor and vulnerable. These categories include the aged, children under five, the sick, and other vulnerable groups. Thus, the model adopted towards welfare provision was residual oriented. Generally, this period recorded negative social development evidenced by a reduction in the standard of living for the average Zambians. This may largely be blamed on the adoption of the principles of capitalism and the implementation of liberalisation and privatisation policies as a conditionality of the SAPs. Thus it can be concluded that the SAPs were largely responsible for the reversal of most of the economic and social gains that Zambia had achieved since independence in 1964. However, despite the challenges that the people of Zambia underwent during this period, Chiluba's administration does deserve some credit to some extent. According to Sardanis (2014), the adoption and implementation of a free-market economic policy opened up the country, politically and economically, although this may have destroyed local industries. This provided opportunities for new initiatives and encouraged the people of Zambia to engage in various business and entrepreneurial activities. In addition, the abolition of the exchange control regulations and the establishment of the Lusaka Stock Exchange enabled people to embark on new ventures. Another achievement that may be attributed to Chiluba's administration relates to improvements in the transport sector. Transport business is currently in the hands of the local businessmen and women and is thriving (Sardanis 2014). The transport industry did not only facilitate easy movement of people from one area to another but it also provided the seed for many new businesses. Thus, Chiluba's administration attempted to create the enabling environment and encouraged people to engage in business ventures. President Frederick Chiluba's term ended in 2001 when he gave way to his successor—President Levy P. Mwanawasa—upon MMD's victory in the 2001 general elections.

Mwanawasa's New Deal Administration Government 2001–2008

In 2001 the new president (Levy Mwanawasa) came into power. This marked the beginning of the New Deal government which pursued the Heavily Indebted Poor Countries (HIPC) initiative debt cancellation programme. In 2005, Zambia reached the HIPC completion point under the leadership of President Mwanawasa. During this period, the country also recorded positive economic growth, which resulted in a real growth rate of 6.8 per cent, and the rate of inflation dropped from 30 per cent in 2000 to single-digit inflation of 7.9 per cent by 2010 (Bureau of African Affairs, or BAA 2011). Debt cancellation provided an opportunity for increased social spending. Considering the prevailing situation at the time, the Mwanawasa government prioritised poverty reduction. During this period, the government came up with the Fifth National Development Plan (FNDP) which emphasized infrastructural development and was committed to promoting socio-economic development. The policies that were adopted during this period focused on poverty reduction through infrastructure development and agriculture support programmes, targeting small-scale farmers. The government also put up an aggressive fight against corruption. Mtetesha (2013) argues that the country also experienced economic growth as the prices of commodities dropped, hence the general improvement in the livelihood of ordinary Zambians. Levy Mwanawasa died in 2008. Following the death of Mwanawasa, Rupiah Banda became president of Zambia in the same year. President Banda adopted similar policies to those of his predecessor, to a large extent. Generally, the status quo with regard to social services remained, although with a record of slight increase in food production. However, unemployment levels were still high.

2011–2014

This period saw the change of government from MMD to Patriotic Front (PF) government led by Mr Michael Chilufya Sata. Mr Sata became the fourth president of Zambia in 2011 amid high expectations from Zambian people. Despite the change of government, it may be observed that the priorities of the Sixth National Development Plan (SNDP) have remained unchanged, and the macroeconomic situation remained broadly positive (EU 2012). The economic growth provides an opportunity for improved social spending and thus general well-being of the people. Nevertheless, the PF manifesto promised job creation, low taxes, more money in people's pockets, and improvement in socio-economic conditions and general standards of living for Zambian citizens. Upon taking office, the new government embarked on implementing the manifesto. The PF government committed itself towards poverty reduction, the fight against corruption, job creation, and equitable growth. In a bid to deliver on the promises, the government implemented a number of administrative and institutional reforms including decentralisation and the creation of new districts. This, it was assumed, would improve service delivery and general living standards of the Zambian people—with a focus on the vulnerable groups. For example, by the end of 2013, President Sata created thirty-one new districts. He also created one new province, Muchinga, and transferred the capital of Southern Province from Livingstone to Choma on the grounds that it has a more central location (Sardanis 2014).

In addition, the PF government launched the revised National Decentralisation Policy in July 2013.

'*Following the lapse of the timeframe for the previous decentralisation implementation plan and in view of the fact that the decentralisation policy has been revised, the PF government needs to prepare and launch another decentralisation implementation plan*' (Mukwena 2014) if the objectives of the policy are to be realised. However, despite the existence of the decentralisation policy in Zambia, Mukwena (2014) observed:

> Local government continues to face the same problems that
> limited its capacity in the previous system to deliver local

services and play any meaningful role in fostering local development. These problems include insufficient numbers of trained staff, lack of coordination at the local level, lack of political will to decentralise powers on the part of national politicians, failure to support coordination mechanisms and citizen participation arrangements with appropriate legal framework, and inadequate financial resources. For instance, the funding to local authorities continues to be very limited to the extent that most of these authorities have difficulties to provide basic local services and even pay staff salaries. As such, the districts in Zambia remain unaccountable and unresponsive to the needs of the local population.

The PF government also adjusted the minimum wage upwards and increased the salaries of civil servants with some getting as high as 200 per cent (*Times of Zambia* 2013). Improvements are evidenced by general decrease of under-five mortality rate, reduction in new HIV infections and other diseases like malaria and tuberculosis. The UNICEF (2012) and EU (2012) reports also indicated improvements in enrolments and completion rates in the area of education as well as in agricultural production.

Despite these developments, Mtetesha (2013) argues that this period has also seen the removal of subsidies on maize and fuel. As a result, the prices for fuel and some essential commodities have gone up, making it difficult for the ordinary Zambians to access some basic needs of life. The EU (2012) report also shows that in spite of economic progress, income inequality in the country remains extremely high, and the poverty reduction rate is also too slow to achieve the 2015 target of 29 per cent. However, it should be noted that the PF policies are still under implementation, and thus, the full impact of the current policies on welfare is yet to be seen.

Social Welfare and Social Work Education in Zambia

Social well-being is an integral component of economic development and any caring government should aim at meeting the needs of its citizens. Before independence, communities and the extended family provided all the needs of members in traditional society. However, this was not the case at the time of colonialism. During colonial rule, it was the work of central government to undertake the responsibility for statutory social services such as probation and the treatment of delinquency, care of the aged and the destitute. However, social welfare services at that time were meant for the colonial masters and not Africans.

The demand for social welfare services increased upon realisation that there was need to raise the standards of living particularly among urbanised Africans. As a result, the copper mining companies started giving serious considerations to the question of African welfare. To that effect, the policy that the Northern Rhodesia government should set up a Department of Social Welfare and Probation Services and should be responsible for financing welfare work was proposed. This resulted in the development of the policy that delineated African and European social welfare services provision in colonial Zambia (Social Welfare Annual Report or SWAR 1952). That meant social welfare services could now be accessed by all communities in the country despite some variations in the quality of services provided. General welfare work then was considered in terms of hobbies and crafts, scouts and guides and women's work. Thus, it can be argued that these services were more of recreational nature than social welfare.

The demand for welfare services increased as a result of the passing of the new juvenile ordinance as well as the increasing need for social welfare services, particularly in casework in European communities and African welfare in urban areas. This resulted in the need to recruit qualified staff to run welfare activities. Much of the welfare work demanded local knowledge which was more easily available among the local people. However, it was difficult to find skilled workers in this regard mainly because of limited educational background among Africans. This meant shortage of qualified social workers to run social welfare institutions including the newly instituted Department of Welfare and Probation Services. According to Noyoo (2000), the department was comprised only of a director who was responsible for the overall work of the department, three social welfare officers who were responsible for the towns of Livingstone, Lusaka, and Kabwe, and two wardens in charge of shelters for children situated in Ndola. This made it difficult for the department to provide the much-needed welfare services to all the people in the country. The shortage of welfare staff had a negative implication especially in African communities as most of the voluntary organizations concentrated their efforts only on white and other mixed-race communities (Noyoo 2000). As a result, unqualified welfare officers were engaged to provide welfare services (SWAR 1952).

In an effort to resolve the challenges regarding the organization and coordination of social welfare activities in Zambia, the colonial government approached the South African government in 1950 to obtain advice in this matter. Thus, the director of social welfare and probation in South Africa visited Northern Rhodesia to undertake a survey of existing welfare services and make recommendations as to how the services should be organized and developed (Noyoo 2000).

However, deliberate efforts were being made to train African welfare officers to run welfare activities in the country. This is evidenced by the consideration of the permanent scheme for training African welfare staff by the government in 1952 (SWAR 1952). This was also meant to ensure that fundamental social problems are met by properly organized and serviced social welfare services. Following serious discussions, a training course for African welfare officers was proposed at Mindolo in Kitwe. This was a junior certificate course in social studies whose aim was to provide a general basic training for all kinds of social welfare work. Following this development, African Welfare Officers Training Board was set. The purpose of the board was to advise as to the general running of the course (including advice on curriculum), to select trainees, and to hear reports on the work of each trainee. The duration of the course was two years; however, an opportunity was taken to offer short courses when the trainees were away on practical training. The short courses focused on group work, refresher courses for women welfare workers, and youth work for those already on post. In 1953, nine trainees were selected for the first two-year course from the mining companies and local authorities (SWAR 1953). In addition, two institutions, Monze and Kitwe community development staff training colleges were established to provide training to community workers for rural and urban areas.

In order to meet the rising demand for high-level trained social welfare officers, the Northern Rhodesia Council of Social Services (NRCSS) established a standing committee for training social workers. This culminated in the government decision to embark on a training course conducting the external diploma in social studies (a one-year course for graduates) under the aegis of London University. Students who wanted to pursue this course had to get university clearance, and then apply on forms supplied by the ministry. These applicants were also required to appear before an interviewing board with representation from the ministry, Rhodes-Livingstone Institute, NRCSS, and the University College of Rhodesia and Nyasaland. Thereafter, the educational department would do the actual examination. In between these extremes of preliminary registration and final examination, students had to study by themselves or they had to attend classes to help them with their studies. This posed a challenge to most applicants, particularly those from other parts of the country because these classes were held only in Lusaka. This meant that the person who wished to take the course needed to be resident in Lusaka. As such, the high requirements of university entrance made it difficult to resolve the main problem of training African professional social workers who were needed in much greater numbers.

A few years later, serious discussions between local authorities, mining companies, and the Department of Welfare and Probation resulted in the introduction and expansion of training institutions in social welfare locally. In 1961, the Oppenheimer College of Social Services was opened in Northern Rhodesia (Zambia) as a symbol of progress in the heart of Africa (*Central African Post* 1961). Oppenheimer College was the first of its kind in Africa, and twenty-five Africans and one European constituted the first students at the college. The college was planned to offer a full professional training for social workers and social scientists to fill vacancies in the social service professions. The aim was to advance the cause of training and education in all branches of social work and welfare work and services. The college also had a provision for research in the field of social and welfare work. It was reasoned the college would meet the particular needs of changing and developing Africa at that time. Short courses such as personal management, housing management, public administration, and other subjects related to social services were also run at the college (*Central African Post* 1961).

In order to cater for the greatly increased need for high-level manpower, the University of Zambia was established in 1965. Following the official opening of the university in 1965, Oppenheimer College of Social Services was formally incorporated into the University of Zambia as the Oppenheimer Department of Social Services in the same year. This led to the introduction of a degree course in social work in Zambia. The university enrolled the first 312 students in 1966. However, despite the high demand of qualified social workers in government departments and society at large to deal with the problems that resulted from urbanisation, migration, and other social change factors, enrolment for training in social work was limited, causing a shortage of qualified social workers. Thus, from this background, it can be argued that social work in Zambia is a product of both industrialisation and colonialism.

Social Work Education and Training Institutions:

Prospects for Developmental Approaches to Social Welfare in Zambia

It is important to reiterate the levels of poverty and vulnerability in Zambia before examining the prospects for developmental social welfare. According to the Bureau of African Affairs (BAA) (2011), Zambia experienced positive economic growth for the twelfth consecutive year in 2010, with a real growth rate of 6.8 per cent, and the rate of inflation dropped from 30 per cent in 2000 to single-digit inflation of 7.9 per cent by December 2010. However, despite the positive economic growth rate, most of the people in the country still live in poverty and experience food insecurity. The BAA report indicates that about 63 per cent of the population is still living on less than $2 per day. Like in other developing countries, poverty is the root cause of many problems that are experienced in Zambia today. The main causes of poverty in the country are many, but they include persistent high unemployment levels, diseases like HIV/AIDS, and deterioration of family structures particularly in urban areas.

The recorded economic growth has not translated into a commensurate increase in the number of jobs. Generally, formal employment has been steadily diminishing as the main source of income in Zambia, yet formal employment is considered to be the main source of livelihood particularly in urban households who rely on markets for food purchases. For example, the Labour Force Survey, as cited in Klaveren and Tijden (2009), indicates that only 10 per cent of the labour force was employed in the formal sector. High unemployment levels can be associated with the experience of the Structural Adjustment Programs (SAPs). The SAPs encouraged radical privatisation, downsizing of public service, and liquidation of enterprises which resulted in massive job losses increasing the already high levels of poverty in the country. The situation is further compounded by HIV and AIDS. Other factors that affect the country's socio-economic situation include fluctuations in prices of the country's main export commodities (minerals) on the international market, inability to diversify the economy, corruption, and conditional aid in some cases.

These and many other socio-economic realities directly affect the fiscal resources and the extent to which social welfare services were to be provided. As a result, many African countries, including Zambia, have failed to meet the needs of their populations. Zambia's poverty reduction strategy plan puts emphasis on empowerment of the citizens and meeting the needs of the people, particularly the vulnerable groups such as women and youth. Thus, it is within this context that social work education and training in the country must be considered.

To enhance the relevance and effectiveness of the social work profession in Zambia and perhaps Africa, there is need to refocus the approach for the profession from residual approach to some developmental intervention measures. Osei-Hwedie (1993) and Nooyo (2008) observe that the beginning of social work in less-developed African countries, especially southern African countries, could be seen as an auxiliary of colonialism as well as the missionary work. This has often meant the development of social services and programmes, policies, and systems that have had a traditional focus of social work; that is, casework, socialisation, custodial, therapeutic, and caretaking models. However, Mupedziswa (2006) argues:

> The social work models that were exported to Africa were based on the Modernisation Paradigm which emphasised social control as opposed to social change, and hence paid particular attention to individual pathologies such as crime, divorce, alcoholism, drug abuse, prostitution and family disorganisation.

Further, Mupedziswa (2006) observed, *based on the Modernisation paradigm, the residual approach does not take sufficient cognisance of the cultural aspects of the people of the African Continent, thus lacking sensitivity to the demands of the African culture such as the traditional informal forms of welfare, the general sense of reciprocity that characterises the social interaction by community members, values as collectivity, consensus, cooperation and harmony, rendering its interventions and programmes ineffective.*

As a result, the more substantive social issues have remained unattended to, rendering the profession inappropriate, hence the argument that social work has failed to meet the demands of the needy people in Africa.

However, considering the nature and uniqueness of social problems and issues confronting most African countries, various African scholars (Osei-Hwedie 1993; Rwomire and Raditlhokwa 1996; Mupedziswa 2006), have called for a different emphasis if social work is to be a meaningful and viable profession in the continent. According to the Association of Schools of Social Work (ASWEA) in Mupedziswa (2006), social work must proceed from remedial social work, foreign by nature and approach, to a more dynamic and more widespread preventive and rehabilitative action which identifies itself with African culture in particular and with socio-economic policies of Africa in general. In the same vein, Mupedziswa (2006) suggests a paradigm shift on the part of the profession, from models informed by the modernisation school to those informed by the development approach. This kind of social work may be referred to as developmental social work.

Developmental social work can be defined as a type of social work which diverges from the residual, service-oriented approach to 'holistic planned' development strategies which place people at the centre of social planning (Mupedziswa 2006). Developmental social work stresses self-reliance aimed at enhancing people's capacity to work for their own welfare. It focuses on empowerment and strengthening the individual's capacity to use resources within his/her environment, and the development of the ability to participate competently within that environment. The developmental approach seeks to enhance the social functioning of all the people, that is, it includes the optimum utilisation of available individual and institutional resources. The approach also emphasizes equitable distribution of resources, income, and other benefits of economic progress, participation of all the people in socioeconomic activities and associated political actions, with focus on the marginalised in collaboration with various agencies involved in the process of development (Noyoo 2008).

Developmental social work proposes adoption of measures such as creation of organizational arrangements at the national level that harmonises economic and social policies, adoption of macroeconomic policies that promote employment and attain people-centred economic development outcomes. This type of social work affirms the profession's commitment to eradicate poverty, recognizes the link between welfare and economic development, and considers welfare as an investment in human capital rather than a drain on limited resources (Midgeley and Tang 2001).

However, Mupedziswa (2001) in 'The quest for relevance' argues that the profession's 'new' developmental orientation has to start at the level of education. That means, therefore, that all social work education institutions (in Africa) are urged to redesign their programmes in the direction of developmental social work. Noyoo (2008) also echoes the need to deliberately reify the African perspective with regard to social work practice and social work education on the continent. Thus, social work education and training must be conducted in such a way as to equip the graduates with appropriate knowledge in terms of relevance to the prevailing conditions. Social workers must attempt to bring about the socio-economic, political, as well as cultural empowerment of their clientele. Rwomire and Raditlhokwa (1996) argue that if developing countries can constructively engage social work in development, significant structural change and socioeconomic improvements can be achieved.

To this end, Zambia's needs in the area of developmental social work are not unique to those of other African countries. For instance, the nature of social problems that are experienced in Zambia, such as poverty, unemployment, deterioration of family structures, diseases like HIV/AIDS, tuberculosis, and general vulnerability, especially among the disadvantaged members of the society clearly shows the limitations of a traditional social work model. Traditional social work focuses primarily on remedial or casework approach as indicated above. As such, the need for developmental approach in social work education and training in Zambia cannot be overemphasized.

Like in other African countries, professional training in social work in Zambia is becoming established. Unlike the early days after independence in the 1960s when Zambia experienced a shortage of trained social workers, the situation is now different. This may be attributed to the increase in the number of institutions training social workers. For instance, the period after independence, Zambia had only one university offering a degree programme in social work, apart from a few other colleges training social workers at a lower level. Currently, there are two public universities (the University of Zambia and Mulungushi University) training social workers at degree level. These public universities are supplemented by several private universities. There is also a notable increase in the number of both public and private colleges getting involved in training social workers at both diploma and certificate levels.

However, despite this positive development, no known measures have been put in place so far to ensure the social work programmes offered by these institutions are relevant to the Zambian and/or African situation. As such, the major concern as at present is not necessarily on the shortage of trained social workers but on the quality and indeed the direction of social work these institutions are providing. Given the above, the need to urge all social work education and training institutions in Zambia to adopt and implement the much-needed and long-awaited developmental approach to social work education and training cannot be overemphasized. To achieve this goal, as advocated for by various African scholars, Mupedziswa (2001) proposes some form of a conceptual model which social work education and training institutions in Africa could use to determine the extent to which they are promoting a developmental approach to social work education and training. If this model is adopted in Zambia, it is assumed that it would strengthen social work education and training in the country, especially in terms of its relevance to the local situation.

One of the measures proposed by Mupedziswa as a way of enhancing the profession's relevance in Africa is curriculum review. If institutions offering social work education are to produce competent and relevant graduates in the country, there is need to review and later on transform the curriculum and other components of instruction. The concerned institutions should endeavour to seriously engage in a rigorous and focused curriculum review exercise. To that effect, there is need to also engage students and other stakeholders in curriculum evaluation. Some other related activities that may be useful in this regard as suggested by Mupedziswa include relevant field placements, progressive lecture delivery methods / classroom interaction, and ensuring the relevance of student projects/assignments. Other measures also include generation and use of indigenous materials, the generation and use of local research and networking with other sister institutions, relevant graduate employment patterns, and meaningful contributions by staff towards local social policy (Mupedziswa 2001). It is also important to ensure that the institutions providing social work training have the right people to deliver lectures. This, it is assumed, would place the concerned institutions in a strategic position to provide social work education that meets the demands of the current social and environmental situation in Zambia, with a particular focus on the vulnerable groups.

One other measure that may help ensure quality in social work training and practice in Zambia is the establishment of the professional body like the national association of social workers, which would oversee all the activities related to social work in the country. However, despite Zambia being one of the first few African countries to provide training in social work, the country is still faced with challenges in regulating the activities related to social work training and practice. While it may be appreciated that the Social Work Association of Zambia (SWAZ) has been established (SWAZ was established in 2005), the association has not achieved much, more so because it has no legal backup as it is not supported by an Act of Parliament. This means, therefore, that although the association has been registered under the Registrar of Societies, it has no authority to regulate social work activities in the country. In the absence of the legal backing, there is a risk that anyone, even unqualified or less qualified persons, could claim to be social workers when they do not meet the basic standards.

Thus, in order to protect the integrity of the profession and to ensure standardized training and practice in social work, there is need to expedite the process of securing a legal framework through an Act of Parliament to give SWAZ authority to regulate or accredit social work practitioners. It is expected that the association would also ensure that standards are observed by all the institutions involved in the training of social workers. As such, this association would be key in the proposed reorientation of the social work training curricula in Zambia.

Summary

The information presented in this chapter indicates some socio-economic transformation trends which have taken place in Zambia since independence in 1964 to 2014. These ideological and policy transformations have translated into Zambia's current social and economic status. At fifty, Zambia has experienced both challenging and good times which have moulded it into a strong state. Despite Zambia's current classification as having some of the worst social and poverty indicators on the continent, it was one of the prosperous countries in Africa at independence in 1964.

The chapter has argued that while certain factors such as colonialism, the collapse of copper prices at the international market in the mid-1970s, and the oil crisis contributed to the country's poverty, the phenomenon can also be attributed to many other factors, particularly the experiences of Structural Adjustment Programmes (SAPs) in the 1990s, which led to the adoption and implementation of privatisation and liberalisation policies. Some of the effects of these policies are still evident in Zambia today.

However, it is not enough to bask in the comfort of a one-time prosperous and thriving economy. This may be better expressed in one of the traditional Zambian (Bemba) sayings, '*ubulimi bwakale tabutalalika mwana*' (meaning, you cannot use the past glories to solve the current problems or challenges). Therefore, there is need for concerted effort to produce a return to the much-discussed economic and social development. To that effect, the Zambian government is determined to provide quality social services to Zambian citizens. This is reflected in the objectives of the Fifth National Development Plan (FNDP) and Zambia Vision 2030. As such, Zambia is poised to become a middle-income country by 2030. However, to achieve this vision, much more needs to be done. There is need to promote socio-economic development and ensure improved equal access to social services.

The chapter also has also reiterated the value of social work as a profession in the provision of social services in developing countries in general and Zambia in particular. Given the fragile socio-economic situation and the resultant vulnerability in Zambia, the value of the social work profession in the provision of social services cannot be overemphazised. The chapter has maintained that, considering the nature of problems experienced in the country, it is vital for all institutions offering social work education and training in Zambia to consider reviewing their curriculum and heed the call for a paradigm shift on the part of the profession, from models informed by the modernisation school to those informed by the development approach (Mupedziswa 2006). This, it is assumed, would place them in a better position to respond appropriately to the prevailing socio-economic conditions in Zambia and perhaps elsewhere. This chapter therefore contends that since social work objectives and principles support Africa's (Zambia) objectives for social development (Osei-Hwedie 1993), there is need for institutions offering social work education and training to review their curricular and align their focus to the nature of problems experienced by their clientele.

Conclusion

Presented above is the evolution of social services in Zambia. At independence Zambia was one of the most prosperous countries on the continent. However, at fifty, despite a rich natural resource endowment and considerable political stability, Zambia is still counted among the poorest countries in the world. Zambia has gone through massive economic and social transformation processes guided by ideological and policy changes. The aim of this chapter was to document the changes that have taken place in Zambia since her independence in 1964. These changes have had significant influence on the current socio-economic status of the county.

The period between 1964 and 1991 saw the prosperous days of infrastructure development, massive social investment, and empowerment programmes mainly to the benefit of all Zambians. This was linked to the booming economy which was as a result of high copper prices at the London Metal Exchange. However, this period was short-lived as the economy could not sustain heavy social expenditure. The situation was compounded by the oil shocks of 1970s, the rise in copper production costs as well as the fall in copper prices at the international market. These developments negatively affected government operations in the long run. In all, despite some identified challenges, it can be argued that Zambia fared well in the area of social services during this period, until in 1991 when the country went through ideological and policy shift from socialism to capitalist-oriented policies. Capitalism brings with it both advantages and disadvantages. Upon the adoption of the capitalist policies, the mid 1990s were characterised by privatisation of the mines, trade liberalisation, and abolition of subsidies as a conditionality of the SAPs. Although the motive was noble, privatisation in Zambia is accredited with massive loss of employment and high levels of poverty which eventually resulted in general reduction in the standard of living for the average Zambians.

Upon change of government from MMD to PF in 2011, the PF government committed itself towards poverty reduction and promised improvements in socio-economic conditions and general standards of living for Zambian citizens. During this period, there have been recorded improvements evidenced by general decrease of under-five mortality rate, reduction in new HIV infections and other diseases like malaria and tuberculosis. There are also improvements in enrolments and completion rates in the area of education as well as in agricultural production (UNICEF 2012; EU 2012). In spite of these positive developments, this period has also experienced some challenges. For instance, the removal of subsidies on maize and fuel have resulted in an increase in the prices of fuel and some essential commodities which may have a bearing on the living standards of the ordinary Zambians. However, it is too early to make conclusive arguments about the performance of the current policies as they are still under implementation. It is hoped, therefore, that the socio-economic situation of the country will improve in the current regime.

References

African Forum and Network on Debt and Development (AFRODAD) (2007), *A Report on the Impact of Wrong Policy Advice on Zambia* (Lusaka).

Bureau of African Affairs (BAA) (2011), Zambia, Republic of Zambia.

EU (2012), Joint Annual Report for Zambia (Lusaka, Zambia).

Hinfelaar, M. (1993), *Conflict and Protests in a Scottish Mission Area, North-Eastern Zambia Centre of African Studies*, Edinburg University, 1870–1935.

Klaveren, M. and Tijdens, K. (2009), *An Overview of Women's Work and Employment in Zambia* (Amsterdam: University of Amsterdam).

Lamb G. (2013), *Disarmament, Demobilisation and Reintegration Program 20 Years Later: Historical Review of the Long-Term Impact of Post-Independence DDR in Southern Africa* (Washington DC: World Bank) 1–41.

Lungwangwa, G. (1999), *The Impact of Cost-Sharing: A Study in Financial and Delivery of Education in Zambia* (Lusaka, Zambia).

Mibenge, B. (2005), *Civil–Military Relations in Zambia: A View from the Military*, 31–38.

Midgley, J. and Leung Tang, K. (2001), *Social Policy, Economic Growth and Developmental Welfare*, 10: 244–252.

Mtetesha, N. (2013), *Zambia Policy Shifts and Reforms: Socio-economic Change and Phases*, accessed in August 2014.

Mukwena, R. M. (2014), 'Decentralisation, Democracy and Development: The case of Zambia', in *50 Years of Local Government in Zambia: Treasuring the past, Reflecting the Present, Shaping the Future* (Lusaka: Local Government Association of Zambia).

Mupedziswa, R. (2001), 'The quest for relevance: Towards a conceptual model of developmental social work education and training in Africa', *International Social Work* 44/3: 285–300.

—— (2006), 'Challenges and Prospects of Social Work in Africa', in Okeibunor, J. C. and Anugwom, E. E. (eds.) *The social sciences and socioeconomic transformation in Africa* (Nsukka, Nigeria: The Great AP Publishers) pp. 271–283.

Noyoo, N. (2000), *Social welfare in Zambia* (Zambia: Multimedia).

—— (2008), *Social Policy and Human Development in Zambia* (Zambia: UNZA Press).

Osei-Hwedie, K. (1993) 'The Challenge of Social Work in Africa: Starting the Indigenisation Process', *Journal of Social Development in Africa* 8/1: 19–30.

Patel, L. (2005), *Social Welfare and Social Development in South Africa* (Cape Town: Oxford University).

Rwomire, A. and Raditlhokwa, L. (1996) 'Social Work in Africa: Issues and Challenges', *Journal of Social Development in Africa* 11/2: 5–19.

Sardanis, A. (2014), *Zambia: The First 50 Years* (London: I. B. Tauris & Co. Ltd).

Social Welfare (1952), Social Welfare Annual Report, 1952, Northern Rhodesia, Lusaka.

The Central Africa Post (1961), Northern Rhodesia, Lusaka.

Times of Zambia (2013), March.

UNICEF (2012), Annual Report 2012 for Zambia, ESARO (Lusaka).

Contributor Profiles

Editors

Royson Mukwena (author of chapter 5) is the dean of the School of Social Sciences and director of Research and Postgraduate Studies at Mulungushi University, Kabwe, Zambia. Before joining Mulungushi University, Ambassador Professor Mukwena was executive director of the Organization for Social Science Research in Eastern and Southern Africa (OSSREA) headquartered in Addis Ababa. Before moving to Addis Ababa, Amb. Prof. Mukwena was Zambia's High Commissioner to the United Kingdom and Ambassador Extraordinary and Plenipotentiary (Resident in London) to the Holy See and Ireland. Prior to London, he was High Commissioner of Zambia to Tanzania and Ambassador Extraordinary and Plenipotentiary (Resident in Dar es Salaam) to the Republics of Burundi, Rwanda, Uganda, and the Union of the Comoros. Before joining the Zambian Diplomatic Service, Prof Mukwena lectured at the Universities of Zambia and Namibia, and served the latter also as head of the Department of Political and Administrative Studies and dean of the Faculty of Economics and Management Science. His articles on local government, decentralisation, and fiscal decentralisation in Zambia and Namibia, and on privatization in Africa have appeared in several international journals. He is also co-editor of *Governance in Southern Africa and Beyond: Experiences of Institutional and Public Policy Reform in Developing Countries* (Gamsberg Macmillan Publishers, Windhoek, 2004) and *Decentralisation and Regional and Local Government in Namibia* (Printech, Windhoek, 2008).

Fanuel Sumaili (author of chapter 11) is director of the Centre for Labour Studies and acting dean of the School of Business Studies at Mulungushi

University. Before joining Mulungushi University, Dr Sumaili lectured at the University of Zambia. He is also a practising lawyer in Zambia.

Other Contributors

Rebecca Banda-Shula (author of chapter 12) is a lecturer of Public Administration and head of the Department of Political and Administrative Studies in the School of Social Sciences, at Mulungushi University, Kabwe, Zambia.

Petra Chinyere (co-author of chapters 2 and 3) is a part-time lecturer at the University of Zimbabwe, in the Department of Political and Administrative Studies, where she is taking political science courses. She was previously a lecturer in international relations at Mulungushi University in Kabwe, Zambia where she developed an interest in Zambian political issues, leading to the contributions made in this book. Her area of interest is political issues in the SADC region, particularly the role of women in peace initiatives and in governance.

Shakespear Hamauswa (co-author of chapters 2 and 3) is a lecturer in International Relations and Development at Mulungushi University, Zambia. Before joining Mulungushi University, he was a lecturer in Political Science and International Relations at the University of Zimbabwe.

Maimbolwa Sepo Imasiku (author of chapter 9) is a lecturer under the Institute of Distance Education at Mulungushi University and has also worked as assistant director under the same institute. She is a marketer and international business specialist, lecturing in Marketing, International Business, and Entrepreneurship courses. Her interests include research in business start-ups, entrepreneurship, and social media marketing

Chilala Kafula (author of chapter 13) is a lecturer in the Department of Social Development at Mulungushi University in Kabwe, Zambia. Her areas of specialisation include gender, social-welfare-related issues, and social policy.

James Mulenga (author of chapter 8) is a lecturer in the Department of Economics at Mulungushi University. He previously worked at the Zambia Catholic University as a lecturer and head of the Economics Department, the

Embassy of Japan, and Zambia Telecommunications Company Limited. His main research interests are on growth and development economics, poverty, youth unemployment, performance of enterprises, foreign investment.

Njunga-Michael Mulikita (author of chapter 6) is Senior Lecturer and Coordinator, Dag Hammarskjöld Institute for Peace and Conflict Studies of Copperbelt University (CBU) located at Zambia Institute for Diplomacy and International Studies (ZIDIS) in Lusaka. Prior to joining CBU, he served as senior lecturer in the Department of Political and Administrative Studies (PAS) and research fellow at the Institute of Human Relations (IHR) at the University of Zambia (UNZA). Dr Mulikita has published papers in *Africa Insight*, *African Administrative Studies*, *African Journal of Public Administration & Management*, *African Security Review*, *Peacekeeping & International Relations*, and *African Yearbook of International Law*.

Christabel Ngongola (author of chapter 7) is a lecturer of Economics and also serving as assistant director of the Directorate of Research and Post-Graduate Studies at Mulungushi University. Her main areas of research interest include development economics and human development. She is also a board member of the Kabwe Chamber of Commerce and Industry.

Torben Reinke (author of chapter 4) is a lecturer in International Relations and Development at Mulungushi University. He is a political scientist who first came to Zambia to do research on the relationship between foreign donors and the Zambian government. His main area of interest has since been Zambia's role in the international political economy.

Samuel Sakala (author of chapter 1) is a lecturer of Public Administration in the School of Social Sciences, Department of Political and Administrative Studies at Mulungushi University, Kabwe, Zambia. He previously worked as a counsellor and coordinator of international students affairs at the University of Phoenix in Arizona, USA. His main research interests include Public Policy Research and Analysis, Creating Public Value, and Seamless Government.

Paul Zulu (author of chapter 10) is Assistant Librarian, Technical Services at Mulungushi University, Kabwe, Zambia. Prior to the current position, he had a stint at the National Library of Namibia on his latest position where he worked as Senior Librarian in charge of bibliographic control from 2005 to 2009. In Zambia, he worked for Zambia Library Service in various departments and positions, which include Librarian, Provincial Librarian, Acting Principal Librarian, and ultimately Chief Librarian between 1995 and 2005. He has vast experience and diverse professional exposure in librarianship ranging from reference, technical, and user services, with expertise in the management of print as well as electronic resources.

15890629R00235

Printed in Great Britain
by Amazon